THEORY AND METHODS IN SOCIOLOGY

3

Theory and Methods in Sociology

An introduction to sociological thinking and practice

John A. Hughes
and
W.W. Sharrock

First published 2007 by
PALGRAVE MACMILLAN
Houndmills, Basingstoke, Hampshire RG21 6XS and
175 Fifth Avenue, New York, N.Y. 10010
Companies and representatives throughout the world

PALGRAVE MACMILLAN is the global academic imprint of the Palgrave Macmillan division of St. Martin's Press, LLC and of Palgrave Macmillan Ltd. Macmillan® is a registered trademark in the United States, United Kingdom and other countries. Palgrave is a registered trademark in the European Union and other countries.

ISBN-13: 978-0-333-77285-0 hardback
ISBN-10: 0-333-77285-7 hardback
ISBN-13: 978-0-333-77286-7 paperback
ISBN-10: 0-333-77286-5 paperback

This book is printed on paper suitable for recycling and made from fully managed and sustained forest sources. Logging, pulping and manufacturing processes are expected to conform to the environmental regulations of the country of origin.

A catalogue record for this book is available from the British Library.

A catalog record for this book is available from the Library of Congress.

10   9   8   7   6   5   4   3   2   1
16 15 14 13 12 11 10 09 08 07

Printed in China

Contents

Figures

Insets

Tables

Preface

What we have tried to do in this textbook is realise an ambition that both of us have shared for much of our professional careers: that is, write a text which better combines sociological theory and method than hitherto. It should come as no surprise to anyone familiar with sociology that we have not succeeded or, rather, not succeeded because it is not possible. Instead what we hope we have achieved is a clear sense of why, at the present time in sociology, this cannot be achieved by us or anyone else. Whether or not it will be achievable in the future is anyone's guess. We ourselves subscribe to a fondness for the idea that sociology will eventually establish itself as a well-grounded empirical discipline and, if anything, we would prefer one informed by symbolic interactionism and ethnomethodology, neither currently at the forefront of sociological fashion. However, we do not want to claim in any way that if all sociologists were to espouse these approaches then everything in the sociological garden would be lovely. As should become clear in the story that follows, sociology is a pluralistic discipline, which for some is a state of affairs to be applauded, and for others an occasion for near despair. In what follows we try not to adopt either of these positions but aim, as best we can, to elaborate the arguments which have prime *methodological* importance in the history of sociology.

We stress the term 'methodological' because, in our view, it characterises and motivates the text which follows. A 'methodological view' in many ways incorporates the theory and method distinction which has so often framed – and institutionalises – what are seen as distinct activities and skills in sociology: those of theory and those of empirical research. The urge to combine more effectively theory and method – and we will provide many instances in the text of such laments – tends to see the problems in a particular way, whereas looking at these matters methodologically, as species of sociological reasoning, enables us to see, hopefully more clearly, the varied places that different approaches accord to the business of theory, the requirement for method and the point of empirical research. Combining theory and method in a more effective way is only a challenge to those positions – and one of these, 'positivism', forms the beginning of the story – which regard a more effective combination as essential to the realisation of their ambitions. Other approaches do not. And not because they think an ineffective combination is what they need, but because they have different conceptions of what function sociological theory is to serve and whether methods as typically understood have any role to play, and because they doubt whether sociology can or ought to be an empirical discipline, and so on.

It is a moot point as to whether sociology will ever be able to attain that methodological unity so often sought after. Even though recent developments in the discipline often call for interdisciplinarity in the social sciences, even 'transdisciplinarity', to the point where what we understand by the sociological tradition is in danger of being lost altogether, our hope is that sufficient remains for a rigorous empirical discipline to emerge. What is more certain is that this will require patience and modest efforts as well as intelligence.

Acknowledgements

As always there are many people to thank for their various contributions, none of whom – no matter how much we might hope otherwise – is to blame for what appears in these pages. First mention should go to our closer colleagues and friends, academics and otherwise, who have helped in various ways: Karen, Kath, Claire and Penny, the members of the Very Sad Bastards (who similarly cling on to a bygone era, this time of rhythm and blues). To Pete, Dave, Mark and Andy. To Graham, Tommaso, Peter and Jason. Special thanks should also be extended to Palgrave Macmillan for their patience. This has proved much more difficult than we imagined – and we imagined it would be difficult. Finally, thanks to Tina and Margaret, Archie and Silver, and to the regulars at the King William IV and the Grafton Arms for very different but very welcome worlds.

Chapter 1

Introduction

Sociology: pluralism or disarray?

The inadequate relationship between sociological theory and sociological method is regularly identified as a central source of the discipline's most basic problems, not least its failure to become the science that it greatly hoped to be. It is, however, unusual to do what we do here: namely, to put sociological theory and method into one and the same textbook. The atypical nature of our venture reflects the situation in the wider discipline, where the need to relate theory and method more closely together is often declaimed, but receives at best lip service.

This is only a textbook, and we are not therefore hoping to make progress in solving the problem of relating theory and method more closely. We are not even confident that the problem can be solved. What we do is try to review some of the major changes in the way in which the relationship between theory and method (or between theory and research, as an alternative formulation) has been thought about in sociology over the last half century or so. The issues we talk about are framed as a story which begins roughly after the Second World War, one which entails an analysis of modes of sociological reasoning that are deeply involved with each other as response and counter-response; a process that took place over time, dealing with issues that are still alive and well. Talking of the Deep South of the United States, the novelist William Faulkner memorably remarked, 'The past isn't dead, it isn't even past,' and the situation in sociology is, we suggest, much the same as it was in Faulkner's South. We present our analysis in the form of an historical story, but it is not a portrayal of a series of successive positions, in which the later ones replaced those that came earlier. To some extent, the movement between sociological positions over time is one of fashion.

Whatever the dynamic of change – and it is one that has produced very rapid shifts over the last 50 years – it is not one that involves the conclusive refutation or displacement of earlier positions which become marginalised by newer, and now more popular, ones. Earlier positions do not disappear from sociology altogether. Rather, they persist (though not always in the same form),

1

along with whatever positions are currently the more favoured ones. This leads some to think of sociology as a 'pluralistic' discipline, one which can, and indeed should, involve a wide variety of rather disparate perspectives, no one of which can legitimately claim for itself the status of *the* sociological point of view. Part of our reason for telling the story historically, however, is to show that in many important respects this 'pluralism' – or in contemporary phrasing, 'multiple voices' – involves a retreat from the ambition to create a unified discipline of sociology and, moreover, in some quarters a unified *science* of sociology.

> Sociology as pluralist discipline

Our story as begins with a short-lived but fateful pre-eminence of what we will call 'the positivist' point of view. Sociology never has been an extensively unified exercise, but around the mid-point of the twentieth century, there were strong hopes, especially in the United States, that it was on the point of becoming a unified and properly scientific point of view. The conviction that sociology should be a science, in much the same sense that the leading natural sciences are, is what we will here call the positivist point of view.

In this introductory chapter we identify in a general way some of the tensions in theory and method that will surface in various forms throughout the book. More detailed discussion of these and related issues will occur throughout the chapters to come.

Of course sociology has a long history, reaching back well before 1950 – and we will say something about this – but our choice of this date as providing our approximate starting point is not as arbitrary as it might seem. Our main aim here is to understand some of the central factors that have shaped contemporary sociological thought on theory and method, and from this point of view it was the dominance of positivist conceptions at that time which was a decisive influence on much – but not all – that came after. This will help us simplify our rather complicated story somewhat, allowing us to treat many of the main theoretical and methodological developments in terms of a reaction against positivism, a reaction that fed into a much wider stream of European thought: the reaction against the Enlightenment where positivism is but one strand of Enlightenment thinking.

Contemporary sociology is certainly in both theoretical and methodological disarray; 'disarray' being a less flattering way of describing the same facts that 'pluralism' identifies. Far from having achieved the unification that many thought both essential and inevitable, it has perhaps further disintegrated, dissolving into an assortment of schools of thought so diversified that they are perhaps not even so much in disagreement with each other as in different lines of business that have almost nothing in common. Sociology proliferates new points of view rather than accumulates or assembles a stock of assured results. Sociology, then, consists of an uneasy coexistence of different theoretical and/or methodological camps, most of which are characteristically dismissive of and otherwise indifferent to each other.

The idea of 'pluralism' suggests that this diversity is merely incidental, that

---

Inset 1.1 The Enlightenment and counter-Enlightenment

The Enlightenment was a major transformation in European thought, around the late sixteenth and seventeenth centuries, which aimed to replace the rule of arbitrary authority – God, the Church, the Monarch – with the rule of reason. Scientific knowledge would give true understanding, and would enable human beings to take rational control of their own, and society's, fate, to put an end to politics as a fight between ignorant armies and recreate it as a rationally conducted pursuit. Bringing in the reign of reason would mean that knowledge could be used to free individuals, make them more self-determining, controlled only by their individual capacity for reason.

Both Marx and Durkheim were deeply influenced by Enlightenment preconceptions, and sociology broadly has often assumed something like the Enlightenment ideal. However, it has never really been entirely devoted to the idea. Indeed, it can be argued that sociology owes more to the counter-Enlightenment movement which sought to question the notion that reason alone was sufficient to provide a just society. Human beings were motivated by more than reason. Religion, custom, tradition, status and ritual were as important as reason in understanding social life. Weber, for example, was much less optimistic than either Marx or Durkheim about what sociology could do to improve the human condition, and the extent to which human life could ever be shaped by the deliverances of reason. The counter-Enlightenment was much less impressed by the developing industrial society and by the idea that, in expanding the growth of both economic productivity and scientific knowledge, it was making progress. For example, the Romantic Movement in the nineteenth century felt that these social changes consisted of more losses than gains, and that a natural, humanised, even sacred order was being destroyed by the reign of intellectual presumption.

---

there is a range of equally valid options, any one of which might reasonably and rightly be chosen in preference to any other, as though there were nothing at stake in the choice. This may now be so, and the best way of treating the assortment of theoretical and methodological angles might be to deal with them in an eclectic fashion. However, this does not, we are convinced, assist in understanding how it got that way, and in consequence, it also fails to give a proper understanding of what the situation now is. The divisions and differences that now demarcate sociology derive from difficulties with and disagreements over the most fundamental and general principles that would decide what sociology might be, and the present 'pluralism' – or 'disarray' – condenses those principled issues.

As an illustration of what we are saying here, let us briefly look at the dispute between quantitative and qualitative methodologies, a distinction which will preoccupy us in various ways throughout the book.

The dispute between quantitative and qualitative methods: a preliminary excursion

There could not be a clearer or starker contrast than that between 'quantitative' and 'qualitative' research in sociology, though it is now more fashionable in methods texts to 'pooh-pooh' the idea that these two kind of research styles are *opposed* to each other. After all, so the argument goes, the difference between them is not utterly sharp, nor are the two kinds of work entirely distinct from each other. 'Qualitative' researchers themselves use 'quantitative' expressions – such as 'many', 'over half', 'several' and so on – so they cannot be *wholly* opposed to quantitative work. The tendency to downplay this contrast these days is, perhaps, due to a feeling that previously too much was made of it by treating them as hostile and antagonistic approaches.

The hostilities did not arise, however, from any failure to recognise that 'quantitative' and 'qualitative' might 'overlap' in the way outlined. The difference was not between those who had an exclusive passion for, to put it crudely, doing things with numbers and those who had an equally strong and exclusive antipathy toward doing *anything* with numbers. Our sociological predecessors were not quite that naïve. The contest between 'the quantitative' and 'the qualitative' was not a contest over using numbers or not, but over *the whole future of sociology*.

The notion that the opposition of 'quantitative' and 'qualitative' approaches can be overcome by pointing out that 'qualitative' researchers use quantitative categories is simply patronising if seen as an attempt to correct a prejudice against quantitative sociology. Rather than objecting to quantification in sociology *per se*, what aroused ire and opposition was the treatment of quantitative methods as if they were *the* template of the best of sociological research. A critique we will examine in some detail in Chapter 8.

Sociology has always been an ambitious pursuit, and it is in recognition of this that we will portray the hostilities we are currently touching upon not as involving opposition to 'quantitative methods' as such, but rather to what we will call 'the quantitative project'. Opposition to the latter does not entail opposition to the former at all, and certainly not merely because the methods are quantitative.

One of the ways in which sociology has often been ambitious is in its desire to turn itself into a science. Further, as if this was not ambition enough, it aimed to turn itself into the equivalent to the foremost of the sciences, such as physics, rather than the less dramatic but no less scientific disciplines such as botany. Making sociology match up to advanced physics might seem ambition enough, but there is also a strong

> The ambition to be a science

streak in sociology of wanting to make this transition *overnight*. Thus, there is a constant quest for the key that, when turned, will *transform* sociology utterly.

One of the things which is characteristic of advanced physics is, of course, that it is a highly mathematical and highly quantitative science. Its work is done in mathematics, and it can achieve astonishing standards of measurement. Thus, it could easily seem that the magic key for sociology was to turn the discipline into a science by turning it into a mathematised and quantitative venture.

However, in sociology we are not dealing with a patient, carefully and steadily thought-through process in which some people have successfully mathematised bits of sociology, and developed some impressive measurement techniques leading, at some point, to the recognition that sociology is turning itself into a quantitative science. Rather, we are dealing with a situation in which some people adopted the idea of making sociology quantitative as a means of making it into a science. We mark this difference by talking of the '*quantitative project*', highlighting the fact that we are dealing here with what was a *programme* for future work in sociology, not an established venture with a stock of substantial accomplishments.

Finding such a programme unpersuasive does not mean, however, that one must reject quantitative methods wholesale. Indeed, we will later suggest that scepticism about the quantitative project in sociology could be motivated in part by respect for the mathematical and quantitative achievements of the natural sciences. The idea that these could be matched pretty much overnight by sociologists hardly seems to pay tribute to the extent to which those achievements in the natural sciences have had to overcome considerable obstacles, an achievement which took many centuries.

The quantitative project was, furthermore, a programme of work marked (not untypically of sociological positions) by a missionary zeal. It is not usually enough, in sociology, to recommend *a* way in which one might go about sociological work. It is, rather, required that one recommend *the* way in which the cause of sociology be advanced. Those adopting the quantitative project were often fervent in their insistence that *theirs* was the only *bona fide* route to progress in sociology and to making sociology a science that could rank alongside physics. Sociological work which did not fit the template was scorned as a waste of time because it was qualitative not quantitative.

The opposition of 'qualitative' sociologists was, therefore, to the quantitative project, not to quantification as such. However, as we shall see, much of this opposition was defensive in character, designed to resist assignment to a second-class status within sociology. The main dispute was over whether immediately, systematically and exclusively taking up 'quantitative methods' was indeed going to turn sociology into a science *in the short term*.

The reaction against positivism was then, in important part, a reaction against the quantitative project that was affiliated with it, and sought to resist the self-appointed pre-eminence of that project. The quantitative project certainly has been – and forcibly – removed from a position of presumed pre-eminence, but, as we have said, it has not thereby disappeared from sociology entirely. It is still very much present in (especially American) sociology and in many other social science disciplines.

The difference between the 'quantitative' and 'qualitative' sides to that controversy was about the direction in which sociology should go. But this did not imply neutrality toward the means by which the quantitative project was to be implemented. Many were sceptical as to whether the sociological quantifiers really understood what was involved in quantification; there were doubts that the methods met the requirements that would entitle them properly to be called 'quantitative', or that the output of these methods did in fact depict the realities they were supposed to portray. In other words, these were doubts about whether quantitative methods in social research worked in the way they were supposed to and whether, even in their own terms, they amount to very much. These were not doubts about the validity of quantitative methods as such but about their deployment in sociology, an issue to which we will shortly return.

The gap between theory and method

Our story will be one of rags-to-rags in one generation. As mentioned, the relationship between 'theory' and 'methodology' has been a continuing theme in sociological thought and became even more pronounced in the period of the positivist project where our story begins. The two do not come together in the way that (at least in anything to be considered a serious science) they might and should. C. Wright Mills (1916–1962) these days is largely remembered for his complaint about 1950s American sociology, that it was divided between 'grand theory' and 'abstracted empiricism'. That was his way of putting the same point that Robert Merton, the functionalist theorist to whom Mills was otherwise opposed, was also putting. Merton argued the need for 'middle-range' theory to bridge the gap between general – or, as Mills called it, 'grand' – theory and empirical (or as Mills disparagingly deemed it, 'empiricist') research.

Inset 1.2 C. Wright Mills (1916–1962)

Mills was born in Waco, Texas, in 1916. He graduated in philosophy at the University of Texas in 1939, and received his PhD, for a thesis on pragmatism, at the University of Wisconsin in 1941. His intellectual heroes were Max Weber and Karl Marx. In 1945 he took up a post at Columbia University, New York, where he stayed until his death. He was highly critical of much of social science for its failure to mount a serious critique of the prevailing structures of power and inequality in American society. Among many other studies he produced three notable works on stratification: *The New Men of Power: America's Labour Leaders* (1948), *White Collar: The American Middle Classes* (1951) and *The Power Elite* (1956). His *Sociological Imagination* (1959) was a study of the evolution of the social sciences in the United States and their failure to retain the critical spirit of Marx and Weber. In brief, his complaint was that American sociology was divided between 'grand theory' – Parsons was his special target – which he claimed more or less endorsed the status quo, and 'abstract empiricism' which was not directed by any critical imagination, but instead devoted to measurement for the sake of measurement, and so failed to contribute to the exposure of political and social inequalities.

Inset 1.3 R.K. Merton (1910–2003)

Born in 1910 in Philadelphia, Merton went on the graduate studies at Harvard University, working with Talcott Parsons. Later he was to take a post at Columbia University, but he remained closely associated with Parsons and structural-functionalism. As far as the latter was concerned, his main contribution was to address particular problems inherent in that perspective. However, his sociological range was broad and can be divided into four discrete, yet interrelated, areas:

- His work on deviance is probably what he will be remembered for by most contemporary students of sociology. Merton took the concept of anomie from the work of Emile Durkheim and adapted it for use in an analysis of the motivations for crime and deviance in the twentieth-century United States. Merton's 'grid' of 'goals and means' is now prescribed reading for all students of the sociology of deviance. In the UK Merton's work has recently gained new authority through 'new left realism', one of the leading criminological theories which justifies much of its analysis of contemporary trends in crime by means of Merton's work on anomie and culture.
- Merton was critical of Parsons' work on structural-functionalism to the extent that it made crude and absolute assertions. Briefly put, Merton contested three main ideas of structural-functionalism: the problem of functional utility, the postulate of universal functionalism and the problem of indispensability. Merton claimed a) that not all social relations and institutions are functionally beneficial to 'social order' and, b) it is only by empirical investigation that a sociologist can determine the role of an institution in society, not by grand theorising alone.
- As a means of bridging the gap between 'grand theory' and 'empiricism', Merton argued that sociologists might be better employed designing and applying what he called 'middle-range theories'. These would have as their central objective the analysis of empirical social reality, but of a more restricted scope than the ambitions of grand theory.

> ▪ Merton also made a considerable contribution to the sociology of science. When all was said and done, Merton remained a functionalist, and this is demonstrated in his work on the 'scientific community'. While this is a valued piece of work, to the extent that it demonstrated the social, cultural and political basis of the community and practices of science and scientists, the analysis is firmly grounded in functionalism.

As we have also mentioned, one of the reasons why 'theory' and 'research' were so remote from each other, as Mills and Merton both suggested, was that they were characteristically done at considerable remove from each other, by different people with entirely different preoccupations. But the question that will eventually need to be considered is whether we are nowadays in a very different situation to that of which Merton and Mills complained almost 50 years ago. If in central respects this remains the situation, it is not one in which contentment reigns throughout. Attempts have, as we will describe, been made to reconfigure the relationship of theory and method in a more appropriate and effective way, but there are also those who have grown impatient with the whole idea. In reaction they have taken – in different ways, it is true – the view that there is something deeply flawed about the general idea sociology has of what is involved in understanding social life, and that the attempts to think of it in terms of theory and research methods address the real issues in only a distorted form. Again, the idea that there is or can be 'pluralism' needs to be questioned, certainly insofar as pluralism implies a comfortable kind of co-existence. Some of the latter-day developments – post-structuralism and post-modernism for example and the concerns of Part III – are, for some thinkers, deeply disturbing rather than comfortably companionable alternatives to their way of thinking.

Thus, a main strand in our story will be that of the *persistently problematic* relationship between theory and methods, depicting the changing understandings of how theory and methods, respectively or in conjunction, are meant to contribute to the overall understanding of social life, and the difficulties that afflict the various manoeuvres that are made within this space.

Sociology's reflexive preoccupation

If one had to sum up what the sprawling, diversified discipline of sociology is about in a single sentence, one might say that it is about understanding social life. What else could it be about? However, we take the view that if sociology is about 'understanding social life', then it is – to a very large extent – in a secondary and derivative sense. We would rather say that sociology's *first* concern is with its own nature. Sociology is, prevailingly, what we can only describe as a *programmatic* discipline. That is, it is (mainly) about *laying down in advance* how sociology should be done, attempting to specify *the right way* to understand social life.

As already mentioned, sociology has always been a very ambitious pursuit. If one accepts the claims of Auguste Comte (1798–1857) to be its founder – a claim which is certainly contested – then sociology was initially put forward as the very capstone on the whole development of human thought. Sociology was to be 'the queen of the sciences' and prevail over all the others. Even if subsequent sociologists have been more moderate in their ambitions, there remains a strong feeling in many quarters of the discipline that it represents:

- a new beginning in human thought, the promise, for the first time, of a true understanding of what society is
- the prospect of radical, knock-on consequences for other areas of human thought which have as yet failed to accommodate recognition of the fact that human life is social life, and also fail to recognise that this transforms their character
- the possibility of a much more rational control over social life, and of putting society right on the basis on sociology's to-be-provided understanding of how society *really* works.

Of course, quite what the implications of each of these might be is, as we shall see, a matter of debate and contention. Nonetheless, the point is that sociologists tend to think of the discipline less as a captivating interest in which they would like to research and more as a very significant development in social and cultural life more generally.

As we have intimated, these important developments are usually given in the future-perfect tense. They are 'what will-have-been-done when a full-blown sociology has been provided'. The question then remains: what will sociology tell us about social life when it is developed? As we have also intimated, one popular way of approaching sociology is through the idea that it will involve the bringing of social life under the frame of reference of modern (that is, post-seventeenth century) science. Sociology will pioneer the understanding of society since it will make the first applications of the scientific approach to social life.

However, it is one thing to say that one will introduce the scientific approach to the understanding of social life, but quite another to implement it. Just what is the scientific approach? Just how is it to be extended to the understanding of social life? In actuality, many of the great sociological theorists were not so much presenting us with discoveries about social life, akin to the discoveries science might make about nature, as spelling out an idea of what sociology might be, offering proposals about what a general approach to understanding society might be expected to say and, as part of this, often incorporating a conception of science. There are, of course, different ideas about the nature of science and different ideas about the ways in which sociology might effectively be turned into one, just as there are serious doubts about whether sociology is, can or needs to be much like a science and different ideas about what it might be instead.

The empirical studies that sociologists do are typically at least as much – and very often even more – concerned with developing and implementing some conception of what sociology might be as they are with the substantive matters that they are engaged in investigating. Be it the family, street corner gangs, work in a giant aircraft engineering firm, religious participation or the movement of fashion that is under investigation, much of the *sociological* interest of the study lies in *the strategy* that lies behind it. The fact that it is a study of religion, of the family or of a giant company does not *necessarily* matter all that much. It is the guiding ideas that are important. Understanding what is going on in a sociological study involves identifying the strategy that governs and informs the study, in seeing how it fits into a project for the further development of sociology.

> Sociology's strategic preoccupations

Given this view of how sociology works, we have tried to examine the development of theory and method in terms of their strategic thinking, to follow *the logic* of the different approaches, and the ways in which they seek to innovate on one another. Unless one understands the problem that the sociological strategists (the theorists and methodologists) are wrestling with in setting out their respective projects as they do, then one will not really understand what is at stake in the ways they develop their positions and differentiate themselves from others. A useful analogy is in the difference between the situation in chess and conversation. It is possible to look at a chess game that is in the middle of being played, and be able to see what the present situation is without needing to know anything about how the players have come to this position; in contrast, to belatedly enter a continuing conversation without knowing what has been said before can leave one at a loss as to what is currently being talked about and where the talk is going. Sociology is, in this way, more like an ongoing conversation than it is like a chess game, and knowing where we are in the present situation hinges upon an understanding of what went on before, of how we got into this situation in the first place. That the ongoing conversation has often been more like a protracted and bitter family row than like an affable exchange of congenial opinions does not diminish the point.

To illustrate further aspects of the above general points, let us return to a contrast we have met before and which, for all its faults, is a predominant one in sociological debates about method.

Quantitative and qualitative research

We have talked about the 'quantitative' and 'qualitative' contrast, and whilst we accept that it is not a *stark* contrast, it is still a very strong and pretty obvious one. Two data extracts can illustrate the contrast. The first is taken from a study of the effects of family and education on the political socialisation process (Dowse and Hughes, 1971). The second comes from an ethnographic study of field service photocopier technicians (Orr, 1996) which, among other things, shows how technicians share their knowledge of the subtleties of machine behaviour through an oral culture. (The extracts were chosen for convenience only: literally thousands of others could have been chosen to make our points).

Extract 1

Relationship between children's party preference and perception of parents' vote in the 1966 general election

	Children's party preference				
Children's perception of parents' vote	Labour	Conservative	Liberal	Other	Totals
Labour	75%	15%	8%	2%	100% (95)
Conservative	4%	90%	6%	0%	100% (82)
Liberal	5%	15%	70%	10%	100% (20)
Total	(75)	(91)	(27)	(14)	(197)

Gamma = 0.79; chi-square< 0.01

Extract 2

An intense group discussion of a machine and its problem occurred over lunch one day. A technician and I had just come from a machine with a recurrent, particularly opaque problem. There had been several service calls on it already, and most of the known fixes had been tried. The machine in its failed state appeared to provide no useful information about the problem. Two of the other technicians from the same subteam also showed up for lunch. A particularly skilled technician not formally part of their group was working with one of them that day and so was available to provide a fresh perspective. Introduction of new persons contributes to the collective consideration in that the summing-up necessary for the new participant to understand the situation permits those who have been working on it to look again at the situation as a whole. Since the difficulty in solving such problems lies in the weakness of the diagnostic information, the summing-up consists primarily of listing their attempts with different strategies known to dissolve the particular symptom. Such a summation is not entirely satisfactory because some of these dissolution strategies are parts replacements, and the technicians know well that even new parts are not necessarily reliable.

The differences between these two extracts could not be clearer. One is a table which numerically expresses the relationship between children's political preferences and those of their parents, as identified in a sample of 627 children at the time of the 1966 General Election in the UK. The other recounts a little story about a lunchtime work-related discussion among the repair technicians and is presented just as one might ordinarily tell a story. There are no numbers, no tables and no attempt to express any of the relationships recounted in a mathematical form.

Of course there are a considerable number of things to be done in order to produce either of these results, things we will be discussing later in the book. The points we want to concern ourselves with for now are more strategic.

Neither result is of particular interest *for its own sake*. There might be someone who found it useful to know how these 627 kids thought in 1966, and there might be someone fascinated by photocopier repair technicians and dying to know what they talk about over lunch – but we doubt it! Of course, these excerpts are not being offered to us because of their specific interest but have been produced for what we have been calling 'strategic' reasons. They are part of very different general strategies of sociological research.

Those researchers who produce statistical tables would be likely to regard the kind of materials presented in Extract 2 as one of the reasons for producing statistical tables. After all, the extract is a 'case study' of some photocopier technicians in California at a particular point in time. It reports a unique event. How could this be the basis of a generalisation about the kind of factors that cause people to behave in the ways they do? In other words, there is an assumption that sociologists are, or ought to be, in the business of seeking generalisations and that different research methods should be judged as means of arriving at generalisations.

> Seeking generalisations

As we have already said, no one has a particular interest in how many of 627 children had, in 1966, the idea that they supported the same or a different political party to their parents, but that is not what the tabular presentation is for. The aim of research of this kind is to arrive at something resembling the *law-like generalisations* of the natural sciences – and that, presumably, would be something worth having, something that everyone would like to know about. That is, it would be interesting and important if we found that there was a pretty general law about the relationship between the political preferences of children and those of their parents. If we could establish this then we might be on the way to understand not only these children in 1966 but the way in which *anyone's* political ideas are formed and endure through generations. In which case we need data that will enable us to start working out what such general relationships might be. And satisfactorily saying what these relations might be really requires a resort to *numbers*.

Galileo (1564–1642) thought that he had proved, by his pioneering and foundational work in the natural sciences, that the book of nature is written in numbers, and this conviction has been bequeathed to us: scientific understanding is cast in mathematical and numerical form. If we do not have mathematical and quantitative ways of expressing our thoughts, then they are not yet really scientific. Such views, however, are not held because previous great scientists held them or in order to ape the most advanced of the sciences. Putting things into numbers is a way of making what we have to say much clearer and more precise than is possible in our ordinary language. The advanced natural sciences are often called the *exact* sciences, inviting the view that real knowledge has to be exact in just this way. Qualitative sociologists might use quantitative expressions such as 'many', 'a large proportion' and so on, but such expressions are not precise. Scientifically, does it say very much to claim that 'many people' who have characteristic X also have characteristic Y? Just *how many* people count as 'many'? But if the claim is made in numerical form, such as '55 per cent of people with X also have Y,' then we can, for example, count up the relevant people to see if the claim is true, make more informed judgements about the significance of the finding, and so on.

A deeper thought behind this is that sociology will not make progress but remain an assemblage of people in chronic disagreement with each other until it is converted into a discipline in which researchers can put their ideas into numerical form and start to establish, with more precision, which ones conform to the evidence and which do not. Keep on producing detailed descriptions of the kind illustrated by Extract 2 and one will be making no contribution to turning the discipline into one that can accumulate attested findings and develop law-like, precise generalities. From this point of view, studies like that reported in Extract 2 are, with respect to the mission to make sociology into a science, effectively a waste of time.

From a different point of view things look very different. A motivation for doing a study like the one illustrated by Extract 2 might be resistance to the idea that sociology needs to be a quantitative discipline or, at the very least, that it needs to be one soon. Indeed, in this respect we can note that despite repeated attempts to make sociology into something like the natural sciences, it is still not very like

> The resistance to quantification

them. The idea of generating a formula which states precisely what kind of influence a parent's political affiliation will have on a child's subsequent attachments may seem attractive, but this is not even remotely within the reach of sociological research. Putting it very crudely – since it is a point that will be considered at length below – might it be that the attempts at turning sociology into a mathematised discipline are basically *half-baked*? Half-baked in that those who want to mathematise do not properly understand the difficulties such a project faces. *Perhaps* sociology is a very different kind of exercise than they envisage. *Perhaps* a lot of it is rather more like anthropology than it is like physics. Society might be like an assortment of very different tribes, and the aim of research is to understand the life of one or another of those tribes rather than formulate equations of the kind that describe the inanimate world. Thus, photocopier repair technicians in Silicon Valley are a 'tribe' that most of us know little about, and this report tells us something of what they do, tells us a little bit about how they think about the machines they are called upon to fix, and how they try to solve tough problems collectively.

Again, though, there is not much interest in such information taken on its own. There is no great reason why photocopier technicians be studied in preference to any other group of people, nor is it a particularly notable fact about them that they do these particular things. But the description is not an end in itself. It, too, is best understood as a part of a strategy, one which might even have the same long-term objective as the point of view that guided the research from which Extract 1 is taken. It might be that this study could contribute to the formulation of general laws about how social life works, but it will do so in a more roundabout and long-term way than does the attempt to move directly to mathematical and quantitative work. Alternatively, it might be guided by the idea that there is something wrong with the idea that human beings are best understood through law-like generalities, and that the whole idea of sociology as a quantitative discipline is at least much more problematic than is often imagined. The ambition to introduce measurement in sociological studies perhaps underestimates the degree to which understanding the way in which the doing of even ordinary social activities is complicated, more so than can be portrayed in a statistical table, or even a series of them.

From this latter point of view, the whole approach of those who would mathematise can seem all wrong. Typically, research of the kind that is reported using tabular presentations is produced by having employee researchers interview the children and then coding the answers given to the questions. The rationale of the approach is that the relationship between political preferences and parental influence can be discovered by working over the initial responses to the interviews and running them through various kind of statistical analyses to see what general relationships are present in the data. But the researchers themselves know little or nothing about the lives that they are purportedly studying, know nothing about the kids and their family situations except what they have been told by them. They know nothing *first hand* about their phenomena at all, and it is surely – as this way of thought can go – necessary for us to *know in detail* about the lives of people if we are to understand them properly. Even if sociology does end up as a highly generalised science like physics, it may nonetheless, have to *begin* by learning first hand, and in detail, about many individual cases.

Perhaps there is a deeper difference still, a difference which challenges the validity of thinking of sociology as a discipline like advanced physics. Perhaps the difference is between an 'atomistic' and a 'holistic' way of thinking. The success of physics has certainly been due in great extent to an 'atomistic' approach; breaking down

> Atomistic versus holistic thinking

phenomena into their component elements, trying to identify the basic constituents that compose those phenomena, and attempting to identify those constituents by isolating them from others with which they are involved with in the real world. Thus, in taking over the idea that sociology should be like a natural science, we may also take over the idea that to become this it will have to follow an atomistic approach. This might involve, for example, isolating the connection between the parents' (perceived by the children) political views and the party preferences of the children themselves from other considerations that might also influence the children's political preference, such as school, peers or even the media.

However, while an 'atomistic' approach *may* be effective in understanding many natural phenomena, though by no means all, there is another point of view which is persuasive. This points out that social phenomena are, in important respects, *contextual*. In which case, proceeding by means of an 'atomistic' strategy will mean that we run the great risk of misidentifying phenomena by isolating them from the context in which they are typically found. An instance often can only be correctly identified by first understanding 'the system' of which it is a part as, for example, one can only understand a sentence in a language if it is recognised that it is a part of a language and not isolated sounds or scribbles. One needs, that is, to understand how the principles of language work in order to understand the nature of its separate components of words, sentences and other elements. In which case, perhaps the kind of explanations that sociologists require are of this 'holistic' (or contextualising) type: that is, attempting to explain some of the things a certain group of people do both by analysing how 'the system' within which they act works and by filling in the detail of the immediate situations in which they do things. The latter entails the kind of detailed descriptions represented by Extract 2.

The main point we have been trying to outline so far is that specific studies gain much of whatever importance they have from the fact that they serve as *vehicles* for the implementation of general strategies for sociological research. We have developed the point in terms of a contrast between the 'quantitative' and 'qualitative' strategies as a struggle to show how their respective ideas about social life can be effectively applied in research. Very often a most important function of research in sociology is that of *illustrating an idea*, of showing, in more concrete terms, what the more abstract theoretical and methodological ideas might imply.

We have given, in gross terms, a simplified contrast between very broad strategies for creating sociology, for working out what its nature is. Sociology's reflexive preoccupation should not be misunderstood as being at the expense of what ought to seem the serious business of a science: namely, understanding the nature of its subject matter, of the phenomena that it purports to deal with. Questions as to whether sociology should be like the natural sciences or not are, of course, argued about on the assumption that the correct answer to this question will depend upon what it is that social life is really like. The attempt to set out programmes for sociology, then, involves trying to say something about what social life is really like.

Although our story begins roughly in the 1950s, sociology is of course much older than this and, in important ways, the ideas of its founders have all played their part in shaping thinking about the nature of the discipline and how social life might be investigated. There is a tendency in sociology these days to denigrate sociology's past thinkers. However, our view is that it is hard to understand the present character of sociology without some understanding of the tradition which has shaped it. As we shall see in the following chapters many of the methodological debates in sociology are informed and fashioned out of themes which have long been of concern to the discipline.

In the next part of this chapter we want to identify some themes and issues first identified by the founders of sociology – mainly Marx (1818–1883), Durkheim (1858–1917) and Weber (1864–1920) – and which are still present in today's debates.

Themes from the founders

The main founders of sociology, especially the two theorists Marx and Durkheim, thought that they were taking a pretty drastic step in the understanding of human social life. In a way, they were taking a stand on the 'holistic' side of the dispute about the nature of society (though they also thought that they were being scientific in their approach). They argued that the trouble with much thinking about society was that it hardly recognised society at all: previous thought was much too 'individualistic'. August Comte, the nominal founder of sociology, had certainly insisted that society, as a form of coherent social organisation, a more or less integrated system of institutions, was a precondition for human life, but he had been preceded by (and would be succeeded by) numerous thinkers – such as Thomas Hobbes (1588–1679), Jean-Jacques Rousseau (1712–1778) – who thought that the individual was the basis for understanding society. Both Marx and Durkheim insisted that this got the situation the wrong way round and that the knack was to understand that society comes before the individual, that the individual's nature is not so much an individual nature as a *social* one.

Furthermore, Marx and Durkheim firmly held that the context in terms of which the individual's activities were to be seen was that of the whole society. It was only in the large view, and the long term, that the nature of social activities become truly apparent. It is only when a way of doing things is seen in the context of *the whole society* that it is properly identified. For example:

- Marx argued that what may look like a fair exchange between individuals – such as the wage transaction between an employer and an employee – when seen in the context of the capitalist *system* can be recognised as an exploitative relationship in which the behaviour of employers and employees as categories are subject to the operations of the capitalist system.
- Durkheim held that what may seem to some a pointless and misguided pursuit – religion – can, when viewed in relationship to the society as a

whole, be seen to play an invaluable part in sustaining the unity of the society. In other words, it is not so much what is worshipped that is important but the act of collective worship.

Marx and Durkheim also agreed that the understanding of our present society also requires seeing that it is the product of a long-term historical development. Society naturally changes, and the present condition is only one by no means permanent stage in the continuing development of the society. Moreover, both strongly suggested that this historical development followed a pattern. Indeed, for Marx one of the objectives of sociology was to discover the laws of historical social evolution.

Also, both thought that sociology should be like the natural sciences, though they each had a rather different idea as to which science should provide their model. Though Marx was hugely impressed by Darwin's evolutionary ideas, he saw himself by analogy with astronomers who, knowing the laws of motion of heavenly bodies and the present position of the planets in the solar system, could predict their future locations. In the same way, understanding the laws of change of society, and knowing its present structure, one can – in principle – predict its future. Durkheim saw biology as a model, entitling him to think of society by analogy with an organism: one understands the nature of the parts of an organism in terms of their relationship to the whole organism, to the part, the function, they play with each other in sustaining its existence. Moreover, if one understands what the natural arrangement of parts for a particular kind of organism is, then one can identify deviations from that norm – pathologies of the organism – and can attempt to repair these. Society's institutions are to be understood in relation to the unification of the whole society – this is Durkheim's pioneering functionalism – and the sociologist can, when these things are understood, operate equivalently to the pathologist, identifying abnormal states of the society and figuring out to how eradicate them.

Both Marx and Durkheim raised an issue which has since bedevilled social thought. There seems to be a conflict between the ways in which we, as members of the society, blithely unaware of sociology, think of ourselves and our lives, and the way that science thinks of them. The presumption is that science is the correct way of thinking about things, which raises the issue that what a sociological science will show about social life will invalidate our ordinary ways of thinking about ourselves and our place in the world. We may think of ourselves as autonomous and self-guided creatures, in that what we do is pretty much up to us and what we want to do. If someone asks us to explain why we are doing whatever it is that we are doing, we can respond by pointing to our intentions, by what we have in mind when we set out to do what it is we want to do.

But the idea that what we are doing can only be identified on the large view and in relation to the long term – this is what *social science* means – suggests that we are not in any position to really know what we are doing, and therefore in no position to explain it either. Moreover, such a science will show us that our activities are governed not by our intentions but by *laws* which explain what we do. The laws dictate how we will act, regardless of what we think. The picture is of ourselves as very small cogs in a large machine and our conduct to be explained in terms of the way in which the cogs fit into the whole machine, driven by its law-governed relationships with other parts of the machine.

Neither Marx nor Durkheim were dismissive of lay ideas and thought. However, they did argue, in their various ways, that a science of society would strip away the illusions about how society actually worked. Society itself can prevent people from seeing the true reasons why their lives are the way they are. They become blinkered by ideological thinking. Implicit in the very idea of a sociological science was that it was capable of revealing the true state of affairs about society, states of affairs of which ordinary members were unaware. In which case sociology would consist of a special set of competences and sensitivities which, if properly applied, gave the science its intellectual authority. But, and this was the awkward question, why should conceptions of a science of social life be exempted from social influences? How do we know that we have the right conception of such a science?

| Science versus ideology |

Max Weber, the third of the great founders of modern society, was unequivocal in his rejection of the idea of sociology as the science of society-as-a-whole. He was far from accepting ideas of the sort that Marx and Durkheim put forward if, at times, somewhat ambiguously. Unlike them, he was sceptical of the idea that 'society as a whole' was any kind of empirical reality, and hence that it could provide a subject matter for the science of sociology. His arguments initiated what was – at least until the present – very much a minority strand of dissenting thought in sociology, often called the 'social action' tradition. Sociology is about individuals not about 'social wholes', and its business is understanding (*verstehen*) rather than discovering law-like generalities. That is, it accepts the ways in which we ordinarily think of ourselves, as acting out of our intentions and beliefs, as the way in which the things we do *are to be explained*. Of course, the kind of intentions and beliefs that we have as individuals differ – often considerably – from time to time and place to place. Accordingly, the explanations of the things that people do, their actions, involves identifying the relevant kind of intentions and beliefs from which their actions arise. Effectively, sociology is done through understanding the point of view of the people in whose conduct we are interested.

Inset 1.4 Hermeneutics

Weber's ideas were not necessarily original to him. He was often involved in attempting to synthesise different strands of thought current in the Germany of his day, where there was a tremendous controversy – the *methodenstreit* or 'debate over method' – over whether historical and cultural studies should be like the natural sciences or completely different to them. Weber's own view on this was that the historical and cultural studies were like the natural sciences in their use of the same basic logic of empirical investigation and proof, but very different in their relationships to their respective phenomena. The idea of looking at society through the eyes of its members was something he inherited from the tradition of 'hermeneutics', a discipline that originated in biblical scholarship, concerned to understand fragments of biblical texts in the light of what was known about the life and culture in which the these texts were created. Wilhelm Dilthey (1833–1911) was an important precursor of Weber's in making the case that the understanding of society is more like such an interpretative (or hermeneutic) task than it is like the generation of scientific laws in the natural sciences.

Like Marx and Durkheim, Weber thought that the long historical view was necessary to understanding social phenomena. It would be quite wrong, for example, to think that the capitalist economic system in which we live is the one and only possible system, and that no alternative to it is conceivable. Seen against the backdrop of its history, the capitalist system with which we are all familiar will be recognised as being historically unusual, and in fact unlikely. It was only a thoroughly specific set of circumstances that resulted in the rise of the capitalism that we have. Indeed, one of Weber's most notorious contributions is his attempt to comprehend the point of view of devout members of (particularly) the Calvinist sect at the time of the Reformation in the seventeenth century. Understanding how Calvinists thought about their place in the world enables us, Weber argues, to understand what led them to behave in hitherto unprecedented ways which, further and unintentionally, anticipated those of capitalist work organisation. We will thus see that the early development of capitalism was, in a central respect, a by-product of the religious Reformation.

Marx, Weber and Durkheim also introduced another contentious issue that has run through much of the subsequent history of social thought. Is society *essentially* a matter of harmony or conflict? Marx and Weber both took

> Society as harmony or conflict

the view that society is *primarily* a political entity, that it is a composite of groups which have aims and interests that are often at odds with each other. The unification of society, insofar as it exists, is a political imposition, effected through the use of power, the whole being held together by the dominance of some groups which can both coerce other groups and also use their power to arrange things so that subordinate groups come to accept the legitimacy of the powerful.

Marx held that the groups which essentially made up society were social classes, groups identified by their economic positions and the different, conflicting interests associated with those. The economic conflicts led to other conflicts throughout social life and politics, so that Marx (and his collaborator Engels) could boldly declare that the history of all hitherto existing societies is a history of class struggle. Weber did not entirely disagree, but was against any kind of essentialism, and insisted that classes were not the only nor, necessarily, the most important groups involved in social conflict: status groups – ones based on cultural commonality – were often more important than classes for example, especially in establishing the predominance of culture within a society. However, for both Marx and Weber, social life is very much a matter of struggle between groups for predominance.

Though he did not deny the reality of class conflict in modern societies, Durkheim thought that this was a sign of pathology in the society, rather than an expression of its essence. Society was not, from his point of view, an ensemble of groups so much as it was a complex of institutions and practices, and his concern was with the way in which such an ensemble articulated itself into a unified entity. Thus, he was concerned with the ways in which religion, education, the occupational structure and the economy, could be fitted together so as to *both* integrate – hold together – the society as a whole *and* integrate individual members into that society, ensuring that they were in strong and supportive relationships that would prevent them from, in the extreme, destroying themselves by committing suicide.

Durkheim's legacy was, in respect of the issue of harmony versus conflict, much more influential on the 'positivist' position at the mid-twentieth century than it has been since, and it is unquestionably the case that Marx's and Weber's perception of society as group struggle which prevails amongst sociologists today.

Concluding remarks and how to read this book

We like to think of sociology as a 'project'; this idea is important to what follows and also implies some scepticism as to whether any approach in sociology is a sound basis for a *discipline* of sociology. We are not saying that sociology is not worth pursuing, that it cannot be a science or that it is trivial, self-indulgent and speculative rubbish – though much of it is. Rather, the point we want to make is that so many of the fundamental problems of sociology remain unresolved and may even be unidentified. It remains a project which has yet to be realised.

> Sociology as a project

There are other aspects of the idea of a sociological project that we want to convey. While we do not wish to offer a false picture of sociology as a coherent, unified discipline, we do want to stress the idea of a common endeavour. Generally, sociologists tend to think of themselves as attempting to *construct* a discipline. But, unlike the natural sciences, this is not to be done by studying social phenomena, learning from studies and developing a richer understanding of such phenomena. Rather, and as we have indicated, from the earliest days, it is by laying out general strategies to fashion the discipline – working from the top down we might say. This way of approaching matters is not only part of sociology's heritage but one which exerts a considerable influence on its current style. It is the extent to which sociology consists of efforts to envision the means to effect its progress which leads us to talk about the 'sociological project'. What tends to go on in sociology is tied to some conception of the right approach to the construction of the entire discipline. So, while there may be a common objective of building sociology, there is often fundamental disagreement as to the most effective way of going about this.

In addition, we also want to emphasise that the 'project' has still to be worked out. Like many projects, be they in industry, in design, in warfare, in government or in engineering, finding out just what the project entails, just what one is committed to, is often only discovered in the course of implementing it. Working out ideas often takes much thought and effort over many years, undertaken, in the case of disciplines, by scholars who work independently rather than under central direction. It is in the attempt to implement the versions of the sociological project that unanticipated problems can arise, especially in trying to move from the general idea of how sociology ought to be done to actually doing it that way. This is one aspect of the issue we started out with: namely, the gap between 'theory' and 'research'.

Regarding sociology as a project still underway is not to see it as a failure. That sociologists seems to be always arguing about fundamental matters does not mean that it is not worth taking seriously. Though physics, chemistry and history, among many others, do not seem quite so preoccupied about their very basis as disciplines, this does not mean that sociology is a less worthwhile pursuit. It should, however, indicate that it is perhaps more difficult than it is often made to appear. As we often say to our students: almost anyone can do sociology, but hardly anyone can do it really well. Be this as it may, it is important to take a more historically tempered view of matters such as these. After all, it took many centuries for physics to attain its present status as the pre-eminent science, and though it is very much an open question as to whether the sociological project could ever match this, or even whether it makes sense to try, as a discipline it clearly has a long way to go.

However, having said this it has to be accepted that the necessary patience for the long haul tends to be in short supply in sociology in the face of anticipations that overnight transformations of the discipline are possible. All that is required is the right key. So, while there is a kind of continuity to the discipline this is as much a matter of wrestling with and returning to the problems of sociology's own identity as of engaging in a continuous accumulation of knowledge. Because many of the problems are fundamental, the discipline is subject to periodic 'seismic' shifts involving drastic movements in its preoccupations. In this text we focus on three such shifts:

- *The positivist project*: the attempt, from the 1940s to about the mid-1960s, to create a scientific sociology through the development of methods of social research. These methods – social surveys, questionnaires, statistical analysis and the like – became the standard tools of social research and are still the methods students learn.

■ *The qualitative turn*: though having antecedents at least as old as if not older than positivism, this developed as a reaction against the positivist project. In brief, its attack was levelled against the model of the social actor and society presupposed by positivism and its methods.

■ *Critique and discourses*: this third shift really represents two strands, one of which, structuralism, attacked positivism's conception of science in favour of an alternative based on linguistics rather than physics. The other movement, post-structuralism and its relative, post-modernism, place language centre stage in an attack on the very idea of an all-encompassing, general account of society and social life. Both sought to refurbish the idea of critique which had been sidelined by the positivist project.

At one level, this is the story of progressive disillusionment with the positivist worldview. While it would be misleading to think of these movements as representing discrete phases in which, say, during the positivist period every sociologist was doing positivist directed research, and then suddenly all switched to reacting against it, and then finally we all ended up doing discourse analysis, they do reasonably represent the dominant modes of thinking about theory and method in sociology over the last 50 years or so. When they were prominent, they were, in effect, the 'leading-edge' ideas, the innovative, even revolutionary, ideas, the latest ideas – a position currently held by post-modern thinking. This does not mean, however, that there are no longer any positivists, or that the problems which, for example, positivism tried to deal with are no longer relevant, or indeed that the latest thinking will prevail for long. There are still positivists around, just as there are interactionists, Weberians and Marxists, to mention but a few, all of whom still make contributions to the debates and arguments within the sociological project.

In what follows we will endeavour to give a clear an account of each style of thinking, dealing with them all as seriously minded attempts to deal with real problems of sociology and social research.

A word about how to read this book

This book is not intended as a methods text which will furnish you with the methods and techniques for doing social research. There are already many such texts available. Our aim is to review and illustrate the logic of the methods. It is intended as a book to help the reader think sociologically by thinking methodologically. Nevertheless, in parts where we think it appropriate for the argument, we have taken some time to provide expositions of the main elements of particular methods. Some of these are set in *Insets* which can be omitted if necessary. This is to preserve as best we can the main flow of the argument.

A selected bibliography is provided at the end of each chapter. Regrettably, finding some of these titles might require the services of a well-stocked library of sociological texts since a proportion of them are old or even out of print. However, we hope that our exposition gives enough flavour of the originals to encourage at least some readers to take the trouble to track down and read some of these worthwhile contributions to the sociological tradition.

It ought to come as no surprise that the authors have their own preferences and axes to grind, and although we have striven hard to be even-handed throughout the various approaches discussed (even when we vehemently disagree with them), it would be no small miracle if these preferences remained invisible. However, the book is about sociological arguments and if it provides a better appreciation on the part of students as to what these consist in, then it will have served one of its important purposes. Certainly, it is no part of our intention that readers will necessarily agree with what we have to say. We will, however, be disappointed if readers do not at least appreciate the force of the arguments.

Selected bibliography and suggested reading

There are many good accounts of social thought since the Enlightenment.

- Nisbet's *The Sociological Imagination* (1967) is still good, although written some years ago.
- Hughes et al's *Understanding Classical Sociology* (1995) provides lengthy expositions of Marx, Weber and Durkheim.
- Ray's *Theorising Classical Sociology* (1999) is a very good thorough analysis of classical social thought.
- C.W. Mills' work is still worth reading, especially *The Sociological Imagination* (1959), which reflects on many of the enduring tensions between theory and research in sociology.

Part I

The Positivist Project

Chapter 2

The Positivist Project: Introduction

By 1950, sociology had been in existence for some time, though it was not to become a prominent university subject in the United Kingdom until the 1960s. Of the classic European theorists – Marx, Durkheim and Weber – it was the latter two who had made an impact on American sociology, which was to become for a time the centre of sociological attention. Talcott Parsons (1902–1979), one of the dominant figures in American sociology from the late 1930s, had attempted to construct a 'general theory' of social action, which comprised, in part, a synthesis of what he saw as the key insights of Durkheim and Weber.

Inset 2.1 Talcott Parsons (1902–1979)

After a short but significant period of postgraduate training in Europe, Parsons spent his academic life at Harvard University. He had a major influence after the Second World War, though he was perhaps as much criticised as followed. His earliest major work, *The Structure of Social Action* (1937) was an extended analysis and synthesis of the thought of Weber, Durkheim and the economists Pareto and Marshall. He argued that sociology was the science of action.

His aim was to provide a conceptual scheme for all the social sciences. His main proposal was for a 'general theory of action', starting from Weber's idea of sociology as the study of social action combined with elements from Durkheim. This he argued would provide a common frame for all the 'sciences of action', ranging from anthropology and psychology to economics, as well as sociology.

However, while sociology, especially in the United States, might be doing well in institutional terms – recruiting students and scholars, forming university departments and research institutions, proliferating research projects – some unease began to develop. Sociology did not appear to be really progressing *as a science*. Much work was being done, some of it very ambitious, but it did not really add up to anything very definite or conclusive. Perhaps something drastic needed to be done. Some argued that the discipline was too preoccupied with its classic heritage and needed to start afresh, unencumbered by what were essentially nineteenth-century concerns. Robert Merton, then second only to Parsons in the sociological hierarchy, however warned his sociological colleagues of an old saw: a science that hesitates to forget its founders is lost. There was a growing feeling that sociology needed to be less concerned with its early founders and, instead, address the idea of making itself into a science more seriously, and in a different way from hitherto.

Sociology looked nothing like the natural sciences, and this needed remedying. Merton was only one of the thinkers (many of whom were, like him, associated with sociology at Columbia University, New York) involved in what we are calling the positivist project, the attempted re-launch of sociology into a more properly scientific status. They did not see themselves as transforming sociology overnight into a science as fully fledged as physics or chemistry. They did, however, think that, almost overnight, a change in sociology could be effected which would 'lift sociology's game' from being something that was, at best, primitively proto-scientific into something that was on the road to becoming authentically scientific. The development of sociology into something comparable to physics might be a long game, but meaningful pursuit of that ambition could be started right away. And it was the natural sciences which they took as their model or, to be more precise, a philosophically inspired version of science which needed to be translated into theories and methods, thinking and practice, which would establish sociology as a true explanatory science.

The key to this transformation was to achieve a more effective relationship between sociological theorising and empirical research. Given the way in which they were done, the two activities could not connect with each other. Both would need to be fundamentally reshaped so that they could connect more effectively, allowing theories to be properly tested against empirical data and to give clear and direct guidance and significance to empirical research.

> The gap between theory and research

It turned out that the transforming method was the social survey. This was not a invention or innovation specifically for sociological research but rather an assembly of ideas and research techniques which had been around for some time. Questionnaires and social surveys were widely used at the turn of century by market researchers, as were interviews. Statistics and measurement techniques were well under way in the 1930s, largely inspired by work in psychology using statistics derived originally from work in botany and agronomy. The achievement as far as social research is concerned was to assemble these methods and techniques into a framework which, it was claimed, was based on a clear conception of how science worked.

To dispel a fairly common misconception about positivism, it is important to note that the project was not simply about methods of social research, even though these are perhaps its most prominent legacy. The point of research methods was to serve the development of theory, and we will acknowledge this by focusing mainly on theory in the next chapter before discussing

> Methods for the improvement of theory

the methods. The positivist project's motivating question was how to put sociology onto a scientific footing and turn it into a properly empirical discipline – one directed toward producing properly scientific theory. For the proponents of positivism, sociology had both too much and too little theory: too much of the wrong kind, and too little of the right.

Throughout its span, sociology had produced a great many different, and radically opposed, general schemes which presumed to explain the whole of history and which were really as much philosophically inspired speculations as anything else. Such schemes might well have their interest and value, but they had nothing of the empirical power of leading natural science theories. Sociology's theoretical schemes were far from being thoroughly systematic and were at best very loose, rambling and rather vague orienting frameworks. None had proved capable of producing cumulative and systematised knowledge. While many of the formulators of these general schemes used empirical illustrations to fill them out, these illustrations were not drawn from systematically collected data, or data which connected systematically to the theoretical scheme being illustrated. They could not be counted as scientific reports on how the social world really was. All that such materials did was support the theory, suggest that the framework was a plausible one, that it appeared to cover some of the things that seemed to happen in social life. For the positivists, the need was to ensure that the methodology of research became as important an issue as that of the formation of theory.

As for the formation of theory, it was necessary to have more modest ambitions. It was too early to aspire to a general theory of social life to match the general theories of physical nature. A much more moderate aim was needed: to build what Merton was to call 'middle-range' theories, ones that were much less abstract and general than the kind of thing that went into Talcott Parsons 'general theory of social action'.

> Middle-range theory

Not only did the theories need to be more limited in their range (applying to a specific area of social life rather than to social life as a whole), they also needed to alter their character, to be formulated in a much more concrete and specific way such that they could make definite assertions about what would happen in that area of social life, and yield *some empirically testable predictions*.

Merton's recommendations for theory building were ideally to be complemented by the programme for developing sociological methods led by his colleague at Columbia, Paul F. Lazarsfeld (1901–1976), methods which took the problem of measurement seriously. These are the methods we will be discussing in this part of the book.

Inset 2.2 Paul F. Lazarsfeld (1901–1976)

Born in Vienna, Lazarsfeld emigrated to the United States as the Nazis came to power in Germany. Prior to this he had occasionally attended meetings of the Vienna Circle, a group of logical positivist philosophers committed to building a philosophical account of science based on indubitable sensory experience of the world. On reaching the United States Lazarsfeld joined the staff of Columbia University and, in the course of a research project designed to evaluate the effects of radio broadcasts, began to develop what became known as 'variable analysis'. In addition he did pioneering research on voting, as well as setting up the Bureau of Applied Social Research which made extensive use of, and contributed to the development of, the social survey – the method which became most closely associated with 'variable analysis'. In addition, the Bureau, largely funded by broadcasting companies interested in the effects of radio upon a rapidly expanding audience, sparked Lazarsfeld's influential interest in the media and the formation of public opinion.

He was well-versed in European philosophy and at one stage attempted to get Theodor Adorno, one of the leading theorists of the Frankfurt School, to provide theoretical contributions to one of the Bureau's empirical projects. The collaboration was not a success. Lazarsfeld deserves to be better remembered as one of the important contributors to modern sociology and social science more generally

Lazarsfeld's initial efforts were immensely influential, and by the 1960s the development of research methods was already well established and generating a fast-growing body of studies covering the effects of the mass media, the determinants of voting choice, deviance, community life, industrial work and much more. There was an imperturbable confidence about the future prospects of such research and its prospects for a scientific sociology.

There are at least two methodological threads which run through the story of the positivist programme during this period and which served, in their various ways, as a backdrop to many of the more particular efforts and developments in method. These were:

- the form and content of theory
- the development of quantitative methods.

The form and content of theory

This issue arose out of philosophical considerations of the nature of scientific knowledge and how it was to be distinguished from knowledge which only masqueraded as science. Science, it was argued, is a superior form of knowledge in that its ideas can be systematically subjected to empirical test to determine whether or not they are true. It was this which had transformed human knowledge of the natural world and enabled growth in the sciences themselves and in technological development. The great success of the sciences in discovering laws of nature of great scope and power – such as Boyle's law, Newton's laws of motion and Einstein's relativity theory – were seen as a testament to science as a form of knowledge. However, even accepting this at face value, it leaves the question as to what it is about science which makes such knowledge possible?

Questions such as this had been the concern of those branches of philosophical inquiry known as epistemology and ontology. While closely related, briefly the latter is concerned with what exists, what is real, and the latter with the ways in which what exists may become known. The point we want to stress here is that, as philosophical concerns, ontology and epistemology are not about empirical questions, questions that science can answer. They are, among other things, about the nature of empirical knowledge, about the nature of science, and as such are beyond empirical inquiry, beyond the remit of science. And since, almost from its beginnings, sociology sought its intellectual foundations in philosophy, such questions continue to be central in sociological debates.

> Epistemology and ontology

As a philosophy, positivism stressed that reality consists essentially of what is available to the senses. Knowledge fundamentally depends upon our sensory experience of the world. However the term 'senses' is not to be understood as, for example, what we might see when we look out of the window. Such perception is mediated by our experiences and cultural knowledge. We know that it is a window we are looking out of, we know that what we see is a street, people walking along it, cars and buses moving to and fro, and so on. But for all kinds of reasons we can be mistaken in what we see. Such perceptions, the positivists argued, could not be foundational to knowledge. What was needed was a specification of indubitable sensory experience which would serve as the bedrock of knowledge. The view, and it had been a persistent one throughout European philosophy, is that in order for something to qualify as knowledge, as opposed to belief or opinion, it had to be grounded in something that was certain, which could not be doubted. For the positivists

> Basis of positivist ontology

this was sensory experience, mainly seen in physicalist terms: that is, in the basic 'sense data' which impinge upon our senses and which are the raw materials out of which we build our more mediated perceptions and experiences. What such 'sense data' consisted in was a preoccupation of positivist philosophy for a long time, and had no ultimately satisfactory solution. But the implication for the positivist programme in social research was the emphasis placed on connecting theory to the empirical world which provided observational data for testing the truth and adequacy of the theories.

However, for such a process to work it had to be systematic. As we have already said, for a long time sociology had used empirical illustrations within its theoretical discussions, but this was not the same as determining whether the theory was true or not. According to positivism, science was distinctive in terms of its method, and any discipline that laid claim to being a science would have to conform to that method. Thus, the natural and the human sciences shared a common foundation: a scientific method. Although the notion of the scientific method was to be the centre of considerable debate, what was clear was that it was a systematic, highly structured and strongly disciplined process. As far as theories were concerned, this meant that if theories seek to explain they had themselves to be both clearly organised, which meant giving them a *logical* organisation, and much more clear and specific in what they said. They must replace vague generalities about the nature of things with specific *and testable* characterisations of how things are. The change to the form of theories was one main part in the attempt to unify theory and method, to ensure that the logical connections between the general explanatory ideas and the empirical reports ran right through the whole. The abstractions of the theory should be connected by logically systematic links, closely and in detail, to empirical data, so that it would be possible to tell unequivocally whether the abstract concepts really did capture the nature of the phenomena as displayed in the data.

The development of quantitative method

The second thread, and perhaps the most salient outcome of the positivist project, was the creation of social research methods which attempted to establish the basis of measurement, or as we shall often alternatively call it, quantification.

Once again, it is important to note that this was not intended as quantifying for the sake of quantifying. Quantification aimed to serve the testing of theories. Since one of the hallmarks of the more advanced natural sciences – to which, further, they seemed to owe much of their power – was quantification, then social research should also begin to devise means of quantifying its phenomena. Although it was realised that the resultant efforts could only be a beginning to proper quantification, measurement quickly became regarded as a central

Quantification and measurement

element of theory testing, as revealing decisively whether or not the theoretical abstractions really did 'fit the facts'. Quantitative data imparted, it was claimed, precision to the research process and represented a set of strict procedures to bring to bear on testing theories: to be able to say that the temperature will be 15 degrees tomorrow is more precise than saying it will be a hot day. A product of natural science, the thermometer, enables us to grade how warm things are in this precise way, degree by degree, and it was thought that the social sciences would massively benefit from tools that would enable them to precisely *and reliably* grade the degree to which any given social phenomena is present.

These two threads were to organise much of the effort of the positivist project, and it was around them that many of the debates flowed. Much of the push was devoted to realising these ambitions in research instruments and procedures. We begin, however, with a discussion of some of the general issues arising from the endeavour to transform sociology into a science.

Perhaps the best way of reading what follows on positivism is to see it as the result of trying to implement a project's strategy – an implementation which involved a number of scholars who were not working according to a fully detailed and worked out plan. If anything they were trying to work out the details of the plan as they went along. Some focused on developing the statistical apparatus, some on the theory, some on developing surveys and interview techniques, some on measurement, but there was no overall direction.

Selected bibliography and suggested reading

- Useful introductions of positivist philosophy more generally are L. Kolakowski, *Positivist Philosophy* (1972) and P. Halfpenny, *Positivism and Sociology* (1982).
- An excellent discussion of the 1950s and 1960s period in American sociology is S.P. Turner and J.H. Turner, *The Impossible Science: An Institutional Analysis of American Sociology* (1990).

Chapter 3

Building a Science of Sociology

Positivism here is being considered as a *strategy* for the transformation of sociology. In evaluating its success we will focus only on the standards that it set for itself in seeking to realise the aims of the strategy. As we will see, positivism's certainly did transform sociology, and introduced into sociology a set of research practices that probably remain the most common ones in use in social research today. But it failed to transform sociology in the way that it intended. We will argue that the positivist project stalled at a comparatively early stage in the game. However, acknowledging that the positivist project did fail (and we review many of the fundamental criticisms that have been made of the project) should not prevent us from giving a sympathetic account of the reasoning underlying it. Assuming that in the intellectual conditions of the time sociology appeared to have the potential to be a science, then the positivist project must have seemed an entirely persuasive one, a wholly plausible direction in which to go.

In the next four chapters we examine the underlying logic intended to link the three main elements of the positivist strategy: the adoption of formal theory, of variable analysis using non-experimental statistics, the social survey and the interview.

The top-down strategy of positivism

The positivist project effectively begins with an idea of what a science is, one based on the natural sciences. One of the main tenets of positivism was that there was – that there *had* to be – a unity of method to all the sciences and, accordingly, if the social sciences were to join that company then they would have to find ways of implementing that method in their inquiries. It was confidently assumed that the social studies were quite capable of becoming sciences; there was no obstacle to this other than the failure to go about building the science in the right way.

It was realised that following the scientific method was not simply a matter of adopting identical techniques and procedures to those used in the various natural sciences. It would be difficult, for example, to carry out proper experiments in sociology. However, the unity of method did not refer to the general sharing of the actual procedures and techniques of any one of the natural sciences, but to following the *logic* of inquiry all the sciences supposedly followed, each in their different way. This was a logic that philosophers of science and knowledge had been trying to formulate for some

> The logic of scientific inquiry according to positivism

centuries (although it had, intriguingly, proven elusive). Desirably, the logic of the scientific method would need to be set out in advance, for sociology's prospects of success would depend on its conforming to the general logic of science, and to know how to fit with this sociologists would need, first, to know what that logic was. Their task would be to implement that logic in the study of society.

As we saw in Chapter 1, this 'top-down' approach of creating sociology to accord with a pre-given image of what science was like was essentially the strategy followed by the classic thinkers, all of whom engaged with philosophical versions of science prior to their more substantive work. The strategy was not *prima facie* implausible. Given the ambition to build a science of sociology, it was not unreasonable to take the natural sciences as setting standards for what any aspirant science need measure up to. Unlike those who had had to figure out the natural sciences without any model to guide them, the would-be social scientists had an example before their eyes, and could see what they needed to do to turn their field of inquiry into something worth calling a science.

The strategy depended upon a crucial presumption. Adopting a logic of inquiry in advance of concrete inquiries has to presume that the reality to be studied can actually be studied by the methodology. Indeed, the methods and the methodology are developed in the first place in order to study the phenomena, the reality. If the method is necessary to make the phenomena available for scientific study then there is no choice but to develop the method, since the phenomenon cannot be identified independently of the method and the methodology.

Inset 3.1 Method and methodology

Sometimes these terms are used interchangeably. Though the boundaries are not always clear-cut, we take methodology to refer to the logic and rationale underlying particular techniques or methods. For example, surveys and questionnaires can be treated as the methods which, for positivists, implement the methodology of the positivist project. So, when talking about the scientific method we are really talking about methodology. However, in this kind of context 'the scientific method' is the more usual phrase used.

To put the point another way and to bring out one of its crucial implications: implementing the general idea of science in sociology is to provide a set of criteria, or the forms, which prescribe what *any* scientific theory must look like, what is to count as data, what is to count as explanation, and thereby to specify what any sociological theory must look like, what sort of things can provide its data, how explanation is to be given, and so on.

There can be no question of empirically testing the adequacy of the methodology itself. Its whole point is to tell us what reality is actually like, so it cannot be independently checked against some reality which the methodology itself is supposed to tell us about. In the case of the positivist project, what was to count as reality was that which could be measured, could be quantified, could be constructed as data, and could be explained by a set of general laws. From the outset, the positivist project set out to state what kind of creature a scientific theory was, what it should look like, the forms it needed to take, and how it should connect to properly constructed data. This is why we call it a top-down strategy, because it works 'downwards' from a general idea of what science must be toward the specification of the variant on that general idea that sociology must be, as a distinctive area of application of the general idea. It is to theory that we now turn.

The form of scientific theory: the hypothetico-deductive conception

The aim of positivism, to repeat, was to create fully general explanatory theories. Theories explain by subsuming particular events under some general law-like statement of regularity. For simple example, we can explain why this ball thrown out of this window fell to the ground by invoking the all-embracing law of gravity: smaller bodies are always drawn to larger bodies (the earth being the larger body, the ball the smaller one). More generally, x happens in this case because x happens in all such cases. This was the kind of explanation that positivism sought. But discovering and proving a theoretical generalisation had to be a systematic process because the different explanatory propositions making up a theory have to be *logically* connected together.

The term 'hypothetico-deductive' is the expression used by positivism to describe the form truly scientific theories should take. A theory is, in this conception, something that is cast in the form of a logically structured argument where the logical structure should make the structure of the explanation wholly apparent. 'Logical structure' in this context means that the statements making up the theory must be arranged in a hierarchy, with the lower-level, less general statements (or 'propositions') of the theory derived by logical deduction from the higher and more general law-like statements: 'this ball fell to the ground' is vastly less general than 'all bodies in proximity to a greater body will, under gravitational

> Covering law model of explanation

force, fall toward that greater body', and it should be apparent that if *all* small bodies (such as a ball) fall to the ground – toward the greater body, the earth – then it *must follow* that this ball will fall to the ground. At the lowest level of the deductive hierarchy are empirical propositions, or hypotheses, which are capable of being found to be true or false by being compared with what happens: the hypothesis (or prediction) is, 'if dropped out of the window, this ball will fall to the ground', and if the ball is dropped and does fall, then the hypothesis is confirmed. If the low-level hypotheses are found to be false then, because of the deductive structure – that is, the relations of implication between the more and less general statements – the plausibility of the higher-level statements is weakened. This kind of explanation is sometimes called a 'covering law' model of explanation because singular cases fall under the 'cover' of the all-inclusive generalisations that 'cover' them.

Take Durkheim's arguments from his study of suicide (Durkheim, 1952). The major theoretical generality is that certain social conditions entail social consequences; for example, the lack of social integration causes high suicide rates. The 'minor premise' was to demonstrate that a particular case fitted this major premise. Saxony lacked a strict religion and, hence, had weak social integration. It followed from the major and minor premises combined that Saxony had a high suicide rate, which could be checked against the suicide rate for Saxony (Abbott, 1998). Importantly for Durkheim's objectives, the sociological theory explained the variations in the suicide rate by showing how particular events could be brought under the general theoretical premise.

Thus, the hypothetico-deductive scheme (HD henceforth) is a hierarchical ordering of statements on the basis of their generality, with the most general at the top and the more specific ones at the bottom logically deduced from the more general ones. In the more advanced of the sciences, the most general propositions will be statements of some all-embracing law and the more specific statements ones which report or predict the occurrence of some specific event. There may be long chains of intervening propositions of diminishing generality between the top and the bottom of the deductive structure. Nevertheless, it becomes easier to see whether a science possesses theories *in this sense*, or at least candidates for them, by looking at their structure. As the positivists noted, such structures were exceedingly rare in sociology, and despite their efforts, they remain so.

The importance of the HD scheme for the positivist project was that it promised fulfilment of the demand for thoroughness and systematicity by providing through-and-through logical integration. The HD scheme was meant to make logical connections more apparent than pages of discursive writing could. In long tracts of prose it is much more difficult to track an argument, and it is therefore more likely that a discursively presented theory will contain contradictions and vaguely formulated expressions which neither its writer nor its readers will readily recognise. Equally, it may contain surprising logical implications which pass unnoticed. By contrast, the HD format exploits the power of logic by placing the skeleton of the theory on full display. It is no accident that the natural sciences sought to exploit mathematics in formulating their theories. But, more than this, logical systematicity helps endow the theory with authentic scientific status.

Inset 3.2 Logical positivism

The HD account of the structure of scientific theories evolved between the wars, mainly due to a group of philosophers known as the logical positivists. Originally based in Vienna, most of them moved to the United States and Britain as the Nazis came to power in Germany and Austria. In brief, they espoused an anti-metaphysical philosophical stance by arguing that there were only two kinds of propositions: the analytic (such as those of mathematics and logic which were true by definition) and synthetic (which were verifiable by empirical observation). Statements which belonged to neither category, such as those of metaphysics, religion, aesthetics and the like, were meaningless, or statements of personal taste or preference, since they were verifiable neither by empirical observation nor logical deduction.

Logical positivism became immensely influential in the first half of the twentieth century. Paul Lazarsfeld, who becomes important in our later discussion of positivist methods, was involved with the group prior to emigrating to the United States. One of its main achievements was that, seemingly, it had resolved many of the problems of nineteenth-century positivism. One of these concerned the latter's failure to provide an adequate account of the certainty of scientific laws. These could not be guaranteed by observational methods since we cannot observe, to take a simple example, all falling objects in the universe past, present and future. Accordingly, the laws of science could only be probable or tentative since it is *logically* possible that we may come across instances that are exceptional to the law of gravity (which will mean that, after all, the law is wrong). However, according to the HD model it was the combination of mathematics-cum-logic and the essentially empirical interpretation of laws that gave laws the highest 'certainty' the human mind could hope for. For social science this was good news and their current lack of success in formulating even half-decent scientific theories could be attributed to the fact that their subject matter was far more complicated than that of the natural sciences.

Good news was to come from another quarter.

Popper's falsificationism, and how science proceeds

The HD schema had evolved during the years between the wars mainly, as we have said, at the hands of the logical positivists. Karl Popper had been much influenced by their writings but was also critical of them, and directed much of his thinking toward the problem of distinguishing science from metaphysics, a concern that had a considerable impact in sociology during the 1960s and early 1970s (Popper, 1959).

Inset 3.3 Karl Popper (1902–1994)

Born in Vienna Popper was, until his retirement in 1969, Professor of Logic and Scientific Method at London University. Apart from his writings on the logic of science he also had much to say about social reform. In *The Open Society* (1945) and *The Poverty of Historicism* (1957), he argued that social theories based on mistaken conceptions of the certainty of science led to authoritarianism and unrealistic programmes for social change. Further, such theories were 'holistic' in their insistence that individuals are of value only insofar as they serve the interests of the whole. His own preference was for a form of methodological individualism which understands all forms of collective actions as due to the actions of individuals. Following on from this, he urged programmes of social engineering that acknowledged competing individual aspirations as well as the spirit of self-scrutiny, as embodied in the principle of falsification, as opposed to utopian and politically dangerous schemes for reorganising society as a whole. He thought that schemes which gave priority to society as a whole would set lesser store by the individual and, when it came to it, would be ready to sacrifice the latter on behalf of the former.

See Popper (1945, 1947).

Popper proposed that what identified a science was that its theories were capable of being proved wrong. However, this is not necessarily as easy as it sounds. The statements of a real science said something sufficiently definite about the world that it was possible to tell unequivocally whether the world was indeed the way the science said it was. By contrast, metaphysics, that is, the *philosophical* attempt to say what reality was like, though it often gave the appearance of saying how reality must be, did not cast its statements in such a form that anyone could tell whether the things said really were either true or false. A statement such as 'It is or it is not raining outside' cannot be falsified because it says nothing definite about the way the world actually is, whereas 'It is raining outside' says something definite about how it is outside and can be falsified. The former statement is more like the kind of thing metaphysics offers, the latter more akin to what science says.

It is important to understand that when Popper is talking about falsifiability he is talking about statements being specified in a form such that they can, in principle, be shown to be false, not that they are in fact false. Very many statements of science are true, but it is not their truth which makes them scientific; many genuinely scientific theories turn out to be false. It is, in Popper's view, the fact that they can in principle be falsified that makes them scientific, not their truth. He places the emphasis on falsifiability because of what he saw as an asymmetry between falsifiability and confirmation. The most advanced of the sciences deal in universal laws or highly general theories which come close to stating universal laws. These have the logical form of 'All X are Y' as, for example, 'all swans are white'. However, as we pointed out earlier, it is impossible to confirm the truth of such statements by observation since it is impossible to examine every swan, past, present and future in order to see if all of them, to the last one, are white. Nevertheless, we can conclusively disprove the claim that all swans are white. All it takes is for us to produce in evidence just one black, green, orange, purple or whatever swan. Science progresses, argues Popper, by ruling out some universal claims on the grounds that they have been definitively shown to be false by the production of a single counter-instance. Accordingly, the HD scheme encourages the formulation of statements that are open to the possibility of falsification, ones which yield a concrete prediction logically derived from the general statements: a prediction which is specific enough about what is the case in the empirical world such that it can be compared with what does happen to see if what is predicted takes happens or not.

> Falsifiability and confirmation

One of Popper's objections to Marxists who interpreted Marx as predicting a revolution in advanced capitalist societies was that they could not set a precise date as to when this revolution was to occur. Of course, one cannot show that a claim that there will be a revolution is false on the grounds that no revolution has yet occurred, for it can be argued that this only shows that it has not yet occurred. If, on the other hand, one sets a date – and the date is not whimsically chosen but logically derived from the theory – then the prediction can be unequivocally supported or disproved. The matter can be definitely settled by whether or not a revolution occurs on the predicted date.

The importance of prediction within the HD model is that if the prediction, the hypothesis, is not fulfilled then this ramifies up through the logical hierarchy and casts doubt on the general law from which it is derived. So, if 'This is a swan, therefore it is white' encounters the report, 'This is a swan and it is black', then not only is the prediction that the swan will be white falsified, so is the general claim that all – not most – swans are white.

One of Popper's objectives was to provide a means of demarcating scientific theories from those which masqueraded as science, many of these being social theories, particularly those of Marx or, more precisely, Marxists. Popper felt that Marx had been scientific and had made proper predictions which actually falsified his theory. His special ire was directed at Marx's followers who, in Popper's view, had diluted the scientific nature of Marx's work by dropping the firmly predictive element. Just in case one might feel that he is being hard on

Marxists, Popper's arguments also cast doubt on the scientific status of Darwin's theory of evolution. Be this as it may, Popper's work not only seemed to resolve the problem of inference that had been a major problem for positivism and other empiricist philosophies in understanding theoretical generalisations, it also emphasised the trial-and-error character of science. According to Popper, science proceeds by subjecting its theories to the most stringent tests, seeking, that is, to falsify them. This is the strongest test for theories since it is impossible to know in advance which theories are the right ones, and confirmatory evidence is always open to the logical weakness of induction. No matter how many more items of evidence we add that appear to confirm a generality, we still cannot *be sure* that something that falsifies it will not turn up. However, we can be *absolutely sure* if someone produces a yellow swan that the claim 'all swans are white' is false. Moreover, the openness of science to criticism by other scientists, enforced as a norm in democratic societies, means that progress in science is not so much a neat linear progression as trial-and-error, in which promising theories are found wanting and replaced by better ones which, in their turn, are exposed to stringent testing by further research, and so the process goes on. Despite Popper's antipathy to much of what passed as sociological theory, his characterisation of the process of science gave heart to sociological positivism (Hughes and Sharrock, 1998). What was needed was a systematic way of proceeding by trial-and-error, and an important part of this was developing the correct form theory should take.

> Trial and error character of science

Inset 3.4 Evolutionary theories

Broadly speaking, evolutionary theories tended to postulate the unilinear and progressive nature of social change based upon an analogy – a mistaken one as it happens – with the evolution of plants and animals as set out in Darwin's theory of evolution. Comte, though not inspired by Darwin but by Saint-Simon, proposed an evolutionary idea of social development as society passed through three stages: the primitive, intermediary and the scientific. Each of these corresponded to progressively more advanced forms of human knowledge. The idea of unilinear stages can also be found in Marx and Engels, and Durkheim. Herbert Spencer, perhaps more directly influenced by Darwin's thought, put forward a linear conception of evolutionary stages. Societies became more complex and differentiated, which marked their progress toward becoming more advanced societies.

In the 1950s and 1960s there was a revival of interest in evolutionary theories, sometimes referred to as neo-evolutionism, among American functionalists who used principles of natural selection and adaptation drawn from evolutionary theories in biology. Such work suggested a unilinear direction of change and that some societies were more advanced than others, suggestions absent from the biological theory of evolution.

Working out a strategy for formal theory

If such ideas were accepted, the inevitable conclusion followed that despite decades of effort sociology had not made much progress toward becoming a science. Indeed, since it was not producing properly scientific theories, then it was no better than metaphysics. What was needed was to introduce into sociology this kind of HD theoretical structure. This would effectively resolve the problem of the relationship between theory and data: that is, it would make sociological theories more responsive to empirical testing. Developing theories in the HD mould would mean having to develop a thorough logical structure for the theory that connected, clearly and systematically, the abstract theoretical statements through a chain of deductions to specific occurrences in the world. Research could be brought to bear on theory, could be used to test it, and the simple cyclical arrangement theory–data–theory (that is, theory is tested against data and revised in the light of what the data shows) could come into operation to build more effective theory.

It would also give an impetus to measurement. The logical relations between statements are most perspicuously displayed in a symbolism which is designed to bring out logical relations, either as formal logic or as mathematics. If theories could be stated in such forms, then it would be reasonably straightforward to derive precise predictions if the data is also expressed in the same logico-mathematical terms. If we can predict, for example, that the pressure of a gas rises by, say, one kilo per cubic metre when the temperature is increased by 2° Celsius – because we have measures of both temperature and volume that will register quantifiable changes in these – then the statement is false if the pressure rises by more or less than this amount under the application of the specified temperature increase. If we can confidently measure the difference in heat degree by degree and the pressure by kilo per cubic metre, then we can unambiguously tell whether the pressure does or does not increase by just the predicted amount.

Accordingly, if the difference between sociology and the real sciences was that the latter had properly formulated theory, then the obvious step was for sociology to acquire such theory. But it is one thing to have a prescription of what needs to be done and quite another to have an idea of what actually to do. It is one thing to criticise existing theories for their shortcomings but rather more difficult to devise sociological theories which conform to the HD model, and do so in an authentic not just superficial way.

The general idea of deductive theory merely talks about the form that scientific theories should assume. It says nothing about what should go into that form: what, that is, should provide the content of the deductive theory. At this point the positivists faced the problem of any sociological theorist: namely, figuring out what scientifically to say about social life. Having condemned existing sociological theory, they now faced the same problem: to put sociological *content* into the formal framework. They did not, however, make an entirely new beginning by proposing wholly new theoretical ideas. Rather, they sought to deal with existing sociological theories, trying to recast them into the HD mould.

> The problem of content

One of their initial difficulties was actually dealing with the complicated character of existing theory as well as trying deal with the complications arising from application of the model of HD theory itself. Describing the basic logic of the HD format – as we have just done – is straightforward enough. But the structures of actual theories in natural science were complicated indeed. Producing something sociologically substantive that would match Newtonian or Einsteinian theories would, accordingly, be no small or instant task. Among the first attempts to recast existing sociological theory was Durkheim's theory of social integration accounting for variations in the suicide rate (Willer and Willer, 1973). This choice was not surprising given that much of Durkheim's own work – though prior to the formulation of the HD format as the distinctive form of scientific theories – was an explicitly positivistic attempt to move toward the development of systematic and testable theory for sociology.

However, the positivist project was imbued with a sense of urgency, impelled by a need to do something quickly to clear up the scandal of discursive and inconclusive theory. In effect, four strategies for general theory building emerged:

- borrowing concepts from other disciplines and appropriating existing theoretical ideas in sociology
- creating a common vocabulary and framework
- 'middle-range' theories
- building mathematical models.

Borrowing concepts from other disciplines and from sociology's own discursive theory

Key ideas in sociology are often 'borrowed' ones and, as we shall see in subsequent sections, this is as much the case today as it was in the classic period of the nineteenth century. However, in the later period of the growing dominance of positivism which concerns us, more was involved than the simple inspiration of a potentially fruitful analogy. The construction of a sociologically meaningful formal theory was a very different proposition than rough-and-ready adaptation of lesser-scoped theories into the HD format as in the case of reformulations of

Durkheim's theory of suicide. Indeed, in the absence of a serious and original sociological contender for recasting into a formal theory, one recourse was to look around for candidates from other disciplines which could be adapted 'off the shelf'. In the 1950s and 1960s such ready-made theories were drawn, variously, from mechanics, biology and especially from economics and behavioural psychology. Both the latter, it could be argued, established human sciences that closely related in their subject matters to sociology.

To illustrate we will look at one example which had a brief but prominent flowering: exchange theory.

Exchange theory: the case of Homans and Blau

Though exchange theory had a long history in anthropology, in its American variant its roots lay in behavioural psychology, particularly Skinner's theories. Skinner held that knowledge or control of the delivery of reinforcements in a situation is both a necessary and sufficient condition for predicting (or controlling) the behaviour of organisms (Skinner, 1938). Arguably, it was a mechanism such as this which made it possible for organisms to adapt to their environments.

Inset 3.5 Behaviourism

Behaviourism took the view that objectivity in psychology could only be secured by abandoning introspection as a source of psychological data and, instead, focusing only upon publicly observable behaviour. A more radical variant claimed that it was unnecessary to postulate the existence of so-called 'mental entities'. All 'mental phenomena' could be described in terms of objective behavioural patterns.

Exchange theory took this a step further by making the assumption that people are rational in the sense that they will seek to maximise the rewards and avoid the costs of some course of behaviour, according to the way they perceive situations (Homans, 1961; Hamblin and Kunkel, 1977). Assumptions such as this became the basis of 'rational-choice theory', which owes much to economics and to a branch of mathematics known as 'game theory' (Heath, 1976).

Inset 3.6 Game theory

Beginning with the attempt to give a mathematical account of poker, game theory is really a branch of mathematics which seeks to elaborate formally the optimum strategies available to participants under various assumptions about goals, number of participants, knowledge of opponents' strategies, resources and so on. It has come to be treated as a theory of conflict. Its applications have included managing international relations and conflicts, arms races, business strategy and elections, among others.

However, from a methodological point of view, one of the attractions of such assumptions was their apparent simplicity. After all, one of the distinctive hallmarks of the HD format, and of the more advanced of the sciences, was the way in which simply stated general principles or laws stood at the top of the schema, from which more specific hypotheses which could be derived and tested. Potentially, such general principles gave the theory great scope since, being general principles, they could be applied to many domains rather than just being applicable to some narrowly specific field of human behaviour. This was certainly the basis of Homans' complaint – made in 1961 (but just as true today) and echoed by Erving Goffman in his Presidential Address to the American Sociological Association in 1983 – that, so far, sociology had failed to establish a single proposition about human behaviour of a kind that would be valid for building a general theory of social life (Homans, 1961). Indeed, in formulating some rules of theory building, Homans states that 'science is an economy of thought only if its hypotheses sum up in a simple form a large number of facts' (ibid.: 16). It must also be recognised and accepted that scientific analysis is abstract and selective, dealing only with a few elements of any concrete situation.

This was effectively the programme Homans followed in *The Human Group* (1950) where he presents an analysis of the interconnected uniformities of the behaviour of human beings in small groups, and the properties and workings of human groups in general. Using case studies of industrial production, the family in Tikopia, street gangs and community studies, among others (all of them drawn from prominent studies of the time), he argued that the observations made by the different investigators could be divided into the same four classes of variable phenomena: 'sentiments', 'activities', 'interactions' and 'norms'. These were, in effect, the four main variables essential to explaining all human behaviour. If interaction intensifies, for example, then so do sentiments of liking among the parties, and so on. It was in a subsequent work, *Social Behaviour: Its Elementary Forms* (1961), that he developed 'exchange theory' as he endeavoured to explain the uniformities he had earlier found in the case studies by deducing them from a set of more general propositions: 'To deduce them successfully *is* to explain them' (ibid.: 10).

Homans insisted that a valid strategy must be parsimonious in seeking to formulate the simplest set of general propositions that, along with subsidiary ones, could be used to explain complex social behaviour. He argued that no new sociological propositions needed to be developed to explain social interaction. Rather, 'from the laws of individual behaviour follow the laws of social behaviour when the complications of mutual reinforcement are taken into account' (ibid.: 31). In other words, Homans' strategy is also reductionist in seeking to explain larger-scale social behaviour in terms of the laws which govern individual interaction. It is reductionist in another sense, too: the principles of sociology (applying to the lives of human animals) were of necessity less general that those of animal behaviour (applying to all animals, human and otherwise). Thus, the principles of sociology were less general than, and could be deduced from, the laws of (behaviourist) psychology.

> Reductionism

Peter Blau took a similar position, but one owing more to economics than to behaviourist psychology. Persons seek to maximise their gratifications. Rewards can only be found in social interactions and, accordingly, persons seek rewards in their interactions with each other (Blau, 1964). Using this basic proposition, Blau develops an analysis which draws upon the method of graphs that has been so successful in elementary economics, and proceeds from interpersonal associations and processes to more complex ones in larger social structures, such as institutionalisation, power and conflict, mobility, status and social norms, among others.

Since our purpose here is to illustrate one of the styles of theory building that is part of the positivist programme, a full-blown critical discussion of exchange theory is not possible. However, one point is worth noting, in that it has methodological import. Most of the criticisms were not methodological at all but, rather, criticisms of the order of 'people aren't like that, they are not always calculative and self-seeking'. In other words, many of the criticisms, as they so often are in sociology, failed to pay any heed to the constraints on theorising that the exchange theorists set for themselves. When theory building, a theorist need not make 'realistic' assumptions in the sense that the above kind of criticism implies for exchange theory. The critics failed to take on board, in other words, the objectives of exchange theory: namely, to explore how much progress could be made toward building a robust deductive general theory for sociology. As we have repeated, often in sociological research what is at stake is not so much the substantive problem and the search for findings, but the strategy which informs the research. In this case, the strategy was one of taking the first steps toward building a deductive general theory, a task which required working from general and simple principles of human behaviour. As in the case of economics, the assumption that persons seek to maximise their gains and minimise their losses is not treated as a description of how real people behave but as a simplification necessary in order to construct an idealised model against which 'real world' behaviour can be gauged and the predictive power of the theory developed. It is a strategy not unlike the idealised models, such as that of the 'perfect vacuum', that physics often employs. Whether or not such a strategy is

> Constraints on theory

> Theoretical simplification

worth pursuing in sociology is another matter, but it does have its own logic and can be argued for on the grounds that it is precisely the insistence on realistic – and therefore complicated – assumptions that prevents sociology building proper theories.

The second strategy of general theory building was to develop a common vocabulary.

Developing a common framework

One of the major problems of developing adequate theory was the vagueness of sociological concepts. Many sociologists had, over the years, produced broad concepts and classifications of social phenomena. While these were often insightful and interesting, for positivism what they lacked was the systematic connection to empirical reality. Assuredly, the concepts could be used to illuminate aspects of social reality, but this was not the kind of connection that could decide between theories. Concepts could be interesting, fruitful and provocative, could even encourage further inquiry, but unless they were systematically connected within a HD schema, inquiry could not scientifically answer questions about reality.

The HD format, because of its deductive character, placed a premium on precise definition because otherwise the strictness of the deductive inference would be jeopardised. The work of Talcott Parsons is perhaps the most notable as an attempt to address the matter of vagueness by producing what he saw as a 'general theory of action systems', a strategy which consisted substantially in borrowing from other sociological theorists such as Durkheim and Weber and from other disciplines, notably psychology.

The case of Talcott Parsons

During his earlier career, Parsons had come to reject all forms of 'radical positivism', such as behaviourism, which treated the world as a closed, determinate system of cause and effect. Such approaches were not theories of 'action'. They left no room for such notions as mind, consciousness, values and norms, or the fact that human beings choose among alternative courses of action. However, he felt that there had been major developments in European social thought (Weber and Durkheim in particular) that had not yet – that is, by 1937 – been appreciated by American sociology. A theory of action must make room for voluntarism, that is, a degree of freedom of action. Without this, 'action' loses its distinctive character and becomes simply 'behaviour', and the subjective and normative nature of social life becomes merely epiphenomena with no causal or explanatory significance. Notions of morality and responsibility are reduced to mythical illusions.

Durkheim and Weber, Parsons argued, had independently converged on the outlines of a radical new 'voluntaristic' approach, so breaking with the framework of social thought that had been pre-eminent from at least 1700 and through the nineteenth century (Parsons, 1937). His own action framework was a distillation of ideas drawn from these thinkers, though it was one which evolved over Parsons' career. In brief, the irreducible elements of an act are as follows:

- an actor performing the act
- a situation, that is, a set of circumstances under which the act will be performed, some of which may be unalterable and some which may be under the actor's control
- an end or result that the act is directed toward bringing about
- rules or standards which govern the selection of means to ends.

Later, this conception of action was to be placed within a systemic frame as Parsons (1952) articulated the idea of the social system, one derived, somewhat reluctantly, from functionalism ('reluctantly' because though not ideal Parsons felt there was no better idea for a general systematic strategy for explanation then available in sociology). Simply put, if any social system is to operate at all, four basic conditions – the 'functional imperatives' – must be met. These are: adaptation to the environment, the attainment of goals, pattern maintenance and tension management, and integration. To solve these problems, and maintain its existence, a social system must have four main structural features: the economy, the polity, kinship and community, and cultural organisations. The forms that these can take in any particular society are influenced by its value system, which directs and motivates social actors to achieve desired ends.

> The social system model

'Social system' is not to be equated with the empirical society and certainly not with the nation state. What Parsons is doing is exploiting the idea of system to think not only about society but also about subsystems within the larger social system. Parsons' idea is of levels of social organisation in hierarchical nested relationships: a given system contains subsystems which themselves contain subsystems, and so on, down to the scale of a two-person relationship and the individual personality system – and even the biological system of the organism.

Parsons' main preoccupation in *The Social System* (1952) was in elaborating the idea of a social system by first focusing upon what needs to be done for the system to retain its identity and functioning *as a system*: its equilibrium conditions. This did not mean that social systems were always in equilibrium. Being highly complex, they always had room for tensions and disequilibrium. The point of first addressing the equilibrium conditions was to provide a yardstick to assess and determine social change and identify tensions in the system.

Parsons' conception of the relationship between scientific theories and the realities they portray was one of 'analytic realism'. This held that the nature of reality is not immediately and empirically given. The phenomena that we see are composed of many different elements which can only be selectively brought to view through scientific

> Analytic realism

analysis. For example, the things we see around us are made of chemicals, but we cannot identify these chemical constituents without decomposing the things we actually encounter by using the methods and theories of chemistry. The chemical constituents are real, but only knowable by breaking down – analysing into their constituent parts – empirical encountered phenomena. The same applies to social reality.

As they are given in everyday perception, social situations are composites of elements that are not immediately revealed in the empirical situation but that nonetheless are real. Again as far as social situations are concerned, these elements furnish sufficient materials for numerous disciplines, each having its specialist focus upon a distinguishable aspect. However, the human sciences deal with the same phenomena, which means that their different frameworks ought to be compatible with each other and their findings complementary. For example, a meeting could be considered sociologically in terms of the interaction of the participants. It could also be examined psychologically by focusing on the personalities of the parties, since their interaction may well be affected by how the different personalities gel with each other. Given that the elements of the situation can be looked at from the point of view of the different human sciences, then these sciences ought to have interconnections between them. If any serious integration of these 'sciences of action', as Parsons calls them, is proposed, then what is required is a shared frame of reference: that is, a general not merely a sociological theory of action. A concrete social situation is a composite of, at least, biological, psychological, social and cultural elements – though since biology is not a 'science of action' it can be theoretically taken for granted. The key idea for Parsons was that of system – that is, an interconnected arrangement of parts which is capable of persistence as an identifiable unit – and the task of the sciences of action was to analyse the organisation of and interrelationships between different systems.

Parsons' conceptual framework came closer than any other synthesis to producing a conceptual linking of aspects of anthropology, economics, political science and sociology. The linkage is, however, very abstract. Indeed, Parsons himself disavowed any claim to have produced a theory of concrete social phenomena. Instead, he makes the case for the advantages of comprehensive and abstract conceptual schemes which were supposed to guide research to produce the data needed to give specific empirical content to the categories and the concepts. If anything, despite its sophistication and thoroughness, the framework was but the first stage of producing theory of the kind positivism wanted, since operationalising it in empirical research was still to do. And, indeed, for a time a number of studies were done using Parsons' schema. Smelser, for example, in his 1959 study of the Industrial Revolution, treated socio-political disturbances as created by the transition from one equilibrium – in which economic activity in Britain in the eighteenth century was organised around the household and in terms of family structure – to a new equilibrium – where economic activity was dissociated from households and located in factories, and where industrial discipline replaced family authority. The approach was also used in studies of interaction in small groups (Parsons et al, 1955), as well as Parsons' own analyses directed more closely to concrete societies (Parsons, 1966) which included discussion of fascism and the strains produced by class and ethnicity, among many other topics.

However, as a strategy for constructing scientific theory, the framework has to be found wanting. It is easy enough to devise some conceptual scheme; the difficult thing is to devise one that is not arbitrary. While it is true that Parsons had distilled much that was interesting and maybe even relevant to sociology from past theories – and, indeed, his account of much of nine-teenth-century social thought (Parsons, 1937) is a prodigious achievement – it does not arise from well-established empirical generalisations and theories; this, by the way, is a problem that affects not only Parsons but also the broad run of sociological theorists.

The virtue of a scientific classification is that it does arise from well-estab-lished generalisations and theories. Mendelev's classification of the elements is built upon a wealth of empirically established regularities concerning the prop-erties of chemical substances and compounds, and this made it superior to the earlier classifications of alchemists (Black, 1961). Mendelev's classification of elements made use of developments in the atomic theory of matter and, in its turn, lent considerable support to that theory. So much so that it encouraged the search for elements which, until that time, were unknown. In short, to be useful in science frameworks and classifications need to be based on well-grounded empirical generalisations and theories, which were not available in sociology.

Even in his own heyday, there were sympathetic dissenters from Parsons' strategy of theory building. Robert K. Merton, as we have already pointed out, felt that grand theoretical schemes of the Parsonian kind did not help sociolog-ical research or, at least, that the attempt to build them was premature. Instead, he proposed a strategy of developing theories of the middle range.

Theories of the middle range

Merton agreed with Parsons that functionalism was a reasonable and useful basis on which to build a scientific sociology, and indeed he did much to develop and complement Parsons' own work (Merton, 1957). Where he differed from Parsons was over the strategy for theory building. Like many others before and since, Merton argued that theoretical sociology was too abstract and lacked significant connections between sweeping generalisations on the one hand, and localised empirical findings on the other. His own use of functionalism was not so much as a general theory but more as an exploratory set of ideas. He subscribed to the HD model, yet fully realised that sociology had failed to develop such theories and was unlikely to do so unless its short-term tactics were changed. General sociological theory, like that of Parsons, was too loosely expressed but, above all, it suffered from the fact that there was no set of more modest generalities between the abstractions and the research findings that could provide the intervening links through which the logical deduction of specific predictions from the generalisations could begin.

As a result, sociological researchers largely carried on without regard for the work of the theorists, forming and testing hypotheses but conjuring these out of thin air on an ad hoc basis rather that deriving them from a systematically formulated theory.

Hence, within American sociology there was a gulf between theory at the 'grand' level at which Parsons was working and, at a lower level of generality, the ad hoc theorising of empirical research. What was needed, argued Merton, was a middle way, one which involved the production of more systematic theory than was usually associated with empirical research, but of more limited abstraction and of lesser generality than that proposed by Parsons: 'middle-range' theory. He defined its hypotheses as logically interconnected conceptions which were limited and modest in their scope 'rather than all-embracing and grandiose' (ibid.). Such a strategy would seek to formulate a set of systematically related theoretical propositions covering a restricted domain of social life, such as 'deviance', the family or bureaucratic organisations, and from these deriving fairly specific and testable empirical propositions. Nonetheless, the focus on middle-range theories was itself a tactical shift within the same basic strategy. Middle-range theories were meant to serve as stepping stones toward a more general theory, but one which was better grounded in research and provided with intermediary propositions that would link general theory and empirical predictions deductively.

An example of the kind of approach Merton had in mind can be gleaned from his explorations of deviance in his 'Social Structure and Anomie' (1938), which is both a contribution to the development of functionalist theory and an explanation of various deviant responses. Grounded in empirical materials, he starts from the assumption that each society stresses particular goals which are seen as worthy of attainment by its members. Further, it is expected that these goals will be sought through normatively acceptable means. For example, in the United States economic success is highly valued and will be sought by the legitimate means of hard work. This combination of valued goals and the legitimate means for attaining them gives rise to the patterns of interaction that constitute the predominant structure of society in which most people adhere to the common norms. However, at times there can be a tension between the goals and the means which puts pressure on some groups to respond in a deviant manner, not least because of the unequal structure of opportunities built into the system of stratification. For example, lower class children may well lack the educational qualifications necessary to obtain high paying jobs and, accordingly, are under some pressure to obtain economic success by illegitimate and even illegal means. It is the dissociation between the imperative to achieve the goals of success and the uneven distribution of realistic opportunities (which manifests a lack of integration between the cultural values of society and the system of stratification) which provokes a tension in the lives of individuals between their aspirations for success

> Social structure and anomie

through their own efforts and their chances of achieving the goals. Since the tension cannot be resolved in a legitimate way, some of them are motivated to use deviant methods, such as crime, political dissension or even withdrawal from society – for example into drug addiction or vagrancy.

This is, of course, but the barest sketch of Merton's analysis. Important to note, however, is his effort to restrict the analysis to the domain of deviance, using well-known empirical generalisations about the distribution of criminal and other activities, such as the association of gangsterism with the lower classes. Nonetheless, he tries to bring together what had hitherto been regarded as unrelated phenomena, for example, crime, political corruption, religious fanaticism and radical political movements, as well as the tendency of bureaucrats to stick mindlessly to procedure. He is not arguing that these are the same things but that all, and more, can be seen as differential responses to the gap between the value of financial success and the realistic opportunity to achieve this by honest, legal means. As his theory is connected to some higher-level principles derived from functionalist theory, although the argument is not set out using the HD format, there is an attempt to connect general functionalist concepts – such as the relation of shared values and socially sanctioned means – to the empirical materials, using the theory of anomie as the 'middle-range theory'.

We now come to the final strategy for scientific theory building, namely, developing mathematical models.

Developing mathematical models

In significant respects this is the most difficult strategy to exposit clearly and succinctly without any understanding of mathematics. Further, some of the mathematical developments which are still used in sociology focus on the measurement and analysis of complex data sets, both of which we will discuss in later chapters.

While the HD format set a standard that sociological theory would need to meet if it was to be properly scientific, it was but a skeletal representation of the general logic of scientific theory. Most theories in the advanced sciences were complex and mathematically expressed. They assuredly conformed to the deductively explicit, empirically refutable form of the HD model, but how could this be matched by sociological theories? The lure of mathematics for positivism was that it epitomised science. When a discipline achieves scientific maturity this is always associated with substantial mathematisation. This was therefore regarded as a step essential to becoming scientifically mature.

One of the benefits of mathematics is that it offers a combination of simplicity and a potential for expansion into complexity (Coleman, 1964). For example, the real number system is composed of simple elements along with the operations that can be performed on them,

The advantages of mathematics to science

but endlessly complex algebraic structures can be created from these basic building blocks. However, for mathematics to have purchase within a science, it must be established that there is an isomorphism between the phenomena being represented mathematically and the combinatorial possibilities of the mathematics. When objects in the physical world are abstractively described in terms of mass, length, time, force, velocity, density – among others – then it can be shown that the relations between these elements are isomorphic, similar to the structure of operations of vector algebra. That is, by manipulating the measurements one can calculate the further behaviour of the object: where it will be in x seconds if it has a mass of m and is being moved by a force f, has achieved a velocity v ... and so on. It is this isomorphism which allows us to take advantage of the algebraic operations, using real numbers, to substitute for the actual manipulation of the physical objects. The power of algebra and calculus in mechanics lies in the fact that once isomorphism has been established, then many things can be done through mathematics that could not be carried out in practice with the objects themselves. As a proxy for the objects, mathematics allow a multitude of results which would be extremely difficult to obtain by using ordinary language, in all its richness, or by manipulating the physical objects (ibid.).

For example, using the concept of 'weight' to refer to the mass that an object, any object, possesses along with some operations for measuring 'weight' we can, knowing only what the respective objects weigh, tell that this bag of carrots – which weighs 2 kilos – is half the weight of this pile of books which weighs 4 kilos. In other words, the concept and its measures are isomorphic to a property of the objects. The objects, as in this example, need not be the same in any other respects but can at least be compared in terms of their weight and, accordingly, allow for all kinds of manipulations in terms of the mathematics of measuring weight.

The catch here is establishing the necessary isomorphism between the phenomena and the mathematics in the first place. An example of how it should not be done is the approach Stuart C. Dodd put forward in 1942, intending to develop a 'quantitative systematics for the social sciences'. This consisted of some dozen symbols for basic sociological concepts, four others for numerical operations and 16 supplementary ones, with a large number of rules for their use. This may have looked like a mathematical sociology but it was nowhere near. It was simply a notation for concepts that did not have any isomorphic relationship to the phenomena it referred to. In science this isomorphism between the mathematics and the phenomena described goes beyond substituting mathematical-looking symbols for concepts. It is only valid if the relations represented in the mathematical relations by the symbols really do parallel the relations present in the phenomena – as the degrees of temperature parallel the even expansion of mercury when heated. Accordingly, when we calculate we need to be confident that the results will be right for the transformations on the numbers – that is, will preserve the relations between the phenomena – and thus render predictions that have a good chance of corresponding to what happens in the world. Achieving this has a lot to do with measurement which is needed, on this scheme, to connect the expressions of the mathematics with appropriate descriptions of empirical phenomena. Fundamentally this has to do with the character of the phenomena for which measurement is sought, as we shall see in Chapter 4.

Coleman (1964), who wrote an impressive text book for mathematical sociology, argued that, compared with economics for example, one of the major problems for sociology is to obtain quantitatively measurable properties which can serve as distance, mass and time do for the physicist, or quantity and price do for economists. Putting the analysis of complex data sets on one side for the present, there have been, and in a small way continue to be, explorations in sociology using such mathematics as set theory, matrix algebra, Markov chain theory, graph theory and more (Mapes, 1971; Boudon, 1974) as a means of expressing sociological theories. But, in significant respects, these are much more exercises in mathematics than they are in sociology, and they have failed to capture the sociological imagination. In effect, techniques have been taken out of the mathematical tool box and applied to various social processes, especially ones that can be most easily modelled using existing mathematics such as diffusion processes, rational choices or networks, using *inter alia* algebra, matrix algebra, directed graphs and topology.

> Mathematical sociology

In other words, it has been assumed that existing mathematics is adequate for treating sociological problems mathematically. But why assume this? After all, in the early days of modern science, Newton and Leibnitz independently developed differential calculus to deal more adequately with the mathematics of motion. Much later, in the early years of the twentieth century, Einstein had to use Riemannian geometry rather than the more familiar Euclidian geometry of 'straight lines' in order to express the 'curved' space-time structure of celestial space. Mathematics consists of a variety of constructed languages and it is more than possible that, if sociology is to become mathematical, then it will have to devise its own, just as in the above examples new forms of mathematics were required to express the theoretical ideas more adequately.

Of course, one reason why mathematical sociology has not made much progress in theory building may well be the fact that most sociologists are not trained mathematicians nor overmuch interested in mathematics, and seemingly those most competent in mathematics are not themselves up to or inclined towards pioneering new forms of mathematics devised specifically for sociology. Newton's scientific achievements were due in no small part to his own mathematical inventiveness. However, even if sociologists were better at mathematics, this would not ensure that the strategy of developing mathematical models would make sociological progress, for reasons that are more fundamental and have to do with problems concerning the nature of social phenomena.

In this respect, a review of mathematical sociology by Skvoretz (2000) makes the point that, after 30 years experience in the field, he finds its problems and prospects are much where they were when he began, and likely to remain so for the next 30 years. He draws attention, first, to the point that we have already made, namely, the difficulty of translating the discursive, ordinary narrative form of sociological theory into mathematical and logic terms: that is, of securing the necessary isomorphism. Second, and relatedly, he notes the tension between the sociology and the mathematics. Mathematical tools, no less than any others, impose their own set of requirements on the necessary process of simplification and selection. Such simplifications are necessary in order to use the tools, but it may be that this is very restrictive on what can be done sociologically. To put it another way: it is the needs of the mathematics not the sociology that drives the model building. In the absence of innovative mathematics, relying only on what is available runs the risk of 'turning a problem that needs a hammer into one that needs a screwdriver because a screwdriver is all we have' (ibid.: 511).

Further, the whole positivist idea of formalisation, mathematisation and quantification aimed to achieve the unification of sociological theory. Thirty years ago, Skvoretz was anxious, and justifiably so, that 'we would get a mathematical sociology in which there would be numerous but nonunified mathematical models, concerned with different areas, thwarting the development of the type of formal unification that constitutes theoretical science at its highest pitch'. This anxiety has been realised. Mathematical sociology has been created in the image of sociology at large, not the other way around. Mathematical sociology has gone the way of general sociology. It has diversified, offering little or no prospect of unification. But, perhaps a concern for unification is premature.

Up until now we have focused on four strategies which have attempted to improve the nature of sociological theory by formal means: that is, by trying to move toward a more systematic theory format which would progress closer toward the HD ideal which was seen as the epitome of truly scientific theory. However, as we have already indicated, the form of theory was one thing, but it could not be divorced from the content of sociological theory.

The persistence of the problem of content

While one can respect the integrity and determination of scholars such as Homans, Blau and Parsons for their respective efforts, as well as those less well-known scholars who tried to create a mathematical sociology, there is no denying that their efforts had little real success in making sociology scientific. This is not to say that their theories were without merit, only that whatever merit they had was not of the kind which served the strategy for which they were developed, namely, that of transforming sociology into a discipline unified around an integrated, HD-cast, sociological theory.

There were very real problems involved in trying to build a scientific sociology by moulding its theories into a so-called scientific format. Adopting a template for the form of a theory does not necessarily ensure that whatever it is that is sociologically worthwhile in the discursively formulated theory can be successfully extracted from it and successfully inserted into the HD format while still retaining whatever value it might have had. Trying to present a set of ideas in a formal deductive system does not ensure that the scheme will be predictively strong and feature genuine law-like statements, rather than just mimicking these. The isomorphism between some physical properties and vector algebra, referred to earlier, was the outcome of many centuries of painstaking work gradually evolving rules of thumb into a full blown mathematised theory. In other words, it may be necessary first to understand a great deal more about relevant phenomena in qualitative terms, with the hope that eventually one may be able to express that understanding in a more disciplined and mathematic manner. A forced march toward formally deductive theories may lend clarity to some existing concepts, but it does not guarantee that those concepts are the ones required to give sociological theory real empirical content.

> Problems of isomorphism

The price that often has to be paid for formal deductive rigour is trading empirical faithfulness for simplicity, as we saw in the case of exchange theory. As Skvoretz (2000) notes: 'it seems formalisation capable of supporting rigorous analysis requires that we discard much of the richness and complexity of a topic. And it is this rich complexity that motivates out interest in the first place.'

The simplification seems necessary to enable any use of formal presentation; it is just too difficult otherwise to satisfy the mathematical requirements. The sacrifice in richness and complexity is justified in the hope that 'complexity can be added (to the considerable simplifications that are needed to enable mathematical expression) by relaxing assumptions, but, as we all know, this usually comes at the cost of analytic tractability' (Ibid: 511). The idea is, in other words, that the simplification will be a first step in the developing theories and models that will enable us to capture complex phenomena. However, this is not how it usually works out, since the difficulty of putting the complexity back in proves too great. In short, mathematical sociology usually involves ineffective simplification – perhaps a manifestation of a common inclination in sociology to take the easy way to get the show on the road – and go for simplifications that will do in order to demonstrate how a particular kind of theory or model might be constructed out of them.

This, however, is not an easy way to overcome the difficulties but merely a way of postponing them. It may be that talk of 'simplification' might be too generous, insofar as it suggests that those who offer the simplicities know what it is they are simplifying. Alas, this is all too often not the case. Simplifying assumptions are often made because the phenomena are not understood in any strong empirical way. In which case this is more like a confession that little is known about them rather than a solution to problems that articulates a grasp on understanding the complexities. Hence, once the demonstrative value of the simplifications has been exhausted, progress grinds to a halt. The 'toy versions' of the theories and models derive their attraction not from what they achieve, but from what they promise will have been achieved when they are elaborated into real theories and models. The trouble is that the 'toy version' says little or nothing about how this elaboration is to be carried through.

It might well be the case that by the standards of mathematics and scientific theory, the ordinary language in which sociologists express their theories is vague, often imprecise, and loosely formulated, but there may be good reasons why this is so. Not because vagueness and imprecision are virtues – these are relative judgements in any case – but because in order to capture the nature of the phenomena, certainly at our present level of empirical understanding, we cannot do much better than this without losing some connection, albeit a less than precise one, to the empirical world.

For example, although economics has been successful in mathematising much of its theory – partly because it has measurable qualities with which it deals, such as monetary values, number of sales or amount of production – there is much that it cannot properly mathematise. It may be able to formulate formal theories of economically rational decision making, say, on the basis of very simplistic views of what decision makers are like, but if one is interested in how businesspeople make the practical decisions that they need to make day to day, then such theories are likely to be found wanting (Anderson et al, 1989). This trade-off between empirical fidelity and simplicity will emerge in subsequent sections as a major issue for sociology.

What we are emphasising here is the 'hard-line' approach to theory and method. It is an approach which highlights the principled treatment of issues in theory and method to the neglect of the pragmatic problems which arise in getting things done, including scientific research. If, for example, we pay some attention to the history of science, what comes across strongly is that the natural sciences did not develop in the way they did by loyally following a pre-given procedure but more by working out procedures to tackle the problems they were dealing with as they went along. Procedures such as the HD format for theories were distilled, mainly by philosophers, out of the myriad of practical solutions that emerged as the respective sciences developed over the years. It is by bearing this in mind that we can better understand some of the key developments in theory and method, especially since these were in essence disputes over principle rather than about practicalities. This is another theme to which we will return.

> Working out scientific principles and procedures

The HD phase of sociology was certainly ambitious, as was the drive toward quantification, as we shall see shortly. And it was perhaps this ambition which inhibited a more realistic attitude to what was achievable. For even if the wholesale implementation of formal theory and quantitative methods in sociology was necessary for its transformation into a genuine science, and even if such a transformation was possible, it may be that the effort was (at least) premature, even precipitate, in the sense that the attempt to develop powerful and all-encompassing conceptions of social life were based on very thin empirical knowledge of social life itself. The problem turned out to be where it had long been: that is, the content, the phenomena, the formal theory would need to incorporate.

It is possible that providing the content to exploit the power of formal theory might involve disproportionate effort. There is no reason to suppose that reformulating, say, Durkheim's or Marx's theories into a formal theory language will, of itself, make much more than a marginal difference. There can be considerable difficulties in translating without loss from the original discursive presentations of such theories, with correspondingly little gain from the formal translation. And, after all, a translation is only that, a *restatement* of what has already been said, adding nothing except, it is to be hoped, a clearer presentation than the original. Such a transformation might make the interconnections of the theory rather easier to assess, but it might not. To argue that it is necessary seems to imply that one could not identify those same merits and weaknesses in Marx or Durkheim except by rewriting them into the HD format. The same objectives might be realised despite the discursive presentation and without the need for formalisation. A deductive formulation of Durkheim's *Suicide* is the same theory, not a better one. And, as we indicated a moment ago, the adoption of a formalised presentation is not guaranteed automatically to deliver the required results. After all, it was a complaint about Homans' version of exchange theory that it was not a collection of empirical propositions at all, but rather closer to an ensemble of tautologies. If such a criticism is true, then it shows that putting the theory into HD form did not automatically make it plain to its author, or to many others, that it failed to fulfil the requirements of the HD model.

The development of formal theory was but one arm of the strategy for scientifically unifying sociology. The other, and complementary arm, was to quantify data so that a more satisfactory fusion of theory, method and data could be achieved. The message, most eloquently put in Merton's appeal for middle-range theory, was really this: that theory without research is blind, and that research without theory is pointless. The point was not to use middle-range theory as a means of developing theory alone, but to give theory a form in which it would be put into closer touch with research. The propositions of middle-range theory would be formulated in a way that enabled researchers easily to see what sorts of facts about social life would be relevant to deciding whether the propositions were true or false. The researchers could thus investigate their truth by establishing those facts through their research, which could then play the crucial role of testing the theory. Therefore, the development of 'middle-range theory' also required the development of *research methods*. One form this took was the drive toward quantification.

The drive toward quantification

The impetus to develop quantitative techniques in social research arose between the wars in the United States, where sociology was reasonably well-established. However, there was a strong feeling among many sociologists that, by comparison with the other human sciences, especially economics and psychology, sociology was lagging behind, not only in producing formal theories but in the development of quantitative methods, with damaging consequences for the discipline's professional standing. Indeed, serious disquiet was expressed that 50 years after the first degrees in sociology had been awarded in the United States (sociology would hardly exist in United Kingdom universities for 30 or so years after these initiatives in quantification were being made), departments were still appointing to senior positions people who had received little or no formal training in the discipline itself. This period was, nonetheless, a period which saw a spate of empirical studies, using a variety of techniques of data collection but in an eclectic and relatively unsystematic manner. What was needed was a framework capable of integrating theory and method so that social research could be much more systematic, and an essential aspect of this was developing quantitative methods and measurement systems.

The aftermath of the Second World War brought a new optimism to social research. Prior to this, big strides had been made in attitude measurement and in statistical sampling theory, which in the 1930s put survey research within the grasp of academic social researchers. However, most of these developments had been undertaken almost independently of current debates about theory. The Second World War brought social researchers into government service to inquire into morale among civilians and troops and into public opinion and, immediately after the war, research institutes were established at many universities (Turner and Turner, 1990). The most famous was the Bureau of Applied Social Research, first at Princeton then Columbia, headed by Paul F. Lazarsfeld. The survey researchers, careers fuelled by wartime resources, advocated a particular strategy for sociology which was to prove fateful for the direction in which empirical social research was to take and for the kind of quantification which emerged.

There is no doubt that by the 1960s quantification had become a strategic priority for the positivist programme. Building a scientific sociology was to be taken forward by harnessing together the formal structure of theory and developments in quantitative methods: a coupling which would drive the project toward the goal of a sociological science.

Measurement and science: the positivist strategy

There can be little doubt that one of the distinctive features of the leading natural sciences is quantification. (However it is not a feature of all of them necessarily; think of botany or anatomy for examples.) And quantification was certainly one of the key elements in the positivist conception of science. We have already discussion in fairly general terms some of the perceived advantages of measurement. The measurement of some phenomenon is purportedly a requisite for intersubjective agreement among scientists. The point about the advanced natural sciences is that scientific observations can be *decisive*. We have discussed how the positivist conception requires that the data collected should, as evidence relative to the truth of an hypothesis, count unambiguously for or against it. Thus, a fine quantitative measure can tell us whether temperature rises by exactly the 1degree it is supposed to, or whether it rises by 1.2 degrees, and thus more than it should if the hypothesis was correct.

Further, such findings are meant to be compelling for the whole scientific community. Expressing results in quantitative terms makes it easier to secure this kind of agreement because variations and unreliabilities in human judgement can be minimised, more easily identified and corrected for, or even cancelled out. Thus, putting one's hand in various bowls of water to determine which of them is hotter than the others, and by how much, is not always likely to produce this kind of agreement. There is no easy way to say by how much this lukewarm bowl of water is cooler than this warm bowl of water, even if we can agree that it is warmer. A thermometer, on the other hand, provides an 'objective' basis for determining such differences. It tells us which is the hotter and by just how much. Objectivity in the natural sciences is very much a matter of intersubjectivity, of agreement in judgements amongst competent observers, and this is massively facilitated in many natural sciences by the development of measurement techniques.

The natural sciences have a number of measures, many of them fairly standardised across disciplines, such as temperature, volume, mass and velocity, and some specific to particular domains, such as ohms, amps, volts, hertz and more. Such measures are integrated into the theories, and in very many cases are themselves the outcome of well-validated theories. In a word or two, the measures can be said to reflect the properties of the phenomena under investigation.

Of course, it was not supposed that measurement in the human sciences could match the achievements of the natural sciences overnight, but it did seem to be necessary to develop some kind of measurement. A start had to be made and, as in the case of theory building, 'off-the-peg' solutions were sought. As in the case of mathematical sociology, a search was made for means of constructing measures that could be used to quantify sociological phenomena. The next chapter begins this part of the story.

Selected bibliography and suggested reading

- For those who want to explore logical positivism further, A.J. Ayer's, *Logical Positivism* (New York, The Free Press, 1959) is still worth reading, even though Ayer was a staunch polemical advocate. Some of the key texts can be found in the collection edited by Robert Ammeman, *Classics of Analytical Philosophy* (Indianapolis, Hackett, 1990).
- Blau's *Exchange and Power in Social Life* (New York, Wiley, 1964) is still an impressive piece of work from a scholar who contributed much, including empirical studies of bureaucratic organisations, to the sociology of his day.
- Homans work these days might read as naïve and overly psychologistic for sociological tastes. Nevertheless his *Social Behaviour: Its Elementary Forms* (New York, Harcourt Brace Jovanovich, 1961) is worth dipping into.

- On 'rational-choice theory', though again rather old, Heath's *Rational Choice and Social Exchange* (Cambridge, Cambridge University Press, 1976) remains a good introduction.
- A good source for Merton's thinking is the collection of his essays, *Social Theory and Social Structure* (New York, The Free Press, 1957, though there are subsequent editions in various formats).
- Parsons' corpus is voluminous. His *Structure of Social Action* (New York, McGraw-Hill, 1937) and *The Social System* (London, Tavistock, 1952) are probably the ones to use to get a sense of what Parsons was trying to do. The edition edited by Max Black, *The Social Theories of Talcott Parsons* (Englewood Cliffs, Prentice-Hall, 1961) contains both favourable and critical assessments of Parson's work to that date.
- Coleman's *An Introduction to Mathematical Sociology* (New York, Free Press, 1964) is intimidating for those without very much mathematics, though the introduction is straightforward and worth reading. By all means press on if you have some ability in mathematics.
- Raymond Boudon's *The Logic of Scientific Explanation* (Harmondsworth, Penguin, 1974) exemplifies the kind of thinking that positivistic sociology sought to develop.
- Willer's *Scientific Sociology: Theory and Method* (Englewood Cliffs, Prentice-Hall, 1967) is also worth a look and is not too daunting.

Chapter 4

Variable Analysis and Measurement

In this chapter we begin to discuss the methods and techniques which were used to implement the positivist strategy elaborated in the previous chapters. We focus on aspects of the logic underlying 'variable analysis': the mode of thinking which underpins the techniques and methods which developed from the positivist project and which still constitute the main methods of quantitative social research to be discussed in the remaining chapters of this part of the book. Many of these methods were originally developed outside sociology, in marketing, advertising and public opinion polling, and were brought into social research largely through the inspiration of Paul F. Lazarsfeld and his colleagues. They had been instrumental in importing the survey from market research and, appropriately, extremely successful in marketing the method to the sociological community immediately after the Second World War.

Lazarsfeld was not the sole originator of variable analysis, though he did much to articulate the framework and establish it as the orthodoxy in thinking about social research. However, it is not the particular methods we want to emphasise in this chapter so much as the framework which gave them sociological voice.

As we have seen, positivism proposed that properly scientific theories had to adopt a particular form, the HD model. So it was with variable analysis. Indeed, both forms were regarded as complementary. Each was to serve the other, for the law-like statements of the leading natural sciences often stated the quantitative relationship between two or more phenomena, such as that between the volume, pressure and temperature of a gas, stating that volume decreases and temperature rises as pressure increases. Accordingly, techniques were required to uncover these empirical relationships between the phenomena of interest. Variable analysis was

Language of social research

proposed as a format to shape the character of the data brought to bear on theory. To achieve this, variable analysis was intended as a theory-neutral language for social research; a language designed to encourage theorists to formulate their theories with a more systematic eye to empirical testing.

Lazarsfeld was fond of talking about the 'two languages of social research', though he himself was primarily concerned with only one of these, 'the language of social research', the title of one of the major collections of readings on the method of variable analysis (Lazarsfeld and Rosenberg, 1955). There was the also the 'language of theory'. The positivist project was intended to bring these into alignment – eventually. For Lazarsfeld's school, empirical work was distinct from theory, with its own rules and procedures independent of any particular vision of sociology theory. Lazarsfeld's own view was that a theoretical sociology was not a reasonable goal for the foreseeable future, given the complexity of its subject matter, hence his attraction to the a-theoretical and experimentalist tradition of social psychology (Turner and Turner, 1990: 107). At best, he felt that a psychological theory could be built on the basis of the social survey method which he was pioneering at the time. Nonetheless, and perhaps paradoxically, he was committed to a programme designed to make sociology more rigorous and scientific, even though he recognised that the goal of building a scientifically respectable theory was long term, if it was possible at all. However, Lazarsfeld's more cautious attitude was displaced in the 'golden era' (ibid.) of sociological research, before the 1960s, by the 'young Turks' – Lazarsfeld's own words – who embraced the positivist vision with more enthusiasm, less patience and not a little arrogance.

Lazarsfeld's approach was tied very closely to a conception of science which held that science did not deal with things-in-themselves but with selective aspects of them (Lazarsfeld, 1977). Thus, for example, the physicist does not study billiard balls but selected properties they have, such as their mass, momentum, angular velocity or molecular composition. The physicist is not interested in the full concreteness of billiard balls, but only in abstracted properties of them – properties they share with other objects – and in seeking to establish general relationships between these properties. In other words, a process of abstraction from concrete objects is involved in the selection of the properties or attributes which any science studies. It is the science's theoretical framework which determines relevant properties.

Such a framework was just what the social sciences lacked. The lack of an agreed theoretical and conceptual vocabulary (though, as we have seen, Talcott Parsons was working on one at the time) meant that identifying and selecting out relevant properties was a major problem – as we shall see in connection with measurement. Nonetheless, a start had to be made somewhere. A promising way forward, it was felt, was to borrow the idea of 'the variable' from mathematics as a tool for thinking about the properties of interest in social research, and as a format for data analysis. It was not necessary to wait upon the creation of an agreed-upon theoretical-conceptual vocabulary to begin building an apparatus for empirical social research. Indeed, variable analysis itself was envisaged as the means for developing such a theory through its ability to identify the relationships among properties, and provide a connecting link between theory, method and data. By thinking about data in terms of variables which can be expressed quantitatively, theories stating the nature of the association between systems of such variables could be tested to provide sociology with a cumulative body of data and theories that were well grounded in that data.

The basic elements of variable analysis: property space, pattern searching and measurement

The basic idea of variable analysis is simple enough. A variable, as opposed to a constant, is something that varies in value. Mathematically, in the equation a + b = c, 'a', 'b' and 'c' are variables and can stand for any number, whereas '+' and '=' are constant operators. The speed of light is a constant, 670 million miles per hour. It is the same, to within the impressive accuracies of ever more refined measuring devices, whether we are measuring the light from a moving or a stationary star. By contrast, the speed of a passenger aircraft is variable, roughly ranging between 0 and 600 miles per hour or, if we include Concorde, 1300 miles per hour.

The idea was that the characteristics of persons (or any unit, be it a group, organisation or society) could be conceived in the same way, as varying over an individual's lifetime or between individuals. Thus, for example, as illustrated in Figure 4.1, the amount of education people have, their wealth, their income, social status, power, political attitudes and so on are all capable of

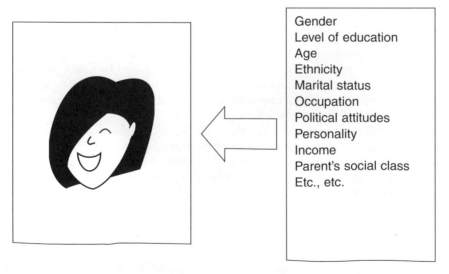

Gender
Level of education
Age
Ethnicity
Marital status
Occupation
Political attitudes
Personality
Income
Parent's social class
Etc., etc.

Figure 4.1 Example of properties which can be asserted of a person

Table 4.1 Types of variables with examples

Types of variables	Examples
Dichotomous	Male–female; voter–abstainer; white–non-white; working class–middle class; adult–child; etc.
Ordinal	Level of education; degree of political conservatism; etc.
Continuous	Income; age; etc.

taking different values. A person may have a very high social status or very low, be wealthy or poor, have a university degree or very little education, have an aggressive personality or a more placid one, and so on.

Property space

The next important idea is that of 'property space' (Barton, 1955). Figure 4.1 is an illustration of some of the properties which can be asserted of a person. The list could, of course, be extended considerably. Each property is capable of taking one of a range of values (even if this is only two, simply whether the person has the property or not). The range of values a property may take is known as the 'property space'. Thus, and again for a simple example, we can say that the property space of gender takes two values: male and female. Some of the other properties we used by way of example in Figure 4.1 may well take more than two values. Income, for example, can take any of a range of monetary values. Other properties may not lend themselves so easily to a convenient metric such as money, but nonetheless can be thought of as properties of which a person can have more or less – 'power' might be an example. A standard way of categorising variables is set out in Table 4.1.

It is important to note that there is some arbitrariness to the typology, in that it is always possible to reduce a continuous variable, such as income, to an ordinal or even a dichotomous one. Income, for convenience, can be reduced to 'low income' and 'high income' on the basis of some procedure which divides the particular distribution of income found in a study into two or more categories. In other words, there is nothing essential, except their definition as variables, about the properties which determines whether they are dichotomous, ordinal or continuous. (Some of the general consequences of this will be brought out later.)

The next step is to translate this idea into practical procedures and methods to realise the aims of variable analysis.

Pattern searching

It is important to remember that one of the main strategic objectives of the positivist project was to build a science of sociology which would, eventually, be capable of discovering general laws as powerful as those of natural science. Despite the aggressive optimism that the positivists sometimes displayed, in their more sober moments they realised that this was not to be achieved overnight. As we have already seen in connection with implementing the HD format for theory, there were a number of difficulties which had to be resolved. General laws are not discovered merely by thinking them up, though a lot of thinking may be needed. General laws in the natural sciences are powerful and general explanations of why physical phenomena behave in the way they do. They are highly predictive, and have close deductive connections with the empirical phenomena they explain; features which are singularly absent from social science theories. Nor was simply trying to impose the HD format on existing sociological theories, as we have argued, likely to yield quick solutions. And trying to borrow the more formally stated theories of economics or behaviourist psychology was likely to fare no better. What emerged was a different strategy to achieve the same end: to seek generalisations in empirical data.

Again, there was much to say on behalf of this move. After all, the regularities of natural science – between, say, switching on the heating element in a kettle and the water boiling at 100°C at normal temperature and pressure, or the expansion of mercury on a warm day – are all specific instances of general laws. When we press the light switch and the light comes on, the regularity is due to the fact that a number of general laws have been incorporated into a technological system. The laws, to put the point another way, are present in the empirical regularities, so if regular connection can be identified between two or more phenomena then we might be able to derive more general, more fundamental relationships which produce not only the regularities found, but the whole range of relationships among these kind of phenomena. However, the natural sciences have received the benefit of centuries of human experience of nature regularities – as astronomy with observation of the stars for travel and navigation, genetics with knowledge of inheritance through stock breeding – which only later were formulated in terms of general laws. The social sciences did not really have such a stock of equivalent experience available.

Variable analysis was, then, a strategy which accorded sovereignty to the empirical; the empirical conceived in terms of interrelating variables. It originated in a recognition of the particular difficulties under which empirical social science laboured: poorly articulated theory, the complexity of its problem, its non-experimental character, the paucity of its measurement, to mention but the main ones. How solving these problems ultimately fared will be discussed later. For now we want to elucidate the procedure variable analysis proposed for pattern searching among variables.

Variable analysis is an engine for finding patterns among variables: that is, looking for the conjoint variation of the values of the variables. The basic idea is the contingency table, or

Cross-tabulation

cross-tabulation, as illustrated in Table 4.2. Two variables, X and Y, are set out so that by inspecting the numbers – usually standardised as percentages – we

Table 4.2 Basic unit of variable analysis: the contingency table

	Variable		
Variable	**Y**	**Not Y**	**Marginal**
X	A	B	A + B
Not X	C	D	C + D
Marginal	A + C	B + D	N = A+B+C+D

can see whether there is a pattern such that from the value of X we can reasonably predict the value of Y. X and Y can be any property of a person, a group or a society: scores on an attitude scale, membership of a political party, ownership of a mobile phone, the level of individualism, religious conservatism, or whatever is of interest to the research. Any property is locatable in terms of the coordinates of the values of the variables on the X and Y axes of the table. We have selected dichotomous attributes as the simplest case, but the logic is the same for more complex tables based around ordinal and continuous variables. In Table 4.2 what we have is the property space of the conjoint values of variables X and Y which, as we have said, could be a multitude of properties of interest to social research.

Table 4.2 is a representation of the basic tool for pattern searching in variable analysis. A unit, which as we have said can be a person, an event, a group or a society, is locatable in terms of the coordinates of the values of the variables X and Y. We have selected dichotomous attributes as the simplest case, but the logic is the same for more complex tables based around ordinal and continuous variables. This, if you like, is the property space of the conjoint values of variables X and Y. (See Inset 4.1 for a worked out example).

Inset 4.1 The contingency table: an example

The simplest way of using such tables is by inspecting the marginal totals. These show how many of the units counted do or do not possess a particular property. Analysis proper begins when the values of the other cells are used since these show, for each pairs of values for the variables, the number of units possessing these values. Accordingly, for example, if the numbers falling into cell A are higher than those in cell B, and the numbers falling into cell C much lower than those falling into cell D, then this would suggest that there is a pattern in the relationship between X and Y such that having X is likely to mean that one also has Y. Such a relationship would be termed a positive association between X and Y. If, on the other hand, X was associated with not-Y, then the relationship would be negative, or an inverse relationship. If there was little difference in any of the cell values then it is concluded that there is no relationship, no pattern.

Table 4.3 illustrates, using hypothetical data, what such a table might look like for two variables, a new teaching method and educational attainment. Once again, the table is a fusion of two property spaces – the new teaching method and educational attainment – each of which takes two values, 'high' and 'low'. Note that the method assumes that we have means of measuring both variables and are able to determine what 'high' and 'low' mean, as we will discuss shortly. Set out this way we can inspect the joint distribution of the properties. The top row of the table shows the number of subjects who were not taught by the new teaching method, with those who scored low on educational attainment on the left and the high achievers on the right. The bottom row shows those who did receive the new teaching method, again with low achievers on the left and the high achievers on the right.

Table 4.3 Hypothetical relationship between new teaching method and educational attainment

Teaching method	Educational attainment		
	Low	High	Total
No	71% (100)	29% (40)	100% (140)
Yes	29% (40)	71% (100)	100% (140)
Total	140	140	280

Such a table would be constructed by allocating each person to one of the four cells, depending upon their joint scores on the two variables. So those who were taught by the new method and scored high on educational attainment would be placed in the bottom right hand cell, and so on.

Another point to note is the placement of the variables. It is conventional to place what is called the 'independent variable', that is, the variable which is the one producing the effect the researcher is intent on examining, on the left of the table, and the 'dependent variable', which is assumed to be affected by the independent variable, on the right. In this example it is reasonably straightforward to identify which is the independent and which the dependent variable, given that it is an examination of the *effects* of a new teaching method on educational

Independent and dependent variables

attainment. However, which variable is to be taken as the independent and which the dependent is not given in the method of the contingency table itself, but is a matter for theory or, in its absence, other preconceptions. So, in the example used, the relationship between the new teaching method and an increase in educational attainment could have been a hypothesis derived from a theory about, say, styles of teacher–pupil relationships and their relative effectiveness.

So the table is read from left to right with the percentages in each cell worked out on the total number of persons who received the new teaching method and the total number who did not. So, reading across, of those who were not taught with the new teaching method, more (71 per cent) scored low on educational attainment. Of those who were taught by it, the reverse is the case. Many more (71 per cent) scored high on educational attainment than did not. If this had been predicted from some theory about teacher–pupil relationships and their beneficial effects on educational attainment, then the theory would have received some support for its claims.

Although the aim of variable analysis is to contribute to the empirical testing of theories and the conjoint variation of variables provides the means of doing this, there are issues that need to be faced. One is that it would be highly unusual in the context of social research to find two variables which are perfectly related. The variation of the dependent variable is not only due to the independent variable but also to the effects of other unexamined (even unknown) variables and measurement error. In the example used in Inset 4.1 neither of these possibilities has been taken into account. We do not know, for example, what the effects of gender might be, or social class or many other factors that might have an effect on educational attainment independently of the new teaching method. In other words, we need to be able to handle more than two variables simultaneously. While the 2 x 2 contingency table neatly sets out the logic of pattern searching in variable analysis, it is by no means the only technique that can be used to examine the relationship of two or more variables. More mathematically sophisticated methods have been developed, and will be discussed in Chapter 6.

What the technique depends upon, of course, is that we have means of measuring the variables so that the units can be allocated to the table cells. In the previous chapter we discussed measurement in general terms. Now is the time to look at it in more detail, particularly in connection with variable analysis.

Measurement

The original idea behind the notion of the variable, imported as it was from mathematics and formal logic, was to encourage social research to think much more seriously about measurement and quantification as an essential element in building a science of sociology. For the seriously committed protagonist of the positivist project, measurement was not simply, as a number of its critics claimed at the time, an attempt by some social scientists to achieve respectability by clothing themselves in the trappings of 'hard-nosed science'. The logic of their position demanded measurement. If the positivist diagnosis of why sociology was getting nowhere was right, that there was no basis for deciding whether its empirical claims were correct, then the positivist project has no option but to try to develop measurement systems to enable the empirically exact comparison of rival theoretical claims. As a result, in the late 1930s and after, much effort was directed at the development of measuring procedures.

Measurement is one of those human achievements that was largely taken for granted before anyone thought to ask how and why it worked (Duncan, 1984: 119). It was not until the late nineteenth century, and even well into the twentieth, that serious attention began to be paid to the foundations of measurement, and this was largely provoked by problems of measurement in psychology. At first, attention was focused on measurement in physics, not surprising given that the philosophy of science had devoted most of its attention to that discipline. It was in the 1940s that a new outlook on the problem of measurement began to emerge, largely in response to scepticism expressed in 1932 by a committee of the British Association for the Advancement of Science appointed to assess the possibility of giving quantitative expression to sensory experiences (ibid.). The response was to acknowledge that measurement can take a number of forms and is essentially a matter of constructing scales.

Measurement, in general terms, is the assignment of numbers to some property in such a way that it makes sense to speak of the magnitude of that property. It should be noted, however, that the assignment of numbers to a property is to be done according to rules, and that the requirements of these rules are very strict. If one does not comply precisely with those rules, then one has not really 'measured'. We can assign numbers to houses in the street or to books in a library, and do so according to rules. Generally, as far as streets are concerned, the numbering is serial and proceeds from lowest to highest the further away from the centre of the town the houses are located. In the case of books this is to classify them according to some system of classification, such as the Dewey, which represents subject matter.

> Number system

However, useful as these are, they are not measurement in the true sense of the term. It does not make sense, for example, to multiply or divide house numbers by each other. Measurement involves using a number system so that the numbers can be manipulated mathematically – adding, subtracting, multiplying, dividing and so on – and, through calculating, being able to infer just what quantity of a property a given object possesses.

If the measurement system is sufficiently general, as in the case of the standard measures of weight, physical dimensions or temperature, we can compare different objects in terms of these properties and say, for example, how much heavier this book is than that rock. In other words, we can compare heterogeneous objects in terms of the properties being measured.

We may in some cases be able to calculate some properties on the basis of the measured values of others if we know how the quantities interrelate. In the case of the mercury thermometer we can turn such relationships into measuring devices. It is known that mercury expands and contracts in a regular way with increases and decreases in temperature. If we enclose mercury in an appropriately calibrated tube, the distance it moves in the tube with expansion and retraction can be used to represent changes in temperature. The importance of this for building a science was discussed in the previous chapter in connection with the ways in which, in the more advanced sciences, mathematical manipulation becomes, in effect, manipulation of the property and its relationship with others.

Lazarsfeld and his colleagues did not underestimate the difficulties of achieving the standards of measurement to be found in the natural sciences, for the measurement problem was a very difficult one for sociology and for social research more generally. The problems can be brought out by contrasting measurement in a well-developed science with the situation in social research.

Science is thought of as consisting of theory and data. The theoretical side consists of concepts and their relations to each other that, in the more advanced of the sciences, are formal, logical relationships as we saw in the previous chapter. The empirical side consists of the data that is observed. Connecting the two are rules of correspondence that define certain of the theoretical concepts in terms of observable data. These rules have to do, in important part, with measurement. Thus, to return to the mercury thermometer by way of example, the theoretical concept of temperature is operationalised by rules of correspondence that will include calibrating the tube so that the distance the mercury moves is a measure of temperature.

Inset 4.2 Operationalisation, operationalism

Operationalisation is the process of constructing an indicator of a concept. Thus, the concept of temperature can be indicated in a number of ways. As in the example used in the text, it can be operationalised as the stable expansion and contraction of mercury enclosed in a glass tube. 'Weight' can be operationalised as the comparison of some object with some other object of a known weight on a balanced rod with the objects placed at either end of the rod. It can also be operationalised in terms of the compression of some spring geared to move a pointer on a scale. Operationalisation is to give a concept some empirical instantiation.

Operationalism is the doctrine that the meaning of a concept lies in the operations designed to measure it. Thus, on this view, the concept of IQ is defined as the property measured by IQ tests. The main objection to this conception is that different measures of the same phenomenon would, in effect, be different phenomena. However, there are often many good practical reasons why different measures of the same phenomenon are used. Nor does the doctrine really answer the question of whether a measure is a valid measure of the concept in question (See Bridgman, 1927; Pawson, 1989).

So, for example, in terms of the notation of the diagram of Figure 4.2 a single line might indicate that the volume of a sphere is proportional to the cube of the radius, and the double line would provide rules for determining experimentally the length of the radius or the volume of the sphere (Torgerson, 1958). So, and again in terms of the diagram, physics would have many concepts and rules of correspondence, and a great many logical connections between the concepts. The rules of correspondence would enable numbers to be assigned to the data, which enables the substitution of mathematical symbols for empirical events.

Accordingly, the connections between the quantitative concepts can be in the form of mathematical equations. In the theoretical space, so to speak, the concepts can be manipulated mathematically, enabling derivation of new relationships from established ones.

Contrast this state of affairs with that in the social sciences. Figure 4.3 is a schematic of what the situation looks like in far less developed sciences. In this case there are two sets of concepts. Those to the right, close to the world, are

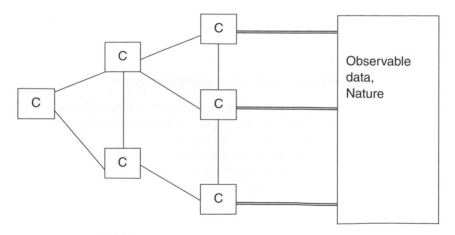

The squares stand for constructs, single lines for formal connections, and double lines for rules of correspondence linking certain constructs with data

Figure 4.2 A schematic diagram illustrating the structure of a well-developed science

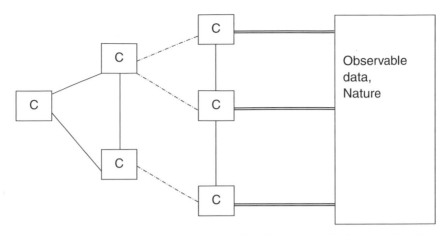

Figure 4.3 Schematic illustrating the situation in a less well-developed science

interconnected, each with a rule of correspondence connecting the variable to the observable data, and those to the left, are also interconnected, but with no logical links to the concepts on the right. The concepts on the left might represent the interrelated concepts of some sociological theory; for example, they might be social class, alienation, cohesion, integration or whatever the theory is concerned with. The connections between them indicate theoretical connection which, however, in sociology is expressed discursively rather than mathematically. The concepts to the-left hand side will be operationally defined in terms of observable data. Thus, we might have social class as defined by whether a person's occupation is manual or non-manual, intelligence as determined by the score on a particular intelligence test, attitude to politics by the score on an attitude scale, and so on.

Whether or not this diagram paints a fair picture of the state of sociology's theory, it does capture sufficiently well how positivist social researchers saw the situation and the resulting need to move theory building forward by making it responsive to data expressed more quantitatively.

The task of the positivist programme was to bring Lazarsfeld's two languages of social research – the language of theory and the language of research as variable analysis – together. The aim was to fuse the two into a single language of a proper quantitative science, moving from a situation where the two are separated to one where, as in Figure 4.2, the concepts have both systematic interconnection and clear empirical import, formally connected within the theoretical structure and connectable to observable data, as in Figure 4.3. However, this remained an aspiration. In the present it is the two-languages model with which social research has to be content.

> Variables and theory building

The main problem area was seen to lie in the middle of the diagram, the dotted connections; one strategy to improve this was to encourage theorists to think in terms of variables and indicators, specifying their concepts in terms of measurable dimensions, attributes or properties. In other words, to begin to theorise in the language of variables: a move which, for example, Parsons took up, though not with any serious import for empirical research (Parsons, 1952), and which also resulted in a number of texts setting out the process of theorising in variable analytic terms (Willer, 1967; Stinchcombe, 1968; Dubin, 1969, for example). Variables were to become ways of thinking about concepts, encouraging the researcher to think about how the concept can be connected to things which can be observed and measured – at least at some level.

For example, a theory might posit that certain kinds of family dynamics related to the cultural values of individualism in capitalist economies predispose children to aggressive behaviour. Such a theory is likely to be expressed discursively and at great length as concepts are discussed, defined, elaborated and connected to others within the theory. However, if we follow the advice of variable analysis we need to discipline our thinking by conceiving the theory in researchable terms. Thus, even as we are developing the concepts, we think about the way these can be identified as variables and, through this, start directing attention to what observables, what indicators, could 'stand for' some of the theoretical concepts. What, for example, might be good indicators of aggressive behaviour in children of authoritarian parenting?

Lazarsfeld's conception of the measurement process

Lazarsfeld took the view that almost anything could be treated as a measure, an indicator. In progressing through their lives, human beings leave traces and records of their activities. Some of these records are, especially in modern societies, institutionally provided – such things as tax records, court records, diaries, birth and death records, examination results, sales receipts, and so on and so on – and have been used as indicators of social trends and changes. The

---

Inset 4.3 Lazarsfeld's Model of Index Construction

Lazarsfeld saw this as a phased process consisting of the following stages:

The 'imagery phase'

The researcher becomes immersed in a theoretical problem, out of which emerges a vague conception of the theme that is of interest. For example, the concept of efficiency might emerge out of nothing more systematic than noticing that some people seem to do their work with less fuss and bother than others, are able to get things done on time, are well organised and so on. Even something as vaguely formulated as this is enough to start the wheels of measurement rolling.

Elaboration into components

The next step is to take this image and divide it into components or aspects. Sometimes these can be derived from the concept itself and/or from other related research. In the example being used, we have an initial notion of efficiency, and it is time to form it into dimensions which can be observed. When we speak of efficiency, for example, do we mean people who work fast but may make many mistakes, or those who make few mistakes but work more slowly? It is by such elaborations that the researcher divides 'efficiency' into 'dimensions', such as 'speed of work', 'quality of product', 'careful handling of tools' and so on.

Construction of indicators

The next stage is to decide upon indicators that can be observed or recorded to 'stand for' the aspects of the concept. In doing so the researcher needs to be sensitive to the context of the research. If we are studying car repair then appropriate empirical indicators might be 'time taken to change a tyre', 'number of rejected components', 'number of jobs completed in a day' and so on. If the setting was a tax office, other empirical indicators would have to be devised. The choice of indicators is very much a practical judgement, receptive both to the concepts and the setting of the research.

Combining indicators

The various indicators, having been decomposed, are then re-combined into as few indicators as possible. One wants, say, to end up with a ranking of auto-mechanics not with respect to their performance on each separate elements in the concept of efficiency, but to provide a ranking of them in terms of their own overall individual efficiency. This involves determining which of the many initial indicators are closely interrelated and can, therefore, be taken together as a single indicator of the concept of interest. This avoids, for example, using indicators so closely related that they are, in effect, measuring the same aspects of the phenomenon.

classic example is Durkheim's use of official suicide records for his study of the social processes of integration (Durkheim, 1952). The trick is to see how these may be adopted as indicators of sociological concepts. However, for most purposes indicators must be constructed anew by the researcher.

For Lazarsfeld the construction of measures was a movement between phases: an initial imagery of the concept, the specification of dimensions, the selection of observable indicators and the combination of indicators into indices (Lazarsfeld and Rosenberg, 1955). See Inset 4.3 for details of this process.

The important point to note about this process is that it is a movement from a concept (an idea of something) to observable characteristics and occurrences that could count as instances of that concept, and could be systematically identified as such. This means that the same concept can be indicated in different ways. This is consistent with the conception of science that informed variable analysis, in particular the notion that science deals not with 'things-in-themselves' but with aspects or properties of them. Indicators can be treated in just this kind of way, as the properties of the things denoted by the concepts. On the face of it, this also seemed to parallel the situation in natural science. Temperature, for example, may be measured using a mercury thermometer, by the contraction or expansion of a metal spring, or by resistance in an electric current, yet, it can be said that these different indicators 'stand for' the same concept, 'temperature'.

Let us accept that there may be a parallel here, but even so the indicators in social research have nothing like the stability, reliability and precision that the instruments for measuring temperature have. In the latter case, the link between the concept and the instrument is a direct instantiation of thermodynamic theories which precisely state by how much a metal, mercury say, will expand or contract consistently and predictably at various temperatures. The measurement instrument is itself designed on the basis of the theory of the relationship between heat and the expansion of metals.

Of course, the proponents were more than aware of the difference between measurement in the natural sciences and what was then possible in the social sciences. At this point one could assume either of the following:

- The social sciences are not conducive to proper measurement. The problems are too tough and any efforts would fall well short of the standards. But a start has to be made.
- The problems are so tough that they would frustrate any efforts at measurement. Therefore, trying to address the problem of measurement directly is a misguided move.

The positivists made the first assumption. A start had to be made through a strategy of 'indirect measurement' (since it could not be true measurement,

> **Indirect measurement**

though some argued that all measurement was indirect and that the differences between the natural and the social sciences are only of degree (Blalock, 1970; Blalock and Blalock, 1968). Despite the difficulties, cause for optimism was found in the successful wartime studies of morale in the American army funded by the army's Information and Education Division. These studies, *The American Soldier* published between 1949 and 1950 in four volumes, used social surveys to investigate a range of attitudes of soldiers (Stouffer et al, 1949). The fourth volume (Stouffer et al, 1950) dealt with methodological issues, especially the measurement of attitudes and methods for constructing scales.

Let us now look more closely at the strategy of indirect measurement.

The strategy of indirect measurement

This approach to measurement arose out the lack of well-grounded theories, of the kind illustrated earlier in connection with heat and the expansion of metals, which led directly to measuring instruments instantiating the theories. What measuring instruments there were in the social sciences were not accurately calibrated against an objective standard as, for example, is the case of measures of length, temperature or weight, and the many other measures used in natural science. This meant that any changes in measures from one study to another had to be assessed in terms of whether the changes were real, or due to vagaries in their use, or to variations in the measuring instrument itself. The response to this was to attempt to apply the axioms of number to indicators in ways which could be presumed to reflect the properties of the concept being measured.

Once again we need to take things step by step, beginning with the properties of a number series. Remember, too, that quantification is not regarded as an end in itself, but as a means of taking advantage of the potential of mathematics for calculation and, through this, working out relationships and quantities of properties not directly measured.

The properties of numbers

Below are set out the main properties of numbers.

- *Numbers are ordered*. This simply means that in a number series a particular number has a place in that series so that it comes before another particular number and after another particular number as in 1, 2, 3, 4 ... n
- *The differences between numbers are also ordered*. That is, the difference between any pair of numbers is greater than, equal to, or less than the difference between any other pair of numbers. For example, the difference between 10 and 20 is greater than that between 15 and 20, equal to the difference between 20 and 30, and less than the difference between 10 and 40.
- *The series has a unique origin indicated by the number 'zero'*. The key point about this is that the difference between any pair of numbers which contain zero as one member of the pair is the number of the other member.

These features of a number system are known as order, distance and origin. The task of measurement, then, is to be able to assign these properties of the number system to properties of the object being measured. However, this is not quite so simple as it might appear. It is not just a matter of assigning numbers.

Isomorphism

As we pointed out in the previous chapter, there has to be correspondence between the property being measured and the characteristics of the number system so that when one starts to apply mathematical operations such as addition, multiplication, and so on, one can take it for granted that the transformations in the mathematics will correspond to actual relations between the phenomena. This means that if one multiplies the quantity of something by two, this will reflect a doubling of the property that the quantity depicts but multiplying House Number 2 by House Number 3 does not mean that House Number 6 is twice as big as House Number 3, or that it is three times the size of House Number 2 or anything like that.

However, it was recognised early on that very few concepts of interest to sociology could sensibly be assigned all of these properties. Income, for example, was relatively straightforward, but what about prestige, power, integration, anomie, alienation and many, many more? 'Prestige' assuredly is a property that is of more or less. An occupation can be said to have 'more prestige' than another, but can we say by how much? Is a garbage collector half as prestigious as a parish priest? Society A may be said to be 'more' or 'less' integrated than Society B, but again by how much? Is Britain 8 per cent more integrated than France? Nevertheless, even if one could not assign all the properties of numbers to some object, one may be able to use some of them and settle, for now, for a lower level of measurement.

Levels of measurement

The idea of levels of measurement involves using only some of the properties of numbers to achieve something that can be called measurement. The ranking of levels of measurement is in terms of their relative weakness in respect of being amenable to mathematical transformation, such as addition, multiplication and the like. Three levels are usually identified and are, from the weakest to the strongest, nominal, ordinal and interval or ratio.

Nominal
This type is hardly measurement at all, though it is a basic requirement of all measurement. Really it is only a classification procedure. If, for example, we classify individuals into mutually exclusive and exhaustive categories, then it is possible to count the number of individuals in each category. Thus, for example, we could classify the citizens of Manchester into three categories: Manchester City supporters, Manchester United supporters, and those who support neither. We could also, using contingency tables, see the extent to which the members of these three categories also belong to other categories, such as income, residential area, religion or ethnic origin.

No ordering is implied by such a procedure. All we can do is count the number of cases in each category and, if we choose, calculate the percentages, which just restates the number in proportional terms.

Ordinal scales
Though classifying properties into a nominal scale is relatively straightforward, it is more difficult to find ways of ordering the categories according to some meaningful criterion. The ordinal scale uses one of the properties of the number system, namely, its serial order, or transitivity. According to this property, if A is

greater than B, and B is greater than C, then A must be greater than C. This allows the researcher to arrange a property into an order such that the serial ordering of the numbers reflects the degree of the property.

There are a number of concepts and properties used in social research which, on the face of it, seem to imply such an ordering. Most of us, for example, are aware that some occupations carry more prestige than others, that having a degree represents a greater level of educational attainment, that some people have more power than others, that some people are more prejudiced than others, and so on. However, while it may be accepted that an ordering is involved, it is not possible to say how much more prestige an occupation has than another, say, or how much more powerful A is than B, even though we are confident that A is more powerful than B.

If we have an ordinal scale we can score units in such a way that the numbers reflect the rank order in terms of the property being measured, but since there is no underlying metric we cannot use the standard arithmetic operations on the numbers. The numbers simply reflect the rank order in terms of the property. We cannot say, for example, that the top team in the Premiership is twice as good as a team halfway down. We can be confident that the first team is better, but not be able to say, arithmetically, how much it is better – being 13 places higher does not measure anything. Many attitude scales used in social surveys are ordinal.

Interval and ratio scales
If we can, however, determine the differences between different amounts of the property being measured and if numbers can be assigned so that their differences reflect the differences in the quantity of the property, then we have an equal interval scale or, if it has a non-arbitrary zero point, a ratio scale. This level of measurement requires a standard unit of measurement which is invariant. Feet and inches, centimetres and millimetres, grams and kilos are examples of familiar metrics which have this property. It is possible to precisely determine the difference between any two points on the scale. We can say that this basket of fruit is twice the weight of that basket or this building is three times as high as that one over there. In short, we are able to use the standard arithmetic operations of addition, subtraction, multiplication and division.

The distinction between an interval and a ratio scale is that the latter has a non-arbitrary zero point. But since there are so few such scales of relevance to social research, this need not detain us further except to reinforce the point that we have been making: that the level of measurement is critical to the kind of mathematical operations which can be performed with it. Many of the mathematically more powerful techniques of analysis in social research – such as correlation and regression – require at least interval or ratio levels of measurement since they involve algebraic operations. In practice, however, all too often such requirements are ignored.

It was clear that social research would have to rely upon levels of measurement somewhat less sophisticated than the highest. This was not, however, an unfamiliar problem to psychology, a discipline which had been concerned with measurement from the beginning of the century. Testing – of which intelligence tests are perhaps the most famous example, or infamous depending on one's point of view – had for long been a preoccupation. Many psychological scaling methods had been developed for constructing measures of psychological attributes. It was perhaps not surprising that as survey research developed in the post-war period, efforts were made to learn the lessons of psychological measurement and derive models of measurement which could be extended in social science more generally (Torgerson, 1958; Turner and Turner, 1990).

We have already mentioned that the roots of measurement in variable analysis lay in social psychological research, especially the measurement of attitudes. In Vienna, prior to his move to the United States, Lazarsfeld had developed a market research tool he called 'reasons analysis' which was, essentially, asking people why they did something (Turner and Turner, 1990: 105). The well-financed and large-scale social surveys done during the war had been led by scholars who were both committed to the idea of measurement and steeped in the then innovative work on attitude measurement and psychological testing (Torgerson, 1958). So perhaps it was not surprising that attitude measurement formed the inspiration of measurement in social research more generally through the development of mathematical theories of measurement as outlined in Inset 4.4.

> The roots of measurement in variable analysis

Inset 4.4 Attitude scale: the exemplar of measurement for variable analysis

Attitude measurement usually consists of giving a respondent a series of questions or, more usually, statements with which he or she is asked to express some degree of agreement or disagreement. The responses are then weighted, with the resulting score indicating the degree of the underlying attitude. In other words, the answers or the responses to statements are seen as indicative of the underlying attitudinal dimension.

A good illustration of the problems that attitude measurement was intended to solve was the frequent practice, exhibited in the early days of the aforementioned study, *The American Soldier*, of using polling results to conclude, for example, that 'Soldiers were 77 per cent against having WACs (female military personnel) in combat units', often based on the answers to a single question (Madge, 1963). Such single questions might have been used in more interesting ways by cross-tabulating them with other variables, such as age, whether located overseas or in the United States. However, the researchers wanted to go further than this. They were committed to the view that social science needed theories which could be formulated in ways that allowed for their empirical verification, and from which predictions could be drawn to apply to new instances. It was necessary to have some provisional theoretical explanations that could be falsified. Before any such theory could be formulated, the objects of study must be described accurately, preferably through measurement.

One of the research questions concerned attitudes to combat. A series of questions was devised to assess this, and was later checked against the rated performance of the soldiers in combat conditions. The questions asked trainees about their feelings about killing enemy soldiers, worries about injury and so on. While there were statistically significant correlations between promise and performance for some of these questions, willingness to kill Japanese soldiers was, surprisingly, not so well correlated. However, another question not directly related to combat readiness but on the subject of going AWOL did correlate highly with performance. The best fighters were the ones who thought that going AWOL was a serious offence (ibid.: 308).

For the methodologists on the team, the procedures of combining answers to different questions was a challenge, and it became an important step in Lazarsfeld's picture of the research process described earlier. Just as the answer to a single question was likely to prove inadequate for gauging the underlying attitude which produces a particular reply, so the ad hoc combining of disparate questions on the basis of their correlation with some other indicator, such as combat performance, was only a marginal improvement. One could only guess how an answer to a question related to the general attitude of the individual on that issue. A more systematic procedure was required. Further, on any particular issue, people can vary in terms of how strongly they feel about it. Earlier work in the 1930s had shown that attitudes have both direction and intensity (Likert, 1932). The same reply by different persons may reflect a deep concern about an issue or relative indifference.

The first step was to replace the single question with a battery of questions, but this raised the problem of which answer to believe and how much faith should be put in it. Until a means of deciding this was found, it was not possible to systematically combine questions to obtain a composite answer that reflected the attitude of the person to the issue. It needed to be shown that the answers to the different questions belonged to the one 'universe' or dimension: that is, whether there was a theme underlying the separate questions and answers that could be measured. If this could be achieved then the responses to the questions could be weighted to give a score for each individual respondent on the dimension.

Louis Guttman, who did much of the work on the methodological basis of scaling in *The American Soldier* study (Stouffer et al, 1950; Guttman, 1954), pointed out that an essential feature of a true scale is that an individual's response to a given item enables us to predict his response to all other

	Items				
Respondents	1	2	3	4	5
1	+	+	+	+	+
2	−	+	+	+	+
3	−	−	+	+	+
4	−	−	−	+	+
5	−	−	−	−	+
6	−	−	−	−	−

Figure 4.4 Scalogram analysis – scalogram of simple ordering

items. If, for example, a person replies that he is over 2 metres tall, then one can be sure that he will also reply that he is over 1.5 metres tall (Madge, 1963: 310). Unfortunately, this kind of confidence that there is an underlying dimension – in the example, the dimension of height – is lacking in social science, so the researcher has to feel his or her way to selecting suitable questions. The technique which emerged was called scalogram analysis. Essentially, the technique involves examining items on a questionnaire to see if they can be ranked without violating the axioms of the ordinal level of measurement (Guttman, 1950).

Figure 4.4 is a scalogram illustrating what a simple ordering of answers to a set of scale items would look like. Suppose that we have a series of six questions tapping fear symptoms experienced in combat: 'urinating in pants', 'vomiting', 'feeling of weakness or faintness', 'feeling sick in the stomach', 'shaking all over', 'sinking feeling in the stomach'. (This is adapted from Stouffer et al, 1950: 13–14, 140–42. Originally ten items were tested; one of them, 'cold sweat', did not fit into the scale). Suppose that the scale has been administered to six soldiers who each have to say whether or not they have experienced the symptoms by replying 'yes' (+) or 'no' (−). In practice, of course, more respondents than this would be used.

In the example, there are two extremes: a respondent who has experienced all the symptoms and one who has experienced none. In between, there are soldiers who have experienced some but not all. However, they do form a pattern that satisfies the axioms of simple ordering. In this example the pattern indicates perfect conformity with the axioms, an extremely unlikely event. If we scored each 'yes' response by giving it a weight of 1, then a score of 6 would indicate that all the symptoms had been experienced, and from any intermediate score between 0 and 6 we could predict which of the symptoms had been experienced.

As we have already suggested, such a pattern is unlikely to occur in actuality. More likely are cases of respondents who depart from the perfect scale type. In scalogram analysis these are treated as errors and if there are a large number the items are discarded. A coefficient of reproducibility is typically calculated (simply one minus the ratio of the number of times a response appears out of order to the total number of responses) and if it is 0.90 or higher, then this is taken as evidence that the scale is unidimensional. In which case, numbers can be assigned to the questions and scores given to respondents in terms of their answers. Normally, the technique is used in pilot studies where a series of questions or statements are given to respondents, and those items which give the best coefficient of reproducibility are retained to form the scale used in the social survey proper.

Although this technique was originally devised for attitudes it can be used for any set of indices which, arguably, could be seen to measure the same underlying dimension. For example, one could take a number of the typologies in sociology, which are often expressed as dichotomies – rural/urban, mechanic/organic, local/cosmopolitan and so on – but which, in any event, normally consist of a number of putative dimensions. For example, Weber's ideal type of bureaucracy is specified in terms of a number of dimensions: hierarchical authority, impersonality, separation of office from office holder, written rules of conduct, clearly defined spheres of responsibility, appointment by qualification, and specialised division of labour and expertise. Each of these can be treated as separate dimensions of 'more or less' rather than 'either–or' categories and, assuming that appropriate measures can be devised of each of them, profiles of actual organisations can be produced as systematically connected empirical types (Pugh and Hinings, 1976). The researcher can then go on to examine the conditions under which each type is likely to occur.

Inset 4.5 Ideal type

In order to gain an analytic grip on a complex and messy reality, Weber proposed that sociologists should formulate 'ideal types': that is, typologies constructed on the assumption that one, and only one, principle operates. For example, his ideal type of bureaucracy is constructed on the assumption that rationality and efficiency are the only principles involved in its organisation. Such a type is an extreme and unlikely to be found in reality. Nonetheless, it is useful as a yardstick for identifying those features of bureaucratic organisations which can then be explored empirically to look for the factors which inhibit an actual organisation from conforming to the ideal type.

'Ideal' in this context carries with it no prescriptive implication. The 'ideal type', in other words, is not formulated as some moral standard. Weber did think that bureaucracy was probably the most efficient form of social organisation ever invented but there are, of course, values other than efficiency (Weber, 1964). The 'ideal type' was intended as a tool for the initial ordering of a complex social reality – not unlike the ways in which natural scientists make assumptions about a 'perfect vacuum' or a 'frictionless plane'. Though not found in actuality they serve as a template against which reality can be seen. The 'ideal type' is an analytic tool for inquiry, not an end in itself. Once it had done its work, it could be discarded.

Indirect measurement: Some considerations

We have taken time to discuss some of the early work on scaling because it illustrates important aspects of the strategy of indirect measurement. In the case of attitude measurement, the task was to test if the items – the statements constituting the scale – conformed to the axioms of ordinality and, in some other types of scale, to the level of interval measurement. If it could be shown that the items of the putative scale were unidimensional, then this was taken as evidence that a general attitude was being tapped, something that was not measured directly. The scale, the items, the questionnaire were regarded as 'gadgets', rather like the thermometer or microscope, by which to measure, in this case, psychological properties (Stouffer quoted in Turner and Turner, 1990: 106).

This exemplifies the strategy of indirect measurement. As we said earlier, the task is to select empirical indicators and, using some systematic procedure, determine whether or not they are correlated and use this as evidence that the indicators tap some factor or dimension which they reflect.

Inset 4.6 Correlation and association

Earlier we mentioned regression and correlation. However, these are but two of a set of methods that can be used to determine the extent to which variables are related to one another. In the discussion, we are not presuming any particular method when we talk of correlation unless specified. Some methods require less stringent assumption than regression and correlation in being able to construct measures of association between ordinal data and some mixture of dichotomous, ordinal and metric data. The statistical assumptions are important in understanding what the measure of association or correlation claims.

As we said earlier, the strategy for measurement is essentially an empirical one. Actually it is a mixture of informed intuition or guesswork, and systematic methods. Indeed, development of systematic procedures has been aided considerably by the widespread availability of data analysis packages for PCs. We will discuss some of these methods in Chapter 8. For now we want to consider some important assumptions that surround variable analysis and measurement in social research. Aspects of these will also be taken up later.

Measurement and the nature of the phenomenon

As we said earlier, the development of indirect measurement was seen as strategically vital in building a science based around systematic social research. However, what it effectively did was elevate the theory of measurement and its mathematics over the importance of understanding the nature of the phenomena supposedly being measured. Much like the attempts to mathematise theory, measurement became exercises in mathematics. In a way, the strategy was an attempt, and explicitly so, at a short-cut by taking the mathematical characteristics of measurement and applying them to sociological concepts rather than – a much more difficult task – developing measures out of the nature of the phenomena.

Let us try to illustrate what we mean here by taking a common concept in sociology: 'power'. As a vernacular notion we are familiar with the kind of things 'power' can mean: the work done by an engine, that some people are more able to get things done despite constraints, some are more able to get valued goods and services, satisfy their wishes, get other people to obey them, and so on. For theoretical purposes – and the sociological literature on power is enormous – we might want to define the notion more precisely in order to measure it so that we can quantify the amount of power that someone has. In which case, we have to think about what kind of phenomenon 'power' is in

> The measurement of power: an example

order to determine how it might be measured. Is it the property of a person, or a role that the person performs, or the circumstances in which persons find themselves, or a property of social relations? This is not, of course, an issue of measurement but something to be determined prior to measurement so that we know what it is we are attempting to measure – if it is at all possible, and it may not be. But what the strategy of indirect measurement suggests is that in the absence of clear theoretical guidance, what we need to do is select some conception, develop empirical indicators and see to what extent it is associated with other variables of interest and, in this way, lead to the refinement of theory.

Let us assume that power is a property of a person (which might, of course, include some of the other possibilities mentioned above) and that it is dimensional in that some people have more power than others. (We might have problems with the extremes of 'total power' and 'complete powerlessness' but we can leave these on one side as conceptual rather than empirical extremes). At this stage we have decided that it can be measured at an ordinal level since we do have available some agreed metric of units of power equivalent to units of length or mass. That is, if we select appropriate indicators, then persons can be ranked in terms of their relative amounts of power. We will not be able to say how much more power a person has than another, but will at least be able to say that A has more power than B.

On the face of it such a step looks to be a major gain in precision and objectivity. We no longer have to 'guesstimate' the relative amount of power but can give it a quantitative expression, albeit at the ordinal level. In practice, matters are not so straightforward. The CEO of a large corporation might well be a powerful woman indeed. But outside the organisation, in her family say, she may well be dominated by her children. Of course, and as is recommended, we can construct multiple indicators for the organisation, the home, among friends, in the leisure club and so on, and look for patterns among these. But, as ordinal scales, we would have to be very cautious about adding the ranks across the various scores to obtain some overall measure of power. We could not be sure, for example, that scores on the scales in the various contexts were comparable or stable. Does a high score in the domestic environment mean the same as a high score in the local gymnasium? The numbers might be the same or different, but what consequence does this have? If it were a ratio scale then we might have more confidence that the numbers on the different scales meant something significant, but this is what is difficult to achieve.

The point is not so much that procedures such as these are nonsensical but that they are dedicated to making progress with measurement on the assumption that measurement is the key to understanding. At the same time, however, they run up against the fact that measurement is extremely difficult, if not impossible, when there is little real understanding of the phenomena to be measured. Relevant to this issue, and a major consideration in measurement, are questions of validity and reliability which are requirements for a proper, working measurement device. However, we want to discuss these issues in connection with 'measurement by fiat', the principle underlying indirect measurement in the positivist programme.

Validity, reliability and measurement by fiat

Validity refers to issues about how well a measure, or an indicator, measures or stands for the thing it is supposed to measure. Reliability is concerned with how stable and consistent the measure or indicator is. In the case of many of the measures used regularly in our daily life, such as length, weight and temperature, issues of validity and reliability tend to emerge when we have grounds for thinking that the measuring instrument is broken. This is because such measures are virtually definitional of the phenomena being measured. Thus, for example, 'speed' is defined as equal to the distance travelled divided by the time taken. Providing we have valid measuring instruments the determination is straightforward. It is normally only when we suspect, say, that the stopwatch is not working that we question the validity of the result.

A valid measure, assuming that it is working properly, is a reliable measure. But we cannot always assume that a reliable measure, in the sense of giving consistent results, is a valid one. A stopwatch that runs slow, for example, will give consistent but inaccurate results. The difficult problem, then, is establishing the validity of the measure or indicator.

There are two kinds of considerations to bear in mind. The first is the question of whether the measure or the indicator actually does measure what it is supposed to measure. The second has to do with the instruments used.

As we have said, in the more advanced sciences, because of their high level of mathematisation and quantification, the measures of a theoretical concept are integral to the theory itself. In many cases, the predicted values of some measure are extremely precise, and small measured differences very consequential for the theory – the fact that light passing the sun 'bent' by only the slightest angle was very important to the wide acceptance of Einstein's theory of relativity.

This assumes, of course, that suitable measuring instruments are available. Indeed, an important element in the advance of the mature sciences is the hand-in-hand development of theories and instrumentation, of which the massive particle accelerators are but the most renowned. But stopwatches, carbon-dating machines, brain scanners, testing equipment of all kinds, lasers, pressure gauges – to mention but a very few – are instruments not only widely used but designed on the basis of well-corroborated theories which enable them to be used as valid and reliable measuring instruments. One has only to think of the development of clocks from the early stumbles of mechanical devices to the electronic digital instruments used today, which are not only more reliable but enable us to achieve an accuracy undreamed of previously. These advances in timekeeping derive from advances in physics and not just from the craft of the clock and watchmakers, and provide an accuracy which is not only valuable for measuring 100 metre races to within thousands of a second, but also for ever more sophisticated scientific measurements.

But, of course, instruments are always prone to errors of various kinds. The most extreme of these is when the instrument breaks down. Nevertheless, there is always room for errors of one kind or another, many of which, in the case of widely used instruments, are known and taken account of in the calibrations. In many respects the margins of error are a consequence of the search for ever more accurate instruments. In other words, the standards of what is acceptable shift as instruments become more and more reliable and more and more accurate.

However, the point we want to stress is that validity is very much bound up with the soundness of the theory from which the measure is derived or, in the mature sciences, the theory in which the measure is integrated. The theory tells us what the measure is. In the human sciences, as should be clear, matters are not so straightforward.

One of the reasons why, in the mature sciences, theory and measurement go hand in hand, is that the theoretical concepts have a precise meaning a relationship to other theoretical concepts. This is what we tried to capture in Figures 4.2

and 4.3 earlier in the chapter. The ability to express theories mathematically is essential to this. Indeed, in such cases theoretical development and refinement are almost indistinguishable from the development and refinement of measures. It is this thorough integration of theory, method and data which positivism sought for the social sciences. But it was a challenge that posed an acute dilemma for the positivist programme. While recognising that measurement depends upon precise theoretical concepts, and recognising too that the theoretical concepts of sociology were vague, imprecise and not at all suggestive of measurement systems, by its own lights the programme needed to develop measurement systems in order to make theoretical concepts more precise. But does the strategy of indirect measurement actually do this?

Concepts and measurement

Consider how the strategy may be used to explore class and stratification.

The case of social class

It is widely known – not only by sociologists – that rewards of all kinds, such as income, prestige, life chances, access to medical services, education or consumption, are unevenly distributed. As we say, this is well known, and has been throughout the history of human societies. More recently it has been documented in numerous studies, both academic and administrative, in many countries. It is an understanding which also underpins advertising, marketing, urban planning, electioneering, social policy and more. It is a familiar feature of our social lives. However, if we introduce some sociological theory into the picture, then we start to have, not surprisingly, a number of sociological problems.

The differential distribution of rewards has, for long, been a prominent preoccupation of sociology. Marx, for one, argued that differential rewards were a function of the economic system and bound up with the division between the ownership and non-ownership of the means of production: in capitalism, the division between the bourgeoisie and the proletariat. Although he recognised that within these two classes further discriminations were possible, for example, in the proletariat between skilled and unskilled workers, it was the basic division with respect to the possession of property which really mattered and which, ultimately, would be the source of the conflicts that would destroy capitalism. By contrast, Weber adopted a more multidimensional view of stratification, giving 'life style', or status, more due as an independent factor in social conflict and change. This did not exclude class, as 'life chances', but could be at least as important, depending upon other social and economic circumstances affecting a particular society, and did not necessarily coincide with class divisions.

Although Marx and Weber are by no means the only sociologists who have addressed the problem of differential rewards and linking them to the system of social stratification, they have been massively influential in subsequent thinking. Further they amply illustrate the kind of problem that positivism faced.

If we return to Lazarsfeld's picture of the measurement process (which, in effect, is a picture of the research process as variable analysis understood this) set out in Inset 4.3, we see the first phase as one of immersion in the theoretical problem: the 'imagery phase'. In the case of both Marx and Weber, this will mean immersing oneself in their extensive, and discursive, arguments. Such an exercise is a formidable one, bearing in mind that both were as much concerned with the nature of industrial society as social stratification and, as part of this, addressing fundamental questions about the nature of social inquiry (See Ray, 1999, for a review of the differences between Marx and Weber). In terms of Figure 4.2 it would be a matter of elaborating the overall theoretical picture and its concepts on the left, of which the concepts of class and status are but a segment.

It is difficult to predict what might come out of this immersion, assuming that one approaches it anew without referring to the extensive subsequent commentaries on both theoretical accounts. However, the next stage, according to Lazarsfeld, is to 'elaborate' the concepts one is interested in – represented by the dotted lines in Figure 4.3. That is, trying to decompose aspects of the concepts into dimensions or variables, and then into empirical indicators.

The indicators, as mentioned earlier, have to be plausibly about the concepts being measured, in this case class and status. At this point the particular instrument being used is likely to make a difference, an issue which we will address more fully in the following two chapters. However, suppose we are using a questionnaire, then we will need to ask questions pertaining to the respondents' occupation, life style, education, attitudes to employers, income, job satisfaction, leisure activities, consumption patterns, political attitudes and views, employment history and so on. We will also have to decide which of these indicators are to 'stand for' the concepts of class or of status: a question of their validity. To complete the process, the indicators need to be intercorrelated to determine which are the relevant ones, which are the ones which best explain the distribution of responses to other indicators of interest.

Let us look more closely at what is going on here. At each stage decisions have to be made. However, this is not the problem. It is the nature of those decisions. The first set – moving from immersing oneself in the 'image' to indicators – involves presuming some relationship between theoretical concepts and their indicators: a process Torgerson calls 'measurement by fiat', which is not measurement proper since it involves a rather arbitrary decision that the numbers represent these phenomena. By this he means measurements that consist of 'presumed relations between observations and the concept of interest' (Torgerson, 1958: 21–2). It is a form of measurement, he argues, which is prevalent when we have a pre-scientific or common-sense concept that seems important but that we do not know how to measure directly. The strategy of indirect measurement is essentially measurement by fiat. It means making decisions and assumptions about the concept and how to measure it: what indicators of the concept are appropriate? However, the form of how to measure the

> Measurement by fiat

concept is already decided by variable analysis. Simply, it means thinking about the concept in terms of variables that can then be decomposed into observable indicators. In the end, it is the intercorrelations between the indicators that will determine the relevance and the validity of the indicators. In effect, the nature of the phenomenon is determined by what can be fitted into the procedures of variable analysis.

However, given the ambition of the positivist programme to achieve a thorough integration of theory, research and data, the question is how any findings produced in this fashion relate to theoretical problems of sociology. This is not really a question about the empirical results of particular variable analytic studies. There is a vast mountain of these, a testament to the difference between accumulating a large collection of uncoordinated studies and the additive effectiveness of studies that a progressing empirical science is supposed to possess. Though questions can be raised about such studies, the point is how we are to systematically connect the results to the theory – the image or picture – which inspired the research. What are we to make of results which state that, for example, a large proportion of the working class vote for 'right wing' political parties? Does this speak for Marx or for Weber? Of course, such a question cannot be definitively answered and, to be fair, nor would variable analysis suppose that in practice, as opposed to in principle, it could. Nonetheless, there remains a problem of determining just what the result means other than as a statement of association between indicators. In terms of Marx, to explicate the point a little more, is the result a refutation of his contention that class is the key division in forming political views, so that we would have expected working class people to support 'left wing' parties whereas what has been found is that significant numbers do not. Or, alternatively, does it direct attention to the mechanisms through which ideologies in the form of 'false consciousness' work? Or, as an alternative, is it the expression of religious affiliation, ethnicity, or many of the other indicators which may also be associated with voting patterns and class?

It is not that we cannot plausibly provide any number of explanations of the finding, many of them based on theoretical perspectives, such as those of Marx and Weber, to name but two. But these are brought to bear on the empirical data to give us alternative ways in which to read that data rather than being adjudicated by the evidence provided through the intercorrelations between the indicators. However, how much of Marx or Weber do we want to bring to the findings? 'Class' and 'status' are but two concepts bound up, in both their cases, with an examination of the nature of industrial society that, in its turn, is bound up with very different conceptions of the nature of social inquiry. In other words, Marx's and Weber's respective remarks on stratification and the distribution of rewards in society are deeply embedded in many other commitments and theoretical positions. In Marx's

> Theoretical commitments and the significance of data

case, the concept of class is tied to a moral metaphysics about alienation, exploitation and oppression that is not incidental to his arguments about class. Do we want to subscribe to these or do we want to regard them as inessentials to the sociological claims Marx is making? The procedures of variable analysis will not answer this question, though given its positivistic origins it is likely to take the view that the metaphysics is so much dross.

The point is that we cannot read the numbers and know what they mean without bringing to them some theoretical picture to give them sense. Each step that is taken to produce the indicators from the theoretical picture involves assumptions, explicit and implicit, on the part of the researcher. But this is not so much the problem as the fact that the assumptions all the way through from theory, to method, to data, are rarely, if ever, thoroughly thought through and systematically integrated. Each step on the way takes us further away from the phenomenon we set out to measure. If this is correct, then it should be no surprise that we have, for example, endless studies of social stratification and endless data, but are little nearer to obtaining any clearer theoretical picture. Instead, what we have are the same competing theoretical pictures, in many ways as deeply divided as ever, and we are no nearer, *on the basis of the data*, deciding between them.

The main weaknesses of indirect measurement are the assumptions that have to be made to achieve the semblance of isomorphism between the measurement system and the phenomenon the concept refers to. While clearly some assumptions are necessary, there can be an irresistible tendency to err on the side of dispensing with the more difficult, even intractable problems, so as to get on with something that might be considered measurement. After all, even if the constraints of measurement are relaxed, numbers can be produced and associations calculated and, through this, patterns found which can be made to 'make sense' through ad hoc theorising.

Conclusion

This is not the end of our discussion of variable analysis since we have also to look at two of the main techniques of research – interviewing and questionnaires, and social surveys – where some of the issues we have raised here regarding the strategy of variable analysis toward measurement will surface again.

Although we have raised critical points about the strategy, this is from the point of view of *sociological* research. We emphasise this because the strategy is, despite the antipathies toward positivism in sociology, far from dead. It remains in the form of many of the techniques of data collection and analysis that are widely used even by researchers, such as Marxist sociologists, who would reject positivist philosophy. In the United States, the approach is still very much alive. In disciplines such as psychology, the measurement systems briefly discussed earlier are still in use, though nowadays even more mathematically sophisticated.

In some ways this is a testament to Lazarsfeld's vision, along with others, in seeking to produce a theoretically neutral language for social research in the absence of clear theories. However, as a strategy for producing a thorough integration of theory, research and data it has fallen short – and in the next three chapters we will raise other questions about the positivist programme for sociological research. Nevertheless, even if we grant this conclusion, it does not follow that the programme is entirely worthless. The strategy was, after all, ambitious in its scope and though, with hindsight, its view of science, measurement and theories left much to be desired, it was not all wrong. And even if its ambitions were too high, it did, one could argue, leave a strong basis for empirical social research. Even though this may not result in the thoroughly systematic integration of theory, research and data found in the mature sciences, it has provided us with the means, the methods, for a systematic empirical exploration of the social world, and through this has elaborated our theoretical pictures a little more. We could, so to speak, disregard its early over-advertisements and settle instead for the methods it has left us. This may be the best that we can do for now.

This is, of course, a claim we need to examine further but it is not an absurd claim. After all, even if we cannot make sociology like physics – assuming that this is what we want to do – we can, *pace* Durkheim, perhaps emulate the science of medicine. The procedures of medical diagnosis are not unlike variable analysis in correlating lots of factors which may or may not be associated with disease symptoms. In other words, it is very much an empirical procedure which can often result in effective theories or, at least, promising avenues for experimental research. Be this as it may, it is now time to turn to the two techniques widely used in variable analysis: the interview and, in the following chapter, the social survey.

Selected bibliography and suggested reading

- It is worth looking at one of the early statements of the strategy of variable analysis, that is, Lazarsfeld's introduction to the reader he co-edited with M. Rosenberg, *The Language of Social Research: A Reader in the Methodology of Social Research* (New York, The Free Press, 1955). The book also contains other material worth looking at, including Barton's paper on 'The Concept of Property Space', as well as reports on empirical studies on a variety of topics.
- Material on measurement is not always easy to read. However, the introduction to Torgerson's *Theory and Methods of Scaling* (New York, Wiley, 1958) is worth some effort although it is not for the mathematically faint-hearted.

Chapter 5

Interviews and Questionnaires

The character variable analysis came to assume was very much shaped by the social survey, and the interview and the questionnaire became the major means of data collection. As Benney and Hughes (1956) remarked in an early seminal paper on the interview, 'Sociology has become the science of the interview.' While perhaps an exaggeration, this nonetheless recorded the prominence that interviewing had begun to assume in social research, and which it retains even today. Just over a decade later, in 1969, it was calculated that 91.7 per cent of research articles based on primary data in the most prestigious of the American sociological journals, the *American Sociological Review* and the *American Journal of Sociology* had made use of interviews and/or questionnaires (Brown and Gilmartin, 1969).

Why did the interview and the questionnaire come to have such importance in social research? What did the method, along with the social survey, seem to offer those committed to taking social research forward as a scientific sociology? In this chapter, we will examine the rationale underlying the interview and the questionnaire from the point of view of the positivist programme. Later in the chapter we will review how far the method achieved the programme's aims.

The rationale of the interview

The interview is a research setting in which a researcher asks a subject, the 'respondent', a series of questions relevant to the topic of the research. The function of the interview is to elicit particular information from respondents, information which can be about their living conditions, their attitudes, their beliefs, their relationships and so on: whatever is deemed to be relevant to the purposes of the research. The aim is to collect this information with a minimum of distortion.

It is difficult these days to imagine how immensely innovative the interview then was for social research, though of course various forms of questionnaire

> Questions and answers as data

had been used as far back as the late nineteenth century. Karl Marx himself had constructed one. But the new idea was that of putting the interview on a distinctly scientific footing. It is obvious to point out that people talk to each other, but the radical step for variable analysis was to use this fact and transform it into a source of data for social research. The researcher is not limited to what he or she can immediately perceive but potentially has access to a vast amount of data: what people can report on, talk about, express about themselves and their lives. They can report on what they think about things, their past, give details of their occupation, home life, express their sentiments about the government of the day, provide details of their material conditions and so on. In short, people can answer questions on as many topics as social scientists can think up, and thus respond in respect of whatever dimensions the researcher wishes to inquire into. By using questions and answers, researchers can obtain a great amount of information from a large number of people in a very short space of time.

It is this latter fact – a practical consideration – that perhaps accounts for the pre-eminence of the survey method, for it is really the only practical method for collecting a substantial amount of data at a comparatively modest cost on many of the kinds of topics sociologists have wanted to study. If one wants to study, say, the effects that early social experiences have on later life, one could study some people in their early life, and then study them later. This is not impossible to do. Television series have been produced on just this basis. But for most social researchers this is impractical. They cannot afford to wait 15 or 20 years to complete their research. Further, if one wants to study issues that involve large numbers of people spread over large distances, such as the voting behaviour of a national electorate, it is relatively easy to observe what a small number of individuals do directly, but very few organisations have the staffing to observe a very large number of the electorate. But one can, with a relatively small staff of interviewers, ask questions in a short interview of large numbers of people, just as one can ask about their early life. Thus, the interview provides a practical, economical substitute for observation. Without it sociologists and social researchers would be denied the possibility of studying electorates and many other large-scale or long-term phenomena.

In the context of sociology, it should be remembered that the aim of the interview is to collect information from individual respondents using questions as the stimuli to elicit this information. However, this information is not intended to be so much about the individual, the respondent *per se*, but about what the individual represents, is an instance of. So what the interviewee says in the course of the interview itself is treated as indicative of more general properties of the population from which the respondent is selected.

There are two key issues involved in the rationale of the interview and the questionnaire. The first is establishing a systematic connection between what people say and what they do or think: the relationship between words and deeds. Many interview questions ask people about how they have acted in the past, or about how they will act in the future. How can we be sure that what people say they have done or will do is the truth? People can lie, change their minds, not recollect accurately, say things in order to try to please the interviewer, want to get the interview over quickly or just say whatever is in their heads, misunderstand the question, and so on. In short, how can we ensure that in the interview the responses are accurate ones?

The second issue, though related to the first, is a slightly different matter and one which we raised in the previous chapter. In public opinion polling, what respondents say about their opinions regarding the government of the day, their voting intentions, support for particular policies and so on are taken as just that, namely, expressions of their opinions, their intentions. Pollsters know full well that people may change their minds, that the movement of public opinion can be volatile. On the whole, however, they are content with treating what respondents say at face value, knowing, by experience just how much confidence can be placed in the results.

> Responses as indicators

However, for variable analysis this is not sufficient. The objective is to test theories not simply to achieve a practical result, the reasonably reliable gauging of public opinion. The ultimate aim is that of explanation and to explain in terms of factors that determine behaviour and the views which people hold. Accordingly, what people say in response to the questions they are asked in an interview or on a questionnaire are intended as indicators of underlying factors which shape their actual behaviour. So, the interest is less in whether a person agrees or disagrees with the item, 'Do you think the government is doing a good job?', but in whether that response is indicative of some more general factor such as, by way of example, political conservatism or political activism. The opinion pollster is interested in finding out who is likely to win a forthcoming election, but this is not the variable analyst's concern. Rather, he or she is more likely to be interested in the more general questions about the kind of social factors determining the outcome of any election. One answer to that question might, at least in part, lie in people's general attitudes towards politics: how they will vote at an election will relate to their broad political orientation.

As we shall see, this second issue surfaces in the efforts to deal with the problem of inferring the properties of some collective entity from the responses of individuals. It arises in a particular form for interviewing and questionnaire studies since the data is gathered from individuals even though the research is meant to examine the nature of collective entities, such as a group, a class, even a society.

For now we want to deal with the various interview methods, organising the expositions around the issue of validity.

Validity

Both of the above issues – the relationship between words and deeds and that of responses as indicators – are bound up with the general methodological issue of validity. A question in an interview or a questionnaire is a vehicle for eliciting material that can be transformed into data. Therefore, it is of paramount concern that the question adequately serves this purpose. Does the question obtain the kind of answers that the research needs? Does the attitude scale actually measure the attitude it is supposed to measure? Is the answer to such and such a question a valid reply? Are the questions phrased so as minimise misunderstandings? And so on.

In everyday interaction these are issues which occasionally surface and we have quite ordinary ways of dealing with them. But, given the positivist project's commitment to the development of rigorous and systematic research methods, these are issues that had to be faced in order to ground the claims being made that these methods are scientific. However, the problem of validity was not one problem but, in fact, a large collection of problems that proved to be an enduring concern to survey researchers.

In what follows we discuss some of the problems and their attempted solutions.

The interview as a social encounter

The interview is, whatever it aims to do, a social encounter between an interviewer and a respondent. It is through the social encounter that the data is collected. Accordingly, it is more than possible that the way in which this encounter is conducted could have a significant effect on the nature of the data produced. An arrogant and condescending interviewer may well deter respondents from expressing what they truly think. Or, to take another example, a woman may be reluctant to talk about her intimate life with a male interviewer, and vice versa. In short, as a social encounter, the interview cannot be presumed to be exempt from the dynamics of social encounters.

One factor which assumed importance in the early days of thinking about the interview as a data collection method was the 'social desirability' factor (Edwards, 1957). In one study, respondents were asked to rate personality traits in terms of whether they considered them desirable or undesirable in others. A separate group were then asked to indicate whether the traits were characteristic of themselves. A strong correlation was found between the desirability of a trait and the probability of people rating themselves as having that trait. The implication is that people are more likely to present themselves in the best light rather than admit to having undesirable characteristics. Since this early study, the issue has been explored with regard to a great variety of factors which may have a bearing on the validity of the replies given in the interview, ranging from the cultural and subcultural variations in the willingness to admit

> Social desirability factor

to experiencing symptoms related to mental illness, the effect on responses of ethnically mixed interview encounters (and similarly with gender, age and social class), the verbosity, aggression and willingness to probe on the part of the interviewer, the presence of others during the interview encounter, to mention but a few.

Similar possibilities have also been noted in respect of respondents. Some, it is claimed, have a strong 'need for social approval' which makes them more sensitive to the demands of a situation and more likely to respond affirmatively to social influences. Some also agree ('yea-saying') or disagree ('nay-saying') with interview questions irrespective of their content. Even on fairly standard information, matters are not much better. The few studies which checked the reports of respondents do not encourage much confidence about the accuracy of, for example, whether or not the respondents voted in the last election. In some cases, these inaccuracies were of the order of 30 per cent after checking the numbers who said they voted against the recorded number who actually did vote. Similar orders in inaccuracy have been reported in the field of birth-control use, health information, deviant behaviour and social welfare (Phillips, 1971).

In light of all of this (the evidence did not emerge all at once), it was eventually realised that the social encounter of the interview needed to be regulated in some way so that effects such as those illustrated above could be taken into account. What emerged was a lore of interviewing: prescriptions of 'best practice' as well as more systematic attempts to maximise the validity of the data collected.

One significant move was to design the interview in terms of the kind of information required. See Inset 5.1 for details of types of interview.

Inset 5.1 Types of interview

Broadly, four types of interview are identified, moving from the highly standardised structured interview to the group interview. Each is designed to elicit particular kinds of information relevant to the purposes of the research.

The structured interview

In the standardised interview the interviewer uses a schedule in which the wording and the order of the questions is the same for all respondents (which is also meant to standardise the stimulus to which the respondent reacts). The role of the interviewer is to direct the respondent according to the schedule of questions. If clarification is sought by the respondent then this, too, should be as standardised as possible. Above all, the interviewer should not behave in any way differently from other interviewers administering the same interview or in different ways between his or her own interviews, so as to avoid unintentionally predisposing the respondent to give a particular answer.

The assumption behind this type is that if all respondents receive the same stimuli, then any variation in their replies cannot be due to variations in the stimuli each respondent received. If one interviewer were to ask a question in one way and another were to ask the same question in a different way, we could not be sure whether differences in the replies were real differences between respondents or artefacts of the way in which the questions were asked. This does not, of course, deal with challenges to validity arising from respondent characteristics. What it does is try to control potential variations in interviewer behaviour in order to standardise the process.

An effective standardised interview depends on good preparation, often through a pilot study, and trained interviewers well versed in the schedule so that they can ask questions in a uniform and non-directive way.

Semi-structured interview

As its name suggests, this type uses specified questions, but the interviewer is given more freedom to probe replies further should he or she feel it necessary, encouraging the respondent to elaborate on answers. The precise mix of structured and unstructured items is a matter for the research.

Unstructured interview

This type of interview is intended to provide qualitative depth rather than answers which are comparable between respondents as in the case of the structured interview. The researcher clearly has a theme in mind for the interview and may well have to do some work to get the respondent to 'open up' and talk freely about the topics of interest. The aim is to provide rich material from respondents, to get them to give long narrative or explanatory or opinionated answers, rather than brief 'yes' or 'no' replies. Such interviews can also be used in pilot studies, using the material gathered as a guide for the design of more structured interviews.

Group interview

These days this is sometimes referred to as a 'focus group' and is widely used in politics, advertising and marketing as well as, increasingly, in academic contexts. It typically involves around ten people who are asked to discuss a particular topic under the direction of a moderator who promotes interaction and discussion, making sure that it keeps on the topic of interest. A session can last up to two hours or more (Merton et al, 1956; Stewart and Shamdasani, 1990).

The rationale behind the different types is that each is suited to particular kinds of research problem. The unstructured interview is claimed to be more appropriate for exploratory studies where little is known either about the problem or the population from which the respondents are selected. Many such studies are often pilots for the design of more structured interview schedules. The standardised and semi-standardised interviews offer advantages in cases where a large sample of people are being surveyed. They allow relatively untrained interviewers to administer the schedule, whereas the unstructured interview requires highly trained and flexibly minded personnel fully cognisant with the aims of the research. Above all, the structured interview simplifies the coding of the responses for machine processing: a not unimportant cost consideration.

The conventions of interviewing

As we pointed out earlier, there has emerged a lore about how the interview encounter should be managed. On the one hand, the purpose of the interview is to gather information that is as objective as possible, but, on the other hand, as a social encounter it must needs be governed by the proprieties of interpersonal relationships between people who do not know each other. The interviewer cannot threaten or chastise the interviewee, for example, or otherwise force anyone to be interviewed. However, it is worth noting that Howard Becker claimed to have gained considerable benefits in understanding the behaviour of teachers from interviewing them in a provocative and offensive manner: a reminder that much of this 'lore' has a rule of thumb character.

Benney and Hughes (1956) identified two conventions which should govern the interaction in the interview: equality and comparability. The first of these, equality, assumes that information is likely to be more valid if it is voluntarily given. The interview should be freely entered into by the respondent and not be compelled in any way. In effect, the interview is a bargain that, in return for allowing the interviewer to direct the interaction, the respondent will not meet with denial, contradiction, competition or any other harassment. To facilitate this the interviewer should try to minimise the effects arising from, for example, the inequalities of gender, age, intelligence or social status which might exist between parties to the interview relationship. Certainly, a great deal of interviewer training is devoted to precisely this point. Of course, the extent to which such a convention actually operates in interviews is a moot point.

> Equality

The second convention, comparability, is designed to minimise the local and immediate circumstances of the particular interview and, instead, to emphasise those aspects which are general and countable. As we have said earlier, the interview is not an end in itself but is one among many others which are part of the same study. Accordingly, idiosyncratic qualities have to be minimised in favour of qualities which are generalisable across the range of interviews. The particular encounter between interviewer X and respondent A should yield information which is comparable to encounters

> Comparability

between X and B, C, D and E, and so on. Similarly, interview encounters between interviewer Y should yield comparable information to that which interviewer X has obtained.

The term generally used to refer to the tone of the relationship that the interviewer needs to establish with the respondent is 'rapport', the development of mutual trust that facilitates the free flow of information. It emphasises the need for the interviewer to establish trust, warmth and reassurance, while remaining detached. The interviewer should never threaten the respondent or erode his or her confidence in the relationship. The respondent should be respected and supported.

> Rapport

Of course, prescriptions are one thing, practice another. However, before discussing these and their consequences, let us briefly look at questionnaire construction.

Questionnaire construction

Along with the interview, questionnaires, either as an interview schedule, self-administered, or as part of a telephone survey, are the main means of eliciting the responses which constitute the data for analysis.

The self-administered questionnaire is normally sent to selected respondents by mail. It is often argued that the anonymity this provides can encourage the expression of strongly held and perhaps unpopular views. It is also a relatively cheap method of data collection since it does not require interviewers. Nevertheless, there is a price to pay for cheapness. The questions have to be kept simple since an interviewer is not there to provide guidance. Further, there is little control over how, or indeed whether, the questionnaire is completed, and there is there is a low rate of return of completed questionnaires. A response rate of 40 per cent is a good one, and many are much lower than this despite repeat solicitations for the return of the questionnaire.

Whether the questionnaire is self-administered or part of an interview, there are a number of guidelines that need to be observed in the construction of questionnaires.

The first step is a careful consideration of what the research needs by way of information from respondents. As we have discussed in the previous chapter, theoretical ideas need to be translated into indicators – in the case of questionnaires, into questions or statements for the respondent. It is important to make sure that there is adequate coverage of the concepts that the research wants to explore. After all, one can only analyse the data that has been collected, and at this first stage the researcher needs to be very thorough in reviewing what the research objectives require. Of course, compromises will have to be made. If a thorough review of relevant concepts is likely to result in a very long questionnaire, then some prioritising needs to be done.

> Choosing indicators

The second stage is actually translating the concepts into questions or statements. In a word, operationalising the concepts: what kinds of questions are the ones that will engender answers that will indeed constitute, say, 'political orientation'? Deciding this is crucial to the relevance of the questionnaire or interview as evidence for the study it is part of. At this point decisions will have to be made about the type of question–answer format to be used. The choice lies between 'open-ended' and 'closed' or 'fixed alternative' questions.

> Open-ended vs fixed choice questions

The 'open-ended' question is one which does not provide the respondent with a set of pre-decided list of possible answers from which to select an alternative. An example would be, 'Why did you come to work in this factory?', leaving it open to the respondent to provide an answer in whatever way he or she chooses. The fixed alternative format, as the name suggests, provides a selection of possible answers. These can be as straightforward as 'yes' or 'no', or 'strongly agree', 'agree', 'no opinion', 'disagree' or 'strongly disagree', or some other listing providing, to use the previous example, alternative reasons why the person came to work in the factory. The respondent's answer must normally be limited to one of the alternatives provided. Although occasionally an 'open-ended' category is provided for the hoped for few cases where a respondent feels that none of the offered alternatives fits the case. Attitude scales are normally fixed alternative questions or statements with which the respondent is asked to express some degree of agreement or disagreement.

Each type of question has its advantages and disadvantages. As open-ended questions put less constraint on the individual's replies, there is less danger of answers being forced into categories which do not adequately reflect what the respondent intends. Unfortunately, such questions tend to be time consuming and the fullness of the response varies greatly between individuals, so making it difficult for those who are to code the interview results to be sure that they are treating the responses in a truly standard way. In self-administered questionnaires, nearly all questions are fixed alternative. In any event, this type of question is easier to code and provides more uniform information, making it easier to quantify the responses. However, it is by no means unusual to find questionnaires containing both formats.

A crucial consideration is the wording of questions. They should ask precisely about whatever it is the researcher is interested in finding out, and in a way that the respondent will understand. The phrasing of the question should be understandable to interviewees, avoiding jargon and esoteric words.

> Question wording

Questions also need to be framed in terms of whether the target population is likely to know the answer. Asking 60-year-olds about the latest hit records – unless there is some theoretical justification for doing so – is likely to result in many blank answers. Ambiguous and loaded terms should be avoided and questions kept as short as possible. Care should be taken not to predispose a particular answer. In the case of questions asking for an opinion, for example, differing wordings can elicit different answers and, therefore, care should be taken in their phrasing.

Also, care should be taken to protect the self-esteem of the respondent. For example, it is better not to ask, 'Who is the Prime Minister?' but, 'Do you happen to know the name of the Prime Minister?' The latter suggests that it is possible, without embarrassment, to admit to not knowing. Questions should be phrased to avoid putting the respondent in an unfavourable light by suggesting that others might feel the same way, or by indicating that the interviewees responses are not exceptional or surprising, and so on.

In the case of fixed-alternative questions, the alternatives provided should be exhaustive, covering the full range of possible responses, be mutually exclusive and, of course, fit the frame of reference of the question. This is especially important with self-administered questionnaires where no interviewer is present to remedy any misunderstandings.

The sequence of questions also needs careful consideration, especially since early questions may predispose answers to later ones. As always, this is largely something which needs to be considered in light of the aims of the research, though there are one or two general principles to be borne in mind. The questions must be consistent not contradictory. Funnelling is often

> Sequencing of questions

useful in guiding the respondent from general to more specific questions. This technique is often used to filter the respondent through subsets of questions. For example, if the respondent only has to answer certain sets of questions depending upon earlier replies, there should be an early question directing the respondent to the relevant subsets. Such as: 'Did you vote in the last election? IF YES, then proceed to question N', and so forth. In an interview, of course, the interviewer can normally handle such movements, depending upon the interviewee's responses.

The sequencing of questions can also play a part in 'breaking in' the respondent smoothly and gently. Conventionally classificatory, or 'face sheet', information is normally asked early in the questionnaire or the interview. This consists of asking about things like age, income, marital status, education, occupation and housing. These are standard items which, in social surveys, are often used as initial classificatory data. More intimate and personal questions are normally asked later when, hopefully, the respondent is fully engaged in the process and more willing to talk freely than he or she would have been before 'rapport' was established. It is important to bear in mind that there is no compulsion for the respondent to answer the questionnaire or take part in the interview. Accordingly, as far as possible the process should arouse the respondent's interest and avoid monotony. In the case of self-administered questionnaires, visual presentation can be important. In any event, all instructions should be clear and precise offering the respondent sufficient guidance and encouragement to complete the questionnaire or interview easily, simply and unambiguously.

Coding

Eventually the results of the interview or the questionnaire (which have been written down or audio recorded by the interviewer) have to be prepared for analysis – and, given the ambition of quantification, turned into numbers. Typically, the data gathered by the interview or the questionnaire is processed to produce cross-tabulations of the kind discussed in the previous chapter. Coding is the process by which the responses to the questionnaire or schedule are transposed to some medium which facilitates counting the responses. In the early days prior to the advent of cheap computing, punched cards were used, one for each respondent, with each question allocated to a particular column containing 12 positions. It was a fairly simple matter to run the cards through a machine which would then count the holed positions to give the number of respondents who had answered a question in a particular way. Successive runs on the relevant questions allow cross-tabulations to be produced. In essence the analytical process remains much the same except that computers have replaced the card processor and questionnaires are often coded directly onto the computer.

Most questionnaires are pre-coded. This involves allocating a numeric code to each category of a variable. For example, if there are five possible answers to a particular question, these could be given a number from 1 to 5, using other numbers for missing or unusable answers. These are often set out on the right hand side of the questionnaire opposite the relevant questions. Pre-coding makes the questionnaire easier to process for analysis.

Open-ended questions represent more of a challenge in that it is not always easy to predict in advance the kind of coding categories that could be employed. Sometimes such responses are simply used as illustration to amplify forced-choice questions. Otherwise, coding categories need to be devised once the replies are available.

Coding is clearly essential to the process of rendering the information collected by an interview or questionnaire into a form usable for research. Although it looks like a fairly mechanical process, it often calls for judgement on the part of the coders to resolve ambiguous and unclear replies, sort out inconsistencies, check out the accuracy of the coding and so on.

The gap between ideal and actuality

The above is a brief outline of some of the considerations that need to be borne in mind when designing and employing questionnaires. There can be little doubt that the proponents of variable analysis took the issue of interview and questionnaire design very seriously indeed. Proper and effective design was crucial to establishing a good case for the validity of the instruments. The procedures which emerged – and which we have merely sketched – were intended to remove sources of bias and subjectivity from the interviewing process and questionnaire design, biases and subjectivities which could affect the validity of the data collected. However, the issue was not simply about bias but more about the menace of unknown and therefore uncontrolled biases. After all, if the gender of the interviewer is likely to inhibit responses, the interviewer can hardly change sex from interview to interview. One can, however, try to make sure that appropriate interviewers are matched to appropriate respondents. Systematising the interview process and the design of questionnaires was one way of trying to achieve this. But, as always, practically executing the recommended principles would be quite another matter.

Indeed, much of the lore of interviewing and questionnaire design was the result of trial and error as the instruments came to be used more and more in social research and questions raised about their validity. What emerged was an amalgam of social proprieties, cultural presumptions and recommendations intended to support the validity of the techniques and meet the requirements of variable analysis, yielding, as we said above, rule-of-thumb recommendations. Let us look at some of these more closely.

The purpose of the interview and the questionnaire is to elicit verbal responses from a subject. But these cannot be just any old verbal responses. The potential offered by the interview and questionnaire in allowing the researcher to cover a wide range of topics, to explore the past, the present and the intended behaviour of subjects depends upon the latter being truthful in what they say. But people are forgetful, try to put themselves in as favourable a light as possible, are not always consistent and do not always do what they say they will.

As we have seen, researchers have not been unaware of these problems as is testified by all the efforts devoted to questionnaire design, interviewing styles, and assessing interviewer effects as summarised above. As early as the 1930s, La Piere travelled with a Chinese couple in the United States reporting the treatment they had received in hotels, campsites, motels and restaurants (La Piere, 1934). Of the 251 establishments visited, only one refused to accommodate the couple. Six months later, a questionnaire was sent to each establishment visited. Half only were asked, 'Would you accept members of the Chinese race as guests in your establishment? The other half were asked about other ethnic groups. Only one 'yes' response was received – a huge discrepancy between verbal and overt behaviour.

> **Words and deeds**

The problems arise from the fact that the interview is an occasion isolated from most of the matters it concerns itself with, namely, the social behaviour of the respondent. With regard to the past, the problem for the researcher is to assess how much of what is reported by the respondent is refracted through the lens of the present. Further, though a respondent may express strong sentiments in the comfort of the interview, when actually confronted with situations where these sentiments may have relevance, he or she is no longer isolated from all the factors which may impinge on behaviour and, accordingly, may act in ways 'inconsistent' with beliefs or attitudes expressed in the interview or on the questionnaire, as the early La Piere example suggests.

What should be no surprise is that these issues are intimately bound up with theoretical problems in the sense that they are not simply about techniques but more about the kind of theories which inform the construction and use of the techniques. As we stressed, the ultimate objective of the positivist project was to create an integrated social science: that is, the development of systematic connections between theories, methods and data. Accordingly, what was needed was a theory which could underpin the rationale of the interview and the questionnaire. Not surprisingly there were no such theories available or, to be more accurate, there were many theories which could be drawn upon from psychology, social psychology, studies of small groups and so on, but none that received anything like universal assent. The net result was an attempt to exploit variable analysis itself as a means of producing generalisations which could inform the design of interviews and questionnaires. As we have already indicated, the end result was a collection of presumptions and recommendations rather than a systematic theory of instrumentation.

Inset 5.2 Theories of instrumentation

The term 'instrumentation' is owed to Cicourel (1964) who uses it to draw attention to the need to disentangle the observer's presence and procedures from the material labelled as 'data'. In effect, it is asking for an account of the connection between the 'data' and the phenomena to which they refer. As has already been noted, in the much of natural science, theories of instrumentation are coterminous with the relevant substantive theories. It is the theory which tells us what and how to measure. In social research, since many of the methods of data collection involve interaction with subjects, theories of instrumentation, if such are to be had, will be sociological theories.

As we have already pointed out, the interview is a social encounter and, as researchers have shown, cannot be exempted from the social processes that characterise such encounters. This is why such stress is laid on interviewing and questionnaire techniques and the management of the interviewer–respondent relationship by the interviewer. Especially important in this connection is the question of the instrumental effectiveness of the interview relationship. Is it, for example, true that establishing a 'detached and trusting' relationship will get the respondent to tell the truth as best as he or she can? It is plausible to argue that it could, just as likely, result in the respondent avoiding potential controversy, offering instead blandness and efforts to maintain conviviality. Certainly few police interrogators or even job selection interviewers would necessarily subscribe to the methods proposed by social research interviewers as the best method for getting at the truth. And, indeed, there were some who eschewed the textbook advice on conducting interviews that was emerging. More recently, some feminist sociologists have rejected many of the prescriptions of textbook interviewing.

Feminist approaches to interviewing

A number of feminist researchers have questioned the recommended interview role of detachment and disengagement, as a one-way process of getting answers from respondents. Oakley (1981), for example, argues that such a relationship is exploitative in concealing the 'subjective position of women' by forcing on the interview relationship a set of procedures which disguise this or, to put it more strongly, reflect a 'masculine paradigm' of social research. In her research on the transition to motherhood, Oakley felt that acting as a disengaged interviewer and expecting someone to reveal important and personal information without entering into a dialogue and sharing experiences was untenable. Disengagement is not, for feminist researchers, a realistic description of what occurs, but an idealised one and should be rejected both in theory and practice (Stanley and Wise, 1982).

This is, of course, an objection from an approach which rejects, in significant respects, the basic tenets of the positivist programme in favour of a more emancipatory conception of the social research process. Nonetheless, even within the positivist programme, by focusing upon gender it raises important considerations of the kind already mentioned about the relative effects of interviewer characteristics. Moreover, in recognising the profoundly social character of the interview encounter, the approach also draws attention to the ways in which, allegedly, everyday conversations between men and women are structured, specifically that men tend to dominate them (Fishman, 1990). In which case, these are inequalities which need to be considered in the selection of interviewers, along with other factors which may have much the same effects, such as social class and ethnicity, to mention only two.

Cultural context of interviewing

The point is, of course, that the procedures of interviewing are as much infused with ethical sensibilities as they are with instrumental concerns. And quite rightly. Social researchers have no licence to force respondents to complete a questionnaire or be interviewed. The point is that the interview and the questionnaire, along with some of the presuppositions on which they are based, derive their plausibility from wider cultural conventions quite apart from the kind discussed earlier in connection with managing the interview: equality and comparability. The method presupposes, for example, a fairly stable social and political order in which the majority of potential respondents do not feel particularly intimidated by requests to take part in social research. They must also be confident in their right to refuse or to agree to take part without fear of recrimination. Further, they must feel confident that remarks made in the privacy of the interview (or written on a questionnaire) will not be disclosed to others who have no right to know what transpired. It also presupposes a literate culture, one in which personal viewpoints are deemed significant, that personal lives can be investigated by properly qualified persons, and so on.

None of this necessarily invalidates the interview or the questionnaire. Cultural expectations such as these make interviewing and questionnaires possible even though, within societies which can lay claim to having such cultures, it is not always easy to interview just anyone. The homeless, vagrants and criminals, as well as the heads of large corporations and senior government officials, are examples of groups who are difficult to interview for the purposes of social research. Of course, social researchers are as aware of these considerations as anyone else, and would be among the first to concede the general principle that any method of data collection has to be evaluated in terms of the prevailing conditions, in this case the prevailing social conditions. Indeed, knowledge of the society and its culture is essential for the social researcher to evaluate how best to go about interviewing, how the effects of particular characteristics of the interviewer may be assessed, and so on.

Earlier, we spoke of the conventions of 'equality' and 'comparability' which should govern the interview. As we said, the convention of equality means that
the interviewer should try to minimise any inequalities that might arise from age, gender, ethnicity, social status and so forth. But it is hard to determine just what the effects of any such properties are. As we indicated earlier, the literature is replete with studies intent on determining the relative effects of interviewer characteristics upon the respondent, but these are not always consistent. In 1968, just after the assassination of Martin Luther King, Schuman and Converse (1971) interviewed 619 residents of Detroit, using a mix of black and white interviewers, mainly older women with experience as professional interviewers, along with white male and female graduate students. For over 25 per cent of the questions, black and white interviewers obtained significantly different responses. However, somewhat against expectations, some questions did not produce strong race-of-interviewer effects. The effect of race was not always in the expected direction. We cannot, in other words, assume that black respondents are more likely to tell the truth to black interviewers than to white. In this case, black respondents might distort their answers in a less racially hostile direction to please white interviewers, and might also express more militant sentiments to please black interviewers. It also appeared that differences in response to the race of the interviewer were greater among low-income and less educated respondents.

However, the point we want to make is not that interviewer characteristics have no effects, but that it is extremely difficult to evaluate just what an effect might have in a particular interview, and near impossible to lay down assured guidelines. Even if we grant, as some feminist researchers argue for example, that there are basic inequalities in the interactions between men and women, it does not follow that this is invariably so in each and every case. Although interviews

> Equality and comparability

– and questionnaires – are normally part of a social survey, and hence the responses from each interview are aggregated across all respondents, at the point of data collection each interview is a single event. Accordingly, it is difficult to know which of the many possible factors that may affect responses are in play at the particular time of the interview. Of course, one may assume that whatever errors there might be will, across the number of interviews, cancel each other out. But, as studies suggest, this is not always a safe assumption to make.

The relation between 'words and deeds'

During the heyday of positivistic research, Deutscher (1968), resurrecting the largely forgotten results of La Piere's work in the 1930s and complaining that this had been buried rather than responded to, drew attention to the relationship, as he put it, between 'words and deeds'. What he largely had in mind was the oft-remarked discrepancy between attitudes and behaviour. However, he also argued that social research had neglected to develop a technology which could facilitate our understanding of the circumstances in which people do or do not 'put their monies where their mouths are'. Interviews and questionnaires were not that technology.

Meaning equivalence

However, we can explore Deutscher's general point another way. In designing a questionnaire or interview schedule, a decision has to be made as to the format of the questions: a format appropriate for the types of interview discussed earlier. This decision is, of course, connected to considerations of cost, sample size, the objectives of the research in terms of whether it is exploratory or hypothesis testing, and so on. In effect, the choice is between standardised and open-ended questions, or some mixture of the two. If the researcher chooses fixed-choice questions in order to standardise the stimuli given to respondents this will, inevitably, restrict the opportunities for amplifying the responses. This not only sacrifices richness, it can also be misleading. Although respondents can and often do answer questions given to them in terms of the categories provided, this is not the same thing as saying that these categories adequately reflect the respondent's meaning. Take the example as set out in Figure 5.1.

The respondents are asked to choose the response which comes closest to their feelings about the satisfaction of their work. Such a question could form

'Most of the time I find my work satisfying'

Strongly agree	Agree	Undecided	Disagree	Strongly disagree

Figure 5.1 Example of fixed choice question

one item of a scale of, say, job satisfaction, with the responses being weighted to give an overall score. Thus, for example, the 'Strongly agree' response could be weighted 5 and the others, in descending order, to 'Strongly disagree' which has a weight of 1.

The problem is about the entitled inferences about, say, a respondent who replied 'Agree' to the question. The question itself asks about 'most times', but do the interviewer and the respondent know what this means? Is X's reply equivalent to Y's who also chose the 'Agree' response? The format of the question has to presuppose that there is an equivalence of meaning in regard to both the question and the answer. It has to presuppose such an equivalence especially if measurement is involved. If the weightings given to each answer are to conform to the requirements of counting, then it has to be assumed that person A's score of 3 is equivalent B's score of 3, and that both these scores reflect a greater quantity of the property being measured than C's score of 2. It has to be assumed that the meaning each item has for each respondent is equivalent in terms of the meaning that it conveys, and also in the 'strength' with which the sentiment it expresses is held, in order for the scale to work as a numerical measure of the property.

Imagine a conversation between some friends about their work. It is possible that an utterance 'most of the time I find my work satisfying', or something like it, could have occurred. After all, one of the recommendations in questionnaire design is that the questions should be phrased in language understandable to the target population. In such a conversation the utterance would have a context of other utterances, the topic of the conversation, the setting, who the people are, and so forth. The utterance might have been said ironically, jokingly, as the justification for working at the weekend or in some other context. It might have also occasioned some further responses on the part of fellow conversationalists: 'Do you really mean that?', 'I agree, I enjoy my work – but the boss is lousy', 'Not many people could say that these days', 'Ha! ha!', and so on.

The point is that in everyday interaction the meaning of utterances can be routinely explored and dealt with for the purposes at hand. What interviewing and questionnaires do is try to rely on ordinary meaning to formulate questions and generate answers which are intended to satisfy the necessary assumptions of counting and measurement. But forced-choice items, it can be argued, put a question mark against the assumption that respondents who answer questions in the same way thereby give vent to opinions of equal strength.

The arguments concerning meaning equivalence do not simply apply to forced-choice items, however. There is a general issue about meaning equivalence, in that it is not clear that in providing an answer to some question a respondent understands either the item itself or the response to it in the same way as another respondent, let alone the researcher. Indeed, we cannot be sure that any respondent would understand an item on another occasion in the same way that it was understood on a previous one. This is not to say that respondents cannot provide answers. They certainly do. After all, such instruments are widely used almost on a daily basis. The issue has to do with the meaning of these answers and whether or not they adequately reflect some underlying property, an attitude for example, such that it can be quantitatively recorded, even if this is only by counting the responses. What can we infer, for example, about a respondent who 'Strongly agrees' with the question in Figure 5.1, but on a later question – 'Sometimes I get really frustrated at work' – also responds 'Strongly agree'? Is the respondent being inconsistent, irrational, or just saying anything to get rid of the interviewer or complete the questionnaire as quickly as possible? Is the response, after all, inconsistent?

The respondent may be any of these things, but the typical way of treating such responses is to regard them as errors. For example, if the items were part of a scale, scalogram analysis of the kind discussed in the previous chapter would probably show this response as falling outside the scale pattern. Even if the intercorrelation of the responses of all the respondents showed a strong relationship between the replies to both these questions – remember that these intercorrelations will be based on aggregating all the responses from all the questionnaires or interviews – this particular pattern would as likely as not be treated as an error and discarded. However, it is perfectly possible to give perfectly reasonable and rationally connected reasons for agreeing with both of these apparently 'inconsistent' statements. It may be, for example, that the respondent is distinguishing between 'the work itself' and the 'frustrations of organisational life', or that dealing with the frustrations is satisfying. But without further elaborations on the part of the respondent it is difficult to judge. Once the data is collected, it is not usually possible to go back and re-interview people about their responses – those coding the survey results will have to make their own decisions as to what people really meant, whether seemingly discrepant answers can be reconciled. There will be, as Harold Garfinkel (1967) has pointed out and illustrated, a huge amount of ad hoc decision making involved in coding survey data. If the data is to be coded, Garfinkel is saying, there will *have to be* such ad hoc decision making. However, this means that the application of individual judgement in the coding process defeats the efforts at standardising the behaviour of interviewees.

Observations such as the above are relevant to understanding why, on occasions, respondents have difficulty answering items since they lack any specification of the context which might give the statements a point. Including them in a questionnaire or asking them in an interview gives them a disembodied, decontextualised character so that respondents often want to ask 'in what circumstances', or answer with a qualifying phrase such as, 'well, it depends'.

It might seem that the kind of questions we are raising here are rather pedantic. As we have just said, after all, people answer questionnaires, take part in interviews, on the whole without too much trouble. Does it really matter if we cannot assume that meanings are precisely equivalent? Surely, if someone replies 'Strongly agree' that is a reasonable indication of how strongly they feel about something even if we cannot be absolutely sure that, in any particular case, this feeling is stronger than someone who replies 'Agree'. In any event, it is reasonable to assume that such differences will not prove to be consequential when dealing with large numbers of people.

Further, getting a survey done at all – conducting the interviews, designing the questionnaires or schedules, selecting the respondents, gaining access to them, organising their coding, and more – inevitably means facing up to the practical problems that arise. It would be a Herculean task to design an interview schedule for all respondents and all the circumstances in which the interview might take place. The injunction of the standardised interview, for example, that all respondents be given the questions using the same wording and in the same order ignores all the various contingencies that might arise at the time of the interview – and studies such as those by Friedman (1967) show just how situationally variable the administration of a supposedly standard protocol could be. Does a respondent going to the toilet, answering the phone or dealing with a fractious child, for example, during the interview violate the principles? Surely we need to take a practical attitude to such matters and strive to implement the spirit of the principles rather than their letter. In this respect, natural scientists are no different. They, too, have to make practical decisions in the course of their research rather than just following something called the scientific method (Lynch, 1985). It can be argued, and is so argued, that pointing out such troubles is far too strict an interpretation of the guidelines and principles. After all, a survey often deals with a few hundred respondents and such departures from the requirements can, for all intents and purposes, be treated as random rather than exerting any systematic bias on the results. Yet researchers should not mindlessly accept the data as if it were pure and uncontaminated, but should rather use their judgement and experience to evaluate whether or not there is any systematic bias in the material collected.

> The practicalities of interviewing

We have no particular quarrel with the argument that in doing social research lots of practical decisions need to be made, otherwise the research will not get done. However, we need to remember positivism's drive toward systematicity; that is, producing an apparatus of theory, method and data that was thoroughly integrated. *The whole point* of the survey approach as positivists conceived it was, remember, to remove this kind of indulgence toward data collection and analysis and put them in a properly scientific footing. The acceptance of these features of survey research as things to be lived with and practically managed as best they can is, *relative to that ambition*, a huge retreat. The survey method was elevated into the very paragon of social research but, if its employment unavoidably depends upon just this practical realism about the difficulties of collecting objective data that all sociologists must acknowledge, then it cannot be so elevated. Sociological data, in this case as in others, is permeated by the 'good sense' and 'practical realism' of the data collector. Accordingly, the question becomes not so much whether people can sensibly answer questionnaires and take part in interviews, but whether relaxing the strict requirements of standardisation is fatal for the rationale of variable analysis *as an unprecendentedly rigorous and strictly scientific project,* with its aim of eliminating the particular encounter of the interview in order to create generalisable results?

To move a little closer to the problem, let us look at how interview and questionnaire data is constructed.

Processing interview and questionnaire data

It is claimed that the great advantage of interviews and questionnaires is that they can be used to collect data from large samples of persons. At one extreme is the census with its near-total coverage of the population of a country, while the smaller-scale surveys often used in social research may still involve many hundreds of people. But collecting the data is but the first step. It needs to be analysed and this means that the data from each questionnaire, from each interview, needs to be put into a form so that it can be analysed, as we have previously discussed.

The coding process is intended to transform the interview from a particular event, a specific encounter, into a generalisable one. The researcher is no longer interested in the interview itself but what, along with other interviews, it yields about general social processes or social structures. Each interview is treated not on its own as a particular encounter between an interviewer and a respondent but as an encounter 'standing on behalf of' other processes which have not been observed by the researcher. In a way, it is a process which treats the members of society, or those that have been interviewed, like the oil in an engine and the interview as a calibrated dipstick. What adheres to the stick is only important for what it indicates about the state of the oil – in terms of the analogy, the members of society (Mehan and Wood, 1975: 49).

To remind ourselves: focusing on what respondents say in the interview, or respond to on a questionnaire, is seen, by positivist researchers, as an opportunity to collect data on social activities that it is impossible to observe directly. Instead, the researcher asks people about them and then treats their answers as indicators of the activities themselves. This is the rationale behind the interview and questionnaire as instruments of social research. The concern with the validity of the responses is an important part of this, in that if respondents do not report on their activities, feelings and attitudes truthfully and reliably then the whole enterprise is vitiated; hence the efforts of interviewers to direct the interview and a concern with the design of questionnaires. But to 'tell the truth' about one's behaviour is a gloss, never a direct exhibition of the activities themselves. By concentrating on what is said in the interview rather than on the activities, by breaking the talk into categories, social researchers ease their way toward general descriptions of the kind sought by variable analysis.

The case of Argentine fertility

In a study of fertility and family planning in Argentina, Cicourel closely examines how the tabular presentations were constructed by the interviewers and

Table 5.1 Duration of engagement prior to present marriage

Duration of engagement	Frequency
Less than **6** months	12
6 months to **1** year	29
1 to **2** years	45
More than **2** years	80
No information	4
Total	170

Source: adapted from Cicourel (1973: 92).

coders from the interview data (Cicourel, 1973; Mehan and Wood, 1975). One example interview analysed by Cicourel was of an older woman who had met her present husband when 43 and had no children. The table for the whole sample had shown that 75 per cent of couples had had engagements which had lasted for one year or more (see Table 5.1).

However, such tabulated results, despite being neatly set out, conceal the intricate work done by the interviewer to turn the respondents' answers into the categories used in the table. For example, when the woman was asked at what age she began to go out with men, she replied, '18'. She elaborated saying that she had a boyfriend of that age who visited 'once or twice a week'. When asked about her parent's attitude toward the boyfriend, she replied, 'I would receive him in my house, he would come in the early evening two times a week. My parents were very "delicate".' The implication from the remark, Cicourel suggests, is that her parents were very strict, suggesting that in this case premarital intercourse was unlikely. Subsequently, the woman was asked: 'How frequently would you see each other? Where?' She answered, 'Every 15 or 20 days because the parents were "delicate", they did not want us to see each other every day.' Cicourel interprets this reply as contradicting the earlier claim that her boyfriend visited twice a week.

The next question asked was, 'Was this the first man you had sexual relations with?', to which the woman answered in the negative. The second part of the question was a probe, 'Could you tell me something more about this?' The question produced the response: 'My present husband wants to have relations every four days, but he can't and becomes very nervous. He attempts it when he is well, but not when he is angry. He then bangs [his head] against the wall.' Although the probe tries to elicit further information to offset the static question–answer format, the woman's remark did not appear to be a response to the question the probe was attempting to amplify. Accordingly, and as we pointed out earlier, one might speculate along a number of lines: she had nothing further to report, she did not want to bring the matter up again, her present marriage was more 'interesting' for the interviewer, her remarks were intended to open up a more serious problem or that she viewed the questions as invitations or opportunities for telling the interviewer about her present life (Cicourel, 1973: 93–4). Because the woman's answer to the probe was ambiguous, a great deal of interpretative work is required on the part of the interviewer and the coder to transform the replies into the categories used in the analysis and in the tabular presentations. Cicourel goes on to detail similar 'interpretative work', including the constraints of propriety, that is an inescapable part of interviewing and transforming what respondents have said into categories developed for sociological analysis: in short, transforming what transpires in the interview (whatever the type), or is written on the questionnaire, into research categories using one's knowledge of social life to make whatever sense of the responses is made.

Cicourel's point is that in interviewing, and much social research besides, there is an inevitable reliance on common-sense knowledge of social life, and this includes reliance on the ordinary language through which everyday social life is conducted. However, positivist methods, such as interviewing, in relying upon ordinary language as the means of data collection, were not only radical in inspiration but opened up a Pandora's box of issues which, in the end, severely damaged their rationale. Much of this damage was inflicted by trying to meet the requirements of quantification by imposing a format on ordinary language regardless of whatever properties that language might have. It assumed a picture of the social actor that, in effect, ignored the fact that persons go about their day-to-day business, talk about themselves and their lives to each other, in ways that make sense to them. It is not that positivist methods did not seek to gather data on people's everyday lives, but that its methods for doing so, despite the efforts to buttress their validity, distorted the very phenomena it sought data on. Nevertheless, it made use of that common-sense knowledge in order to deploy the very research instruments that were producing its distorted picture.

One can see similar effects in the production of official statistics.

The case of official statistics

The criticism of the social scientific use of official statistics is well documented, especially as it arises from Durkheim's pioneering use of them in his study of suicide (Durkheim, 1970). At the time, Durkheim himself voiced doubts about their accuracy as have many commentators since (see, for example, Coleman and Moynihan, 1996). However, the point we want to make here is that those responsible for the compilation of such statistics – in the case of crime statistics these will include the police as well as legal officials, coroners, court personnel and others – have to decide upon the appropriate categorisation of the purportedly criminal act. As studies have shown, such personnel rely upon common-sense typifications which enable them to make sense of the activities with which they are faced (Cicourel, 1968; Atkinson, 1978; Eglin, 1987). They have to assemble, as does an interviewer or a coder, the particularities before them in order to achieve a description of *this* event so as to be able to classify it as 'similar to' or 'different from' other events, using the classifications provided. The so-called objective facts of official statistics are the outcome of practices relevant individuals use to make sense of, and decide the identity of, the events they are confronted with (Hughes and Sharrock, 1998). The official record, like the tabular presentation, is the product of practices and negotiations among those involved in producing them even though it does not – could not – capture, record or reflect the process which produced them.

The above points are not solely concerned with the technical validity of methods, though they are deeply relevant. While positivism recognised the fact that the interview was a social encounter and tried to develop the means by which this could be managed to improve the validity – as it understood this – of the data collected, its approach ultimately failed by imposing a method intended to serve the purposes of a deductive and generalising science, again as it saw this. The conduct of interviewing, for example, is based on procedures intended to obtain 'clear' and 'unambiguous' responses which can be coded for machine processing and statistical analysis. Unfortunately, as has been argued, these procedures do not necessarily reflect the way

> Research categories and ordinary language

respondents, as ordinary members of society, ordinarily talk about their social lives. Transforming such talk into abstract entities called 'attitudes', 'beliefs', 'values', 'actions' and so on is presumed to provide an adequate description of what people say and do. Yet, as we saw in the case of measurement in the previous chapter, it is the format which is supposed to achieve the move to scientific description but without examining the phenomena it was supposed to describe. The interview is detached from the circumstances in which people act. The coding and the manipulation of the data further removes and abstracts them from the social lives of those who are the objects of study. The positivist conception of the interview and the questionnaire produces a version of the social life being investigated that is refracted through the methods themselves: methods which do not so much discover facts about social life as construct a version of that life by its methods. The methods do not so much explore the nature of social phenomena as force them into constrictions of the format which is applied to facilitate quantification (Hughes and Sharrock, 1998).

Conclusion

Our treatment of interviewing and questionnaires is not an argument against their use in social research, only that such use does not signify any singular merit. Survey research is very much in the same boat as other sociological methods. Our emphasis has been to look at these methods in light of the ambitions the positivist programme set itself, namely, the thorough integration of theory, method and data. In the Introductory chapter we raised the issue facing any science: namely, whether what we have before us are facts worthy of being admitted to the corpus of knowledge. We also noted that an important part of this process was showing that the fact was established by following a method. This is a significant element in establishing the objectivity of the research process. Accordingly, if positivism was to acquire a corpus of knowledge, then there had to be criteria for admission to that corpus. Among those criteria would be well-grounded theories of instrumentation. In which case, the points we have been raising about the interview and the questionnaire are, from this standpoint, far from pedantic considerations but strike at the heart of the positivist programme. The development of variable analysis and the survey method was meant to be a way of addressing what was seen to be a difficult problem, but it has proved, we suggest, to be one which, in practice, is much more difficult than was envisaged in advance. The survey did not move the positivist project forward, but resulted in a retreat from the ideals that project had set. The rationales for the survey became entirely practical – it is efficient, comparatively low cost, can be handled by machine processing and converted into forms which can be analysed statistically. However, survey research is *admittedly* inadequate with respect to the theoretical issues it was supposed to address.

Part of the problem was using a variable analytic mode of thinking to try to secure the validity of the methods; a mode of thinking which, it can be argued as in connection with measurement, obscured the very phenomena the methods were designed to explore. In seeking out the factors which might affect the validity of replies, researchers tended to follow the variable analytic strategy of looking for properties, variables, associated with various biases. For example, they looked to properties of the interviewer and/or the respondent – gender, age, social status, ethnicity and the like – and then tried to find other properties associated with identified 'biases'. They tried, that is, to discover general principles which could be manipulated during the interview process. However, it is not clear how any such general principles applied to any particular interview encounter. Are we confident, for example, that the category 'women', or any of the usual ones invoked, adequately encompasses all that might transpire between a female interviewer and a male or female respondent? The interview is a particular encounter and it is perfectly feasible that what transpires has little to do with gender (or ethnicity, social status, etc.) but may have to do with the manner of the interviewer, the time of day, the topic of the interview, or the myriad of other things that might affect the interviewer–respondent relationship. It cannot be assumed that gender, or any category for that matter, universally operates in all encounters.

This is an issue we have met before in connection with variable analysis and one we will meet again. In essence it has to do with the relationship between general categories and concepts, supposedly tied to sociological theory, and those of ordinary language. However, this is not simply about meaning equivalence, important as this issue is, but fundamentally about the picture of the social actor and interaction that is implicit in the presumptions of the research techniques. On the one hand efforts are devoted to making the interview encounter as non-threatening and as relaxing as possible, the questionnaire accessible to 'ordinary people', yet on the other hand, what is produced is detached from the actual encounter and treated as a set of indicators of categories derived from some theory. But what is missing is an understanding of the ways in which in everyday interactions persons describe, report on, talk about and otherwise relate their activities to each other. In Cicourel's (1964) terms, there is a lack of isomorphism between ordinary concepts used in the interview or questionnaire and their treatment as indicators of theoretical categories. The methods use the vernacular as a source of data but then virtually denounce it in favour of a version formatted according to the needs of variable analysis. There is, to put it another way, a double detachment of the interview not only from the circumstances it purports to inquire into, but also from the interpersonal processes which make it possible to collect that data in the first place.

As we said at the beginning of this chapter conclusion, we have looked at interviewing and questionnaires from the point of view of the positivist programme and its ambitions. But, of course, showing that the positivistic justifications for interviewing and questionnaires leave much to be desired does not necessarily vitiate the methods for social research. In some ways, it is difficult to imagine social research without talking to people, without taking notice of what they say, listening to them and asking questions about what they do; interviewing and questionnaires are one way of doing this among others. Also, there is much good sense in following the practicalities and proprieties of interviewing and questionnaire design when using such methods. But such a use of the method would be hard put to justify in positivistic terms.

However, we are not yet finished with variable analysis. Interviews and questionnaires are typically part of social surveys and it is to these we now turn in the next chapter.

Selected bibliography and suggested reading

There are many methods texts which provide the basics for interviewing. See, for example:

- May, *Social Research: Issues, Methods and Process* (Milton Keynes, Open University Press, 1997).
- Oppenheim's, *Questionnaire Design and Attitude Measurement* (London, Heinemann, 1966) is still a good source of the principles and practices of questionnaire construction and interviewing techniques.
- Benney and Hughes' article, 'Of Sociology and the Interview' is to be found in the *American Journal of Sociology*, 62, 1956.
- If it is still available Converse and Schuman's *Conversations at Random: Survey Research as Interviewers See It* (New York, Wiley, 1974) is a salutary read of extracts from actual survey research from the point of view of interviewers.

Feminist approaches include:

- Anne Oakley's 'Interviewing Women: A Contradiction in Terms', in Helen Robert's edited collection *Doing Feminist Research* (London, Routledge).
- Also useful is Stanley and Wise's *Breaking Out Again: Feminist Ontology and Epistemology,* 2nd ed. (London, Routledge, 1982), though its remit is wider than interviewing.

Critiques of the interview include:

- Phillips' *Knowledge From What?* (Chicago, Rand McNally, 1971), which mounts a sustained attack on many of the orthodox sociological methods.
- A.V. Cicourel's *Method and Measurement in Sociology* (New York, The Free Press, 1964) remains highly relevant.

Chapter 6

The Social Survey and Multivariate Analysis

Much of the thinking behind variable analysis, along with many of its research techniques, was influenced by developments in the social survey pioneered by Lazarsfeld and his colleagues after the Second World War. The social survey even then was not a new instrument of social research. Its history goes back at least as far as the population censuses which most industrialising states undertook in the nineteenth century as regular instruments of national accounting. These were designed to gather – in the form of statistics – facts about material conditions – income and expenditures, living conditions, employment histories, and so on – often promoted by the state with its increasing interest in the social and economic conditions of its population. This period also saw the advent of the 'social psychological survey', encouraged in the main by the growing field of market research and public opinion polling, which showed that the more intangible aspects of people's lives, such as their attitudes and opinions, could be accessed by survey methods. What this seemed to offer, along with the ability of the survey to gather information from large sections of the population, was a data-gathering method ideally suited to the needs of a sociological science. This was to be achieved by developing statistical techniques for the analysis of the numerical data being gathered that, it was argued, would transform the social survey from a data-gathering instrument to one which could also be used to test theories and, by this means, develop genuine general theories.

In order to understand how this transformation was achieved it is important to grasp the logic underlying the use of the social survey as a means of testing hypotheses and, through this, building a properly scientific theory, according to positivism. As we have said before, the positivist project did not move forward as a whole in a steady step-by-step manner. Rather, fuelled by its enthusiasm, it grew in a rather ramshackle way as borrowings of methods, including the social survey, from other pursuits and disciplines whenever it seemed these borrowings could be made to fit in the emerging framework, without overmuch thought being given to the overall consistency of the programme. Further, it was, as we have elsewhere remarked, characteristically sociological in that it sought its solutions 'off the shelf', borrowing from a heterogeneity of disciplines, rather than working them out *de novo* and for itself. Measurement theory was taken from psychology, social surveys from public opinion polling, interviewing from market research and inferential statistics from agricultural botany and genetics, though many of these statistical techniques were already being applied in psychology. Much effort was made to patch up the methods and techniques in order to give the semblance of a coherent framework which was also making progress. This often meant that the justifications for particular methods were *post hoc* rather than thought through from the beginning. Having said this, however, it is as well to bear in mind that such matters are not easy or straightforward, in that what was being attempted had never before been tried in sociology.

In this chapter we want to focus the discussion on the social survey, in particular its role in the positivist programme as the means of developing theoretical generalisations. It is important to note that this is not the only role of the social survey. It is widely used in a variety of endeavours – marketing, public opinion polling

> Survey as a means of theory building

and planning, among others – but, the positivist programme sought to take it further as a means of theory building. Behind this move was the incorporation of a style of statistical thinking that sought to emulate the logic of the experiment in research which was non-experimental in character. It is, of course, impossible to arrange in sociology anything like a properly strictly controlled experiment of the kind that is commonplace in some of the natural sciences. The role of the controls in the controlled experiment is to manage, to manipulate the relationship between the variables so as to limit the interactions among them to the ones that are of interest in the experiment. However, it was felt that statistical analysis of the right kind could achieve much the same conditions as the experiment by subjecting survey data to suitable experimental controls.

The exposition of this 'thinking', in which we will try to avoid what are sometimes complex mathematics, will have to be steady and slow as we try to convey what are sometimes difficult ideas and ones which have multiple ramifications for the social survey as hypothesis testing and, more generally, for the ambitions of the positivist programme of social research.

The search for generalisations

In Chapter 3 we discussed the hypothetico-deductive model of theory. This had emerged as the model of what a proper scientific theory should look like. The aim was to devise empirically tested theoretical generalisations. However, it was recognised that achieving such a goal would inevitably be long term. As we argued attempts to build general theories were less than satisfactory. The companionate strategy adopted was to develop research techniques for bringing data to bear on more restricted theories – 'middle-range theories' in Merton's terms –which would at least give sociology some well-grounded generalisations. These techniques were built around variable analysis.

However, a serious problem was the non-experimental character of social research. As said earlier, it is clear that sociologists are not able to control the behaviour of even a small number of people in ways that will enable them to set up very finely regulated experiments, and they are certainly not able to do this with large numbers of individuals. In any event, the same point made with respect to instrumentation in the previous chapter applies. The ability to develop refined instruments or precisely focused experiments depends upon having some sound knowledge of how the phenomena work in the first place. Sociologists are, in both cases, in the same bind: trying to adopt sophisticated methods at the beginning of the enterprise before they have acquired anything other than primitive knowledge of their phenomena.

> Non-experimental character of social research

The impossibility of real experiment in the social sciences has been the oft-cited excuse for the lack of progress in them: that is, that the phenomena with which they had to deal were too complex and not amenable to experimentation. Although 'complexity' is a relative judgement and experiment is not perhaps as essential to the development of the sciences as is often supposed, the excuse did direct attention to the agreed upon and well-grounded procedures that the developed sciences had for simplifying their problems so as not to be overwhelmed by the complexity of their phenomena.

Quite how the natural sciences managed to simplify their problems was a matter of some debate. Some views, as we indicated earlier, stressed the regularity of natural phenomena. The universe was a mechanism beating with the regularity of a clock, repeating its cycles endlessly. By contrast, human life, human history was shaped in significant part by the fact that human beings had a choice in what they did. Human life, society, did not work like a clock but was more organic in quality and much more complex. Unlike natural science, the complexity of the world meant that the social scientist could not be confident that all the variables of relevance could be taken into account. Nor could the social

> Complexity of social phenomena?

sciences, for practical and ethical reasons, so easily resort to experimentation for dealing with unwanted variables. Although psychology had, from its earliest days, made use of experimental settings in its investigations, sociological research, given the focus of its inquiries into society and the scale of the phenomena it proposed to encompass, could hardly follow this path. Most of its inquiries must be non-experimental in character. According to the positivists, this was a challenge which could be met – at least in part – by the use of inferential statistics. This, however, required some modification of the notions of generalisations: the idea of what sociology could and should do was adjusted to meet the needs of the method that was adopted, rather than the other way around.

Karl Pearson (1857–1936), a pioneer of statistics, at the turn of the century argued that the precise, pristine laws of science are idealisations, the products of averaging, and not descriptions of the real universe where all kinds of 'contaminations' are present (Pearson, 1911). Even for the most advanced of the natural sciences, all kinds of factors are present in the natural world which affect the causal relationship of interest. The result is that data are prone to variability due to errors of all kinds, including errors of measurement, of data collection, of unknown variables and the failure to control variables adequately. Accordingly, the distinction between a causal relationship as expressed as a law precisely stating an invariable relation between two phenomena in a scientific theory and an empirical correlation among variables is a spurious one. The former is simply an idealisation, concealing the fact that the latter are all that we can really have. In the messy world in which most investigations are done, we would not expect to be able to reach this idealisation – a perfect correlation – since it is impossible to exclude everything that might affect the causal relationship of interest. Instead, what we would expect are strong but less than perfect correlations.

> The nature of generalisations in science

Such an interpretation seemed, on the face of it, highly accommodating to sociological research since, for the most part, it had to be conducted in the messy world in which it was extremely difficult to separate out all the potentially interacting variables. The pursuit of generalisations was to be the pursuit of highly correlated variables. In other words, inferential statistics were to be the means for discovering generalisations. According to the Pearsonian view, sociology could thus be subsumed under the general method of science.

We will have more say on these matters later. For now we want to focus on how the social survey evolved as a central method in the positivist programme along with the multivariate statistical analysis techniques which emerged as part of the package.

The social survey

The social survey is a systematic collection of standardised information from a sample of people chosen to represent some larger population. The idea of population here is not to be equated with the population of a town, city or some other geographically defined region, though it may consist of such. Population in this connection refers to some collection of people who are of interest to the research and could include categories such as 'manual workers', 'single mothers', 'clubbers', 'readers of this book' and so on. In other words, social surveys could be focused on groups, collections or types of people of interest to sociological theory.

The method also offered the means of getting around the problem of small-scale studies, which could be idiosyncratic. How do we know, for example, that Whyte's study of an Italian slum area of Boston is typical of such areas? Effectively he spent most of his time studying a small group of men who hung around one street corner in a particular city in the United States. How do we know that this is typical? And if it is, what is it typical of? Moreover, would another fieldworker have discovered the same things that Whyte did? How can we generalise from findings such as these? The social survey seemed to offer the opportunity for resolving such problems, and in three ways.

- It was not limited to the efforts of a single fieldworker who could only study a small number of people. By contrast, if sufficient resources were available the social survey could cover many thousands of respondents.
- If used in conjunction with the interview an immense variety of information could be gathered from a large number of people. This could be about their attitudes, their opinions, their beliefs, their hopes and fears as well as about the material conditions of their lives.
- Using the interview and questionnaire, data collection could be controlled by standardising the questions and the format of the responses to remove any possible effects of the researcher's own inclinations and views. Such standardisation would also facilitate measurement not only by removing any influence the researcher might inadvertently have on the results, but by making sure that all respondents received the same stimulus in order to make sure that there were no variabilities arising from the research instrument itself.

As we shall see elsewhere, the problem of generalisation was not a simple one and the route proposed by variable analysis was to prove a dead end to developing the wished-for generalisations of the kind achieved in the more developed of the natural sciences. This is, however, to run ahead of the story. To see why and how the solution failed to achieve the goal of generating theoretical generalisations, there are other matters to consider. The first of these is the turn to statistics especially the statistics of probabilities.

The turn to statistics

For our purpose there are two main kinds of statistics, descriptive and inferential.

Descriptive statistics

Statistics are commonly used to describe the distribution, the frequency, of some phenomenon, be it the ownership of mobile phones, the number of burglaries in an area, births, deaths, marriages and so on. Such a use is very nearly as old as human society itself. Indeed, many of the earliest forms of writing have proved to be records of various kinds of goods in the ruler's possession. This form of record keeping became a more or less standard procedure in societies with a central authority which needed to extract resources from those subject to its authority. Not unnaturally some form of record keeping was useful in determining who had and who had not paid their dues. The *Domesday Book* of Norman England, compiled 1083–6, is but one of the more prominent survivors of an attempt to record the wealth and the liabilities of a population. With the advent of the national state, such activities became a standard element in government administration. By the nineteenth century various countries and city-states were conducting censuses of their populations (Duncan, 1984). It was a movement associated with the increasing standardisation of weights and measures and currency, within and between societies. These days the compilation of such statistics is endemic in all societies and a source of much social science data.

However, important as such statistics are, from the point of view of variable analysis it was inferential statistics which were seen as the key. In essence, these procedures were designed to estimate whether some event, some relationship could have occurred have occurred by chance. Thus, for example, if we know that some extremely unlikely event occurred, then this is some evidence that the event did not occur by chance but was caused by something else.

Inferential statistics

Given the long history of gambling and games of chance, it should be no surprise that the idea dawned that supposedly chance events, such as tossing a coin or throwing dice, might after all display some regularity which could be described. After all, it is easy to assume, for example, that in tossing a coin if two heads in a row are thrown then it is unlikely that the next throw will be heads, as if somehow the previous throws have a bearing on what the next throw is likely to be. Although this is a fallacy that has no doubt lost many gullible people money, the seed of the idea that chance events had some describable regularity began to bear fruit in the late seventeenth and early eighteenth centuries.

This was a decisive move in the history of thought, representing, as Hacking (1990) calls it, the 'taming of chance'. It was the beginning of the attempt to systematically formulate the idea that chance events had a regularity to them – albeit remaining chance events – and showing that chance was not chaotic but predictable, a predictability which could be expressed in terms of probabilities.

The idea of probability

Lotteries are a popular pastime. They offer very large prizes because lots of people take part in them, paying into the central pool from which the prizes are taken. Everyone knows that the odds of winning are astronomically small. If you took part in the lottery every day of your life and extended that life by a couple of thousand years, the chances of winning are not much improved. People still take part. Though the odds against winning are very, very high, somebody has to win and it might be you. The odds do not tell us what will happen, only how likely it is that something will or will not take place. Statistics themselves do not tell us what will happen but rather, *if* something does happen, they tell us whether that event was a very likely or a very unlikely one. Thus, statistics tells us that it is a near certainty that someone will win the lottery this week, but it is unlikely in the extreme that it will be you. This does not mean that you cannot win it, only that if you do, then something very unlikely has happened to you.

Statistics can seem both puzzling and forbidding. Some of its ideas seem counter-intuitive, and once one gets into serious statistical reasoning matters can become labyrinthine. Hopefully the lottery example can help ease some of the puzzlement about how statistics works.

If one thinks of the 'laws of statistics' as being like 'the laws of physics', then one may be puzzled as to how the laws of statistics govern phenomena, how chance or random events can be subject to laws. But, as the lottery example shows, the 'laws of 'chance' are not like the laws of physics. The latter, if properly applied, can predict what will happen (or could until they, too, began to take a statistical form in the shape of quantum theory).

Even so statistics can be very useful. Designing a modern passenger plane requires taking measures against all kinds of risks. But there are endless imaginable risks. Which ones should one try to guard against? How long are the odds against a particular kind of malfunction? If they are extraordinary long – once in every 2 billion flying miles, say – then one might decide not to design against that possibility. The statistics may say that it is incredibly unlikely that a particular set of circumstances will ever occur, and the designer may therefore decide that it is not worth providing against these. But the statistics do not say that this configuration of events will not occur, only that if the designer is caught out by them occurring he or she will have been very unlucky.

In this mode, statistics is a way of calculating the likelihood of various events, which it seeks to do by identifying all the possible outcomes of a situation, and then calculating what proportion of that range of possibilities a particular outcome comprises. If we throw two dice aiming to get a score of seven or two, we can work out how many different ways in which the dice can possibly fall. There are only six faces on each die and each die must fall on one of these faces. So, out of these different ways, the question is how many combinations of two faces make up seven or two? There is only one way two can occur – where each dice shows a one – but there are different ways of making seven: six and one, five and two, four and three. So, out of all the ways that the dice can fall, it is more likely that they will give a seven than a two. Three times more likely. Which is not to say that on any throw one will get a two or a seven, or that over any run of throws one will get seven three times as often as one gets two. It remains, however, that the likelihood on any throw of getting a two is less than the likelihood of getting a seven. This is true because it is a matter of calculation not of empirical prediction.

Statistics is nothing more mysterious than the above example, though it can become mathematically much more complex. If one can work out the total number of all the possible things that can happen, then one can work out the probability – the likelihood it will occur – of one of those possibilities. So, working out all the combinations of circumstances that affect an aircraft's operations, it is possible to calculate the probabilities of all the possible circumstances that could cause a particular thing to go wrong. If there are only a small number of such combinations, when measured against all the possible ways in which relevant circumstances can combine, then we can consider that kind of accident highly unlikely.

But, of course, unlikely events do happen. The statistics only tell us how probable an event is. The challenge was to work out a mathematics for describing probabilities: a mathematics which could be used to calculate the relationship between the number of outcomes and the number of theoretically possible outcomes, using that calculation to disentangle complex and messy problems. To do by calculation what cannot be done by research, and so approximate to the natural scientific experiment. Statistics in sociology is a tool, a means to sociological ends. The statistics themselves have no sociological content, and so are only as good as the sociology that governs their use, which, as we shall see, is a serious limitation. They are of use mainly because mathematicians have worked out very sophisticated ways of calculating.

At this point – and we recognise that not many of the likely readers of this book will have overmuch proficiency in mathematics (like the authors we might add) – Inset 6.1 is an attempt to provide an account of the logic underlying probability in statistics. Although the account barely scratches the surface of statistical mathematics, its intention is to convey the basic elements. Shortly we will discuss how they are applied to the analysis of social survey data. Meanwhile there are one or two general points it is important to note.

The first is that statistics is a mathematical discipline. This means, as we saw in Chapter 3 on mathematical theory and in Chapter 5 on measurement, that when we apply the mathematics we have to be sure that the mathematical assumptions are isomorphic with the nature of the phenomena they are intended to model or measure – does a real population match the characteristics of the statistically normal one? In Inset 6.1 we talk about theoretical distributions, which are mathematically derived distributions based on certain assumptions. The normal distribution is one example. These are compared with actual distributions. But, of course, such a comparison is only worthwhile if the assumption of a normal distribution for the phenomenon itself is plausible. If not, then serious doubts have to be cast on the appropriateness of the use of the mathematics. Of course, determining such isomorphism is not a straightforward matter, and sometimes we just have to try in order to see whether or not the mathematical application is worthwhile. However, the point we are drawing attention to here is the importance of thinking as clearly as possible about the mathematical assumptions and the nature of the sociological phenomena the mathematics is intended to illuminate.

The second observation follows from the first, and is one which gets us closer to the social survey and its hypothesis-testing role. Earlier we spoke of the 'taming of chance': that is, the conception that seemingly chance events are not chaotic but have a regularity to them which can be mathematically described. One important interpretation of this, and it is consistent with Pearson's thinking described earlier in the chapter, is that probability is not an argument against the idea that events in the world are caused, but that what we have is an extremely complex world of multiple causation. The choice is not between the orderly world of causation that is subject to scientific investigation on the one hand, and a world of chaos not open to scientific investigation on the other. In fact, there is no choice to be made. The world is a causal world and the problem is one of disentangling causal relationships from the complicated multi-causal world with which we are confronted. In other words, statistics offers itself as a tool for disentangling complicated relationships. But, of course, like any tool it needs to be appropriate for the task to hand. In other words, not all complex relationships can be disentangled by the use of statistics.

> Multi-causality

Inset 6.1 An excursus into the logic of probability

The ideas of statistics may seem strange and unintuitive but they are actually in principle easy to understand once one knows how they basically work.

Given a coin, we would say without too much trouble that the odds of a head (or a tail) occurring in a single toss would be 0.5. (Probabilities are expressed as a number between 0 and 1, inclusive). But what if we tossed the coin ten times, or 20, or 500 times? Would we expect to get heads 50 per cent of the time and tails 50 per cent of the time? What if we had two coins? What is the probability of getting two heads or two tails? These are the kind of questions that belong to the mathematics of probability theory.

Let us stick with the simple example of tossing a coin. If we toss the coin once the probability of getting heads is 0.5. If we toss it again the probability of getting heads is still 0.5, as it is for every other toss since they are independent events. The first toss cannot influence the second one. If we went on to toss the coin ten times, say, we might end up with six heads and four tails even though the probability in each toss of the coin is 0.5. If we went on tossing the coin 20 or 500 times, it is still unlikely that we would get 50 per cent heads or 50 per cent tails. This is why statistical ideas may seem counter-intuitive. People who are gambling on the toss of a coin expect that, if one face has consistently shown over a number of tosses, the other face must show soon; that is, they assume a 'heads' becomes more likely the longer the sequence of 'tails'. But this makes the false assumption that if one face has consistently shown over a number of tosses, then the other face must show soon – that a 'heads' becomes more likely the longer the sequence of 'tails'. The results of the previous tosses do not affect the current one. The current throw involves just the same probabilities of a head or a tail as all the previous throws. These probabilities are worked out just by consideration of the ways in which a coin can fall: heads or tails. These remain the same however many previous throws there have been and how ever many throws there may be in the future. The throws of the coin are statistically independent of each other. The probabilities do not change with the number of throws. Hence, there is no more reason, on any particular throw to expect a head than there is on any other throw even if this throw follows a long sequence of tails.

Mathematically the assumption can be made that in an infinite number of events where one of two states of affairs can occur, then the probability of one of these occurring is 0.5 in any single occurrence. In our mathematically imagined coin, over an infinite number of tosses, heads would occur 50 per cent of the time and tails 50 per cent of the time. But, of course, real coins are not mathematical objects. With use they may have worn unevenly, we cannot be sure that in each separate toss the forces setting the coin spinning are identical, cannot be certain that the ambient temperatures and minute movements of air are the same in each toss. And we certainly cannot toss the coin an infinite number of times. Nonetheless, the mathematics of probability can be used as a standard to inform hypothesis testing. In the case of the coin tossing example, we can, by comparing the way that the actual fall of heads or tails over some sequence approximates to the 50 per cent distribution between heads and tails, begin to suspect that if too long a run of tails goes on, the coin may not be an unbiased one. Of course, the fact that the sequence of tails might be ludicrously long does not tell us for certain that the coin is unfair. That there are such sequences is certainly one of the possible distributions that chance can produce even though, unless aided by some form of cheating, it is a very, very unlikely one. But very, very unlikely events do occur. With statistics we are stuck in the realm of chance. The statistics can tell us what the chances of a coin being biased are, but we are likely to have to made empirical investigations of the coin, the user and other relevant factors to determine that the sequence was not just a very unlikely one but the result of bias or interference.

The decision an investigator has to make is whether the coin is a fair one on the basis of a number of tosses. 'Fair' is defined as the situation where the probability of heads occurring is 0.5 (pH=0.5). Two possible states are under consideration: the coin is fair or the coin is not fair, where the latter state is defined as a probability of not 0.5 (p<>0.5). In addition, there are two alternative decisions to be made: the coin is fair, the coin is not fair.

Thus, there are two alternatives states of affairs and two alternative decisions, as set out in Table 6.1. What we have here is a combination of decisions and states schematising two cases where the investigator makes the correct decision as to whether the coin is fair or biased, and two cases where the investigator makes the wrong decision: that the coin is fair when it is biased, and biased when it is fair.

Let us assume that the researcher begins with the hypothesis that the coin is fair. This starting hypothesis is known as the null or tested hypothesis (H_0). An alternative hypothesis is that the coin is not fair (H_1). The investigator has two alternatives decisions, accept H_0 or reject H_0, and the decision may or may not be correct.

Table 6.1 Alternative states and alternative decisions

Alternative states	Alternative decisions	
	Coin is fair	**Coin is biased**
	pH=0.5	pH<>0.5
Coin is fair	Correct decision	Type I error
Coin is biased	Type II error	Correct decision

As can be seen from Table 6.1, there are two correct decisions: accepting a true null hypothesis and rejecting a false null hypothesis. In either case a decision is made in favour of either the null hypothesis or the alternative hypothesis.

However, in the world of probability matters are rarely as straightforward as one might hope. Even if the coin were tossed a million times and it came up heads every time, there is still – in the world of probability – a very small probability that the coin is a fair one. In this case, the probability would be p(1million heads) = (0.5) (0.5) (0.5) ... 1 million, which equals $0.5^{1.000.000}$. This is very close to but is not equal to zero. In other words, even in the face of very strong evidence, a wrong decision is possible. Acceptance of a null hypothesis which is false is known as a Type II error, and the rejection of a null hypothesis which is correct is termed a Type I error.

We are not yet done. If there is always room for uncertainty, no matter how small, as to whether the correct decision has been made, how then is any decision to be made? (Note: in gambling we have no trouble in using calculations of the odds to decide what to do. Good odds do not guarantee that we will win, but they increase our chances of winning, and for gamblers that is good enough.) What if we only have the time and resources to make far less than a million tosses of the coin? There are, in fact, standard formulae for calculating the probabilities of, to stay with the example, the distribution of the number of heads under N tosses of the coin under various assumptions, for example, that the coin is fair, that is, p(H) = 0.5. The application of such formulae will provide a listing of the expected probabilities of obtaining 0, 1, 2, 3 ... N heads in repeated tosses of a fair coin. Note that these will be expected frequencies: what theoretically we should expect on the assumption of a fair coin, p(H) = 0.5. Table 6.2 sets out the expected relative frequencies of a fair coin tossed ten times. (This calculation is derived from an application of the binomial theorem which, to put it simply, can be applied to events which have only two possible outcomes, where each outcome has a constant probability of happening at every trial, and the outcome of every trial is independent of the outcome of other trials. There are other techniques which can be used where such conditions do not apply.) Note that the expected relative frequency piles up around a central value, in this case around 50 per cent heads and gets progressively smaller as we move from this value. Further, although not shown here, if the number of trials were increased, say, from 10 to 20 to a 1000, and so on, the distribution would be more and more concentrated around the central value. In this case the central value is around 0.5, namely, the probability of getting a single head in a single trial.

Table 6.2 Expected relative frequencies of heads on ten tosses

Number	Expected relative frequency
0	0.001
1	0.010
2	0.045
3	0.117
4	0.205
5	0.246
6	0.205
7	0.117
8	0.045
9	0.010
10	0.001

However, and it is important to stress this, what we have is a listing of probabilities, expected relative frequencies, of an assumed fair coin tossed ten times. (Similar tables could have been constructed for an assumed fair coin tossed any number of times.) The table is not a listing of empirical events but of events derived from the application of a mathematical procedure under certain assumptions. If, in fact, we were to toss a coin ten times, the likelihood is that sometimes we would get four heads, sometimes seven, sometimes ten, sometimes two, sometimes none at all, and so on, though with a large number of repeated trials the profile would – at least if the coin is fair, it should – approximate closer and closer to those expected from the formulae. Nevertheless, even the relative frequencies calculated from the formula *are* probabilities and though the likelihood of obtaining three heads in ten tosses of a fair coin is smaller that the likelihood of getting five, it is still possible. This means that we could reject the hypothesis that the coin is fair if we were to get three heads, say, out of ten tosses of a fair coin: make, that is, a Type I error.

Accordingly, we need some way of guiding our judgements as to when to reject and when to accept a hypothesis. We have to decide on the observations upon which we will base the assessment; that is, we must decide which data are relevant and choose a measure based on these data that can be used as a test statistic. This test statistic is a standard that will tell us how far the data is away from support for the tested hypothesis and toward the alternative one. The next step is to set up decision rules for deciding on the basis of the test statistic whether the tested hypothesis is to be rejected in favour of the alternative. These rules are usually informal rather than calculated mathematically.

The final step is the crucial one of evaluating the worth of the procedure by determining the probability that the decision rules will lead us to reject the tested hypothesis if, in fact, it is true. Rejecting, in the example, the hypothesis that the coin is fair when, in fact, it is. The probability of a test procedure causing us to reject a tested hypothesis when it is true is known as the level of significance. The lower the level of significance, the more confident we may be that the procedure will not lead us to reject the tested hypothesis mistakenly. Note that a high level of significance does not indicate that the hypothesis is true. It indicates that the data are not incompatible with the tested hypothesis. But the data could also be compatible with the alternative hypothesis. A test of significance is like someone who is always happy no matter what the circumstances. The state of the world cannot be inferred from that person's demeanour.

Suppose we do not know whether coin is fair, so decide to test this hypothesis. It is decided to toss the coin 100 times. If the tested hypothesis is correct then approximately 50 of the results should be heads. If the results depart from 50 this would offer support for the alternative hypothesis, that the coin is not fair. But, after all, and as said earlier, even a perfectly fair coin, for all kinds of reasons, need not result in 50 per cent heads. So, how far from 50 are we prepared to accept? We need another statistical concept to enable us to calculate this: that is, the measure of standard deviation.

At this point we need to introduce another idea. Statistics deals with the distribution, the frequency, of some property or event, and describes these distributions mathematically. One of the standard measures of a distribution – of scores on an IQ test, the income of a group of workers, goals scored in successive games of soccer and so on – is its central tendency, or average. There are a number of such measures, corresponding to whether our data is nominal, ordinal or interval – the mode (the most frequent value), the median (the middle case in a ranking) and the mean (the average or the value every member of the distribution would have if the aggregate of the distribution were spread evenly among the members). This last is the 'average' we are familiar with from ordinary life such as when we speak of the average number of runs a batsman has scored in test cricket, or the average mark gained from a series of essays, and it is the important measure of central tendency in statistics. However, the average of a distribution tells us only one thing about the distribution, its central tendency. We might also want to know how the frequencies are dispersed. Two distributions of income, for example, may have the same average but one may have a high range while the other shows income clustering more around the mean. Measures of dispersion are known as measures of the variation of the distribution and, again, vary according to the level of measurement of the data. The most important for our purposes is that for interval data and is known as the standard deviation, or σ (sigma) though sometimes other symbols are used. To put it simply, the standard deviation measures the average deviation of all observations from the mean (for mathematical reasons it is the square root of the sum of the average deviations from the mean) and is expressed in terms of the units being measured, say, income, scores or whatever. So now we can compare distributions in terms of their central tendencies and their dispersion.

At this juncture we can return to a distinction we have been alluding to throughout this discussion of inferential statistics, namely, that between a theoretical distribution (that is, a statistically calculated one) and an empirically observed one. The latter is what we get when we investigate and plot the distribution of some property. Such curves may well turn out to exhibit a variety of shapes; some skewed to the left or the right, some flattened, some peaked, some having more than one peak, some symmetrical, some asymmetrical, and so on. By contrast, the theoretical one is a mathematically derived distribution based on certain assumptions. One of the more

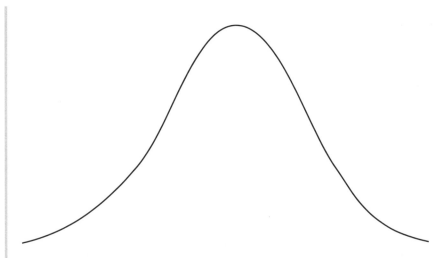

Figure 6.1 Normal distribution

important of these is the normal distribution. Figure 6.1 gives an example of the main properties of a theoretical normal distribution. What we see is a bell-like curve with a mean of 0 and a standard deviation equal to one unit. Every normal distribution is like every other normal distribution except for its unit of measurement, and by the proper transformation of these any normal distribution can be made exactly like any other. This has enabled statisticians to decide on a standard normal distribution and construct tables for it, telling us just what proportion of the normal distribution lies between the mean and other values. For example, from such a table we can say that 34 per cent of the population of a normal distribution will fall between the mean and one standard deviation beyond the mean. (Which, again, does not mean that the distribution of something in any actual population will conform to this. It is a standard not a prediction for not all populations are 'normal' in the required statistical sense.) Since the normal distribution is symmetric, this means that 68 per cent of the population will fall between minus one standard deviation and plus one standard deviation. 95 per cent will fall between plus and minus two standard deviations.

A major reason why theoretical distributions are important in statistics is that by reference to the appropriate distribution – and the normal distribution is but one theoretical distribution – we can judge whether an empirical distribution is compatible with some hypothesised underlying process. If we know the theoretical distribution that will result if a particular process is at work, then this enables us to judge whether an empirical distribution could have occurred as a result of that process.

We can now return to the coin-tossing example, but must make one preliminary remark. The coin tossing is a binomial distribution since we have the possibility of two states, heads or tails. So, plotting the frequency of heads and tails would give us a distribution with two peaks. However, given a large number of trials the normal distribution is an excellent approximation of the binomial distribution, so we will stick with the normal distribution. In practice, some correction is necessary since the normal distribution is continuous whereas the binomial deals with discrete states, for example heads or tails.

Accordingly, referring to tabulations of the normal distribution, this will show that approximately 95 per cent of cases will fall between plus or minus two standard deviations from the mean. In this particular case of tossing 100 coins, the standard deviation is 5 per cent. So, applying the formula, 95 per cent of the cases will fall between (x-2a) and (x+2a). This means that if the tested hypothesis were true, that the coin is fair, then 95 per cent of the time we would find between 50–2(5) heads and 50+2(5) heads in a trial of 100 tosses. Therefore we can reject this hypothesis if there are 39 or fewer heads, or 61 or more heads, at a 5 per cent level of significance. If we go ahead with the test and find that 30 heads result, then we reject the hypothesis that this is a fair coin in favour of the alternative that it is unfair. But, note: what this states is not that the coin is in fact unfair but expresses the confidence we have in rejecting the hypothesis that the coin is fair.

The social survey and multivariate analysis

We want now to pick up on the last point and begin to examine the logic underlying the social survey as a tool for unravelling patterns of causal relationships in social research, given that one cannot isolate variables through real experiments, and has to try to work out their relationship through calculation. The problem, as we have suggested, lies in the difficulty of disentangling genuine causal relationships from the immensely complex connections there are in the world. To reinforce the point we need to look at the experiment.

The experiment

Earlier we spoke of the lack of an ability to experiment as one of the excuses often offered as to why scientific social research had failed to progress as rapidly as hoped. While overrating the experiment as a tool of scientific investigation, nonetheless this feeling encouraged the search for other ways in which social research could approximate to the experiment. It was this context which stimulated the development of the social survey as a hypothesis-testing tool in nonexperimental situations.

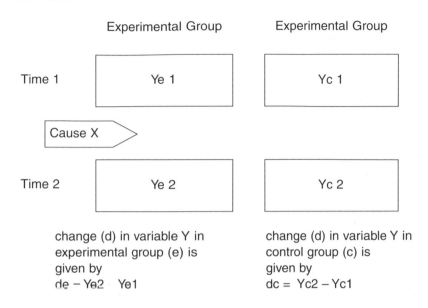

Figure 6.2 Diagram of 'classic' experimental design

However, to see why – and how – this was the case, we need to progress in a step-by-step manner and look first at the logic of the experiment

Figure 6.2 is a schematic of the 'classic' experimental design. We say 'classic' advisedly since the control group, which is a cardinal feature of the design, was incorporated when the design was introduced into psychology to take account of experimenter effects, of which more anon (Boring, 1969).

The basic purpose behind the design is to isolate the purported causal relationship – between X and Y – from any other factors which may affect Y. It does this, first, by comparing two groups: one to which the causal factor X is applied and the other from which the causal factor is withheld. If there is any difference between the two groups at the end of the experiment, then this must be due to the effect of the causal factor. In principle, nothing else could have affected the groups since other possible causes have been excluded by the way the experiment is set up. However, this is a conclusion that can only be drawn if the two groups are thoroughly alike to begin with. Suppose the experimental group consisted of boys and the control group of girls. We would not know whether gender had an effect on Y independently of the causal factor.

Accordingly, two methods can be used to try to make sure that the two groups are as alike as possible on all relevant factors which might affect the relationship of interest:

- *Matching*. This process selects the subjects according to relevant characteristics and pairs them – as far as this is possible. The end result would be two groups of subjects identical in the relevant respects.

■ *Randomisation.* In order to eliminate the effects of possible unknown factors which might influence the result of the experiment, one of each pair is randomly allocated to an experimental group, and the other to a control group. Randomisation is intended to avoid the systematic interference by unknown factors on the hypothesised causal relationship, because the likelihood of a systematic effect is very small if the group is put together randomly

If both these principles have been followed and the two groups are as alike as possible on all possible factors, then any difference in outcome between the two groups has to be due to the one thing they do not have in common, namely, the application of the causal factor.

Clearly, this is a powerful design for testing putative causal relationships – if it can be stringently deployed. This is not simply about carrying out research under laboratory conditions but, more importantly, whether the research can be designed and implemented in the way required. Nonetheless, it is a method which has been used in a variety of domains and has become a standard research tool in psychology and education, and a number of variants of the classic design have been developed. But its utility in social research is limited, in that many of the problems of interest are not amenable to strict experimental designs. If one's concern is with the relationship between inflation and employment, the effect of the death penalty on crime rates, the effect of religion on suicide rates, or differences in voting behaviour between two-party and multiparty democracies, then it is hard to see how one could devise a strict experimental design to answer these kind of questions. The critical question is whether non-experimental strategies can be designed that emulate the power of the experiment.

Inset 6.2 Quasi-experiments

In some ways, social experimentation is a continuous process in modern societies, carried out by governments, business and sometimes by natural forces. Government policies, business strategies, slow but persistent shifts in climate, for example, to the extent to which they introduce changes in patterns of behaviour, can be regarded as equivalent to 'experimental' treatments (Campbell and Stanley, 1963).

The logic of the quasi-experiment was predicated on the notion that the purpose of control in the classic experiment is to rule out plausible alternative hypotheses, many of which are artefacts of the experimental treatment itself. Accordingly, although physical controls are often impossible in social research, nonetheless, steps can be taken to try to rule out as many rival hypotheses as possible even when strict experimental controls are impossible.

Table 6.3 Summary of rival hypotheses in Connecticut crackdown on speeding

Plausible rival explanation	Example
History	Specific events other than experimental treatment which occur between pre-test and post-test and which might also account for the change, e.g. a dry winter, improvements in safety features of 1956-model cars.
Maturation	Regular, routine changes, e.g. becoming older, more experienced, increased efficiency of medical care, better roads.
Testing	Variations in measuring instrument independent of any change in phenomenon being measured. A classic problem in public records. In earlier versions of study, death rate per 100m vehicle miles was calculated from an estimate of number of gallons of fuel sold in the state. Decrease in actual miles driven, either by using engines of larger horsepower, driving at higher speeds, etc. could masquerade as lower mileage death rate by inflating number of miles driven.
Instability	If a drop in fatalities had occurred in a small township, it would have seemed less impressive since small size can make for greater instability in measures.
Regression	Where a group having an extreme score on a variable is selected, on average the post-test measurements will be less extreme than the pre-test ones. A crackdown might be expected in those states with high road casualty rates.

A good early example of this kind of research, and one which has contemporary relevance, was the early study of stricter law enforcement of speed violations in Connecticut (Campbell and Ross, 1970). During the first six months of the campaign, traffic fatalities and speeding offences declined, and this was hailed as a great achievement. The question was whether this decline was due to the stricter law enforcement or to other factors: a type of problem typical in social science where change has to be evaluated in non-randomly selected groups and in the absence of controls. The argument was, however, that the lack of control and randomisation are only damaging to inferences about cause and effect to the extent that they suggest alternative explanations are plausible.

Using the 1955 figures as the 'pre-test', the crackdown as the experimental treatment, and the 1956 figures as the 'post-test' data, and then looking for plausible rival explanations, the effect of the 'experimental treatment' was assessed. The factors considered are summarised in Table 6.3.

Campbell and Ross tested out these and other, rival explanations and concluded that while the crackdown had some effect, no unequivocal case could be made that the decline in fatalities was entirely due to its influence.

Of course, not all of these sets of rival hypotheses need apply equally in all studies; nonetheless, they are factors which must be ruled out before the original hypothesis can be accepted with any confidence. These days such thinking is typical of much of the statistical analysis of social and economic policies.

Multivariate analysis

So far we seem to have covered a lot of background without yet getting to what is supposed to be the focus of this chapter, namely, the social survey as a hypothesis-testing tool. However, such background is important since not only does it display the breadth of the positivist programme but, and more importantly perhaps, it illustrates the scale of the challenge that the programme set itself: a challenge and ambition that would be hard to fulfil even by its own standards. More prosaically, but nonetheless important for all that, such background is vital to understanding the arguments underlying the justifications for methods of social research such as the survey, which provide the logic for statistical analysis of survey data of the form that is widely known as 'multivariate analysis' that prevails throughout social research.

In the nineteenth century, as a result of the accumulation of large amounts of descriptive statistical data, it became clear that new ways would be needed to study social phenomena (McKim, 1997). What had become apparent was that the frequency and distribution of phenomena such as crime, suicide, poverty, disease and much else besides appeared to show a regularity over time. It was also discovered that the relative stability of such rates coexisted with different rates in nearby populations which had similar economic and demographic profiles. (It was such observations that Durkheim was to use in his study of suicide. In fact, statisticians had already noticed the regularities in suicide rates that Durkheim made so much of.) This is an aspect of what we earlier referred to as the 'taming of chance'. Disease, poverty, birth and death, famine and the like were not a consequence of Bad Luck, Misfortune or Sin but were occurrences in a world of causation. The problem was how to identify such causal relationships.

There were two related problems, both in different ways having considerable relevance for sociological thinking.

What kind of phenomena?

The first had to do with the fact that these regularities were statistical descriptions of collections or aggregates of individuals and their actions. But what sort of phenomena do they point to? Durkheim, for example, argued that such stable rates of, in his case, suicide, indicated 'social facts' which were not simply the same as facts about a large number of individuals and that needed to be explained in terms of other social facts. No doubt every individual suicide had its own circumstances and reasons, but these could not explain why much the same proportions of individuals in a population killed themselves year after year, why the rate of suicides was constant. Instead, what was required was a means of identifying other phenomena on a comparable level to that of the regularity to be explained which might vary with the phenomenon of interest. However, and against this view, it could be argued that the statistical regularity was simply the summation of individual decisions in much the same way that the outcome of an election is the summation of the individual votes cast or, for a further example, consumer choice of some commodity. For all intents and purposes these aggregate consequences – the outcome of an election, the rush to buy the latest CD by the Grovelling Newts – imply nothing more than the statistical description of a large number of individual decisions.

In an important sense this issue is closely related to that of indicators that we discussed in Chapter 4 when discussing measurement. What does a number, a measure indicate? Its relevance in the context of sociological research has to do with some fairly predominant pictures in sociology of the relationship of the individual to society, particularly those pictures, as we discussed in Chapter 3, which proposed that sociology dealt with supra-individual phenomena, such as social systems, groups of various kinds, organisations, structures of stratification and of exploitation, and more. Durkheim's notion of social facts was but one prominent expression of this idea. So, one important task we might ask of aggregate statistical description is to indicate such phenomena. Whereas the early statisticians tended to use official statistics collected from ecclesiastic or municipal districts, one might wish to extend this idea to groups defined in terms of sociological categories, such as social class, gender, ethnicity or whatever. We shall have more to say about this issue later, but before moving on we want to remind ourselves that this is not a problem of statistics but how they fit into the theoretical pictures which make use of them.

> Social facts

Methods and techniques

The second problem had to do with constructing the techniques themselves to identify the causal relationships. An early method, used especially when dealing with rates over time, such as those dealing with births and deaths, diseases, marriage rates, the trade cycle and the like, year by year, was to graph the fluctuations to see if the patterns correlated with the patterns of other rates. If they did, then this could be treated as evidence of some causal relationship between the various rates (Morgan, 1998). Although there were problems with such analyses, during the early part of the twentieth century correlational methods began to be used more and more, and became more and more sophisticated.

... and the social survey

As we have already stated, the social survey grew out of the movement to investigate social problems, but began to be used more extensively as a key instrument of the positivist programme in the years immediately following the Second World War. By the 1960s, survey research had become dominant in the United States. This was related to the movement to develop measurement techniques, as discussed in Chapter 4 and, importantly, methods of analysis which, it was hoped, could approach the logic of experimental design in the non-experimental survey (Turner and Turner, 1990).

Essentially, what this involved was – following the strategy of variable analysis – to treat the social survey as a means of collecting data on a range of variables using, as we discussed in the previous chapter, the items on the questionnaire or the interview schedule as the indicators of the variables. The task was to develop techniques for identifying patterns of (hopefully causal) association among the variables of interest. By the 1940s, from a variety of sources, valuable technical groundwork had already been laid. The first of these we need to set out is sampling.

Sampling

The social survey is inextricably linked with the idea of sampling. Even though the survey offers access to much larger numbers of individuals than does a localised case study, the cost of collecting survey data is a constraint. It would be impractical, if not impossible, to collect survey data on all members of any large population, and it is only feasible to interview a comparatively few of them. It may be surprising how few people one needs to interview in order to get statistically adequate results to allow generalisation to the whole population from which those few are taken. It is the need to make just the right kind of selection from the population to ensure that the generalisation to the population will be valid which raises the issue of representativeness in sampling.

Sampling is a method for selecting members of some population – in the sense described earlier – in such a way that the distribution of some property of that population can be reasonably estimated using the distribution of the property among the sample. Thus, instead of enumerating the total population of some city or town to see which of them possessed a home computer, if we draw a suitable sample from that population we can provide a reasonable estimate (that is, subject to the statistical calculation of how much confidence we can have in our estimate, as discussed above) of home computer ownership for the population on the basis of the distribution of ownership in the sample. This clearly offers immense gains in the cost of social surveys. However, there are two key phrases here: 'suitable sample' and 'reasonable estimate'.

The purpose of sampling is to provide a statistical basis for generalising to a population. What is wanted is a basis for being able to say, for example, that if 37 per cent of the sample own a home computer, then it is very likely that 37 per cent, or very near that, of the total population will own a home computer.

The sample must, in a word, be representative of the population. For example, suppose we

> Representativeness

selected a preponderance of people of low income; then, since home computers cost money and people on low incomes tend to have less room for discretionary spending, such a sample is likely to underestimate the distribution of ownership in the population. What is needed is a means of selecting the sample in such a way that the appropriate proportion of people on low incomes and high incomes, along with any other factors which may be relevant, are represented in the sample.

The notion of representative sample is an important one. A representative sample must include, in approximately the same proportions as in the population from which it is taken, people of various ages, occupations, economic status, religion, gender and any other classification that might be of relevance. But, of course, there is the practical difficulty that a very large set of factors – some unknown to us – might have a bearing on the property of interest. Accordingly, rather than try to balance the sample for all of these factors, it is more realistic to take a random sample. This means that every person in the population of interest has an equal and known probability of being selected for the sample. So, suppose the population of the town is 250,000 and we want a sample of 250 persons, then the probability of each member of the population being selected for the sample is one in 1000.

Selecting a truly random sample is a non-trivial matter, in that randomisation is a form of control. Earlier, when discussing the experiment, we talked

> Random sampling

about matching and randomisation as the means by which the researcher can control for other potential factors which might affect the relationship of interest. So not only is randomisation important to securing a representative sample for accurately describing the distribution of some property in a population, it is also essential to uncovering relationships among properties where the opportunities for matching and other controls are not open to the researcher.

In the coin-tossing example used earlier to illustrate probability and hypothesis testing, we could potentially have introduced physical controls for the coin tossing – a machine to toss the coin with exactly the same force, in a sealed container to remove air currents and so on – in which case we would have expected the frequency of heads to come very close to 50 per cent in 100 trials. In the absence of such physical controls, reliance is placed on comparing the actual distribution of heads with a statistical model derived from assumptions about the distribution to be expected if the coin is fair. The actual distribution of heads will be affected by all kinds of factors but, it is assumed, that in a suffi-cient large number of trials these effects will be randomised. While this will not necessarily result in a frequency of heads 'very close' to 50 per cent, using the level of significance we can make an informed judgement as to whether or not the coin is fair. Similar arguments are relevant to randomisation in sampling to explore patterns of relationship among properties.

Inset 6.3 Types of sampling methods

In social research, four types of sampling method are usually identified: simple random sampling, stratified sampling, cluster sampling and quota sampling.

Simple random sampling

As the name suggests, this uses a random sample of cases drawn from some listing. All units have an equal probability of being selected. Normally the researcher will list the population and assign to each member a unique number. Using a table of random numbers, a sufficient number of units are selected for the sample size required. Random sampling is not hit-or-miss sampling. The chances of each unit – be it a person, firm, community, organ-isation or whatever – being selected must be known in order to calculate probabilities. Practically, pseudo-random sampling is often employed, for example, by selecting every nth name from a list on the assumption that there is no systematic bias in choosing every nth name. This is not something that can be taken for granted.

Stratified random sampling

This form of sampling is used to offset the occasional risk that a random sample can result in a biased or lopsided selection or, alternatively, when we wish to compare groups and require a sufficient number of cases in each group. The population of interest is divided into strata, each of which is homogeneous with respect to some characteristic. Each of these strata is then randomly sampled according to its proportion in the population. Thus, if 'gender' is of special interest, then the proportion of males to females in the population is determined and then sampled within these strata according to this proportion. This method can increase the representativeness of samples of a given size even though each individual will not have an equal chance of being selected. However, the probabilities of being chosen from within the strata are known and can be duly weighted in any calculation.

Cluster or area sampling

This is a method in which groupings of units to be sampled are first selected by a probability sample and, second, units are randomly selected within the groupings chosen at the first stage. For example, in a large city one might group different neighbourhoods together and sample within these. This can often save time and resources but can be prone to misrepresentation unless the initial clustering is based on a sound knowledge of the population in terms of the geographical distribution of interest.

Quota sampling

This is a non-random method in which an interviewer is given a list of types of individuals and required to interview a certain number of each type. While this is useful for some purposes – such as opinion polling or market research – the accuracy of the results cannot be statistically determined because the selection of cases is not based on any random sampling procedure.

An important consideration is, of course, determining how large a sample is required. Intuitively we have a sense that a sample of 20 is not likely to provide us with a good estimate of, say, the voting choices of some electoral district. We would have little confidence in generalising from the results of such a small sample since the effect of categories disproportionate to their distribution in the population is likely to be great. This is not to say that a sample of 20 would not give an accurate estimate of the distribution of some property in a population. It might just do that, but the point is that statistically the likelihood of it doing so would be very low indeed. A sample of 2000, on the same intuition, would seem better and an even larger one better still.

According to probability theory, if successive samples of the same size are taken from a population, the sample values will differ between the various samples. But if the sample size is increased, the sample values will approximate closer and closer to those of the population. As sample size increases, so chance variation of the sample from the population will be reduced and the chances of securing a representative sample increased. There is nothing certain about this: it is simply that the larger the sample, the greater the probability that it will give more accurate estimations of the population values. However, after a certain sample size, increasing the size of the sample only gives marginal improvements in accuracy, and does little to improve the chances that the sample will represent the population. In other words, it is the sample size which matters, not the proportion of the total population which the sample represents. A properly drawn sample as small as 2000 could be an adequate representation of a national population of many millions. (Technically, choosing a sample size for a randomly drawn sample involves consulting the sample distribution of the statistic, calculating its standard error, and consulting the sampling distribution of the statistic to provide some idea, according to probability, of how closely the sample statistic should approximate to population values within stated limits.)

We have spent some time discussing sampling not only because it is regarded as essential feature of the social survey but also because it is crucial to the use of inferential statistics which constitute the core of multivariate analysis.

Multivariate analysis

In Chapter 4 we discussed the basic idea of variable analysis, namely, establishing the joint variation of two variables. Although the contingency table of two variables, as used in the example, instantiates the logic of pattern searching in variable analysis, it cannot take us very far in that we do not know whether any other variables might affect the relationship. Real-world situations must be the product of very many contributing causal variables, not just the small number of variables that we are interested in, and these variables may all be interacting with one another. In experimental situations, randomisation and symmetrical designs can take care of many of the effects of other variables, including unknown ones. In non-experimental situations, on the other hand, variables are likely to come already interrelated in many kinds of ways. This is the 'messy situation' we spoke of earlier, which needs to be disentangled if we are to identify the genuine causal relationships of interest, and to disambiguate the many correlations which non-experimental data produced, not all of which indicated genuine relationships.

To illustrate the problem here we can use Lazarsfeld's own example. Suppose we found a close positive correlation between the number of storks in an area and the birth rate. Although this used to be an explanation given to children to account for where they came from – either that or the gooseberry bush – it is not a relationship that many would entertain as involving a direct causal connection. In other words, the relationship is likely to be a spurious one; that is, other factors are responsible for the increase in both the stork and the human population, such as an increase in the standard of living which encourages people to have more children as well as disposing of more food waste on which the storks can feed, so increasing their population.

Let us take a simple example of a supposed relationship between, in this case, political affiliation and attitudes toward minority groups, to see how multivariate analysis proceeds.

Table 6.4 Hypothetical relationship between political preference and attitudes toward minorities

	Party A	Party B	Total
Negative	62	38	100
Positive	38	62	100
Total	100	100	200

An example

The attitudes toward minority groups have been measured using an attitude scale and the distribution divided into two groups: those with positive attitudes and those with negative ones. Suppose that we find the results shown in Table 6.4. (The figures in the body of the table are numbers that have been selected to total 100).

What we have is what looks to be a fairly strong relationship between attitudes to minorities and political preference: those with negative attitudes tend to support Party A, and those with positive attitudes, Party B. What we have is an association between two variables.

We do not, however, know the direction of any causal connection between the two variables. Is it the attitudes which predispose party support or party support which stimulates either positive or negative attitudes toward minorities? The table does not tell us and we could, as far as the tabular data is concerned, plausibly treat either variable as the cause. In other words, this is not a matter for the data but, rather, how far the data supports, or fails to support, some theory about the direction of the relationship. Nonetheless, let us stay with the interpretation that political support is at least partly 'caused' by attitudes toward minorities.

We also have to worry about the *ceteris paribus* – 'other things being equal' – conditions or assumptions. Since persons are not assigned randomly to the negative–positive groupings as they would be in the classic experiment, kept under laboratory conditions and later asked about their political preferences, then the claim that attitudes toward minorities affects political preference is harder to sustain than it would be under experimental conditions. In other words, *ceteris paribus* conditions have not been met: other things are not equal since they have not been controlled or taken into account.

Ceteris paribus conditions

We know that there are many other factors which could affect political preferences as well as attitudes to minorities. As a host of studies have shown, one of the biggest factors associated with both variables is occupational type. Manual occupations, for example, tend to support 'leftish' parties, while those in non-manual occupations tend to support 'rightish'

Table 6.5 Hypothetical relationship between political preference and attitudes toward minorities, holding occupational type constant

	Manual				Non-manual		
	Party A	Party B	Total		Party A	Party B	Total
Negative	56	24	80		6	14	20
Positive	14	6	20		24	56	80
Total	70	30	100		30	70	100

political parties. It is not implausible to argue that it might also affect attitudes to minorities if the minorities represent additional competition in the form of cheap labour for scarce manual jobs. In which case, if occupation is important, and if we were to hold occupational type constant, the relationship between attitudes toward minorities and political preference might weaken or even disappear. If we construct separate tables for 'manual' and 'non-manual' occupations, the relationship might appear as in Table 6.5.

The first thing to note is that Table 6.5 is a decomposition of Table 6.4 to control for type of occupation. Every person in the subtable to the left is a manual worker just as, in the right subtable, every person is in a non-manual occupation. Within the limits of the crude dichotomy, occupational type is being held constant. What we see is that within both the sub-tables there is no relationship between attitudes toward minorities and political support. Among the manual group, for example, 80 per cent of Party A and Party B supporters have negative attitudes toward minorities, whereas among the non-manual group 20 per cent of the supporters of both parties have negative attitudes. With a control for occupation the original relationship has disappeared.

A possible explanation for this is that the relationship between the original two variables was spurious which we can more formally diagram, following Blalock (1970), as in Figure 6.3.

Z represents the control variable, occupational type, X attitudes toward minorities and Y political preferences. Common sense suggests that if Z were

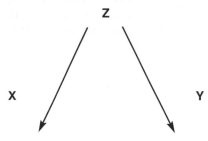

Figure 6.3 Spurious relationship between two variables

a common cause of both X and Y, then Z ought to be more strongly associated with X *and* Y than X and Y are to each other. It must however be noted that there will be other, and numerous, variables operating. Accordingly, we need to make the further assumption that the aggregate effect of these other variables is random. In which case, and according to this model, the correlation of X and Y can only be accounted for by Z. If Z were held constant, there would be no reason to expect X and Y to remain associated.

We can note, in the hypothetical data of Table 6.5, that occupation is strongly related to party support: 70 per cent of the manual workers support Party A, and the same proportion of non-manuals support Party B. It is also strongly related to attitudes toward minorities, in that 80 per cent of manual workers have negative attitudes, and only 20 per cent of the non-manuals have such attitudes. Thus, an alternative explanation has been found by locating an additional variable, Z – occupational type in our example – which is highly related to both X and Y and which can be assumed to be a common cause of both X and Y.

The above is, in essence, the logic of multivariate analysis: crudely, given that we have the right sort of data on the members of the population, we can calculate and recalculate the aggregate figures so as to 'play off' the effect of one variable on another. As we shall indicate, multivariate analysis has become statistically very sophisticated indeed, much more than our exposition might suggest.

Next we want to explore some further ramifications of the strategy of seeking causal relationships in non-experimental research. Setting out the essence of the logic of multivariate analysis is one thing; following it through in terms of practical methods is another, and so is determining the sociological relevance of what one has found.

Earlier we discussed multivariate analysis using three variables and highlighted the method of scrutinising the data: that is, manipulating the variables to see if a relationship is, in fact, a spurious one. In some ways spuriousness could be regarded as a complication. But in other respects, exploring a relationship in this way can add to the richness of the material as well as the complications involved in working out just what has been found. Below we briefly set out some of these 'complications'.

Alternative explanations

Even in the three-variable case, there is another explanation which could account for the same data used in the above tables. Z, instead of causing X and Y, may be an intervening link between them. That is, X may cause Z which, in turn, causes Y. Although this might seem implausible in the example, given that it would suppose that attitudes toward minorities 'cause' occupational type which, in turn, 'causes' political preferences, we need to remember that the variables are indicators which have an (unknown) probabilistic relationship to the supposed phenomena they stand for. It might be, for example, that attitudes toward minorities are associated with motivational dispositions which themselves have an effect on the choice of occupation or the lack of ambition to secure the qualifications for non-manual work. Alternatively, there may also be structural impediments at work, as is the case, for example, in Northern Ireland where religious affiliation still has an effect on the kind of occupation a person could expect. According to this kind of interpretation, attitudes toward minorities affect occupational type (for whatever reason) which, in turn, affects political preference.

However, the general point is that there will always be more than one explanation for any set of variables, and it will, accordingly, be necessary to look to supplementary information to choose among them.

Temporal sequences

Among such additional information is the temporal sequence of the variables. If it can be shown that occupational type precedes the development of positive or negative attitudes to minorities then we could rule out alternatives which suggest that it is the latter which 'cause' occupational choice. Apart from anything else, this suggests that it is important, where possible, to have research designs which collect data at more than one point in time.

Additional sources of spuriousness

Another source of complication is if there are two or more sources of spuriousness as in the Figure 6.4.

The relationship between attitudes toward minorities and political support may be due to two common factors, occupational type and urbanisation for example. In which case it would be necessary to control simultaneously for occupation and urbanisation. In this simple example, this can be done by setting up a series of tables, one for urban manual workers, one for urban non-manual workers, one for rural manual workers and one for rural non-manual workers. This would mean four separate tables, each of which related attitudes to minorities and political preference.

In principle this could be extended to any number of control variables but, as can be imagined, it soon becomes cumbersome. But, more than this, a point

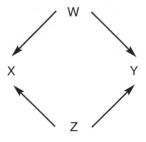

Figure 6.4 Multiple sources of spuriousness

will be reached where there are insufficient numbers of cases in each table. If, for example, we added gender, ethnicity and age to occupation and urbanisation – and, somewhat dubiously treated each of them as dichotomous variables – as being a matter of 'yes' or 'no' – this would lead to 32 separate tables. Since there are only 200 cases to start with, this would mean an average of just over six cases per table so aggravating the consequences of any errors.

Correlated independent variables

In some cases a number of independent variables can themselves be highly inter-correlated. A good example of this would be the poverty syndrome of low education, low income, low employment prospects, broken families and low aspirations, all of which might be possible sources of high crime rates (Blalock, 1970). The problem is to separate out the effect of each variable, a task which might have immense relevance for public policy expedients for lowering the crime rate, in that different strategies are implied depending upon which variable is the more important as a cause of high crime rates.

One of the advantages of the experiment is that several causal factors may be independently manipulated so that their effects do not confound each other. But, of course, in the real world such factors *are* confounded. This means that any measurement of their correlation will not be perfect, in that there will be some with poor education who have high incomes, some unemployed who instil high aspirations in their children, and so on. Providing that samples are very large and there are good measures for each variable, individual effects can sometimes be separated out, but this often requires complex statistical analysis. More often, such instances are treated as a single 'syndrome' or a cluster of variables which are considered all at once.

Measurement errors

All the techniques we are discussing depend upon valid and reliable measurement. Without this there will be additional unknowns in the analysis. Nor can it always be assumed that measurement errors are random. Indeed, it has been argued that the progress of variable analysis, especially in its more sophisticated forms, depends crucially upon solving measurement problems (Blalock, 1968). As we have seen, in sociological research, such problems are not straightforward.

Interaction effects

When we think of something being associated with more than one variable, we tend to see the effects of the independent variables as additive. For example, if we know that education, gender and ethnicity are associated with income, we might surmise that adding these variables would have a more or less linear effect on income, so that if one was highly educated, male and white then one's income would be higher than if one was highly educated, female and non-white, and so on. But this may not be the case. It may be, for example, that there is not much difference between the incomes of whites and non-whites at low educational levels but much larger ones at higher levels of education. What if the incomes of white and non-white women were much lower than those for men at the same level of education? Or what if education made a bigger difference to income for men than for women? (Blalock, 1960). In effect we might have different kinds of relationship between while males, non-white males, white females and non-white females. In other words, the effects are not linear and additive but interact in complex ways.

Reciprocal causation

Many relationships we want to think about in social research are not straightforward causal connection in which X directly leads to Y, but ones where there are reciprocal effects such that X might affect Y which, in turn, leads to further effects emanating from X, and so on. Much system thinking in sociology, and in other disciplines, assumes relationships much like this. The difficulty boils down to deciding whether X or Y has the bigger effect on each other, an assessment which requires complex estimation procedures that have been developed by statisticians and econometricians.

We started out talking about the social survey as a hypothesis-testing apparatus and, indeed, within the framework of variable analysis this was seen as its main purpose. However, as the kind of complications itemised above might suggest, this has proved less easy than the early optimism hoped. To put it simply: the problems are horrendously difficult despite the increasing sophistication of the statistical tools available. Indeed, very often these days hypothesis testing has been reduced to 'data dredging': that is, correlating everything with everything else and seeing what significant correlations come out. On a less sarcastic note, there are statistically respectable techniques which have been developed over the years to systematically simplify complex data

Other techniques: factor and cluster analysis

Factor analysis arises from the ideas of Galton (1822–1911), who sought to identify some 'general intellectual power' which underlay the range of human aptitudes. It is a technique which uses correlational methods to determine if there is some factor common to a set of interrelated measures. Starting with a set of measures which show many correlations among them, the aim is to end up with a few factors or dimensions (Child, 1970). While mainly used in personality and intelligence studies, it has been extended to other disciplines, including sociology, biology, medicine and economics. As a technique it is very dependent upon the mathematics of correlation coefficients, and therefore depends upon strong assumptions about the levels of measurement which must be robustly interval or ratio. There is also the problem of having identified the factors determining what it is has been found.

A similar set of techniques which have been applied across a range of disciplines, including psychology, zoology, biology and, to a much more limited extent, sociology, is cluster analysis. These techniques seek to group objects or individuals rather than, as in the case of factor analysis, variables. (Everitt, 1974). In other words, and to put it simply, in the case of factor analysis the output would show those variables which are strongly associated, whereas in cluster analysis one would uncover groups of individuals in which the degree of association is strong between members of the same grouping and weak between members of different groupings. So, if one subjected a selection of individuals who have scores on various properties, in factor analysis one would find those few factors which best summarise the properties, in cluster analysis one would find the groupings of individuals among whom the association between the properties is strongest. These are not the same thing from a different perspective.

There is another approach, and one perhaps more attuned to sociological problems, which is a logical extension of multivariate analysis, namely, causal modelling.

Causal modelling

The term 'model' can be the cause of considerable confusion. Often it is used interchangeably with 'theory' and, on the whole, in sociology no great harm is done is doing so. However, a model in

---
Models and modelling
---

simple terms is a representation of some theory or an object constructed to highlight some properties, and their relationships, which are of interest. In some cases a model may be an analogy, as in the case of likening society to a system or the distribution of status and prestige to the deposition of rocks in strata. Turning an analogy into a model usually involves going a little further than merely pointing out the analogy, in that some effort is devoted to setting out the implications of the analogy and building some systematic representation of what the model is supposed to picture. In the more advanced of the sciences, constructing models is a very precise procedure – often carried through in mathematics – making use of theories (though often combined with guesswork) and measurements to provide a representation (which can often be actually constructed as a physical representation) of the phenomenon or process.

A famous example is that of the structure of DNA as a double helix, which Crick and Watson actually built in their laboratory. The model was based on what was known about the chemistry of DNA, X-ray photographs, and suppositions about what the structure needed to look like in order for it to carry and reproduce the necessary genetic information. What the model did was demonstrate for the first time the structure of the DNA in a way that was consistent with existing knowledge and which could direct further research.

A model is a simplifying device. It is not intended to be a perfect copy of what it models but to bring out those features which are of interest. Although the distinction is not hard and fast, a model is not a theory, even though it may instantiate a number of theories and may be very useful in the construction of theories.

Models may also be mathematically expressed. Earlier when discussing the use of statistical methods in multivariate analysis, we talked about the ways in which actual distributions of some property, or a relationship, is compared with a distribution derived from the application of probabilistic assumptions about what the data would look like if due to chance. This, too, is a form of modelling. In this case comparing an actual distribution with a representation derived mathematically, and using the latter as a standard against which to make a judgement about the actual distribution. Causal modelling is a more thoroughgoing application of this principle. It is an attempt to use statistical analysis as a means of methodically working out the causal interconnection between a number of interlinked variables.

As we have already pointed out, the motivation behind multivariate analysis was the effort to emulate the logic of the experiment in non-experimental situations. This meant dealing with data produced in situations one could not directly manipulate as in a laboratory experiment. Accordingly, recourse was made to statistical modelling to disentangle the real causal relationships from the spurious. However, causal modelling sought to go further than identifying relationships in complex data sets. Rather it aimed to advance toward developing what are often considered 'proper' theories – that is, formal deductive ones – by forcing theorists to recast their informal verbal theories to fit within the tighter constraints of mathematically presented causal models (Blalock, 1961, 1969). However, one cannot just throw a verbal theory into a mathematical form. The complaint against verbal theories was a familiar one. The concepts of value are often too abstract from empirical testing, and make reference to but do not clearly identify a very large number of variables.

Let us look at an example of the kind of problem that causal modelling seeks to tackle.

Figure 6.5 sets out some of the general factors which have an effect on the inequalities that affect minority groups (Blalock, 1970). These are general factors each of which may consist of a number of other variables. The model also makes assumptions about the causal direction of the variables (indicated by arrows). It assumes, for example, that patterns of family upbringing and socialisation shape attitudes and dispositions, of which attitudes toward minorities is a component. There may also be 'contextual factors', which might affect not only the patterns of upbringing but also the attitudes and dispositions which might arise from these patterns. 'Contextual factors' might also have an influence on the actual behaviour of the majority group toward minorities. If, for example, the economy is booming and there are plenty of jobs, overt discrimination might be more muted than if there was a recession. There are also reciprocal causal loops (indicated by double headed arrows) in that some factors may initially cause others – such as attitudes toward minorities and the actual behaviour toward minorities that, in turn, reinforce the attitudes.

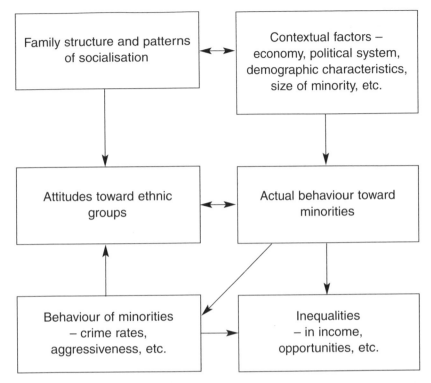

Figure 6.5 Schematic of general variables affecting inequalities
Source: after Blalock (1970).

Matters become even more complex and difficult if we want to determine the relative importance of the variables. This is a particular concern if the research is to be used to inform and guide policy and determine where scarce resources might need to be directed to mitigate the effects of discrimination. There are systematic ways of attaching weights to the variables in each block, but these require careful conceptualisation of the variables and their accurate measurement. And this should apply to *all* variables equally, otherwise systematic judgements of their relative importance will be unsound. Small-scale studies cannot be 'added up' to achieve this effect.

It would be a very tall order indeed to try to explore a model such as this using social research data. More usually, the techniques which have been developed for causal modelling are used, as in econometrics, where complex data sets are reasonably readily available, normally as a consequence of the routine activities of government and other agencies. Nonetheless, as with the application of mathematics to sociology, of which causal modelling is really a branch, over the years some effort has been directed at exploring the method as a tool for the analysis sociological data. Unfortunately, the mathematical operations involved are usually complex and beyond the background of most sociologists, so only a flavour of the techniques can be given here.

Essentially, causal modelling is about trying to find a mathematical formulation for the paths of cause and effect – hence, sometimes the term 'path analysis' is used – within a complex collection of variables, and then seeing how closely the model approximates to the data. This requires constructing a set of equations which it is assumed describe the model underlying the data. Earlier, when discussing multivariate analysis, we referred to some simple models of causal paths and the implications they might have, in particular elaborating the relationships in terms of whether or not they are 'spurious' in the sense discussed earlier. A similar logic is followed in much of causal modelling.

In Figure 6.5, for example, we set out some of the possible causal connections among sets of factors which might affect inequalities. The model is based on certain assumptions about the nature of the factors and their possible causal directions. Further, the factors as set out are not really single factors so much as composites of a number, possibly a large number, of variables. There will also be a number of logically possible causal relationships among the variables both within each block of factors and between the variables in the respective blocks. For example, attitudes to ethnic minorities may be composed of a number of different measures, some measuring attitudes toward different ethnic groups, some measuring attitudes presumed to be closely related to discriminatory attitudes, such as 'authoritarianism', as well as indicators of level of education, political awareness and so on. Other blocks of factors may be similarly decomposed. There are also very likely to be numerous correlations among such variables, some of which will be spurious. The problem is to disentangle these from the 'genuine' ones and, by this procedure, determine which of the logically possible models best fits the data. In this way the number of logically consistent models is reduced.

As always with the use of mathematics, the assumptions underlying the mathematics are critical.

Importance of mathematical assumptions

The first assumptions have to be made about the direction of causality. In the case of the 'Family structure and patterns of socialisation' block of variables, the assumption is that the causal direction is toward attitudes; an assumption based on the not implausible supposition that early childhood experiences affect later adult attitudes rather than vice versa. However, as far as the lowest four blocks of factors in Figure 6.3, what we seem to have is a loop of cause and effect rather than a simple unidirectional one. Although this is not a mathematical problem as such, in that it is up to the theorist to determine the most plausible interpretation of the causal direction, it does have mathematical implications of a serious kind (See Blalock, 1961, 1969 for an early review of these problems). A number of different mathematical techniques have emerged to deal with various models, such as simple chains, single equation dynamic models, simultaneous equation dynamic models and, more recently, directed graphs linked to probability distributions (Glymour, 1997; Humphreys, 1997).

The second, and more directly mathematical, assumptions are the assumptions to do with measurement. Many of the causal modelling techniques depend upon regression and correlational methods which require at least an interval level of measurement. Moreover, all measurement is prone to error, none more so that social research measurement. Accordingly, assumptions have to be made about the distribution of these errors, whether they are systematic or random.

Third, and relatedly, causal models are intended to disentangle the causal paths in complex data sets. In other words, they are applied to data which is already available, whether collected by means of a social survey or part of a data archive. Although this may seem an obvious point, its import is that the models can only be explored on data which has already been collected. This means that there may be other relevant variables about which there is no information but which, nonetheless, have causal effects. Again, estimations must be made of the effects of unmeasured variables.

The development of causal models is, in some respects, the ultimate refinement of the positivist strategy and the methods of variable analysis intended to implement that strategy.

- The causal modellers sought to discover causal generalisations within non-experimental data and, through this, offer a means of testing hypotheses.
- As part of the this, they sought to recast verbal theories as causal models, and develop a systematic language which can be used to think about theory-and-data as a more coherent unity. By borrowing the formality of mathematics (in the case of causal modelling, the mathematics of probability and statistics), they sought to move closer to the HD ideal for the formulation of theories.
- Causal modelling was intended to move closer to creating a quantitative science in which measurement issues were paramount and theories were decided upon by a more objective way of testing hypotheses.

The development from Lazarsfeld's early formulations of the idea of variable analysis to causal modelling seems, on the face of it, to make considerable progress toward implementing a positivist science of sociology. Of course, this was a far cry from the thorough integration of theory–method–data, but significant steps had been taken toward that objective. There are still problems, of course, many as much mathematical as sociological. However, the blend of the social survey and multivariate methods of analysis had brought the dream nearer to fruition. Or had it?

Conclusion

We have tried to explain the logic of multivariate analysis so that its connection to variable analysis will be quite plain, the use of statistical manipulations being intended as a non-experimental equivalent to the use of the experimental method for the identification of law-like relationships between changes in 'dependent' variables brought about by changes in 'independent' variables. The logic is a statistical logic. Multivariate analysis is a method that can be used in any empirical discipline provided that the materials and the problems of that discipline are suitable to handling within the strict requirements of the statistical procedures. Multivariate analysis, like so many ideas and techniques in sociology, is a borrowed one, and the question is whether the analogy between variable analysis and sociological use of multivariate analysis techniques is a sociologically effective one.

As we have suggested, high expectations about the transforming effect of multivariate analysis on empirical sociological research have not been fulfilled. Certainly, the use of these techniques, and similar mathematical and statistical approaches, is predominant in American sociology but the results are less than overwhelmingly impressive in sociological terms. Part of the reason for this is that multivariate analysis faces that common problem in sociology: one may adopt a very sophisticated technique from some other discipline or pursuit, but the sociological content that will have to be inserted into that technique will consist of just the same problematic theoretical ideas that are already around. As with variable analysis, multivariate analysis is likely to involve recasting existing sociological ideas into its form in the hope that placing tighter restrictions on their expression will improve their sociological quality. This may not be the case.

Selected bibliography and suggested reading

- For those interested in the history of probability, see Hacking's two books, *The Emergence of Probability: A Philosophical Study of Early Ideas about Probability, Induction and Statistical Inference* (Cambridge University Press, 1975), and *The Taming of Chance* (Cambridge University Press, 1990). Pearson's *The Grammar of Science*, 2nd ed. (Adam and Charles, 1911) has its own historical interest for those keen to explore the topic.
- The procedures used in multivariate analysis are covered in numerous research methods texts, some extremely statistical, others less so. Lazarsfeld and Rosenberg's edited collection, *The Language of Social Research: A Reader in the Methodology of Social Research* (Free Press, 1955) is still a good source as is P.F. Lazarsfeld, A.K. Pasanella and M. Rosenberg (eds), *Continuities in the Language of Social Research* (Free Press, 1972). These are old now but do set out the basic logic well. It is, however, important to remember that statistically matters have become much more sophisticated.
- On experimental thinking in social research Blalock's early statement, *Causal Inferences in Nonexperimental Research* (The University of North Carolina Press, 1961), sets out the problem well. Much attention was given to this issue in the 1960s. See D.T. Campbell and H.L. Ross, *Experimental and Quasi-experimental Designs for Research* (Rand McNally, 1963). Their study of the crackdown on speeding is to be found in 'The Connecticut

Crackdown on Speeding: Time Series Data in Quasi-experimental Analysis' in E.R. Tufte (ed.), *The Quantitative Analysis of Social Problems* (Addison-Wesley, 1970). Time series analyses are widely used in economics.

- On causal modelling Hubert Blalock's *An Introduction to Social Research* (Prentice-Hall, 1970) is fairly clear even though it demands careful reading. Also his 1969 work, *Theory Construction: From Verbal to Mathematical Formulations* (Prentice-Hall, 1969), remains a good statement of one of the main objectives of the positivist project. Finally his article 'The Measurement Problem: A Gap between the Languages of Theory and Research' in H. Blalock and A.B. Blalock (eds), *Methodology in Social Research* (McGraw-Hill, 1968) reiterates the measurement problems and causal modelling's proposed solution. V.R. McKim and S.P. Turner (eds), *Causality in Crisis? Statistical Methods and the Search for Causal Knowledge in the Social Sciences* (University of Notre Dame Press, 1997) contains a wide selection of papers bringing the issues up to date both conceptually and in terms of new statistical techniques. The Introduction is especially useful but do not ignore other contributions.
- On factor analysis, D. Child, *The Essentials of Factor Analysis* (Holt, Rinehart and Winston, 1970) sets out the basics with useful examples. B. Everitt, *Cluster Analysis* (Heinemann, 1974) does likewise.
- On the aggregation problem and its relevance to theory see Lazarsfeld and Menzel, 'On the Relation between Individual and Collective Properties' in A. Etzioni (ed.), *Complex Organisations: A Sociological Reader,* 2nd ed. (Holt, Rinehart and Winston, 1969). H.R. Wagner's, 'The Displacement of Scope: A Problem of the Relationship between Small-scale and Large-scale Sociological Theories', *American Journal of Sociology,* 69, 1964, is still worth looking at. K. Knorr-Cetina and A.V. Cicourel (eds), *Advances in Social Theory and Methodology: Toward an Integration of Micro- and Macro-Sociologies* (Routledge and Kegan Paul, 1981) contains papers dealing with theoretical and methodological issues.

Chapter 7

The Demise of Positivism?

This part of the book has discussed the main methods which are the legacy of the positivistic conception of empirical social research. Of course, and this is important to note, the methods themselves – interviewing, questionnaires, social surveys and the rest – are not necessarily nor irrevocably tied to the positivist programme. We highlighted the connection between the concept of variable analysis and multivariate statistics because of the importance that this attachment had in promoting, first, an idea of how real progress was to be brought about, and second, the use of statistical techniques in sociological analysis generally. The use of survey methods, however, can take place in practical domains, such as market research and government information gathering, without any attachment to theoretical ideas at all. The methods do not depend upon the positivist programme that they were associated with in sociology at a crucial time in its development.

As we have indicated many times, in our view the positivist programme failed even though it remains the most consistent effort to date to realise the nineteenth-century dream of a science of society. We emphasise that positivism failed by its own standards, at least insofar as the adoption of those standards was meant to render sociology 'genuinely scientific'. If the positivist programme for the thorough reconstruction of sociology now looks very unconvincing, it would be false to say that the spirit of positivism has entirely departed the body of sociology and social research. In some respects the spirit still looks strong and remarkably vital. A glance at the major American journals will show just how much empirical research is still being done using surveys and questionnaires, and analysed using extremely sophisticated statistical methods, many now readily available for use on desk-top computers. Many of the methods are still widely used in various forms of social research, in education, in political science, in economics, in social administration and in government, and are emphasised by various training bodies and research councils. More subtly, many of positivism's critics, as we shall see in

Parts II and III, are perhaps more positivistic than they would allow, at least to the extent of buying into many of the ambitions that positivism sought to realise.

When we say that positivism failed, and failed by its own standards, we have in mind its failure to identify any sociological laws, to develop any convincing or powerful formal theory, or to bind theory and method into an apparatus which was thoroughly integrated. Positivism failed, in sum, to become the integrated research mode for sociology that it envisaged.

At such junctures it often seems that the choice is either reform or revolution. One can attempt to operate within the tradition, trying to improve it, reform existing practices, face up to the problems and, in the main, do one's best to carry the project through. Alternatively, one can abandon the project entirely. Both responses have been tried in sociology, and the remaining parts of the book will deal with many of the revolutionary responses to the failure of positivism. However, in this chapter we want to stand back a little and examine aspects of positivism's strategy for social research. In the main the critique which follows is an immanent one rather than one which is perhaps more common in sociology, namely, a critique from outside the perspective – which is often an argument that effectively says: 'I wouldn't do it that way.' As we have already indicated in the various chapters of this part of the book, there were intimations of the mortality of positivism well before the reactions against it we will discuss in the following parts – problems to do with interviews, with social surveys, with data analysis and the like, which were the methodological bread and butter of social research methods

Also, we intend this chapter to serve as a bridge to Part II, where we examine one mode of sociological thinking which emerged as a response to the rise of positivist social research even though its antecedents were at least as old. In particular we want to discuss the following related themes:

- positivism as a short cut to science
- the supposed theoretical neutrality of variable analysis
- the causalist conception which underpins the enterprise.

These will not only allow us to bring a critical eye to bear upon the positivist project but also draw out some points which will be important in the parts which follow.

The short cut to science?

One hallmark of positivism was its almost messianic pursuit of its idea of science. It was not intended to be a milk-and-water exercise but set out criteria that were meant to be tough, stringent and definitive. It was often aggressive and contemptuous in its attitude to anything that failed to conform to its preconceptions. A live-and-let-live approach is not, on the whole, a characteristic of sociological positions, and so it often was with positivism. The project was conceived as a ruthless rejection of previous sociology.

In significant part, the problem positivism thought that it faced was the pluralism of sociology. Here were all these different approaches and no real way of definitively choosing any of them as the way forward. For such as Popper, this very fact was a reason for rejecting much of sociological theory in that, since it was not amenable to potential refutation, then it was not authentically scientific. Positivism had a firm view of what science consisted in, a view derived largely from positivist philosophy which, on the whole, took the more advanced of the natural sciences as the model to elaborate what distinguished science from other claims to knowledge. These disciplines are characteristically unified within a single framework of shared theory and method in a deductively integrated way.

> The problem of pluralism

Assuming that the methods of the natural sciences explained their success, then it followed that if sociology, or any other social discipline, was to become a science, it would need to follow these same methods. There was no alternative; the logic was inexorable. If positivism emulated the practices of the successful natural sciences as the means of finding out about reality, if there was to be a proper social science then it had to be done according to the method of the natural sciences and these are positivistic. It was a vision of science that was imposed from the top, that is, adopted from successful natural sciences – or, to be more accurate, from philosophical accounts of what made those sciences successful. Thus, the shape of sociology was to be carved out in accord with general principles identifying the nature of science. The positivists, and they were not alone in this, thought that they had a short cut to creating a science of sociology by using a philosophical account of science based on the natural sciences. Marx and Durkheim followed much the same strategy. The natural sciences had pointed the way and by following their example, their underlying logic, their method, sociology could save itself centuries of effort.

> The top-down strategy

Not surprisingly with such an ambitious project, there proved to be a gap between forming the strategy and working out what it would take to implement it. After all, the advanced sciences had taken many centuries working out how to do what they do. What positivism did was try to model itself on the finished sciences, not on what they had to do to get there. As we will argue, with hindsight the strategy was misconceived from the beginning. We say 'with hindsight' because the strategy was not, in the beginning, self-evidently stupid even though no science hitherto had been built in this way. With the impressive examples of the natural sciences before us, what could be more natural than to suppose that the success in understanding nature scientifically should be a precedent for understanding society, and that the means of doing this must be broadly similar to those in disciplines which have been tried and tested. The challenge was to instantiate the principles into appropriate methods and techniques of research and achieve that apparently seamless connection of theory, method and data that supposedly typified the more advanced sciences. Success would show up in the form of a potent sociological understanding of life in society. However, the effort required to meet this challenge was seriously underestimated. Reading a basic textbook on criminal law would not equip anyone to become a trial lawyer, and reading books in the philosophy of science does not tell anyone how to do successful science. Positivism only succeeded in matching the methods of science in a superficial way.

The case of method

In important respects, one of the problems of implementing the strategy was the emphasis on method. To talk of 'method' sounds like we are talking about a means to an end. The methods of the natural sciences (whatever they actually are) are presumably those procedures which enable, for example, astronomers to find out where a black hole is, or physicists to find out if there really is a Higgs boson. The methods, including the use of giant radio telescopes and enormous particle accelerators, are means to these kind of ends and the methods of sociology should presumably be of the same order. However, let us note the following:

- The methods actually implemented as part of the positivist programme for sociology were not tried and tested *in* sociology, but were developed or borrowed because they, at best, approximated to the picture of natural science method drawn from the philosophy of science. They were not, on the whole, developed out of tackling *sociological* problems.
- These methods were not, therefore, ones which could be shown to identify the true nature of social phenomena on the basis of their results. Rather, the results were to be recommended solely on the grounds that they represented an application of the *scientific* method.

The presumption that the methods of natural science are *the* methods is exactly that: a presumption. It begs the question as to whether the subject matter of the social sciences is at all of the same kind as that of the natural sciences and to be handled by the same methods. As we shall see in the next chapters, this question resurrected the 'struggle over method' that had taken place in Germany in the later years of the nineteenth century.

Inset 7.1 Struggle over method

The 'struggle over method', or *methodenstreit*, was central to debates in the cultural sciences in Germany during the 1890s. The key issue was whether the cultural sciences, including sociology, could be based on the methodology and epistemology of the natural sciences or whether it required methods especially suited to the study of social action. (See Inset 1.4 for further details.)

The advance stipulation of method makes sense if one accepts positivism's basic assumption of the unity of science and, further, that this unity is basically a unity of method. In which case, it follows that the method of the successful sciences defines the general method with, of course, necessary adaptations which recognise the diversity of the different branches of science.

> The emphasis on method

The positivists did not expect that the social sciences would be exactly like the natural sciences, but maintained that they must conform to natural science logic and work within the same broad principles. Accordingly, on this argument, conformity to the method provided a basis for appraising the success of *all* inquiries, including lay inquiries. A general standard of rationality was set out according to which inquiries which used the method were endorsed as science.

It was arguments of the kind sketched above which gave the impetus for positivism's concentration on methods of research. Everything, of course, depends on the assumption that there is a general method of science and that the positivists have identified it. If there is, then, only that which fits the general method can comprise the substance of sociology, and so method moves into the driving seat and starts to dictate what sociology can be. As we shall see in the Part II, these assumptions were to be challenged.

Even if we accept these assumptions, however, there is still the problem of translating the general method into techniques adapted to the domain of the social – remembering, of course, that the nature of the social is already presumed in the initial assumptions rather than by independent understandings of the phenomenon itself. In practice, what happened was the attempt to recast much of existing sociological ideas and theories into a form which had the appearance of implementing the scientific method.

Take the case of the attempt to produce successful theories conforming to the HD model of theory. Recall that conformity to this model was thought of as a means to an end, not as an end in itself. Casting sociological theories into the HD model would make them theories that would enable the acquisition of assured knowledge of social reality. For all the work to this end, including writing textbooks on how it should be done, none of the attempts to produce such theories – not that there were really that many – nowadays survives as being of much interest. One of the foremost examples of the attempt to mathematise theory, James S. Coleman's *Introduction to Mathematical Sociology* (1964), was a brave attempt to push the enterprise forward, but at the end of the day it turned out to be an exercise in mathematics rather than sociology and little worthwhile came of the effort. One might also consider the work on 'expectation states theory' that has continued for three (rather lonely) decades and more in an attempt to develop a rigorously deductive theoretical structure around the fact that social categorisations shape people's expectations of what others do (Berger et al, 1966).

However, it is worth dwelling on this a little longer.

Prospects for the mathematisation of sociology

The tendency is for the strength and interest of the 'mathematical social sciences' to be rather more in the mathematical that the social. Econometrics is a good example, as are subjects such as 'decision theory' and 'game theory'. In order to make their topics tractable to sophisticated mathematical formulations, these disciplines have characteristically tended to adopt unrealistic assumptions about their subject-matters. Anatol Rapoport (1966, 1974) gave a robust statement in an introduction to game theory to the effect that this is a mathematical rather than an empirical discipline. Game theory was developed out of an attempt to give a mathematical account of poker and has, subsequently, been treated as a theory of conflict. It is famous for its formulation of the Prisoner's Dilemma which, specifically, has to do with two prisoners charged with a common crime and offered a deal if they inform on each other. The interest is the mathematical solution to each prisoner's maximisation strategy – the attempt to work out the 'best' solution for this taking some decades. In Rapoport's view, game theory (which is close kin to 'rational choice theories' which have periodic bouts of popularity with sociologists, James Coleman in the United States, and John Goldthorpe in the United Kingdom being two recent enthusiasts for its theoretical potential) is mathematically interesting but not really packed with lessons for how to deal with and resolve real-life conflicts. In Rapoport's words: 'lack of sufficient acquaintance with the essential ideas of game theory has frequently led to regrettable misunderstandings and confusion; for example, about the uses and misuses of game theory in policy making, and about the relevance of game theory to the social sciences' (Rapoport, 1966: 6). This is a conclusion one can easily extend to much of the use of mathematics in the social sciences.

> Game theory: an example

It is also worth noting that the mathematically more successful social science disciplines, such as economics and game theory, are ones in which measurement problems have largely been solved – not by them but for them. Economics has the invaluable measure of 'price' which, in money economies, gives a ready numerical value for at least some of the key factors in which it is interested. Poker has quite clear-cut situations and outcomes – people win, lose, have so many cards of value and so on – so that one can work out the odds, which is the objective of game theory. This is not the case with sociology. Simple situations work for mathematics but, before too long, the mathematical equations become too simple for sociological purposes or, conversely, involve too complex mathematics to model the sociology adequately. What is needed to continue to carry the mathematics through is not what is needed for sociological plausibility. 'Mathematical sociology' characteristically involves off-the-shelf solutions, taking over bits of mathematics which have been developed for use in other disciplines but have not been tailor-made for sociological purposes – recall Skvoretz' reflections detailed in Chapter 3. Thus, there have been enthusiasms for catastrophe theory and chaos theory, and currently complexity theory is being vigorously promoted. But these enthusiasms are commonly short-lived as while they seem attractive in principle and can appear to apply effectively to one or two carefully chosen exemplary cases, the difficulty of applying them to specifically sociological problems once one moves beyond a few simple and especially suitable examples soon becomes apparent.

We are not saying here that the mathematisation of sociology is an impossibility. It may or may not be. What is at issue is that the strategy of mathematising sociology followed by the positivist project failed to produce much which was sociologically worthwhile. To repeat the point: the problem lay in the form of mathematics that was adopted – as though it was just a matter of fitting sociological content into a pre-built mathematical framework rather than developing a mathematics that would really raise sociology's game and capable of doing better work than was otherwise possible on something of sociological substance. And even this pre-built frame turned out to require more mathematics than would-be mathematical sociologists could do.

Of course, scholars should be free to pursue their ideas to see where they might lead, and the attempt to develop a mathematical social science should be no exception to this. But it is not too unfair to say that it has a long way to go before it can produce much that is sociologically worthwhile. Be this as it may, as it happened most effort was devoted to the development of measurement techniques as a complementary strategy to the mathematisation of theory. If one could quantify the relationships found in data then, at some point, this would serve the former objective of mathematical sociology and, ultimately unify theory and data as exemplified in the advanced sciences.

Not forgetting measurement

However, there was a tension at the heart of the positivist enterprise as applied to social research. In the advanced sciences there is an intimate connection between theory and measurement. Theory tells us what the phenomenon is like – though it is more complicated than this – what its properties are and what measurement systems are appropriate. In variable analysis, as we have seen, working out how to do measurement was treated as a largely abstract enterprise isolated from any theory on the simplistic positivist assumption that the data could be used to test theories, as though 'the data' could be identified and measured without necessary reference to the theory being tested. Accordingly, and as variable analysis recommended, sociological theories and their concepts needed to be recast in the forms of measurement identified by the theory of measurement. One result of this, in the heyday of positivist social research, was that there were almost as many different measures used by sociologists as there were studies of social phenomena (Bonjean et al, 1967). After examining every article over a 12-year period in the main US sociology journals it was concluded that in 3609 attempts to measure various phenomena by the use of scales or indices, 2080 different measures were used. Only 589 of these were used 'more than once' though 'more than once' does not imply anything other than 'used a couple of times'.

This is a very different picture to that of the natural sciences, which make use of far fewer measures and, moreover, measures which mathematically interconnect (as temperature, pressure and volume do, for example). In hindsight, the situation in the social sciences should not be surprising, given the emphasis of variable

> Ad hoc character of measurement

analysis on indirect measurement through indicators. An indicator is anything that can plausibly be argued to 'stand for' a theoretical concept and depends upon the empirical situation that is the focus of the research. Onto whatever is selected is imposed a structure intended to provide some level of measurement, with the kind of consequences noted in Chapter 4. Although positivism attempted to be principled about measurement, it turned out to be an ad hoc affair which, while mathematically sound enough, bore little connection to what the phenomena being measured might be. Anyone could, more or less, propose a 'variable' or two and offer a way of 'sort of measuring' them whilst admitting that, strictly speaking, they did not actually measure the variable. It was very much a 'make do' operation.

Further, the social survey is a primitive measuring device. It cannot do much more than ask people questions and, moreover, is constrained by the need to ask questions that people can understand and answer. It is not really directly measuring anything much beyond the frequencies with which certain kinds of answers are given by a particular popula-

> The social survey

tion. Anything else it measures only indirectly, and often so indirectly that the measure is very tenuous indeed. One of the more amusing examples is Arthur Stinchcombe's attempt to measure rebellion in high schools (1964). Looking for a quantifiable indicator of this he was compelled to resort to using the frequency with which pupils did not answer questions on his questionnaire which, one might rightly think, has no assured connection with rebellious conduct generally.

Given the above constraints, improvement in the measuring instrument seems to be limited to what can be done to ask 'better' questions – as this is understood relative to the needs and standards of survey work – and perhaps to contrive more imaginative ways of questioning. Much improvement in the survey will have to come from the use of more sophisticated statistical techniques to manipulate the resulting data but, again, this will be within the limits of what can be done with the survey rather than any development of the survey itself.

The net effect of this measurement strategy was, for positivism at least, to make measurement *the* sociological problem – a displacement of means and ends! Method and theory were intended to solve sociological problems but, in the end, the methods themselves became the problem.

They also became a problem in another way, to do with the supposed theoretical neutrality of variable analysis.

The theoretical neutrality of variable analysis

We said earlier that one way of thinking about methods is to see them as means to an end. In the case of positivism the methods were intended as a means of building an empirical social science (itself a partisan commitment to the notion that sociology could be a science). In the absence of any worthwhile sociological theory to speak of, methods, particularly variable analysis, were the means of forcing existing theory into a form which enabled hypotheses derived from the theory to be empirically tested, or of attempting to force the development of new theory that would fit the HD framework and that could, from the start, be connected to measurement procedures. Indeed, in the beginning, the positivist project was more concerned with theory than it was with method, although it is the latter which is perhaps its most enduring legacy.

It is probably fair to say that variable analysis, the main vehicle for translating positivism's vision of science into a set of practical research procedures, was assembled as a 'quick fix', as a way of getting things started. And, in important respects it was a successful beginning. Following the Second World War, in a short space of time bureaus of survey research were established, and training in the techniques of variable analysis became a central part of sociology teaching throughout the United States and, rather later and less densely, in the UK. Much of this was achieved by taking already existing methods from other fields and placing them within a framework which, on the face of it, lent them coherence as a strategy for building an empirical science of sociology. The price of this was that the idea of variable analysis was formulated independently of any sociological theory, and deliberately so. It was intended to be neutral between sociological approaches so that, ultimately, choices among approaches could be made on empirical grounds.

Of course, the methods were not sociologically neutral. They were not methods that could be used for any sociological purpose, but carried with them strong conceptions of what allowable sociological purposes were. They were not tools that could be used for any sociological conception but themselves incorporated such conceptions. Positivist methods were sociologically partisan, as we can see from the model of the actor and society which it imposed upon sociological research.

The model of the actor and the social

From the beginning, positivism was beset by the considerable range and diversity of sociological approaches and theories with varied pictures of society and the social actor. In effect, it sidestepped the issue of choosing between them by speaking instead of properties and variables. It was not supposed to be necessary to subscribe to any particular sociological picture in order to use variable analysis. Whatever the picture, it was necessary to translate the concepts into properties and cast them as variables. It would ultimately be up to empirical research to decide which picture, so to speak, yields properties and variables which, through empirical research, provides the most promising generalisations. But, of course, the very procedure of casting concepts into properties and variables makes a difference to the ways in which sociological phenomena might be conceived. In effect, the 'unit of analysis' as defined by the methods of variable analysis was substituted for 'sociological phenomena'.

This is a subtle but important distinction that needs more elaboration. Lazarsfeld espoused the Kantian view that science, including natural science, did not deal with 'things-in-themselves' but with the properties of things. The whole idea of variable analysis is built upon this notion: the emphasis on developing indicators, the very idea of variables, looking for patterns of relationship among variables; these were regarded as the means of getting at phenomena which could not be directly inspected but only glimpsed through the measurement of their properties. Kant's argument, however, was a metaphysical one about the nature of reality and how it is known. It was part of his extended, and not always easy to follow, arguments about the nature of reason, morality, the nature of experience and the limits of knowledge. If anything, and this is generally true of metaphysics, it was an argument about the logic of concepts, such as knowledge, perception and reality, rather than an inquiry into the nature of things themselves as science might understand this.

> The notion of property in variable analysis

Thus, for example, although we might talk of things, such as cats, dogs, cigarette lighters, doors and windows or books, our perception of these 'things' is indirect, it is not of them 'in themselves'. We perceive only their properties, for example their colour, their shape, their heaviness, their smell or whatever properties they are deemed to have. In other words, in effect Kant is saying that the concept 'the-thing-in-itself' cannot be discovered by empirical means. The question is: how far is such a metaphysical conclusion relevant as a guide to the practice of science? Indeed, in making his argument Kant was drawing upon the science of his day and its understanding of the nature of perception. His interest is not in the practice of science or the knowledge it has produced. His concerns were metaphysical and, among other matters, to do with the nature of scientific knowledge, its limits and its relationship to morality.

Nonetheless, Kant's supposed influence apart, it is true that scientists rely upon indicators incorporated into instruments of all kinds. These indicators are generated as consequences of the theories, and not as self-standing indicators independent of any theory. They are generally not seen by scientists as offering a unique insight into a metaphysical reality. As far as our own story is concerned, whatever the metaphysical origins of variable analysis were, it was partisan in that it imposed a conception of science on sociology and, in so doing, created a situation where the methods began to drive conceptions of society and the social actor, and did so through a serious misunderstanding of the nature of theory in science.

We said earlier that to talk of methods is sometimes to talk of a means to an end. But the end is important to devising whatever methods are necessary to achieve it. This may not be easy but the end is important to the exercise. Positivism's frustrations with the state of social theory were perhaps understandable and, further, made it appear that a concentration of method might bear earlier fruit than trying to tidy up sociological theory in an appropriate scientific form. But it presented a fundamental problem. To put it in simple terms for now, since it is an issue which will resurface in many forms later in the book, in science it is the theory which tells us what to observe, what methods we can use to do this, what the implications of our observations might be, and so on. Method alone cannot tell you any of this. Positivism knew this, as shown for example in its emphasis on variable analysis as hypothesis testing, an activity which gets its very point from the implications that a true or false hypothesis has for the theory. Otherwise there is little point to hypothesis testing. Its strategy of emphasising method, however, proved fateful for this being anything more than 'abstracted empiricism', to use C. Wright Mills' term, rather than the truly scientific theories looked for.

By way of illustration of these points let us return to the social survey.

The case of the social survey again

Perhaps more than any other method, it is the sample survey which illustrates the problems which positivism set itself right from its inception as variable analysis. To repeat: variable analysis was proposed as a ubiquitous framework for thinking about the connection between theory and data, between theory and the world it set out to explain. Remember, Lazarsfeld and his colleagues developed variable analysis out of their experiences with social survey work, originally focused on radio audience research. And, in its own way, the social survey was not an inappropriate method to find out about such things as who listens to which programmes, how often, and what they think about them. In many ways, such research is not unlike market research and, in its own terms, perfectly respectable. It does not really matter for audience surveys that the measures might be inaccurate in various ways, even seriously so, as long as they provide some plausible figures that can guide, for example, the setting of advertising rates. What will do for the needs of advertisers or policy makers, however, does not necessarily provide an appropriate foundation on which to base a framework for a strict scientific approach to social research in general.

In Chapter 2 we pointed out that sociology began as a reaction against the individualism of the Enlightenment and its efforts to construct accounts of human behaviour entirely in individualistic – what we would now call psychological – terms. The body of social thought that became sociology sought to remind thinkers that individuals lived with other individuals and that out of this grew social organisation, cultures, language, morality, religion and the other elements of human life. Of course, working out what this implied and how it may be studied was, and still is, the continuing objective of the sociological project.

The way variable analysis operationalises this idea is as properties of the individual. So, for illustration, individuals can be characterised, as we have seen, in terms of a host of properties including the number of friends they have, marital status, level of education, attitudes, life histories and more, all of which, on the face of it, are social properties. Moreover, there is a convenience to this formulation in that one can easily sample individuals randomly – in modern societies listings of individuals are readily available in the form of electoral registers, street listings and the like – and use the supposed power of inductive statistics. Correlations of all kinds can be found in the data, and can become the grist to the mill of some theory. But are we convinced that randomly sampling individuals is an adequate way of implementing the originating idea of sociology? Random sampling assumes that the individuals sampled have a known probability of being selected, yet a key sociological idea is that people, as individuals, are not randomly assorted in society but, rather, are interconnected to one another in numerous and overlapping relationships. In which case, should we not be sampling these rather than individuals, no matter how convenient it is to do the latter? Of course, individuals can report on their relationships, among many other matters, but is this the same as sampling such relationships directly? Of course, we can use what individuals report about their relationships, but then have the familiar problem of 'words and deeds'.

> The asociological character of random sampling

In may be recalled that one of the ideals of positivism that the social survey was intended to implement was to link theoretical ideas with what was empirically observable as a way of finding out about social organisation. Hence, the idea of variables and their indicators. The social survey was a surrogate for doing that observation directly. Observing large numbers of people doing things would be impractical. One cannot observe enough people to make up a meaningful sample for a large population, one cannot wait for people to manifest relevant behaviours which they may do only rarely and on unpredictable occasions, and so on. The social survey seemingly gets around these kinds of problems. But what makes it seem mandatory for positivism is the assumption that sociological research should take the form of hypothesis testing. If a researcher is concerned with the effects of racial attitudes, for example, then following someone around to observe what they did directly might mean that the researcher was doing this for a long time before any situation relevant to the expression of racial attitudes might occur. But you can ask people questions about their racial attitudes, or ones whose answer in understood to manifest racial attitudes and, if they are willing, you can right away collect data on racial attitudes as a kind of substitute for observing what they might do. Accordingly, using interviews and questionnaires in conjunction with the survey as a hypothesis-testing tool on the face of it brings theory and empirical observation closer together. But what kind of theory?

The outcome of social survey research is a set of correlations and associations among indicators. These correlations and associations have to be explained. Part of this is distinguishing, as we have seen, the genuine from the spurious ones. Assuming that this has been done – and it is no straightforward matter – the task is to bring theory to explain the genuine ones or, alternatively, to use these to rule out theories whose hypotheses are inconsistent with the correlations produced. But this could only work for theories formulated within the variable analytic framework and, even then, did so in an ad hoc manner.

This section of the chapter is challenging the idea of variable analysis as theoretically neutral, and at the core of the challenge is that, despite its claims, it had to have a conception of the social in order to work at all. But, this conception of the social was little more than sociological commonplaces rather than a systematic connection of theory to data. To illustrate this point let us turn to a problem which looks statistical, and is one which emerges in survey research, but in fact has important sociological ramifications: the problem of aggregation.

The problem of aggregation

Essentially, the problem arises in variable analysis from the attempt to provide a statistical solution to a sociological problem. As we mentioned earlier, the sociological reaction to Enlightenment individualism was to argue that individuals live among other individuals, and it is this which gives rise to the intellectual focus of sociology. It is an idea reflected in concepts such as 'group', 'culture', 'institution', 'social structure', 'social class' and 'society' itself: concepts which are intended to direct attention to phenomena which cannot be understood in individualistic terms. Again as we have said previously, quite what this involved has been an enduring theme and argument throughout the history of sociology. Again briefly (and it is another of those issues which will surface in a number of guises through the book), the problem is the ontological status to be accorded to the 'entities' that such concepts point to. Durkheim, for example, argued that supra-individual phenomena emerged out of collectivities of individuals and were as real, enduring and constraining as any of the 'facts' of nature. For Weber, on the other hand, terms referring to collectivities, such as 'state', 'class', 'group', were shorthand expressions for the socially organised *actions* of aggregates of individuals and had no additional ontological qualities.

Variable analysis' approach to the problem was to seek a 'solution' mainly through methods of analysis. It was recognised that the social survey tended toward an individualistic, or 'atomistic', bias in that its raw data was obtained from individuals, either through interviews or questionnaires, and was essentially data about individuals. (It also needs to be remembered that many official statistics are also derived from the actions or characteristics of individuals, so the issue is not confined to the social survey.) However, it was also recognised that what was wanted was data not simply about individuals but about the collectivities and relationships of which individuals were a part.

> Individual vs collective as methodological problem

For example, one of the more persistent sociological claims is that people have the beliefs and the attitudes they hold because they are members of a particular group, and such membership affects the beliefs they have, beliefs they would not hold unless they were members of such a group. There is, to put it simply, a notion here of levels of social phenomena from the individual, rang-ing from the small group, to the aggregate, such as a crowd, to the large collec-tive or group. Moreover, there are many sociological studies which purport to focus on units above that of the individual, such as comparisons of states in terms of such things as their relative economic growth, their propensity to develop authoritarian modes of government and, a recent interest, the effects of globalisation on a variety of economic activities and sense of national iden-tities. The problem for variable analysis was to construct indicators of 'group properties' out of raw data that was derived from individuals.

> Levels of phenomena

There are, of course, standard mathematical operations for summarising the values of individual units. For example, enumerating the wages of the individ-ual members of an occupational group and calculating an average will produce a summary figure which can be compared with the average wage of other occu-pations. Such data, which Lazarsfeld and Menzel (1961) called 'analytic prop-erties', were obtained by performing some mathematical operation upon an individual property. They could be contrasted to 'structural properties', which were calculated from data about the relations of individuals to other members of some collective. Examples would be the degree of cliquishness as measured by non-overlapping sociometric choices of friends, as would the concentration of power in a state or organisation by the relative measure of the influence of key groups or individuals over decisions. The last class, 'global properties' were, Lazarsfeld and Menzel opined, not derived from individual properties and included, by way of example, the density of settlement of a region or the 'warlikeness' of nations (as measured by the density of national budgets allo-cated to armaments as opposed to education and welfare). Similar efforts were made to distinguish between individual and collective properties of one sort of another (Blau, 1960; Tannenbaum and Bachman, 1964, for example) as well as explicit efforts to develop social survey designs less prone to the 'atomistic' bias. One such was the technique of 'snowball sampling', aimed at collecting data on individuals and their relationships. An individual would be chosen at random and then, when interviewed, asked to name closest friends or colleagues (thus providing data on his or her social networks, for example). However, the statistical apparatus for handling the analysis of such data is by no means straightforward.

However, the quarrel here is not with the techniques used to construct the indicators, but that they are being constructed without benefit of any clear theoretical statement of the phenomenal status of what the indicators are supposed to be measuring. While there are likely to be plenty of correlations among such indicators, in order to make sociological sense, recourse is made to rather vague sociological presuppositions about levels of phenomena, presuppositions which are fundamentally contentious within sociology itself. Durkheim's arguments on behalf of the reality of 'social facts', for example, do not demonstrate their existence. Rather, his account explores some of the arguments for their existence, and the study of suicide a brave attempt to illustrate the argument he is making (Durkheim, 1952). But, as others have pointed out (Douglas, 1967, Atkinson, 1978), very serious flaws, both methodological and theoretical, can be found in Durkheim's arguments. Admittedly, many of the counter-arguments arise from very different sociological positions – positions which will be discussed in the next section – but, in an important way, this is the point. Positivism's claim that variable analysis was a ubiquitous theory-testing apparatus has at least to be a much more restricted one. It can only test theories framed within an appropriate framework and not all sociological perspectives or positions can be so framed, and these must remain outside the remit of variable analysis.

> The case of suicide

But even from within variable analysis, the source of theoretical concepts left much to be desired. In the absence of adequate HD-formatted theory, variable analysis had to make recourse to what was available. Lazarsfeld himself, in talking of the process of translating variables into indicators, spoke of beginning with a 'vague image' of the process to be examined, culled from existing literature and ideas. The ultimate test of whether or not these were to prove any good was to see if they were consistently correlated with other variables. However, there was an aspect of this kind of thinking which was to prove extremely contentious.

Causal thinking in variable analysis

As should be clear, the ambition of the positivist project was to create an apparatus capable of putting sociology on the route to becoming a science. This meant discovering strong theoretical generalisations akin to the laws of nature or, at least, akin to the best that the social sciences had to offer. Hence the emphasis on the HD model of theory and methods of quantification. As we have already pointed out, there was a tension between the ambition to build an integrated approach to a sociological science and, in the end, the practical ways in which the positivists went about its realisation. A major stumbling block was that sociology could not be an experimental science but had to test its theories, discover its theoretical generalisations, by investigating relationships found in non-experimental situations, mainly relying on the social survey. Underlying this strategy was the understanding that theoretical generalisations were causal generalisations.

In the previous chapter we reviewed some of the thinking which led to the development of inferential statistics as an aid to identifying causes of complex and non-experimental situations. In a way this was a deflationary interpretation of the notion of cause, partly because the notion was under attack from prominent physicists and philosophers as well as by statisticians themselves, such as Karl Pearson. All that science required, it was argued, is the discovery of relatively invariant relationships among measured properties. Even the most fundamental laws of physics are but idealisations of such invariant relationships.

We have already, in the previous chapter, briefly looked at causal modelling and path analysis, and indicated that there were a number of technical problems which raised serious issues about the interpretation of the models. Among the most important of these was the inability of current techniques to unequivocally rule out the large number of alternative models consistent with some data set.

However, the problems about causalist thinking begin earlier, paradoxically with doubts expressed by philosophers who had laid the foundations for what became positivist philosophy. One such was David Hume (1711–1776). Briefly, his argument was that the foundation of human knowledge is in our experience of the world. In that experience there is nothing to suggest that one thing causes another except that the two things are in constant conjunction. In other words, all that a causal relationship can consist in is the habitual association of two things, and to infer anything more than this is to drift toward metaphysics. Hume was making an epistemological point as to how our knowledge of physical necessity could arise. What in experience accounted for the origin of the idea of physical necessity? (Wright, 1976). Nevertheless, it was these kind of arguments which were embraced by the logical positivists and the physicists who were influenced by Hume's philosophy, such as Ernest Mach, leading them to suggest the abandonment of the concept of cause as unnecessary to science and, instead, propose Hume's principle as an ontological claim.

Such views had implications for how we are to understand the laws of nature. Do they express simply regularities or uniformities in nature – that is, they are descriptions of the way the world is – or are they principles which govern the natural world in the sense that the world 'obeys' the laws of nature? While this dispute between the 'regularists' and the 'necessitarians' is a continuing one in philosophy (and which we do not have the space to go into but see Swartz, 1985, for overview), its implications for the practices of inquiry, natural or social, are not easy to see. As far as the social sciences were concerned, the regularists view seemed to lend support to variable analysis, which explicitly sought regularities in data as a means of uncovering more general theories. However, there was an equivocal attitude to the notion of cause, given the aim of providing 'not only genuine explanations of social phenomena, but knowledge relevant to policy-makers anxious to make effective interventions in the social world' (McKim, 1997: 5). The problem was, as we have seen, to devise techniques which could uncover regularity in non-experimental data.

> The nature of causal laws

It is instructive to return to the logic of multivariate analysis for a brief time and look at Turner's exposition of the debate over the causes of cholera (Turner, 1997).

The cause of cholera

It was Yule, in 1897, who revived the idea that social statisticians might be able to identify the causes and effects of social phenomena on the basis of statistical data (Yule, 1911). He accepted that statistical representations were not direct representations of causal relationships. However, empirical association must represent a mixture of the effects of known and unknown causes even though their proportions are unknown. Accordingly, if an observed association could be 'corrected' in some way that would identify other causal influences apart from the main, or 'primary', cause, then we would have a better estimate of the effect of the main cause. This 'correcting' could be done, he argued, on the basis of other observed associations. This procedure is, in effect, that discussed in the previous chapter on multivariate analysis. We take the observed correlation between a suspected causal contributor and the outcome of interest, and then subtract it from the total observed association to get a 'corrected estimate' of the magnitude of the primary causal relationship.

The supposed advantage of this procedure is that it only makes use of known associations. The problem, however, is that all of these are unknown mixtures of known and unknown causes, none of whose magnitudes are known independently of the correlations themselves. The procedure can, of course, be repeated for a third variable – as in testing for spurious correlation – and a fourth, and so on. If this could be done for all of the relevant correlations then one would arrive at the true causal effect of the primary causal variable, the true 'net effect'. But, in the end, all the pieces of evidence used to support the claims about the primary cause themselves only imperfectly represent actual causal processes.

However, the crucial issue for Turner is that in the absence of any clear indication of what causal mechanism, or law, is involved, then the apparatus cannot resolve the issue of causality.

In the mid-nineteenth century, William Farr, the foremost biostatistician of the day, studied the distribution of cholera and the correlates of the occurrence of the disease. He believed that cholera was primarily transmitted through the air and had substantial statistical support for this idea. He found a strong association with altitude, which he took as an indicator of 'miasmata' in the air. Indeed, the data for one epidemic fitted this neatly. He proposed a 'law' with the following property, namely, that halving the elevation doubled the mortality since this fitted the mortality figures. We know this to be wrong as an explanation of cholera, but could Farr have discovered that cholera is waterborne from statistical methods alone?

John Snow, an epidemiologist, adopted a different approach by trying to determine the manner in which the disease was transmitted. This led him to examine many non-statistical, qualitative facts and details that ordinarily would not have presented themselves in even the most elaborate listing of background variables, such as the fact that the poor often kept food under their beds near the chamber pot. However, the most impressive statistical relationship, exemplified in Farr's 'law of elevation', pointed to the wrong hypothesis. In fact, the 'law' held only for the 1849 epidemic. Snow concluded that the relationship was the result of coincidental circumstances specific to that epidemic and, accordingly, ignored it. Indeed, he did not attempt to explain the many associations that Farr had discovered in the health statistics. What struck Snow as more interesting were reports about the spread of the disease. His conclusion was that cholera was transmitted in the evacuations of its victims and that this explained all the cases. In light of Snow's hypothesis, Farr tried to modify his own theory to allow for the possibility that impure water had a role in the transmission of the disease by treating Snow's mechanism as one contributory variable among others and calculating the net effect. The impurity of water was a net effect established by subtracting the supposed main effect of elevation. However, the causal process was not an additive one, not a combination of impure water and something else. It was only after further epidemics and experiments that Farr accepted Snow's hypothesis about the causes of cholera. But Farr could not have justifiably accepted Snow's conclusion on statistical evidence alone. The facts of the case were established on the basis of a series of experiments that identified the actual mechanism of transmission.

The point is that to identify a cause requires clear knowledge of the relevant causal mechanisms or laws in addition to adequate measurement and accurate estimates of the effects of other causes. However, the logic of causal thinking in statistical analysis only assigns a causal interpretation to the correlations, it does not, and according to Turner cannot, demonstrate a causal connection in the sense of providing strong grounds for inferences to the true explanation. With the benefit of hindsight it is seriously doubtful if the strategy could ever have worked to produce the kind of generalisations sought.

One of the early exponents of causal modelling, Stanley Lieberson (1985), raised serious objections to the whole procedure. In particular, he drew attention to how little we know about the properties of phenomena independently of the format of variable analysis – a point we have made earlier. The result is that modellers have to make assumptions which may be wildly wrong. Again as we have pointed out, such assumptions, while

> Critique of causal modelling

necessary for the mathematics, may not be consistent with sociological assumptions or, more likely, may be mathematical assumptions masquerading as sociological ones. Matters are made worse, of course, by the regrettable tendency of many to be careless about the employment of the techniques. Too often researchers select variables for examination because available data is ready to hand or can be easily measured. Too often data sets are examined only to conclude that some additional variable might be 'of interest', with little or no improvement in our sociological understanding of the processes being examined. More fundamentally, Lieberson asks the question: how might social researchers, using their methods and ways of thinking, go about studying the question of why objects fall?

He visualises a study, based on an analogy with the typical multivariate, non-experimental social science study in which the characteristic objective is to explain the differences, the variance if you will, in the behaviour of different instances of the phenomenon, namely, falling objects. He asks us to imagine a variety of objects dropped without the benefit of strong controls, such as being dropped in a vacuum. This parallels the conditions of much of social science research, in which controls usually enter *post hoc* at the data analysis stage.

Suppose the objects are a dining table, a feather and a lead ball. Without a vacuum the objects will vary in the time it takes each of them to reach the ground. The lead ball is likely to reach the ground first, followed by the dining table, while the feather floats gently to the floor. Accordingly, the question becomes: What characteristics of the objects determines the difference? Air resistance and the size and density of the objects are likely to be determined as the factors which affect the speed of the fall. Assume that these factors, and any others we might think of, taken together account for all the differences in the velocities of the objects. In a social research context, this would be a tremendous achievement since all the differences had been accounted for; the result far exceeds the typical standards of social research. But, and this is the point of the example, we still would not have come up with the idea of gravity. An analysis of the rate of fall of various objects might tell us why they differ in their rate of fall but not why they fall. What we would not have available is the power of the theory of gravity and its statement of the constant rate of acceleration of falling objects within a vacuum, a theory which can be used to great effect in various calculations, including calculations of the rate of acceleration in a non-vacuum.

Lieberson's point is not dissimilar to the one Turner raised in connection with the cholera example and the determination of 'net effects', namely, the importance of a causal mechanism or law. The generalisations that variable analysis produces (which are all it can produce) are derived from a sample of some population and the measures of correlation summarising the relationships among the variables found in that sample. But these can only be empirical generalisations, and no empirical generalisation can logically entail a law.

The fact that empirically A has always been followed by B does not imply that it will always be followed by B. Indeed, not all statements of the logical form 'Whenever A, then B' can be treated as law-like in the sense required by science. What are sometimes called 'nomological generalisations' – the laws of science – support subjunctive and counterfactual conditional statements whereas 'empirical generalisations' do not. For example, the law concerning the effect of dissolved solids on the boiling point of a liquid entitles a subjunctive conditional such as, 'If this solid salt were dissolved in this pan of boiling water then the boiling point would be raised'. The law, along with statements about the initial conditions stating that the law is applicable to this particular case, entitles us to make such a statement. Similarly, it lends support to counterfactuals such as, 'If this piece of solid salt had been dissolved in water, though it was not – the boiling point of the water would have been raised.' In short, 'nomological generalisations' enables us to make inferences about cases that do not now

> **Nomological and empirical generalisations**

occur, have not occurred in the past and may not occur in the future. None of these characteristics apply to empirical generalisations. The generalisation that all the people in this room are under 6 feet tall does not entitle the inference that any future incomer to the room will be under 6 feet tall. Although a number of such generalisations may have always held, this will be a contingent fact rather than a consequence of a law-like connection between the properties in question or, more basically, of there being a scientific theory from which the generalisation can be derived.

Suppose, for example, that after intensive studies of samples of individuals we find a high positive correlation between the number of siblings in families and poor educational performance. If we wanted to use the generalisation to explain why little Johnny with 12 brothers and sisters is not doing very well at school, then it might be offered as an explanation. But what about the other factors which play a part? How do we know, in this particular case, whether it is the number of siblings which causes the poor performance rather than, say, Johnny's passion for soccer, his dyslexia, or whatever else might characterise little Johnny's life and circumstance. Could, to put it briefly, little Johnny's educational performance be deduced from the generalisation? Equally briefly, the answer is no and for two major reasons:

- The laws offered in natural science establish the *ceteris paribus* conditions under which the applicability of the law is judged. In this example – and in most social science examples – these conditions have not been determined.
- The lack of a theory from which to derive the generalisation and, importantly, of a the statement of the conditions under which the theory will apply, means that any application will have to be determined *post hoc*. Though the mechanisms involved here have an intuitive plausibility – for example, a large family means less time for study, less parental attention for any one child, sibling rivalry and so on – this ad hoc process is not quite what is to be expected from a scientific theory and the observations that might be deduced from it.

There are, in fact, any number of theories which could explain little Johnny's poor educational performance, some which are consistent with the generalisation but many which are not, and for which the empirical connection between the number of siblings and educational performance is an irrelevance. There is no way to derive measurements which would enable us to calculate the relative effects of the different variables. Since the generalisation is drawn from samples, all we have is a statistical generalisation stating that a property (number of siblings) is associated, with a particular strength and direction, with another property (educational performance). From this nothing follows about any particular instance. A deductive conclusion cannot be found, only an inductive one. Premises made up of such generalisations can only lend support.

Yet, one might argue, surely such analyses show something. They strike us as intelligible, as at least suggestive of possible causal relationships. Indeed, there are principled arguments, notably those of Weber, that this is all we should want from social science (Turner, 1997; Turner and Factor, 1994). Anything more would result in pseudo-science if not drivel. In making the kind of practical decisions that governments, business and administrations need to make, testing causal beliefs against available data as effectively as possible is the best that we can do even though we may know that the real causal mechanisms are misrepresented by the models we use. After all, and to mention but one example, these days most governments make use of such models, often highly complicated, for economic and financial planning and, occasionally, adjustments are made to them in light of changing economic circumstances, or shifts in consumption patterns, or changes in taxation policies and so on. And, in important ways, these are classic statistical problems. For us, the issue is whether they can work for sociological problems.

However, the more fundamental issue in all of this is not so much a technical matter about the statistics, despite the fact that efforts continue to develop more sophisticated causal modelling techniques (see, for example, Humphreys and Freedman, 1996; Glymour, 1997). It is a question of whether the statistical assumptions that are necessary for the mathematics 'fit with' sociological assumptions. But, as Freedman points out, in the social sciences statistical assumptions are rarely made explicit, let alone validated. Instead, when this approach is seriously called into question, what we have is a range of responses from 'indignation to obscurantism' of the kind he offers below, and which plead the practical difficulty of doing better than this rather than answering the serious question being asked:

> We all know that. Nothing is perfect. Linearity is a good first approximation. The assumptions are reasonable. The assumptions don't matter. The assumptions are conservative. You can't prove the assumptions are wrong. The biases will cancel. We can model the biases. We're only doing what everybody else does. Now we use more sophisticated techniques. What would you do? The decision-maker has to be better off with us than without us. We all have mental models, not using a model is still a model.
>
> (Humphreys and Freedman, 1997: 154)

Of course, this is a debate which will simmer on, mainly because causal modelling is a technique whose use goes well beyond sociology to include economics, biology, agriculture and medicine, among others. But, as we reiterate, our focus has been on how far they meet the ambitions of the positivist programme and, from this point of view, the answer must be 'not very far'.

Conclusions

Much of this chapter has been concerned to discuss the failings of the positivist programme from the point of view of the ambitions which the programme set itself. However, as we said earlier, it survives happily, though in sociology not perhaps with the same zest and confidence that it once had. Social surveys are done, interviews carried out, questionnaires filled in, data banks developed, reports written, papers published. Methods teaching is almost a mandatory part of a sociological education, and much of this consists of the methods associated with positivism. However, in Europe particularly, the programme no longer has the legitimacy it once claimed for itself for many reasons, not all of which were problems inherent to positivism; some of these will be discussed in the following sections.

But positivism cannot entirely escape blame for its loss of pre-eminence. In view of its ambition to create an integrated apparatus of theory–method–data, in the end it failed to think its problems through. By trying to make progress as fast as possible, it endeavoured to patch things up when they proved difficult, and let things pass hoping that eventually they would come right. During the early years serious effort was put in and the work of Lazarsfeld and his colleagues, among a growing number of others, remains an important testament to the ambition to turn sociology into a science – albeit a particular version of science. At the time it amounted to an intellectual revolution of no mean achievement. An apparatus of methods of social research was assembled in relatively short order, often by begging, borrowing and stealing from other domains. However, despite the commitment to producing an integrated apparatus of theory–method–data, the infrastructure of the positivist project was constructed out of opportunistically connected elements, ones that were readily available, even if they could not be combined in the tight way that a principled integration of theory, measurement and research would have needed. The combination of aspirations to formal theory, variable analysis, non-experimental statistics and the social survey proved not to be synergistic in practice in the way required to fulfil the ambitions of the positivist project. In fact, the project suffered just as much as sociology at large from the very problem it had diagnosed to begin with: that is, that the development of supposedly needed resources was always someone else's problem. Theorists could continue to complain about the quality of research and data, researchers could continue to complain about the lack of proper and usable theory, and both theorists and researchers could decide, independently of each other, which sociological ideas they would favour and cultivate. Within the positivist project itself, therefore, effort was disproportionately concentrated on developing a framework for measurement and hypothesis testing, with the result that methods came to be in the driving seat.

But, and this was another respect in which the positivist project turned out to be in the same boat as the rest of sociology, when the going got tough, when many of the central assumptions of the methods began to look sociologically suspect, the requirements stemming from those assumptions were often relaxed, a move which frequently was tantamount to abandoning them altogether. However, the point of setting such strict requirements in the first place was to impose a firm discipline on sociological practice. In other words, it is one thing to outline a programme for a scientific sociology, but something rather different, and endlessly more problematic, to realise such a programme and to achieve much more than notional examples of the kind of things the programme could potentially do if it was followed through.

One indicator of the practical difficulties in which the positivist project became becalmed was the 'confessional literature' which briefly flowered in the 1960s when positivism was coming under threat by forces outside sociology itself. In this literature many prominent sociologists 'came clean' about the way they had actually conducted their research (Hammond, 1964). It turned out that this was not the way they had outlined in the methods sections of their initial research reports, nor in strong accord with the requirements set by the strategies their studies were supposed to instantiate. What comes across strongly in much of this literature is how difficult it was to meet the strategy's requirements, and that sacrificing them seemed necessary if the research was to be done at all. The practical difficulties had to be dealt with in ways that were not themselves recognised as recommended procedure but that were nonetheless critical in making the research the success that much of it came to be. However, little of this led to a questioning of the whole enterprise of variable analysis.

> 'confessional' literature

With the wonderful privilege of hindsight one of the basic mistakes of the positivist project was commitment to the idea that it was possible in effect to plan to take sociology into an fully quantitative science, whereas the natural sciences themselves had developed under emergent and unforeseen conditions. As things stood, the positivists' efforts were caught in an unresolved tension between their promotion of stringent methodological standards and their failure, in practice, to live up to them (a tension that was unresolved because it was largely not addressed, except in the ad hoc manner necessary to fix enough practical problems to get the research done). Positivism ended up as another instance of a common phenomenon in sociology: namely, an ambitious manifesto for the future of the discipline with a subsequent failure to follow through. Despite the initial hopes and aspirations, and at times downright arrogance, it failed to deliver itself as the paragon of social research. But given its assertiveness, the reactions against it were bound to be strong.

> Quantitative vs qualitative research

We do not apologise for presenting the controversy between positivists and their opponents as one between 'quantitative' and 'qualitative' approaches to sociology since we regard these as providing a historically sensitive way of understanding the antipathy between the 'quantitative' and the 'qualitative' in sociology. It is often argued that the opposition to quantitative work in sociology involved some sort of stupid animosity to the quantitative *per se*, rooted perhaps in the innumeracy of many recruits to sociology. As a supposed correction to this antipathy, it is often pointed out that the quantitative and the qualitative are not utterly distinct. Quantitative research involves qualitative elements – and unavoidably so – while, in certain respects, qualitative work can and does contain quantitative elements. However, we do not think that the historical or contemporary situations are at all well described as an opposition between the quantitative and the qualitative as such. We are not denying that there were, and continue to be, powerful antipathies, but it is important to understand the reasons for them rather than treating them as though they were a kind of over-sight. The opposition is between the 'quantitative' and the 'qualitative', the former as the supposed bearer of positivism's ambitions and, therefore, as the exemplar of methodological virtue in sociology.

The appearance of numbers or quantitative expressions in sociological texts does not necessarily qualify those texts as quantitative if, as the critics argued, the numbers are rather arbitrarily assigned to the phenomena they are alleged to describe and if, further, those numbers are not assigned in a manner which conforms to the requirements of measurement and do not, therefore, really qualify for mathematical manipulation. In other words, 'quantification' in sociology was criticised for being only a make-do version of measurement.

Much the same point can be made in respect of the opposition to science where it is a complaint against 'science'. There is no reason why someone who opposes 'quantitative' methods in sociology should necessarily be seen as opposing science, anymore that someone who declines to be treated by a person wearing a white coat in necessarily showing an antipathy toward being treated by doctors. Wearing a white coat is not a medical qualification and arbitrarily assigning numbers is not a scientifically justified quantification. As we will shortly show, Herbert Blumer's critique of variable analysis is that it has only superficial and inessential resemblances to comparable practice in the natural sciences. Accordingly, it cannot be exemplary of a particularly scientific way of doing things, let alone be the only scientific way of doing social research. In brief, below are some key 'qualitative' oppositions to quantitative sociology, in that the former:

- does not involve any intrinsic opposition to quantification
- shows perhaps a greater rather than a lesser respect for science in that it sees that the achievement of the natural sciences involved the overcoming of serious difficulties and, perhaps, a greater unwillingness to indulge the practical need to compromise the strict requirements of mathematics and measurement than is present in contemporary social research.

In a fundamental way, the critics and defenders are apt to agree on a basic point: that if quantitative methods are truly to be developed in sociology, then doing this will be formidably difficult, as the persistent failure of the positivist project to achieve lift-off shows. Both sides agree that the 'successes' of the positivist project – such as they are, and they might be many – are largely inconsequential in relation to its larger ambitions for sociology and social research. The difference, over which the two sides do not see eye to eye, is whether 'biting off more than one can chew' is, in this case, a virtue.

But if the positivist project failed so signally, why progress through the logical structure of its approach so extensively as we have done? The main reason is that the great bulk of practice in and writing about 'social research methods' is within the framework of the social survey, multivariate statistics and hypothesis-testing conception of the role of sociological research, although this now continues without dependence upon the positivist project, and without the sense of purpose provided by it. The revolt against the positivist project was a successful one but not because it eliminated the positivist influence from sociology. On the contrary: this influence remains a strong, though not as a *project*, even a dominant force in sociology in terms of practitioners, especially in the United States, working by means of the survey, variable identification and hypothesis testing, and multivariate statistics. Thus, understanding the logic outlined and discussed in this part of the book is necessary to understanding why social research methods are constituted in the way that they are, why those who use the social survey use it in the way they do, and what the rationale for all this actually is.

What the revolt against positivism did achieve was a demotion of positivist research methods from positivism's status as a convincing project-in-hand, and from its intellectual predominance. Certainly within American sociology the vast bulk of the sociological research undertaken is closer to the positivist tradition and its legacy than to the positions that rebelled against it. However, most of those working within the positivist tradition are now largely making routine applications of its resources and essaying incremental improvements in its techniques, rather than attempting to overcome the frustrating difficulties that the initial foray into the project had failed to overcome.

However, along with its orthodox practices of social research, the project has bequeathed a sense that there is something rather more scientific and meritorious about continuing in the ways of this orthodoxy. There is perhaps a residual sense of the project that leaves a hard-to-eradicate impression that one ought to be working toward making sociology a true science. And there is often an air of wistful disappointment that things have not turned out as hoped and that sociology still fails to make progress in this regard. Those who persist in the conviction that sociology should make progress toward a properly scientific status are apt to be realistic about their own efforts, realising that they have not made the hoped-for advance and are unlikely to do so in the foreseeable future. Nonetheless, they tend to retain a sense that there is something meritorious about what they do. John Skvoretz (2000), for example, reviewing his own involvement over 30 years in attempts at mathematical sociology, confides that, 'as personally frustrating' as the failure of mathematical sociology to make any impact may be, those who engage in this exercise 'can take solace in the belief that we are doing the kind of work that must be done to construct a cumulative body of knowledge about social processes and structures' (p. 510). Thus, in this case, the idea of sociology as an empirically cumulative, quantitative discipline modelled after the natural sciences persists, along with the conviction that – although these days sociology-at-large resists, even rejects, such ambitions – nonetheless this is what sociology actually needs. However dubious the immediate prospects are, persisting with the methods is necessary so that sociology will eventually flourish in the way desired.

Nevertheless, for sociology the positivist project has been demoted and it no longer has the pre-eminent status it once had; its claim to exemplary status have been marginalised. The whole point of the opposition to positivism was to enable the pursuit of alternative conceptions of what sociology might be and, especially, to affirm that qualitative research was in no way inferior to the flawed practices of positivistic quantitative research.

Selected bibliography and suggested reading

■ See the previous chapter for material on causal modelling, especially the collection edited by McKim and Turner, *Causality in Crisis? Statistical Methods and the Search for Causal Knowledge in the Social Sciences* (University of Notre Dame Press, 1997). In addition, Stanley Leiberson's *Making it Count: The Improvement of Social Research and Theory* (The University of California Press, 1995) is not always an easy read for the mathematically unsophisticated but is very well worth looking at.

■ The 'confessional literature' includes P. Hammond's *Sociologists at Work: Essays on the Craft of Social Research* (Basic Books, 1964), which was, perhaps, the most notorious at the time.

■ See also J. Berger, M. Zelditch and B. Anderson, *Sociological Theories in Progress*, Vols 1–3 (Sage, 1989).

Part II

The Qualitative Turn

Chapter 8

The Contest over Realism: Introduction

We have tried to show that neither the positivist project nor its quantitative offshoot were pieces of stupidity. In their context they were plausible, even seductive, ideas that sought to remedy pretty obvious shortcomings in much of extant sociology. Those who took up the project were aware that working out how to fulfil their ambitions would be a long-term affair that would have to face many difficulties and surely encounter numerous setbacks. As we have shown, they were often quite self-conscious about the divergence between the ideals of the project and the often compromised state of their practice. For many this was an unavoidable transitional phase in the project's development. However, for others these difficulties were symptomatic of deeper problems, ones that were either profoundly strategic or, perhaps, even constitutional.

Without necessarily casting doubt on the ultimate viability of the positivist project, the strategy used to carry it out could be regarded as inappropriate to realising its objective. Though it might seem to make moves in the right direction, this was only a misleading impression of progress. Mao Tse-tung once proclaimed that the longest journey must begin with a single step. On the other hand, making the highest jumps into the air that one can does not achieve even the first moves toward landing someone on the moon. More searching critics of the positivist project, such as Herbert Blumer (1956) in his condemnation of 'variable analysis', subscribed not to the Maoist epithet of its efforts but to the latter reservation. As we shall see, Blumer does not challenge the aim of variable analysis. Rather, he questions whether its practices, particularly as far as measurement in sociology was concerned, were a sound and sensible basis for fulfilling the aims of the positivist project.

Other critics did, however, raise doubts about the ultimate viability of the project. The difficulties it faced were not temporary problems that would eventually be overcome. They were much more stubborn and perhaps insuperable for a sociology conceived on positivist lines and according to the strategy described above. Maybe the requirements of formal and quantitative representation can be satisfied in at least some of the natural sciences, but – perhaps – they cannot, except in the most superficial way, be satisfied in the case of social phenomena. Harold Garfinkel and Aaron Cicourel raised this possibility (and it is, as we shall see, an issue which eventually blew up into the intellectual storm often called, 'the crisis of representation') by pointing to the lack of the necessary 'isomorphism' between the categories of natural language and those of a logico-mathematically formulated apparatus. In sum, and we shall elaborate this point later after a review of Blumer's critique of the variable, the positivist methodological apparatus looked to them more like a Procrustean bed, that is, a kind of forcing device rather than an instrument for the sensitive exploration of the lineaments of social life. The methodological difficulties of positivism were much more than temporary problems and, moreover, were not only about methods.

Inset 8.1 Procrustes

Procrustes, or 'one who stretches', was a robber who preyed on travellers along the road to Athens by offering them hospitality on a magical bed that would fit any guest. He then either stretched his victims or cut off their legs to make them fit the bed. Hence, the notion of a 'Procrustean bed'. In the context of the positivist project, it is a critique which claims that positivism and its methods became the arbiter of what social reality must be like, and anything that could not be handled within its terms of reference had to be excluded from the reality as specified by positivism.

Procrustes came to a suitably ironic end. Theseus cut off his head to make him fit his own bed!

As we have already pointed out, reactions against the positivist programme were already under way even during its heyday. As early as the mid-1950s, Herbert Blumer, in his presidential address to the American Sociological Association, mounted a strong critique of variable analysis (Blumer, 1956). However, the critique is not simply about methods; it is more fundamental than that in raising the issue of the nature of sociological inquiry itself. Blumer's inspiration was the tradition which became known as symbolic interactionism, deriving from the early pioneering studies of the Chicago School of Sociology in the years after the First World War blended with the social psychology of George Herbert Mead (1863–1931).

In this relatively long introduction to Part II we discuss three thinkers who set out clear reactions against the positivist programme and identified some of the main issues involved in the qualitative turn.

Blumer's critique of 'the variable'

Blumer's critique begins with a diagnosis of a problem of sociology that we have met before, namely, the gap between sociological theory and empirical reality. Theory is glaringly divorced from the empirical world that it putatively claims to say something about. To a large extent it is compartmentalised in a world of its own. Theory feeds on itself. Theoretical critiques follow theoretical critiques but little of this is systematically connected to any empirical checks. Theory has its own courses and its own literature, and consists primarily of the exegesis of theoretical schemes old and new. Old ideas are translated into a new vocabulary, with the occasional addition of a new notion based upon reflections on other theories. Schemes from outside sociology are readily imported – the organic analogy, behaviouralism, psychoanalysis, economics and, one might add as more recent examples, catastrophe theory, structural linguistics and complexity theory – but the result is that when applied to the empirical world theory becomes primarily a way of interpreting the world, 'not a studious cultivation of empirical facts to see if the theory fits. In terms of both origin and use social theory seems in general not to be geared into its empirical world' (Blumer, 1954: 53).

> The gap between theory and research

So far such a critique of social theory would be recognisable to the positivist programme. Indeed, it was just such a diagnosis that fuelled the development of its own cure. Nor would the positivists demure from Blumer's recommendations about what needs to be done. Social theories need to abandon their navel gazing and, instead, get more in touch with the empirical world. Stop taking in each other's washing but work with empirical data. Stop importing fanciful ideas from other disciplines and, instead, cultivate one's own empirical fields. Abandon the practice of interpreting things and determine to test theories, which will mean casting theories into a form which makes them testable.

However, for Blumer such recommendations merely state the problem not its solution. By themselves they cannot provide the answer to what is wrong with social theory. He concurs with the positivists that the deeper problem is the lack of precise meaning of sociological concepts. It is at this point, however, that he departs from the positivist line. Though acknowledging that, as variable analysis, it has made a serious attempt to grapple with the problem by developing procedures to give concepts a definite empirical content, he does not think that these efforts have succeeded. Nor does he believe that the zealous and persistent pursuit of trying to make the procedures more and more refined will improve matters.

Blumer has no desire to eliminate variable analysis altogether since it has made a worthy contribution to sociology. What he does oppose, however, is the inclination to treat variable analysis as if it were *the* model of sociological research, as if it were the standard against which all sociological research should be judged. The fundamental objection to the positivist programme and variable analysis is that it misconceives the nature of sociological concepts and, accordingly, efforts to improve the methods cannot succeed.

Sensitising concepts

As we saw in Part I, the ideal for variable analysis was to create definitive concepts, that is, concepts which could be given a clear abstract and general definition, and which could be applied to diverse instances by identifying common characteristics from the specification of the concept. Of course, it was realised that this was no easy task, but the procedures of indicator construction, measurement and pattern searching were all intended to aid this ideal. However, Blumer holds that the concepts of sociology are not definitive but sensitising ones. Concepts such as 'norms', 'institution', 'social process', 'social system', for example, are less than definitive, as the positivists would agree. At best, such concepts point to possible phenomena, direct our attention, get us to think about what social life might be. They rest on a vague sense of what they might mean rather than on any precise specification of properties. What the positivists sought to do, however, was repair such 'deficiencies' by turning them into definitive concepts through stipulation and indicator construction. In Blumer's view, this would not improve such concepts since the 'deficiencies' are part of their nature and the positivist approach would, accordingly, transform them out of all recognition. It would divest them of the value they have for assisting our understanding of social life.

Blumer does not intend to mount an unqualified defence of sensitising concepts. Indeed he accepts that they need to be made as clear as possible but insists that this must be 'patient, careful and imaginative'. What he is arguing for is a slow cure not a quick fix. As he says:

> It is not achieved by inventing new technical instruments or by improving the reliability of old techniques – such instruments and techniques are neutral to the concepts on behalf of which they may be used. The clarification of concepts does not come from piling up mountains of research findings. ... By the same token, the mere extension of research in scope and direction does not in itself offer assurance of leading to clarification of concepts.
>
> (Blumer, 1954: 55)

Blumer's complaint is very much directed at what is, in his eyes, a premature and misleading effort on the part of variable analysis to solve the problems of sociological theory by means of procedures which impose a set of preconceptions onto the phenomena they are claiming to investigate. However, if we want to remain faithful to social phenomena then, for the time being at least, we will need to work with sensitising concepts.

Sensitising concepts do not pick out their instances directly. They give no clean-cut identification of instances but provide only a general – 'vague' as the critics would say – sense of what is relevant to identify an instance of a concept. The phenomena we seek to bring under our sociological concepts are hetero-geneous and we cannot eliminate, by arbitrary decision, the distinctive features of the diverse instances to arrive at some common core characteristics. What sensitising concepts cover is 'shaped up' in a different way in each instance. What the concept provides, as the name suggests, is a direction for the researcher, sensitising him or her to certain issues, giving an orientation to the examination of the instance. One moves out from the concept to the concrete distinctiveness of the instance instead of embracing the instance in some abstracted framework. The researcher has the obligation to make the concepts match up with the circumstances at hand rather than moulding the data to fit the concepts. The concept itself points one toward certain kinds of consideration, giving only 'clues and suggestions'. Blumer holds that if we are genuinely to understand the phenomena that our concepts attempt to capture, then we will be forced to work with sensitising concepts. Such concepts can be improved, but this process will not be a miraculous trans-formation. It will only come through the deep investigation of a growing diver-sity of instances, so giving the concepts 'more fitting abstraction and keener discrimination'.

> Nature of sensitising concepts

What Blumer has in mind here can be illustrated by the concept of negotia-tion. It is an idea relevant to many domains, ranging from politics, through industrial relations, legal proceedings, interper-sonal relations and international politics to busi-ness life, and studied by economists, psychologists and conflict theorists as well as sociologists (See, for example, Raiffa, 1982; Pruitt, 1981; Strauss, 1978). If we were to follow the procedures of variable analysis, what we would have to do is distil from the many studies some conception of the concept, deter-mine its properties and then derive indicators for them. It is this very process that Blumer is questioning. For one thing we could only do this if we ignore the differ-ences between the ways in which different disciplines conceive of negotiation. Such differences are not simply incidental characterisations of the same concept but are often deeply rooted in the respective disciplines' theoretical and analytic interests. Economists, for example, might well be interested in negotiation from the point of view of business behaviour or what it says about economic ration-ality. Moreover, such conceptions are likely to be idealisations which, in their own terms, might well serve some purpose. However, Blumer's point is that proceduralising concept formation in the way that variable analysis proposes is doomed to failure. In sociological terms, all such a concept can do is direct our attention toward the kind of things in the empirical world which might be char-acterisable as negotiations, without any presuppositions that the kinds of nego-tiations one might find in businesses, in markets, in law courts, in the United Nations, between trade unions and management and so on have qualities in

> Example: negotiation

common. They might well have, but equally they might well not. It is up to empirical research to fill out the notion and, as part of this, also illuminate other concepts with which it is affiliated, such as rationality, influence, commitment, decision making and role performance, among others.

In many respects, what Blumer is proposing does not look radically different from what variable analysis in its earlier incarnations was recommending. But this was before procedure and method began to dominate. In fact, Blumer is reversing the positivist strategy by arguing that general concepts should be used as tools to explore complex instances instead of, as variable analysis proposed, accumulating large numbers of – in Blumer's view – cursorily considered instances from which to extract a generalisation.

Of course, the difference between the proponents of variable analysis and Blumer's subtle but radical proposal will remain hard to resolve. The former will insist that capturing the phenomena by developing definitive concepts is what scientific understanding involves. Equally, Blumer can simply reiterate that all this does is impose a set of preconceptions on social phenomena rather than investigating them. For him, the results of variable analysis are, at best, interesting but bare. They provide only a superficial understanding of the phenomena which they seek to represent as variables. So, while variable analysis is not devoid of merit, it is limited and should not be accepted as providing the general form of sociological inquiry, but must co-exist with other, and potentially more sociologically effective strategies that, though they would not satisfy positivist criteria, are not thereby outlawed. But then, variable analysis failed to satisfy positivist criteria.

So far Blumer's complaint against variable analysis looks tactical rather than strategic, radical rather than revolutionary. It is when he starts to raise the issue of meaning and context that matters become more serious.

Meaning and context

Meaning and context are central to the issues that Blumer is raising as concepts; they play a pivotal role in the campaign against positivism and, as we shall see, originate in a number of sociological traditions. The point that Blumer is drawing attention to is that social phenomena consist, in important respects, in the meaning they have for people (Blumer, 1969). However, meaning is not intrinsic to any kind of phenomenon, social or otherwise, but is attributed by the members of society. How a person responds to an event depends upon what meaning the person assigns to it. People who see a red light at a crossroads will respond to it as a signal to stop, whereas if they see a red light in a window, they are likely to treat it as something else entirely.

A 'red light' does not, *of itself*, mean either 'stop!' or 'come in'. Further, even if the light is understood to mean the same thing to two different individuals, it does not follow that they will each react to it in the same way. Some will accept the invitation in the window, while others will be repelled by it. In the language of variable analysis, what connects the 'independent variable' – the 'red light' – with the 'dependent variable' – the behaviour or action – depends upon the meaning given to the 'independent variable'. As such it is not the 'independent variable' which impacts upon the 'dependent variable' but the 'independent variable as interpreted' by the members of society.

However, Blumer is saying more than that a process of interpretation connects the 'independent' and the 'dependent' variables. The variables themselves are also phenomena of interpretation. Thus, sociologists who operate with variables as abstract conceptions do not know what meaning these variables might have for those who react to them and, as a consequence, do not know what relationships variables have to social behaviour and conduct.

> The process of interpretation

Contrary to positivist precepts, variable concepts cannot operate as definitive concepts but are sensitising ones and, what is more, operate in this way for the members of society. Variables, for example, are often tied to given historical and cultural situations for their meanings. The examples that Blumer himself cites are 'attitudes toward the Supreme Court', 'intention to vote Republican', 'interest in the United Nations', a 'college education' and 'factory employment', and one could go on and on. Even though such variables might be treated as indicators of supposedly more general concepts, such as 'social class' or 'political preference', the fact remains that at the level of data collection, the meanings of the variables and their application are restricted to groups or categories at the time the research was done.

Other and more abstract sociological concepts, such as 'social cohesion', 'social integration', 'assimilation', 'authority', 'morale' and the like, have no fixed or uniform indicators. Instead indicators have to be constructed to fit the research problem. Thus, certain features are chosen to indicate the social integration of cities, say, while other indicators are used to represent the social integration of teenage gangs. Even such generic variables as 'sex', 'age', 'birth rate' and 'time period,' while applicable universally to social life, in their use in the field do not, and cannot, function as generic variables. Each has a content that is given by the particular instance of its application. Thus, and again following Blumer's own examples, we have the sex distribution *of* Nebraska, or the age distribution *of* St Louis. In short, variable analysis can only provide 'here and now' findings, wherever the 'here' is and whenever the 'now' is timed.

However, to adequately understand a 'here and now' relationship it is necessary to understand the context, which variable analysis fails to do. It identifies a single relationship stripped bare of just those things that sustain it in a 'here and now' context. The very business of abstracting from the process of interpretation that goes on in social life can only give an impoverished picture of actual social phenomena. Not only is the social process an interpretative one for Blumer, it is frequently collective and complex and not to be captured by definitive concepts, since the empirical reference of a true sociological variable is neither unitary nor distinct.

Admittedly, variable analysis has claimed that it can look at context and meaning. Attitude scales, for instance, could be construed as attempts to obtain data on the subjective meaning that social phenomena have. Similarly, gathering data on the wider context in which some relationship of interest is embedded could be argued to provide a better understanding of the variable relationship. However, Blumer's point is more fundamental, attacking not the intentions of variable analysis but in the way it treats concepts as determinate rather than as sensitising ones.

Critique of variable analysis

Let us take one of Blumer's own examples, that of the relationship between a birth control programme and the birth rate among some population. If we look at the actual social character of variables we are likely to find these to be both an intricate and changing complex. For example, there would seem to be a fairly clear-cut variable relation between a birth control programme and the birth rate. As variables the 'programme of birth control' and the 'birth rate' can be given a simple and unitary character. For the programme of birth control one can choose merely its time period or select some other reasonable measure, such as the number of people visiting a birth control clinic. The birth rate is even more straightforward, being simply the number of births per 1000 of the population over a time period.

However, a scrutiny of what the two variables stand for in the life of the group gives a very different picture. If we view the programme of birth control in terms of how it enters into people's lives, we would need to take regard of such things as the literacy of the people, the clarity of the printed information, the manner and extent of its dissemination, the social position of the programme's directors and other personnel, the way in which people define attendance at birth control clinics, the views of influential people about the programme, their status and power, and the nature of the discussion among people about the clinics and the programme. And these are but a few of the matters to consider in determining how the programme enters into the life of the people concerned – and this is only the independent variable. A similarly complex understanding will be required for the dependent variable. There are many social considerations affecting, for example, sex acts, including the prescribed relations between mean and women, conceptions of manliness and womanhood, the organisation of home life, and more.

Blumer's general lesson is that the corrective to positivism and variable analysis is to look closer at actual cases in order to gain a better sociological understanding of what it is that the abstractions actually stand for. In this way, the clarity of the concepts can be improved and sociological understanding furthered. However, he does not hold out hope of a sudden and drastic leap from sensitising concepts to definitive ones. Indeed, Blumer can be construed as suggesting that, in principle, no such move can be made. Thus, positivism and its tool, variable analysis, while not expelled from sociology is denied its claim to premier status as *the* method of social research. It remains a viable but limited mode.

Blumer's critique was very much directed at the failure of variable analysis, as he saw it, to adequately grasp the reality of what it was purportedly examining. Despite positivism's efforts to improve the ability of sociology to understand and explain social reality, the apparatus it developed distorted the very phenomena it was designed to investigate. Accordingly, as a sociological project positivism failed.

However for many, including Blumer, this did not necessarily mean abandoning the idea of a sociological science. It did mean abandoning the idea of a sociological science according to positivism. That was both premature and a misconception of what a science of social life would turn out to be like. Another strategy was needed if an adequate empirical sociology was to be developed.

Many of the critics of positivism during its heyday agreed with the diagnosis of what was wrong with sociology, but were less unanimous as to how its ills might be cured. What was rarely questioned was the need for sociology to produce theory, and ideally formal theory. What was challenged, however, was the idea that this could be achieved by formalising existing theory. As we argued in Chapter 3, in practice positivism had concentrated on the form of theory to the relative neglect of its sociological content. The idea was that presenting theories in a logically tight format would expose their weaknesses but, as we have suggested, the attempt to formalise existing theory did little better that provide translations of them. If a theory is not much good to begin with, then a cleaned up translation will not make it better. We do not need formalised theory or mathematical formalisation to tell us that sociological theories are rough and ready constructions at best, often with major inconsistencies (or 'tensions' as they are sometimes more charitably identified). Positivism did not pay enough attention to the fact that the weaknesses of sociological theory were sociological weaknesses, not ones of presentation or form.

Moreover, in positivism the role of research is essentially the passive one of testing theory. This was, in important respects, the burden of Blumer's complaint against sociological theory, namely, that it is developed without much reference to, or in conjunction with, empirical research. This was also, as we have pointed out previously, the point of Merton's proposal for 'middle-range theory' as a bridge between the 'grand theory' of such as Talcott Parsons and empirical research. However, and importantly, the complaint voiced by scholars such as Blumer was that in effect sociology needed to step back and examine the nature of its phenomena – namely, the lived experience of the members of society – rather than tinkering with positivism and variable analysis which, in the end, could not give an adequate account of social reality.

The next part of this chapter will review the work of Glaser and Strauss (1967), who took up the challenge of providing an alternative, and inverted, strategy for theory construction to the one deployed by positivism.

Inverting the strategy: grounded theory

The whole thrust of Blumer's critique was that positivism distorted the phenomenon of social life, namely, the lived world of social actors. The task for social research, then, was to gain access to that lived world. Glaser and Strauss accepted this challenge and also accepted that sociology should provide more than a rich description of ways of life and try to develop abstract theories which explain social action. The problem was how to do the latter? What they proposed, in contrast to the positivist strategy, was that theory should pay more attention to its content than to its form and by this means move toward developing theory. In other words, research should play a much more active role in developing theory than hypothesis testing and, in the first instance and probably a few instances after this, aim to develop less-than-general theories. Theories should be developed, grounded, in the results of research and apply to specific areas of social life.

The logic of their position is that, as a first step, the social researcher should gain access to the ordinary world of the members of society; more specifically, the members of some group or collectivity which is of interest to the research. As a next step the researcher needs to understand the what and how of what he/she does. To do this it is not necessary to immerse oneself in the sociological literature before entering the field. To do so could well mean that one's perceptions became shaped by those of sociology rather than gleaning the conceptions and perceptions of those being studied. More often than not, the kind of research Glaser and Strauss are recommending puts the researcher in the position of a stranger and having to find out the whats and wherefores of this new territory.

However, Glaser and Strauss recommend using preconceptions, sociological or otherwise, as 'sensitising concepts' in the way outlined by Blumer. Preconceptions give the researcher things to do and ask immediately. But they must not be treated as firm research orientations. Their purpose is to provide an initial orientation, used so that they can be abandoned, used to find aspects of others' lives that can confirm, rebut or transcend the initial preconceptions.

In grounded theory, unlike variable analysis, data collection, observation, coding and categorising the data go on simultaneously so that they are mutually supportive of each other. Coding is the general term Glaser and Strauss use for conceptualising data; it is dependent upon the aims of the research and should be open to modification. If, for example, a researcher is interested in negotiation, to use an earlier example – and it could be observations or informal interviews – the researcher would note, and code, instances of what initially look to be aspects of negotiations, comparing and refining the codes as the research proceeds. The main guideline offered is that of 'process': that is, the patterned interactions of persons over time which create and sustain what is often referred to as the social structure. This guideline arises from Glaser and Strauss' commitment to symbolic interactionism and its assumptions:

- that the social world is created and sustained by temporal patterns of social interaction among individuals
- individuals' interpretations of meanings and taking other individuals into account, determine their actions and, thus, the course of interaction itself.

As to what to look for in the field, what to compare, what to count, Glaser and Strauss propose a procedure of 'theoretical sampling'. This differs from that typical of variable analysis in which units are selected on the basis of how representative they are of some larger collection, in that one's initial coding – a first stab at 'what's going on' – is used to select further observations. The researcher needs to clarify 'what's going on', resolve uncertainties and anomalies, fill in parts of the process not yet observed, and so on. Coding and observing proceed together in a feedback process of constant comparisons. If, for example, by observing the process of 'becoming a mental patient' one has gained a good descriptive grasp from observing in a single mental hospital, then one needs to look at other hospitals. By comparing different groups undergoing the same process one can better determine similarities and differences and build up an even richer understanding of the process.

> Theoretical sampling

The whole approach, and the above is merely a sketch, is directed at making substantive theory grow out of the observed data derived from actual situations. This is achieved by constant feedback by first proceeding in a fairly ad hoc manner and then refining the data, and the categories used, by further observation. The observations and their coding force one to become progressively more and more abstract, so building theory out of the investigation of the lived world of social actors.

The grounded theory approach has, over the decades since its first promulgation, slowly gained prominence as a systematic method of qualitative social research, and has even received the dubious accolade of computing support for the development of grounded theory (See, for example, Strauss and Corbin, 1990; Fielding and Lee, 1991). It has even become an important mode of research in management science (Turner and Williams, 1983).

It is not perhaps so difficult to see why the approach has become so established as a counterpart to variable analysis since, in many respects, they share similar ambitions and, what is more, can be treated as if they were complementary. But more on this later.

The final set of ideas we want to consider in this introduction again takes issue with the claimed objectivity of the positivist programme's research procedures and develops the theme of 'faithfulness to the phenomena' but, this time, with a hint of a more radical sociological approach.

Bittner and faithfulness to the phenomena

Egon Bittner's (1973) attack on the positivist programme takes as its point of departure the claimed objectivity of the research procedures and findings that were so important to positivist claims. This emphasis on objectivity arises out of a commitment that the objectives of rational inquiry could only be served by strict compliance with the canons of objectivity. Failure to do so was condemned as 'subjective' and, hence, any resulting findings were not to be trusted as knowledge. The preoccupation of positivism with methods of research, techniques and, in its philosophical guise, the theory of knowledge, were a reflection of such a commitment. Bittner concurs that such a point of view, both of research methods and as a philosophy, might well be adequate for the growth of natural science. What he questions is whether this is adequate for the development of the social and cultural sciences.

The norms that govern objectivity in science are:

- the operational definition of meaning
- the strict formalisation of the rules of inference.

These are also the norms that positivism, in the form of variable analysis, sought to meet in the formalisation of theory and, perhaps more significantly, in the proceduralisation of methods of research and measurement. Conformity to the procedures should eliminate 'the unruly factor of subjectivity' (although, as we pointed out in previous chapters, this was harder to achieve than it first appeared). While such conceptions might be indispensable in the physical sciences, this is because they are attuned to the phenomena to which they are applied. Does it, however, make sense to apply them to the social sciences?

Bittner illustrates by asking whether it is worth the attempt to treat the notion of prestige in the same way that physical scientists treat velocity. His conclusion is that, despite many studies operationalising prestige and using mathematical modes of analysis, the normalisation of usage has not occurred in any way remotely like that achieved for the concept of velocity. Moreover, there are few grounds for hoping that such normalisation might be forthcoming about the concept of prestige or any other concepts of this kind. In other words, there is no promise of developing concepts in the way positivism proposed that will contribute to our understanding of society in the way that the concept of velocity, for example, contributed to our understanding of the physical world. In which case, taking a sceptical view of the principle of objectivity should be no loss.

However, Bittner is not proposing that we abandon scholarly endeavour nor that 'anything goes'. His argument is about the relationship between the canons of objectivity as set out earlier and the nature of social phenomena. He points out – an observation which will loom large elsewhere in the book – that sociologists always produce accounts about, provide theories of, phenomena of which accounts already exist. To use his own example: in analysing kinship structures the sociologist is analysing patterns of social relationships which are already known to those involved in them – kinship structures are the arrangements which people live by, the basis on which they allow marriage, assign responsibility for the raising of children and so on. Indeed, the sociologist is bound to base his or her analysis on what the social actors involved know; the interview and the questionnaire were explicitly designed to do just this. But, to meet the canons of objectivity, what social actors know has to be transformed into concepts which are, to use Blumer's term, determinate.

So far the argument should be a familiar one from the previous discussion. Bittner goes further, however, by drawing upon ethnomethodology and Harold Garfinkel's claim that all accounts – by this he means all the means of describing, analysing, questioning, criticising, believing, doubting idealising, schematising and so on – are 'unavoidably and irremediably tied to the social settings that occasion them or within which they are situated' (Garfinkel, 1967). This condition of what is known as 'reflexivity' involves more than simply the notion that ideas are influenced by their social setting. The claim is much stronger than this. It means that the factual realities of social settings are permeated through and through by the ways in which participants in them know them for what they are and how they might change. Thus, say, the sense of what goes on in an encounter between two persons in terms of what they say, what they are doing, depends on whether they are mother and son, shop assistant and customer, children at play, actors on the stage, policeman and offender, or in any other relationship. What transpires in the encounter derives its sense from the kind of encounter that it is and, in its turn, the encounter itself takes its character from what transpires within it.

> Reflexivity

The force of this argument, which will be developed in Chapter 10, is that accounts and actions – what people say, report on, describe, complain about, criticise, believe, what they do and so on – derive their sense from their occurrence within the lived social world. Accordingly, if we try to examine any particular encounter between persons in terms of 'definitive', or objective concepts, we will be forced to relax the canons of objectivity in order to apply them to this particular case and feel that it is accurately capturing the features of the case in hand. As we argued in the previous chapter, it is by relaxing the requirements of the methods that they can be made to work at all. Thus, concludes Bittner: 'paradoxically, it is the violation of outward stringencies of formalized research technique, not compliance with them, that betrays the researcher who feels a sense of doing justice to the object of his inquiry' (Bittner, 1973).

The ideal of objectivity embodied in the norms of operational definition and the formalisation of inference is unobtainable in sociology, because using them fails to do justice to the nature of social reality, fails to capture the features which make the phenomenon what it is.

Are there any prospects at all of having a science of society if we abandon the canons of objectivity? Here Bittner turns to a sociological tradition mentioned earlier in connection with our discussion of Blumer, namely, that associated with what became known as the Chicago School and the research done in the 1920s. What this research stood for, according to Bittner, was realism in the sense of 'faithfulness to reality'.

> The Chicago School

The work to which Bittner is alluding consists mainly of ethnographies of urban life. One of the distinctive features of these studies was that the researchers immersed themselves in the ways of life they were studying, using only the competencies and resources they possessed as members of society. Their focus was on the everyday life of the people they were studying with the aim of understanding that life as the social actors themselves understood it, and this Bittner wants to propose as the central task of the sociological project.

For Bittner, 'faithfulness to reality' is the methodological equivalent to the positivist canons of objectivity. But there is a fundamental contrast in the reasoning here. The positivists would no doubt want to maintain that they were no less concerned with remaining faithful to reality than their critics, but what is being objected to is their idea of what is required to remain faithful. The positivist idea is that remaining faithful to reality involves adhering to pre-given rules of inquiry, so that what does and does not capture reality is defined by those rules. The critics are attempting to raise the question as to whether the results that are obtained by loyal adherence to the rules of scientific inquiry provide anything that looks like the reality it is supposed to capture. They are suggesting, rather, that if anything approximating to the effective methods of the natural sciences is to exist in the social sciences, then it will have to be forged anew. Extending the 'scientific project' to social phenomena is not just a matter of picking up where the natural sciences left off, but one of starting afresh.

Bittner's arguments put three issues on the table:

- Does the positivist conception reflect an adequate understanding of the successes of the natural sciences, or does it mistake superficial aspects for profound ones?
- Is rigorous compliance with the positivist requirements of procedure a practical possibility in sociology? Does the failure of positivist research to live up to its own requirements show that there is a need to put the shoulder to the wheel in a much more determined fashion? Or is it a sign that the needs of real research into actual social life will inexorably compromise the positivist ideal?
- Have the results of positivist inquiries been at all proportionate to the sophistication of positivism's methodological conceptions? Have they identified any laws, do they give us a richer and deeper understanding of the phenomena they portray, or do they, rather, render impoverished, even distorted, portrayals of the phenomena, surrendering the realistic depiction of the phenomena to the dictates of method?

Even if one allowed the validity of positivist ambitions (for measurement, mathematisation and formal theory), one could reasonably argue both that this was a much longer-term project than contemporary positivists acknowledged, and – more profoundly – that following the positivist strategy in the short term was not the way to go about this. One could fault the strategy if not the aims. Indeed, one can echo Thomas Kuhn's (1977) comment about the rise of quantification in the natural sciences. Genuine, cogent measurement was born, he argues, out of a rich, accumulated qualitative understanding of the phenomena. Accordingly, the failure to appreciate the futility of measurement from nowhere is at least one part of positivism's failure to grasp the precedent of the successful natural sciences that they sought to emulate.

For these critics of the positivist project, then, the commitment to qualitative work was not a step backward but a step forward. Equally, from the critic's point of view, there was no loss of 'rigour'. The positivist's rigorous methods were only supposedly so, were more honoured in the breach than the observance, were deployed in a relaxed and indulgent rather than a genuinely stringent manner. Indeed, the transformation of qualitative data into purportedly quantitative representations was typically cavalier in its treatment. The accumulation and examination of qualitative materials need be no less principled and scrupulous than what was actually achieved in 'quantitative' work.

In any case, the stage of qualitative study might not be one which could be bypassed: if a rich qualitative understanding is a precondition of genuine quantitative work, then such an understanding was lacking.

Conclusion

What united these critics was their claim that positivism in the form of variable analysis must fail as the basis of a scientific sociology because its very methods misrepresented the nature of social reality. Methods had become merely ways of processing data rather than a means of exploring the actual nature of social life. Positivism had focused on the form of theory and method to the neglect of the content, namely, the social reality that should have been the objective of the theory and the methods. The theory and the methods which did emerge as variable analysis were simply not attuned to the nature of that social reality.

This argued for two important and related shifts in social research: first, adopting a different attitude to theory, and second, developing and using methods which were more attuned to the nature of social reality.

One of the things which comes out strongly in the critics just discussed is the complaint that the positivist strategy toward theory building, despite its own complaints against what had passed for theorising in sociology previously, had produced theories which were just as divorced from social life as lived, experienced and understood by the members of society. Though collecting data from the members of society, positivist methods transformed them into abstracted and, in the end, distorting concepts which served more the purposes of method than that of understanding the social reality they were originally designed to explore. The idea that theory needs to generate hypotheses to be tested may be appropriate for a mature science, but it is certainly premature for an underdeveloped one such as sociology.

> Problematising theory

What this did was to problematise theory building by insisting that theories should strongly connect to the everyday world of the members of society. This, in turn, led to an emphasis on looking at the social world from the point of view of the social actor in whatever milieu might be of interest. Although working out quite what this meant was to take some time, it was from the 'actor's point of view' that theory building should begin. There were two important consequences which flowed from this.

The first was to eschew the approach embodied in theories such as structural functionalism which were holistic in their focus on the total society as the main unit of theoretical analysis. Rather, the unit of analysis should be the social individual in interaction with others.

Second, theory building should cease to be a distinct activity in the discipline but become an integral part of the research process. Rather than deductive theory, with research having the role of testing theory, it should become more inductive in character, in that general theoretical claims should emerge out of the detailed study of cases. What was also denied, again in contrast to positivism, was the idea that theory had a canonical form. It was this insistence by positivism which, it was argued, had resulted in versions of the social actor, social activities and sociality itself which distorted the phenomena which should be the concern of sociology.

Similar arguments were advanced with respect to methods. The mistake of positivism was to try to adapt and develop methods which were regarded as conforming to the conception of science that positivism sought to implement for sociology. But this was simple to ape some version of the scientific method not to produce anything of substance. Instead, what was required were methods which actually captured the phenomena of interest. This was what we should have learned from the example of science: not the form but the substance.

> Problematising method

Research is a social transaction and the extent to which this is presupposed in methods needs to be made explicit. This positivist methods failed to do, despite the fact that the employment of common-sense knowledge of persons and society was essential to making the methods work. But more than this, if we are to take seriously the notion that social research needs to begin with understanding 'the actor's point of view', then we need methods which can accomplish this. Data collection, to put it in terms of the standard model, needs to access the members' points of view and understandings of the world in which they live out their lives. Data analysis needs to provide an exposition of members' points of view. It is by these means that sociology can begin to develop theories which have content and not merely form.

Selected bibliography and suggested reading

■ Blumer's paper 'What Is Wrong with Social Theory?' appeared in the *American Sociological Review*, 19, 1954, and his 'Sociological Analysis and the Variable' in *American Sociological Review*, 21, 1956. Also worth reading is his *Symbolic Interaction: Perspective and Method* (Englewood Cliffs, Prentice-Hall, 1969).

- Glaser and Strauss' *The Discovery of Grounded Theory; Strategies for Qualitative Research* (Chicago, Aldine, 1967) remains the standard text for this approach. However, a more recent account is A. Strauss and J. Corbin, *Basics of Qualitative Research: Grounded Theory Procedures and Techniques* (London, Sage, 1990). For those interested in computer-based techniques, see N.G. Fielding and R.M. Lee (eds), *Using Computers in Qualitative Research* (London, Sage, 1991).
- Bittner's paper, 'Objectivity and Realism in Sociology' is to be found in George Psathas' edited collection, *Phenomenological Sociology* (New York, Wiley, 1973).

Chapter 9

The Method of Fieldwork

In the previous chapter we outlined the theoretical and methodological reasons that drove some to reject the positivist project, particularly as instantiated in variable analysis and its drive toward quantification. Naturally enough, such criticisms led many to conclude that the alternative strategy must, of necessity, be 'qualitative'; at least in the short term.

Though the methods and approaches we are discussing in this part of the book are typically grouped under this more recent label, their lineage is, in sociology at least, older than variable analysis. The dichotomy 'quantitative and qualitative' gained its strength as reaction to the positivist project began to build and, as is not unusual with sociological dichotomies, simplifies rather more than it clarifies. This apart, we have already outlined the direction in which the approaches to be discussed here were inclined to move, arising out of what was seen as the *sociological* failure of positivism and variable analysis. Important in this regard was the insistence on recovering 'the actor's point of view' and using a method of research which was attuned to this task. The method was that of ethnography – or, as it was often called within sociology, 'participant observation' – which belonged to the older anthropological tradition.

In what follows we will begin with a brief outline of the ancestry of the method but the more important task is to relate the method to the sociological concerns which motivated it, along with an exposition of the practicalities of what the method involves.

The ancestry

Ethnography owes its origins to travellers' tales of foreign climes, and ultimately came to be refined and incorporated as *the* method of research in anthropology. Given anthropology's concern with the lives of exotic peoples, most of whom were preliterate and hence kept no records which could be used by researchers, there was little option but to study them by living among them. However, as far as sociology is concerned, the roots of ethnography retrospectively lie in the studies associated with the University of Chicago in the early quarter of the twentieth century.

There are three elements important to this story:

- the distinctive research style which came to be the hallmark of the Chicago School
- the notion that the way in which social actors thought of their world was consequential for their actions
- the elaboration of a set of ideas which came to be known as symbolic interactionism.

However, these ideas did not develop 'of a piece', so to speak, but rather were brought together as a coherent methodological approach in the late 1940s and 1950s, stimulated in large part by the success of the Lazarsfeldian programme, by proposing what was argued to be a more properly sociological strategy for theory building and research.

A distinctive research style

During the second decade of the twentieth century, the Sociology Department at the University of Chicago under the leadership of W.I. Thomas, Robert Park and Ernest Burgess, began a series of studies into various aspects of the social life of the city of Chicago. Interestingly, in that it presaged similar complaints voiced by the positivists some years later, one of the prime motivations for the studies was to improve the then current state of sociological theory. In the United States of the time, evolutionary and holistic theories tended to dominate. These were vast discursive constructions dealing with the evolution of human society, and poorly based on empirical research. Nor was the situation much better in Europe.

Park and Burgess were also strongly interested in social reform and felt that sociology could, potentially, make an important contribution to improving the conditions of large sections of society, and there was nowhere better to explore this possibility than Chicago. From the 1870s onwards, the city had grown into a major metropolis and the dominant city in the mid-west. It was also a conglomeration of various national and ethnic groups, including Irish, Poles, Scandinavians, Germans and Russians as well as the growing number of Blacks from the southern states seeking better jobs and an escape from the racism and rural poverty of the South. Park and Burgess urged that Chicago should be treated as a laboratory for the study of the social processes of assimilation and adjustment within a rapidly growing urban milieu (Bulmer, 1984).

In terms of methods, the studies done during this period were eclectic; indeed, the researchers involved over the years pioneered many of the methods which were to become the staples of variable analysis, including surveys and interviews as well as quantitative methods of data analysis. This eclecticism was not surprising in view of the fact that the early school was a meeting place of intellectual cross-currents ranging from theories of instincts, moral reform, evolutionary theory, organic and functionalist models, to ecology and city mapping, to the sociology of George Simmel and the social psychology of George Herbert Mead. Methodologically it was equally diverse. Ultimately, the Chicago School came to be best known for the use of fieldwork methods known as ethnography or participant observation, but at the time neither Park nor Burgess were committed to any particular method of social investigation. Indeed, there were few guides as to research methods or, for that matter, very much conception of the idea of method which was to emerge with positivism and variable analysis.

Park's greatest strength was in working out how studies could be done by giving the abstract concepts of the discipline a practical twist. His natural inclination was to send students into the city to get at the way things really were and to write about them in a jargon-free manner. The research style which eventually emerged depended on Park's charisma much more than it did on any formal training. For the Chicago School researchers, methods had to be worked out during the course of the research. However, both Park and Burgess insisted that whatever methods a study eventually came to use, the research was to be informed by first-hand knowledge of the setting and the people being studied. As it turned out, many of the notable studies involved researchers using ethnography: that is, participation in the way of life under investigation.

> Working out methods in the course of research

At the time this insistence on first-hand knowledge of the research domain was little more than sound advice given to researchers, on a par with the kind of advice one might give these days to 'always back up your files'. It was not seen as a method that was somehow distinct from the research itself or as a set of principles to be learned and applied. The School espoused no particular methodological principles akin to those which emerged from the positivist programme. However, there were glimmerings of a methodological principle which served to integrate ethnography with a distinctive sociological approach. It was a principle which built upon W. I. Thomas' dictum: 'If men define their situations as real, then they are real in their consequences'.

The definition of the situation

One of the more famous studies which came out of the Chicago School, and one of the first, was the *Polish Peasant in Europe and America* by Thomas and Znaniecki (Thomas and Znaniecki, 1918). The data used consisted mainly of letters written by Polish immigrants in the United States to friends and relatives in Poland, along with letters written to a Polish newspaper. The study was a landmark of American sociology because it integrated theory and data in a way that no other study had done before, though not perhaps as systematically as it might have done. It marked a shift away from abstract theorising and library research to a more empirical style of social investigation, something which Thomas had always stressed from early in his career.

The personal documents provided the researchers with the possibility of understanding why Polish immigrants acted in the way they did from their own 'definitions of the situations' in which they were placed when trying to create a new life in Chicago. One of Thomas' main reasons for choosing Polish immigrants was their often 'incomprehensible' behaviour, which swung from a passive acceptance of authority to behaving as if America gave them a licence to do anything they wished. The immigrants had brought with them to the United States relatively 'old' rural values and tried to apply them in what was a new culture. The lack of correspondence between the old and the new values led to social disorganisation. For Thomas and Znaniecki, however, the deviation from the norms of the new culture had to be understood as culturally patterned behaviour and not simply an individual pathology or explicable in terms of abstract concepts such as 'social strain'. It had, to put it another way, to be understood in terms of the meanings through which the immigrants themselves saw their social world. The materials Thomas and Znaniecki used were more than suggestive of the interpretative nature of human group life and set the scene for further investigations along these lines.

Though the study was to become one of the unread classics, at the time it played a considerable role in the encouragement of empirical sociology. It did not, however, result in a distinctive sociological approach. This was to come later as Blumer, among others, formulated a sociological approach developing Thomas' dictum, an approach which became known as symbolic interactionism. Nevertheless, prior to this the School was to produce a range of studies of Chicago life which have also assumed classic status. They include Thrasher's study of teenage gangs (Thrasher, 1927), Anderson's study of the hobo (1961), Shaw's study of a teenage criminal (1930), Cressey's study of 'taxi-dance halls' where patrons paid to dance with women of their choice, among others (Prus, 1996).

Symbolic interactionism

Symbolic interactionism was a relatively systematic formulation of a sociological approach by Herbert Blumer, drawing on the work of the Chicago School and the social psychology of George Herbert Mead (1863–1931). Mead had been at Chicago during the Park and Burgess era, although he had little direct influence on the sociological research done at this time. Nevertheless, it was a reworking of his ideas which were to form the conceptual core of symbolic interactionism.

Much of the psychology of the time was behavioural in conception, seeing the social as a kind of external influence on behaviour. Mead, by contrast, saw human behaviour as intrinsically social, as social action. While he did not deny that humans were animals like any other creature, what was he saw as distinctive about them was their capacity to use symbols, the prime example being that of language. Human beings, accordingly, encounter the world and each other not in terms of stimulus and response but through the meanings carried by language.

The problem which preoccupied Mead was to reconcile the uniqueness of the individual with the requirements of social life. His solution was, in brief, to see the individual as the creation of the social process of socialisation. From the moment they are born, human beings are involved in group life and through this learn language and, in doing so, learn what the world consists

> The ideas of G.H. Mead

in. Language and the world are learned together. It is the process through which the social individual is formed in such a way that each of us has a sense of our own individuality and a sense that we are also part of a world which includes other individuals with whom we interact. Unlike the instinctive co-operation of insects and the lower animals, human collectives display not only considerable variety but also change. Human co-operation is based on the human ability to ascertain the intentions of the actions of others and respond to these on the basis of that knowledge. Human action is not a response to some immediate stimulus but is anticipatory and sensitive to the intentions and purposes of others.

This capacity to interpret and respond to others implies that each individual possesses a 'self': that is, a conception of who and what he or she is. Persons can be the object of their own actions, can praise or blame themselves, be pleased or disgusted with themselves and so on. It is the ability to look at ourselves as others see us which enables individuals to interact with others and understand what they intend and what they do, to comprehend what it is to be an object of attention by others.

The social world – its people, objects and activities – is a world constituted through symbolic meaning. It is this into which persons are socialised and through which they interact with others. Socialisation is itself an interactive process through which we learn not only language and what is in the world, but also what we ought to do, how we should behave. The social world is normatively regulated and much of this consists in our

> Socialisation

own self-regulation, as members of society, knowing what is he right thing to do, knowing what not to do, knowing that if we do some things we will earn the disapproval of others. The social world is also a world known in common with others, in that our actions are informed by what we understand others will understand about what we ourselves do. And here Mead is offering a solution to what Talcott Parsons would later refer to as the primordial question of sociology, the problem of order. For Mead we do not only learn to see the world in our own personal way, but also learn to see ourselves as others might see us.

Blumer's formulation of Mead

Blumer, in the 1950s, began to develop Mead's ideas for the study of social life (Blumer, 1962, 1966, 1971). Human interaction consists in the ability to understand the meaning of each others' actions. The key feature, as it was for Mead, is the self which can be the object of its own actions. This is the prime mechanism through which human beings deal with the world. The conscious life of a human being is a constant stream of self-indications from the alarm in the early morning, the smell of the coffee brewing, the slam of the front door, the sound of the traffic and the beeps of the word processor. A person's social behaviour is not the result of environmental pressures, stimuli, motives and attitudes, as it is conceived of in psychology, but instead arises from how these things are interpreted and dealt with in the actions and activities that are being performed. It is this idea which reformulates earlier ideas such as Thomas' 'definition of the situation' as well as Park's insistence on researchers obtaining first-hand knowledge of the experiences of those being studied.

As we saw in the previous chapter, Blumer makes the process of interpretation central to his conception of society and social life. Human society is made up of individuals who have selves, who build up actions through interpreting the features of the situations in which they act, and who align their actions with those of others. This represented a radical

> The process of interpretation

departure from the sociological theories in vogue, which saw individuals as responding to forces lodged in the make-up of society, forces that were part of the causal effects of the social system, the social structure, in institutions, in social role and in custom. Individuals were the medium through which such forces operated and their actions the expression of such forces. None took the self, the process of self-indication, the process of interpretation, seriously. As a result, social behaviour was regarded as the expression of forces playing upon individuals rather than as acts built up by people through their own interpretations of the situations in which they found themselves.

Symbolic interactionism treats social organisation very differently from other sociologies. As just indicated, these tend to treat social actions as an expression of social structures or 'hidden' forces. While symbolic interactionism recognises the presence, and the importance, of so-called supra-individual levels of social organisation, it does not see these as the determinants of actions. In themselves they do not have any direct effect but have to be mediated through the understandings, the beliefs, the conceptions that people themselves possess.

Methodological implications

Blumer's formulations brought together in a more systematic framework the ideas which were first explored during the early days of the Chicago School. To a large degree Blumer's endeavour had been stimulated by the growing hegemony of variable analysis. As we have elaborated in the previous chapter, he mounted a serious *sociological* attack on variable analysis: that it was not informed by any mature conception of the nature of social phenomena. To recapitulate briefly, there were no guides as to what was to count as a variable; the technical apparatus was insensitive to the nature of the phenomena; variable analysis could only provide a superficial account of the phenomena since it lacked an understanding of its specifics; it was ignorant of what variables meant in the lives of the people being studied; and it lacked a rich and prior understanding of the nature of the phenomena.

Variable analysis left out what was, for Blumer, the core of group life, namely, the processes of interpretation that go on and that constitute the basis of social interaction. As social beings we act, singly and collectively, on the basis of the meanings which people and things in the world have for us. Social life is a 'vast interpretative process' in which people guide themselves by defining the objects, the events, the persons and the situations they encounter. Variables would have to operate through this process yet variable analysis says nothing about it. All it can tell us is that there is a relationship between variables, not about the interpretative process which connects them as elements in social life. The real operating factors in social life are glossed or unexamined.

Given this critique of variable analysis, the main task of any research built upon symbolic interactionists' precepts would be gain access to the meanings and understandings of the social actors in situations where they had a voice, rather than through a detached and distorting instrument such as a questionnaire or a formal interview. Hence the emphasis on participant observation or ethnography. In other words, what had started out as a piece of good advice to research students, namely, 'get first-hand knowledge of the people being studied', now becomes a methodological requirement for symbolic interactionism. Given this theoretical picture, the researcher had to come to understand the meanings and the definitions that social actors use to construct their courses of action, and this could only be done by a close involvement with those being studied.

> The importance of first-hand knowledge

In significant respects this methodological implication that the researcher, the observer, should become part of the way of life being studied was a radical change to that proposed by the Lazarsfeldian programme of variable analysis. As we have already discussed, one of the objectives of that programme was to develop methods by which social research could be proceduralised and so serve the goal of objectivity. The methods could be taught, people could be trained in their use and, accordingly, the observer, the researcher, should play no part in the outcome of the data collection process. The researcher becomes part of the apparatus of research, so to speak. By contrast, for symbolic interactionism the researcher has to find out about social life in just the same way that anyone else has to find out about it: that is, by taking part.

A key premise was the idea that the social world, even of people or groups with whom the researcher has no prior acquaintance, was available for the researcher to discover or otherwise report on. In just the same way that the members of the group 'know what is going on' by using their modes of inter-pretation and definitions of the situations in which they are placed, so can the researcher learn to 'know what is going

> The visibility of the social world

on' by taking part in the way of life. The social world is, to put it another way, highly visible, available and acces-sible. It is not a world determined by 'hidden forces', variables or whatever, but is there for anyone to see if they take the trouble to go and find out.

However, there was precious little guidance as to how one did the business of ethnography. The early Chicago researchers were encouraged to gather all manner of materials relating to life in the city but, apart from that, it was very much learning by doing. Indeed, in the early years there was little discussion of methods or their reporting. Nels Anderson, whose ethnography of the homeless (Anderson, 1923) was one of the first of the Chicago studies, noted that the only direction he was given by Park was to 'write down only what you see, hear and know like a newspaper reporter' (Ibid). Although Anderson had little formal sociological training he had been a hobo for some years, which meant that his own personal experiences permeate the study. But, as to techniques – what to record, how, when, whom to talk to and so on – there was little guidance.

This style of working things out as one went along is apparent in what has endured as one of the classic ethnographies, *Street Corner Society*, by W.F. Whyte, which nicely illustrates some of the practicalities of fieldwork.

Whyte and *Street Corner Society*

In 1936, Whyte, then a junior fellow at Harvard, decided to study a slum district, a place in Boston he dubbed 'Cornerville'. The method he adopted, though as far as one can tell driven by his interests in the social dynamics of the community rather than any explicit methodological guidance, was ethnography. Like the early ethnographers in Chicago, Whyte had to work out the practicalities of the method as he went along. For example, an early discovery was that acceptance by any social group in the district depended more on the personal relationships he was able to develop than on any explanation of what he was doing. He fell in with one of the residents of the area, 'Doc', who introduced Whyte around. Through 'Doc' he met people from a variety of groups and became accepted. Cornerville was almost entirely an Italian community and eventually Whyte took lodgings above a restaurant owned by the Martini family and was soon treated like a family member. He realised that as long as he had the support of key indi-viduals he was fairly confident that he could get what he wanted from others. This was the importance of his friendship with 'Doc'.

He also learned the importance, and the art, of 'hanging around', just taking part in the activities 'on the corner', talking about gambling, baseball and horse racing, listening rather than trying to direct conversations to matters which were germane to his research. Learning, in a word, patience rather than trying to drive the conversations into topics that were of interest to his research. He also discovered that fieldwork often involved delicate dilemmas. It was one thing to be accepted in the community but quite another to pretend to be like those who lived there. Because Whyte had been vouched for, he was accepted by the corner gangs and was able to study their way of life. But he was not one of them and was not expected to be. He was regarded as 'one of the boys' but also as someone whom they knew was different from them.

Of course, 'hanging around' is but part of the task of fieldwork. Its point is to gather material from the lives of those being studied for sociological purposes. The fieldworker has to record what is seen and what is heard. To this end, Whyte kept copious notes, intermittently going up to his room to write up what had happened. At first he kept these notes chronologically but this soon became unmanageable. Eventually he started to file them by social groups which, after all, was the focus of the study. Later, as he began to write up the study, although in some respects and on some aspects of life in Cornerville it was extremely rich and detailed, he became aware of the gaps in his material. Nevertheless, though he had not covered the whole of Cornerville, he does provide a portrayal of the 'structure and functioning of the community through intensive examination of some of its parts – *in action*'. (Whyte, 1955: 358).

The point of fieldwork

A fundamental reason for the abandonment of the positivist method was that it distorted priorities. *A priori* conceptions of method had been placed in the driving seat so that they, in effect, defined social reality. At least one opposition to this can be expressed in the phenomenological slogan of 'faithfulness to the phenomena' or, as Garfinkel put it, 'following the animal' (Garfinkel, 1967).

The positivist project's position might make more sense if it had a *proven* method. In that case it might be legitimate to let the method dictate the nature of the phenomena. But in sociology, these methods were not proven. Qualitative methods, then, can be seen as attempts to redress the imbalance by letting the phenomena, so to speak, show itself. Rather than deciding in advance what kinds of methods could capture the nature of social reality, qualitative methods sought to see what social phenomena presented themselves, essentially through fieldwork.

> Faithfulness to the phenomena

Though there are different elements in the qualitative method, it is mostly about fieldwork, about the first-hand observation of people's activities. Its whole purpose is to be present to social phenomena as they unfold themselves. Often it is a matter of just being there to see. Fieldwork is often undertaken in social settings unfamiliar to the researcher, areas of social life largely unknown prior to the fieldwork.

If we are realistic about sociology, then the discipline is at the beginning of analysing actual social life. Despite the energies devoted to it, the positivist project failed to produce studies which grappled with the elementary questions of sociological analysis. By contrast, fieldwork is often an occasion for working out what a sociological approach and scheme of analysis might be. Therefore, there ought to be no sense of embarrassment to the idea that when one sets out to do fieldwork there is a real sense in which one does not know what one is doing. To regard this as a weakness is to give too much credence to the positivist tradition, as perhaps did Becker and the grounded theory approach.

Fieldwork is not a method in the way that the use of surveys is a method. It is more akin, on the methodological level, to a means of finding out the kind of problems a sociological method would have to contend with. If we were to regularise sociological inquiries in a way which would entitle us to make a strong claim that certain procedures did capture the sociologically essential features of reality, what would we have to do? There is no way of answering such a question in advance of some inspection of the phenomena that we need to deal with. Thus, fieldwork is potentially a means of accessing social reality without preconceptions.

The last comment is not to suggest that fieldwork is done without any preconceptions whatsoever. We are talking about accessing social reality without firm methodological preconceptions. Qualitative research often makes use of broad, guiding sociological preconceptions about social life. But these do not provide deductive expectations about what will be found. They provide 'sensitising' directives pointing one in certain general directions. They must be recognised as tentative and provisional. They are not preconceptions to be projected – imposed – on observations. Their main role is to make certain kinds of things notable. In symbolic interactionism's case, these were the interactional nature of activities, the diversity of definitions, and the distinctiveness of definitions.

- *The interactional nature of activities.* The imperative is: don't just look at things done by individuals, look at things done between individuals, the ways in which things get done by individuals acting together. Don't, for example, think of the achievements of students in medical school as being their own individual attainment, but be aware of the large amount of collective effort that students put into organising their efforts so as to help each other out.
- *Diversity of definitions.* Recognise that people act in response to situations in different ways, depending on their point of view. Look out for people reacting differently in the same situation. For example, recognise that professionals and their clients often define the situation very differently. The defence lawyer will go home after a day's work; the client may go to prison. The client's situation may well have an urgency and intensity that is entirely lacking for the professional, for whom, after all, this is just another day's work. Try, therefore, to identify social encounters in which such differences in definition are at play, and see how the interaction handles the tensions associated with them.

▪ *The diversity of group definitions*. Recognise how definitions of the situation are expressed through language, and expect that groups of people with shared interests will develop words which 'belong' to their group, and which they use to organise their relations among themselves and with outsiders. For example, shoe salespersons have coded ways of talking among themselves, so they can say things to each other in front of customers that the latter will not understand even though they are in plain English.

These guidelines provide direction for fieldwork, but they do not qualify as a method and are none the worse for that. As we have pointed out, the early ethnographers had to find out the practicalities of the method in the course of doing their studies. And, despite efforts to alter it, fieldwork remains very much a practical activity. By this we mean that it is difficult to proceduralise in the way that attempts have been made to proceduralise data collection and analysis in positivistic methods. Fieldwork is a means of accessing the actor's point of view as this is exhibited in 'real world' settings. The setting will involve a host of exigencies with which the fieldworker will have to deal, and accordingly it is difficult to set out in advance the how's and the what's of what a fieldworker should do beyond some guiding principles, as set out in Inset 9.1.

Inset 9.1 Practicalities of fieldwork

Below are set out some of the main practical considerations involved in fieldwork.

Gaining access to research sites

The kind of research site required – be it a factory, a hospital, a power station control centre, a school, a street gang, a court room or other location – will obviously depend upon the research interest. Not all settings will be equally accessible, though one can be surprised. Unless the fieldworker intends to be a covert participant in the setting (and this is something that needs to be thought about very carefully before embarking upon the study), normally it will be necessary to get 'official' permission to conduct the research. This may well involve reassuring a number of interested parties about the bone fides of the research, what it will involve by way of possible disruption and, importantly, protection of the confidential information.

This last point can often be tricky, especially when those who give permission might also have an interest in what the research might uncover. The relatively small scale of most fieldwork sites means that individuals could be easily identified in research reports. Accordingly, it is vital that the fieldworker protects his or her fieldnotes and recordings and anonymises them in any research report, and makes it clear right from the beginning that this will be done.

The character of the researcher's involvement in the setting

We mentioned earlier the possibility of covert participation, in which a fieldworker's research role is hidden from those being studied. This is a role which tends to be used where there are grounds for thinking that a researcher's presence would significantly change the character of the interaction between the parties to the setting. This is most likely with groups whose activities are illegal, but it may also occur in settings where issues of professional confidentiality are involved, such as doctor–patient consultations. However, covert fieldwork is fraught with problems and dangers, not least those arising if the research role is revealed. The fieldworker is constrained by the need to maintain the deception, along with bearing the risk of discovery (Gold, 1964; Homan and Bulmer, 1982, Van Mannen, 1988). There are also important questions of research ethics in that it is a widely held view among the sociological research community that the subjects of any research should be aware of the researcher's involvement. In most cases, however, covert fieldwork is unnecessary, with the proviso that the requirements of confidentiality are observed.

Researcher interaction

Closely related to the above is the recognition that fieldwork is itself an interactional transaction between the fieldworker and those being studied, a transaction which needs to manage in some way the researcher's presence in a setting where this is likely to be uncommon. Once again this is an issue about which much unnecessary fuss can be made. As we stressed earlier, the task of the fieldworker is to recover the actor's point of view as exhibited in a 'real world' setting. This means that the researcher's presence and activities should not disrupt the setting.

What this means in terms of the conduct of the research depends very much on the circumstances and the organisation of the setting. It is also important to remember that in fieldwork there is no particular place to start in a setting, no place dictated by any theoretical or methodological requirement. One can, so to speak, begin anywhere. The important point to take on board is that those involved in the setting, whatever it might be, are not there for the convenience of the research. They are there to do a job of work, process forms, direct air traffic, repair photocopiers, 'hang out' on street corners, serve customers or whatever. This means that the fieldworker will have to conduct him or herself accordingly. No matter what the problem inspiring the research, no matter what the sociological point of the research might be, the fact remains that the fieldworker will have to make do with whatever material he or she can manage to get. It is the fact that the fieldworker is studying people going about their daily business which means that the setting is recalcitrant to organising it for the purposes of research. The people will have their own interests to pursue, their own commitments, their own motivations, which are not those of the researcher. But, and it is important to remind ourselves of this, the intractability of the research setting is not a methodological impediment but connected to just what it is that the field-worker needs to find out: namely, how the parties to the setting organise and conduct their practical affairs, be they air traffic controllers, drug dealers, 'squaddies', police officers, nurses, marihuana smokers or whomever. Arthur Vidich once described the role of the fieldworker as that of an 'interested incompetent' who can benefit from remedial instruction. Finding how and in what ways the setting is intractable is part of this.

This will also have a bearing upon what data, what material, the field-worker is able to collect. One of the more troublesome issues in doing field-work is what to record and how much. The typical temptation at first is to try to record everything, a task which is clearly impossible. Some selection must take place. In Whyte's case, for example, his initial motivation was to study rackets, and he felt that a slum district was a good place to find out about them and how they fitted into the lives of the people living there. But this hardly furnished much detailed guidance as to what to look for, what material to collect and record. This emerged during the fieldwork itself, and this is very much part of the rationale of fieldwork.

A similar problem is how long a fieldworker should spend in the field. Anthropologists often spend years doing their fieldwork and even studies of the scale of Whyte's can take two or three years. However, as with the previous issue there are no precise answers to this problem. In the social survey it is necessary to precisely determine sample size for example, determine what and how many questionnaire items there are to be, what the items will consist in; however, there are no equivalent specifications for ethnography. There are no systematic ways of determining whether a researcher should stay in the field for six weeks, six months or six years. There is no systematic means of – or sense to – determining how much material will need to be collected. In the end what determines these is the judgement of the fieldworker that he or she has learned enough.

'See the phenomenon for itself'

The commitment to investigate the actor's point of view through ethnography is an insistence that the phenomenon should show itself through inter-actions in the setting. This means that it is important not to import inappropriate assumptions and preconceptions into the fieldwork, important not to project onto the phenomenon but to identify it.

Clearly this cannot mean that a fieldworker goes into some setting without any preconceptions whatsoever. The very selection of the research site as, say, a factory, a school or an air traffic control centre, will involve the researcher knowing at least in general terms what kind of places these might be and what is likely to go on there. This may not be known in detail, but sufficiently to inform the selection of the site as worth research time and effort. The important point is not to project *sociological* conceptions and presuppositions onto the setting since these – and the point of the method – need to emerge out of the research itself. As we said earlier, the method relies on the same resources that anyone has for finding out about the social world, namely, taking part.

Exhibiting to other sociologists

We now come to two other considerations both of which perhaps deserve more attention than they have received. This principle refers to presenting the study which preserves the properties of the setting as they have been observed and making them available to other sociologists. The typical mode of ethnographic reportage has the flavour of a 'day in the life' story of air traffic controllers, photocopier technicians, street-corner gangs or whatever, through which sociological ideas and concepts are illuminated. Orr's (1996) study of photocopier technicians, for example, brings out the importance of 'war stories' in communicating technical knowledge and 'know how' among a community of workers whose task is to maintain extremely complicated machines. In this way it connects to sociological interests in, to mention but a few, informal organisations, person and machine interaction, and the nature of skilled work. Such studies also illuminate the perspective of the actor's point of view since this is the way that the story is worked up. A good ethnography convinces because it brings out the 'real life', flesh and blood character of those who have been studied.

Of course, 'working up' the story involves considerable analytic work. But the data, the material, that has been collected is not so much used for hypothesis-testing as for illustration. The fieldworker typically collects far more material than can possibly be used, so it is a matter of selecting and expositing the elements which perspicuously illustrate the sociological point being made.

Portraying the actor's point of view systematically

This last principle tends to be neglected and, to anticipate a little, constitutes a divergence between symbolic interactionism and other so-called qualitative approaches which we shall discuss in the next chapter, namely, ethnomethodology. The issue of divergence has to do with portraying the actor's point of view systematically and thoroughly. Much of what we have said so far about fieldwork could, if we are not too fussy, be said about both symbolic interactionism and ethnomethodology. However, and to briefly anticipate, symbolic interactionism tended to think of fieldwork investigations as processes of data collection leading to analysis; that is, assembling a corpus of data and then inspecting it for the social organisational features that it exhibits. The analysis – despite claims that data collection and analysis go hand-in-hand – has a retrospective character to it, in that it looks for social features of the collected materials which show themselves after the fact. The 'definition of the situation' is an ongoing process and, accordingly, it is perhaps natural to think that the defined situation is an outcome of the process. To see how the process works, it is necessary to be able to see how it turned out, what the eventual definition was. As we shall see in the next and the subsequent chapters, ethnomethodology departs from this conception.

However, as symbolic interactionism was developing a more coherent sociological approach in the 1960s, there was a parallel tendency to attempt the same with fieldwork: that is, in the debate with variable analysis to make fieldwork seem as systematic a method as the methods of variable analysis.

The debate with variable analysis

It might seem from the foregoing discussion that, compared with the techniques of variable analysis, ethnography is an haphazard process in which considerable reliance is placed on the fieldworker as to what data to collect, how much and for how long. Whereas variable analysis had attempted to proceduralise and routinise the process of research, ethnography seems to relish the personal dependence of the research process on the fieldworker. However, this was by no means the whole story since the proponents of the method, in the 1950s and 1960s, engaged in debates about method in response to the dominance of variable analysis.

Although, as we have said, in the years of the Chicago School there was relatively little formal discussion of research method, and little concern to report on the methods used in the studies, there had been some attempts to give method a higher profile. Around the time of the early ethnographies, Eduard C. Lindeman, in 1924, published a book, *Social Discovery*, which not only tried to raise the issue of method more systematically but, in doing so, was highly critical of social surveys in ways we would find familiar today. He rejected the notion of trying to make questionnaires and interviews impartial and neutral, arguing that this was doomed to failure since the premises on which the questions were based implied overly simple conclusions. Instead, he argued that more emphasis should be given to observation as a method of social investigation, and in his scheme of things observation 'from the inside', or participant observation, was at least as important as 'objective observation' from the outside, if not more so.

However, it was in the late 1950s and 1960s that the defence of ethnography became more spirited with the efforts by Howard S. Becker to set out the basic analytic operations of ethnographic social research (Becker and Greer, 1957). This effort, like grounded theory which owed much to Becker's original formulations, strove to give the process of fieldwork a more systematic shape, and was a response to the strident claims of variable analysis that it had placed social research on a more properly scientific footing. In the previous chapter we have outlined Blumer's critical rejoinder to that claim; nonetheless, the sociological approaches which espoused ethnography wanted at least to make claims that their method was systematic and certainly as deserving of the label scientific as positivistic methods, if not more so. However, and fatefully, they chose to debate on positivistic territory which meant, to a large degree, having to accept the terms of the debate as set by the positivist agenda. It meant, in more practical terms, having to defend against the argument that ethnography was unsystematic in lacking clear procedures for data collection and analysis.

As we have pointed out, one of the main aims of positivistic methods was, in effect, to remove the person of the researcher from the research process. Properly scientific research, by its lights, should be anonymous, a matter of applying appropriate and formal procedures so that who the researcher is, what views or opinions he or she holds, play no part in the outcome of the inquiry. Objectivity was to be secured through the rigorous application of method down to the last detail: the selection and phrasing of questionnaire items, their ordering on the schedule, the specifications of how the interviewer should behave, coding instructions, sampling selection and so on. All of these, and more, were as we have seen the subject of intense investigation in an effort to eliminate biases of various kinds.

The issue of objectivity

Although, as we have seen, the realisation of this ambition was less than satisfactory, it nonetheless, as Bittner warned, set the context in which the proponents of ethnography felt they were judged and would have to defend themselves. In particular, they felt that they would have to defend against the charge that their method depended far too much on the quality and personality of the fieldworker, the circumstances in which the research took place and the contingencies that inevitably arise, not to mention the views and the opinions of those conducting the research. The ideal for positivist methods was that, using the prescribed methods, two entirely different groups of researchers studying the same problem would come up with the same results. No such claim could be made, it was argued, for ethnography. Becker's article was a contribution to the debate about the role of ethnography but within, to stress the point, a broad context of agreement about the point of methods and research set by the positivist agenda.

The first point Becker makes – basing his illustrations on an extensive student of medical students, *Boys in White* (Becker et al, 1961) – is that participant observation research is carried on sequentially and important parts of the analysis are done while the fieldworker is collecting the data. This is in contrast to the social survey where there are distinct phases of data collection and then analysis. For ethnography this has the consequence of directing further data gathering in the light of the provisional analyses. It also means that because preliminary analyses will be limited by the exigencies of the fieldwork situation, a final comprehensive analysis will have to wait until the fieldwork is complete.

There are, according to Becker, three distinct stages of analysis in the field itself, with a fourth which follows on from the completion of the field work. Each stage is dependent on some analysis done at a preceding stage of the fieldwork and has different relevances for the continuing research. The stages are also differentiated according to the criteria used to assess evidence and conclusions. The stages are as follows:

- *Selection and definition of problems, concepts and indices.* In effect, this is setting initial observations in the context of some sociological theory as a means of selecting concepts and problems for further investigation. It may rest upon only one observation, but constructing a theoretical model to cover that one case makes it open for refinement in light of subsequent findings. Becker's own example is, 'Medical student X referred to one of his patients as a "crock" today.' This finding may be connected to a sociological theory suggesting that the occupants of one social category in an institution classify members of other categories according to criteria reflecting the kinds of problems that such persons raise in the relationship. This directs research to look for other instances, other problems in medical student–patient relationships, and explicate further just what the term 'crock' elucidates. Other issues which are raised at this stage include assessing the credibility of informants, making judgements about volunteered statements or ones directed by questioning, the effect of the presence of other members of the group as well as the effect of the observer, and so on; all of these are important in assessing the validity of the material being gathered.
- *Checking the frequency and distribution of phenomena.* In light of the first phase, the observer wants to know which of the many provisional problems, concepts and indicators are worth pursuing as major concerns of the research. Which are typical, which are exceptional, and how are they distributed among the organisation? These are essentially 'quasi-statistical' conclusions which do not require precise quantification but, nonetheless, give an adequate estimation of the frequency and distribution of phenomena.
- *Construction of social system models.* This final stage of the fieldwork consists of incorporating the findings into a generalised model of the social system or the organisation which is being studied. At first these may be theoretical models of parts of the organisation, which are then successively refined, and gradually an overall model of the organisation is assembled.

■ *Final analysis and presentation of results.* After the fieldwork is completed, the models are rechecked and rebuilt as carefully as the data will allow. It is a process of looking closely at the character of the conclusions, seeing how well they are supported by the evidence and considering alternative hypotheses. Presenting the results is not easy since the data does not lend itself to tabular summaries. One way is to present a natural history of how the conclusions emerged, as the evidence came to the attention of the fieldworker, so enabling evidence to be assessed as the substantive analysis is presented.

What is striking about Becker's attempt to portray ethnography as a systematic process of gathering data and attending to the chains of inference to theoretical conclusions is how much it resembles Lazarsfeldian accounts of the research process. Indeed, articles by Lazarsfeld himself are cited with approval and the theoretical models which are taken as the outcome of the research are spoken of in terms of the 'complex interconnection of variables'. And, as we have already indicated, the paper, along with others, was part of an attempt to portray participant observation not only as worthy of the name scientific but, in the context of sociology, better able to investigate the phenomena than variable analysis.

However, it would be wrong to dismiss this as simple a way of currying favour with the growing powers of variable analysis. This was a period of serious methodological debate undertaken by people who were profoundly committed to the attempt to build a scientific sociology. It was this ambition which provided a sense of belonging to a common endeavour even though there were profound differences which were to surface later, with more serious consequences for the direction of social research. Meanwhile, the efforts of Becker and others placed participant observation firmly in the debates over social research methods, but on terms which were dictated by the positivists.

For example, proponents of participant observation were concerned with questions of inference, the validity of the concept indicators, the generalisability

Participant observation and interviewing

of findings and theories, and so on. In another paper, Becker with one of his colleagues, Blanche Greer (Becker and Greer, 1957), wrote comparing participant observation with interviewing. Their argument is woven in terms of participant observation and interviewing as complementary methods, but with participant observation having the edge, so to speak, in being able to observe and collect rich and detailed information about the lives of those being studied, which cannot be collected using the standard interview methods. This 'rich experiential context' makes the observer more aware of incongruous or unexplained facts, sensitive to their possible implications and connections to other facts. It forces the revision and adaptation of the theory so that it has greater relevance to the phenomena being studied. There is still a place for interviewing, but its use would be much enhanced if it were informed by fieldwork.

Of course the debate, which we have barely sketched here, was a debate about methodological matters, about inference, about generalisation, about theory building, about validity: about all the kinds of things which preoccupied the positivists. Hence, there was considerable discussion of such matters as how the conduct of the fieldworker could affect the validity of the data collected and, consequently, the theoretical conclusions drawn. In other words, ethnography – along with the sociological approach which inspired its use in research, symbolic interactionism – became embraced within the conception of social scientific research of positivism. In effect, it was arguing that it could be more scientific, in the sense of being faithful to the phenomena, than could positivist methods. However, this strategy was to produce a number of tensions that had consequences for the development of post-positivistic conceptions of sociology and social research. Some of these we will consider in the next chapter. For now, and by way of intimation, we need to look closer at what ethnography aimed to do, and some of its implications for sociology.

Explicating the actor's point of view

Symbolic interactionism's choice of ethnography as a required method of social research arose from its insistence that social life was an interpreted order in which social actors, using their understandings, constructed courses of action with others. The very stuff of social life was produced and reproduced in and through the meanings that were employed within various settings. It is this which made ethnographic fieldwork mandatory for symbolic interactionism. Moreover, in contrast to the kind of theory-building exercises associated with the positivistic stance, ethnography was predicated on a 'bottom-up' rather than a 'top-down' approach. The positivist research apparatus, variable analysis, was ultimately designed to test hypotheses but, and despite its original intentions, this created a division between theorists and empirical researchers. Variable analysis was offered as a theory-neutral apparatus in the sense that the methods were derived not so much in any systematic way from a sociological theory but from a vision of what science was. Accordingly, it was presumed that any sociological theory, once formulated in terms of the format of variable analysis, could be tested. It was this which was, as we have seen, the basis of many of the charges against the apparatus, not least by the symbolic interactionists: namely, that it was a format devised with little or no attention being paid to the nature and characteristics of the phenomenon it was intended to investigate.

Symbolic interactionism and fieldwork represented a better worked out fusion of sociological approach and research method though, as we shall see, this did not mean that it was devoid of methodological problems. However, in the context of a debate whose parameters had been set by positivism, its lack of formal procedures presented a serious problem. This was the source of both criticism and some of

'Bottom-up' approach of fieldwork

the anxieties and confusions that are still expressed about ethnography. Its 'bottom-up' approach, given also the lack of procedure and the reliance on the personal capabilities of the fieldworker, meant that studies were unlikely to be reproducible and, hence, unable to produce the theoretical generalisations required by a social science. All that the method consists in are litanies of advice rather than systematic procedures.

In some respects, such criticisms had, and still do have, a point – and one which has more general import for the nature of sociological inquiry. Much of this centres around the issues involved in what it is to explicate the 'actor's point of view'.

The expression, 'the actor's point of view', in common with such summary phrases, leads to misunderstandings. The task of explicating 'the actor's point of view' can be made to seem bizarre, even mystical, a matter of gaining some deep communion with others. However, if we focus on the task as a practical one then the mystery of the process disappears, although it remains a process which requires thought and care.

The actor's point of view

The task of the analysis is to bring out, and convey, a strong understanding of the ways in which the participants in the setting construct, organise and make sense of their activities. Out of the accumulated notes and other materials that have been collected, the ethnographer needs to construct a picture of the patterns of interaction and social processes of the setting. The early Chicago ethnographers, for example, emphasised the life story and 'slice of life' approach to their reportage, making much use of the language of the persons studied. Of course, what else one might do depends a great deal on the point of the research. Nonetheless, whatever the point of the research, an important stage, if we remind ourselves of the point of ethnography and fieldwork, is to gain a good sense of what life is like in the setting, using much the same personal and social resources that one uses in making sense of any setting. There are two related issues here which need discussion, both of which arise out of the reaction to positivist methods: description and explanation and the generalisability of findings.

Description, explanation and generalisability

These related issues, in the context of ethnography, stem in large part from the emphasis on the requirement that sociology, as a discipline, should explain its phenomena: that is, should explain, to put it simply, why social arrangements and regularities have the character that they do. Why, for example, with industrialisation, do extended family patterns decline in favour of the growing prominence of the nuclear family? Explanation, and we have seen this in the case of the positivist apparatus of social research, is by means of theory. Indeed, as we have discussed in the previous section, the whole thrust of variable analysis was the testing of theories in the effort to

Explanation

identify the ones which best explained the empirically described patterns and regularities. The apparatus was predicated on the covering-law model of explanation: an empirical instance was explained if it could be shown to be logically connected to some law-like generalisation: showing, in other words, that it was an instance of some general process. This is an important part of what we mean by a 'top-down' approach. Developing theories, general explanations, are the point of the apparatus and everything is subordinated to this objective.

Closely related to this issue, though not straightforwardly, was the extent to which one might generalise from what are, in effect, case studies of particular social settings. To what extent, for example, are the street-corner gangs described in Whyte's study similar to those one might find elsewhere? Or the extent to which the experiences of 'hobo' life described in Anderson's study generalisable? Or the processes of transition from a medical student to a doctor the same for other settings or for other professions? There are really two aspects to the issue of generalisability: one to do with the case study, and one to do with the problem of a single observer.

> Generalisation

The case study

This is an interesting notion in terns of the presuppositions upon which it draws. To describe something as a 'case study' is to suggest that what is being studied is an instance of some more general category, and that by studying the instance one can obtain a richer understanding of the general category. Studying a single teenage gang, for example, can be taken as throwing light upon the social organisational features of other teenage gangs, but not necessarily on gangs of all kinds. And, indeed, this may be what is required of the research: that is, trying to find out as much as one can about some phenomenon.

In practice, in social research, selecting cases is often a rough-and-ready affair. One might, for example, choose a particular business firm because it can plausibly be seen as an instance of a more general category, say, small as opposed to a large manufacturing company. A more detailed study of such a firm might well, in light of what else is known about business firms, enhance our knowledge of manufacturing firms more generally. Another example might be Weber's explorations into the nature of Western rationality through a series of case studies of different societies at different periods of their history. By comparing such cases he was able to tease out what was distinctive about rationality in the West and how, among other things, it encouraged the rise of capitalist industrialisation. Yet another example of the comparative method is what is called 'deviant case analysis'; that is, selecting a case for detailed study because it differs from the general pattern (Merton, 1957). One might, for example, select for more intensive study a city district that has a higher average crime rate than would be expected from knowledge about its social composition. Here the intention is to identify further factors which might enhance our knowledge of the relationship between social conditions and crime rates. In all the above examples, the rationale behind the case study depends upon being able to effect comparisons with what is known, and it may not be a great deal, about some general category from which the case is drawn.

However, there are issues here which are worth airing.

Put simply, the problem is how to secure any inference from the instance to the general? Or, to put it another way, what is the relationship between the particular instance and the some general characterisation of it. In the case of a falling object, we would presumably want to say that this was an instance of the law of gravity. It might be other things as well – a suicide, a bomb, a raindrop – but it is at least an instance of a general law. Further, and following Popper, if we are interested in testing a hypothesis deductively arrived at from some theory, then a single instance is sufficient to falsify the hypothesis. In this example, the relationship of the single instance is to test the theory through the hypothesis. If, of course, the instance confirms the hypothesis, then the process goes on. However, it is not a question of generalising from the single instance.

Closer to the strategy of variable analysis, the issue of generalisation is typically one of representativeness. That is, instances need to be selected according to some proper procedure which enables us to infer from the sample to the general population. In this case, the instance becomes an instance of whatever property (or

> Generalisation and variable analysis

properties) is being sampled. The mention of 'properties' is a powerful clue to another way in which variable analysis tries to achieve generality, namely, by the use of so-called general concepts. These, along with the standardising procedures of the questionnaire and the interview, attempt to provide a sense that the data produced is not unique to a particular interview or a particular questionnaire. As we have argued in Chapter 6, at best what such procedures produce are empirical generalisations not the law-like generalisations sought. As Blumer's arguments for 'sensitising concepts' strongly suggest, we have no reason for any strong confidence that such a procedure actually does produce well-grounded generalisations about social phenomena.

In terms of ethnography, it is a central feature of the method that, in one sense at least, it is a case study method. However, in another sense, this is a problem only if one buys into, as it were, the presuppositions of variable analysis which emphasise representativeness and the standardisation of methods and concepts. As we shall see in the next chapter, in symbolic interactionism – though this is by no means the only source – we begin to get a glimpse of a rather different attitude to the detailed study of particular cases: namely, the discovery of the generic properties of social phenomena which take a different tack to the issue of generalisation.

Is it the same for different observers?

Related to the issue of generalisability, and again one often cast in a variable analytic form, is the question of whether different fieldworkers are likely to produce the same results. As we have said, variable analysis devoted considerable efforts to proceduralising and standardising the research process to remove the effect of any individual bias in interviewers, coders and analysts, whereas the relative lack of procedure in ethnography leaves open the strong possibility of personal bias. Much will depend upon the ingenuity and skill of the fieldworker as well as the contingent opportunities, or lack of them, furnished by the site of the research. However, before buying too much into positivist criteria, it is worth asking the prior question: what is to count as the same, or different, results? The variable analytic approach depended on a combination of research design, specification of variables, assumptions about the distribution of measurement error and unmeasured variables, and the relative stability of measures of association and the like, which, as we have seen, are not unequivocally likely to resolve the problem which the initial question raises. Even panel studies – a research design in which the same sample, often along with control samples drawn from the same population, is compared over time – have to face up to the fact that changes often occur. In which case, the problem is one of identifying genuine changes from change that is an artefact of the instruments used and the assumptions about the distribution of error. The point is that the issue of whether two or more studies of putatively the same domain will produce the same results is as much a problem for variable analysis as it is for ethnography. Though the respective approaches to the problem are different, there is no reason to take the view that one is any better than the other at providing a solution.

Further, one also needs to take account of the different objectives of the two approaches to social research, and how these affects the criteria for judging whether or not any results are the same. In brief, and there are other considerations which we will come to in the next chapter, ethnography seeks, as an initial achievement, to describe what is 'going on' as an essential preliminary to developing any more general theoretical concepts. Variable analysis, on the other hand, sought to test general theories. The 'bottom-up' approach which ethnography represents has to place an initial emphasis on describing rather than theoretically explaining 'what goes on' in the setting. This, after all, is the point of doing fieldwork, of 'being there' to see how people interact with one another and how they understand their activities within the setting. Accordingly, the material that the fieldworker will collect will consist of notes and descriptions closely based on what he or she has seen and heard within the setting, often using the very vernacular expressions that parties themselves use in the conduct of their daily lives. Let us call these, following Schutz (1962), 'first order constructs': that is the concepts and expressions that members of society employ to talk about and do the activities in which they are involved.

However, the 'bottom-up' approach is not an atheoretical one but an approach which is advanced to produce, it claims, better theory than does the positivist framework. In other words, it is not content with simply producing a description, albeit a selective one, of a way of life, but uses this to generate general sociological theories which are better attuned and grounded in the way of life studied. The problem was how to do this given that the material, the data, gathered has the character described above. What principles are available to effect the transformation of 'first order constructs' to theoretical 'second order constructs'?

Of course, variable analysis had the same problem. Questionnaires and interviews had to be couched in ordinary language to elicit responses which were also framed in ordinary language. These were treated as 'indicators' and subjected to further transformations to 'stand for' theoretical concepts. However, given the critique of the kind of procedure which the 'bottom-up' approach of ethnography is based upon, this is not an option open to the fieldworker – or at least not in that form.

The pioneers of the Chicago School, despite their relative indifference to fulminating about method, certainly did not see themselves as merely engaging in description of particular and unique settings but as making a contribution to a more general understanding of societal processes. Its dedication to investigate the facets and processes of Chicago life was motivated, in large part, by interests in assimilation and social disorganisation. Though uneven in its theoretical contribution there was, nonetheless, an effort to move beyond the unique and the particular.

Later, of course, Blumer's conceptual scheme for symbolic interactionism laid the groundwork of a general framework for ethnographic studies. Though in no sense a recipe for how to conduct fieldwork, it stressed the importance of blending theory and research. However, in contrast to variable analysis, it laid much more stress on the importance of developing fruitful concepts out of the research study itself. In other words, and again using Schutz's formulation of the problem, the task was to move beyond 'first order constructs' to more general theoretical ones.

> Blending theory and research

Essentially two strategies emerged to give fieldwork a more systematic cast: analytic induction and grounded theory.

Analytic induction

In contrast to deduction which reasons from general premises to particular conclusions – and is the cornerstone of the hypothetico-deductive model of theory – induction is a process of inferring a more general conclusion from the observation of a number of discrete facts. Sampling is an example of induction. From a properly drawn sample from a population one can infer the values of the population from the sample values. Two types of inductive procedure are normally identified: enumerative and analytic. Statistical generalisations are an example of the former in which, in effect, the instances are 'added together' to produce an empirical generalisation. Analytic induction, in contrast, seeks to develop universal statements about the 'essential features of a phenomenon, or those things that are always found to cause or lie behind the existence of a social occurrence' (Manning, 1982). It is argued that essential features are revealed when they are always present when the phenomenon is present and absent when the phenomenon is absent. So, to use an example from Becker, continued marijuana use for pleasure occurs when a willing person first learns the technique of smoking, then learns to perceive the effects and, finally, defines these effects as pleasurable. If these conditions are absent, a person will not continue using marijuana (Becker, 1953).

Inset 9.2 The main steps of analytic induction

Define the phenomenon to be explained:

1. Formulate a tentative explanation of the phenomenon.
2. Examine a particular case in order to see if the hypothesis holds.
3. If the hypothesis does not fit, either reformulate it or redefine the phenomenon to exclude the case.
4. Practical certainty is achieved using a small number of cases. However, negative cases disprove the explanation and require a reformulation of the hypothesis.
5. Examination of cases, redefinition of the phenomenon and reformulation of the hypothesis continues until a universal relationship is shown.

The antecedents of analytic induction lay in Thomas and Znaniecki's classic *The Polish Peasant in Europe and America*. A major objective of the study was to remain as close as possible to what they called human documents – the newspaper files, the letters, biographies, magazine files and other records – so as to present an account of the actor's perspective. In subsequent years there was some debate about the method, resulting in the distinction noted earlier between enumerative and analytic induction. Indeed, it is out of this debate that sampling and scaling methods emerged as more efficient ways of tapping into human experiences and attitudes, and there were to be further developed as part of variable analysis. However, and importantly, those who remained firmly with analytic induction were not content with discovering a pattern of association which covered a large majority of the cases, as in enumerative induction methods, but with providing complete causal generalisations.

However, and not surprisingly, there is a continuing debate about the merits or otherwise of analytic induction. In many cases, the criticisms of the method have been mounted by those committed to statistical methods who question its logic of explanation and cast doubt on whether it is feasible to think of universal statements applying to all cases. Certainly it does not clearly establish causality nor, in the end, could it sustain the claim to provide universal statements. Nonetheless, proponents of the method argue that it is best suited to the development of sociological theories by its capacity to generate concepts closely tied to empirical studies. In this respect, it incorporates Blumer's argument that the basis for theory must be sensitising concepts which are open to revision through the careful analysis of exceptions. Moreover, it could be claimed that analytic induction offered a more suitable mode of proceeding for a discipline still in its methodological infancy that the theory-testing model proposed by variable analysis. Deduction, it can be argued, depends on prior principles or, to put it another way, upon already well-formulated theories. Where these are not in evidence, the search for fruitful concepts on a case-by-case basis offers much.

Grounded theory

This approach we have already met in the previous chapter. Though it departs somewhat from analytic induction, it is similar in being an attempt to place fieldwork, and the qualitative data it produces, on a more secure scientific footing. As a methodological strategy it was first formulated by Glaser and Strauss (1967), though it owes much to Becker's earlier formulation of the process discussed earlier that was designed to generate theories from data. Using Merton's notion of 'middle-range theories', its proponents draw a distinction between 'substantive theories' and 'formal theories'. The former are ones developed for a substantive domain of sociological inquiry, such as race relations, delinquency, patient care or classroom interaction, while the latter are developed for a conceptual area, such as deviant behaviour, power and authority, reward systems, stigma or formal organisation. They are 'middle range' because both types fall between the 'minor working hypotheses' of everyday life and the 'all-inclusive' grand theories. The distinction between 'substantive' and 'formal' theories will, as we shall see, be an important one, with significant ramifications for the nature of sociological thinking.

Inset 9.3 Stages of grounded theory

1. Researcher compares incidents applicable to each category. This requires coding of the data and generating theoretical properties of the category.
2. Categories and their properties are then integrated.
3. The theory is delimited in order to reduce the theory and limit the saturation of categories. This will require the researcher to check the criteria used to select and delimit categories.
4. The period of writing up and generating major themes for further publication.

As the term 'grounded theory' suggests, the strategy accepts that theory is the point of research and, secondly, that sociological theory needs to be adequately based on empirical data. However, in contrast to the positivist programme, it is less concerned with testing theories than with generating them on the basis of a close acquaintance with the ways that social actors talk and conceive of their social worlds. Its emphasis is on qualitative data, which can include not just ethnographic fieldwork but also informal interviews. In other words, the approach is not quite so tied to the case study that ethnography inevitably involves. Indeed, one of the main purposes of the strategy is to facilitate the development of more general sociological theories.

At the heart of the approach is comparative analysis. In the case of a substantive area, this might involve, for example, studies of classroom interaction within and between schools. The aim is to generate and develop categories, properties and hypotheses rather than to test them. In contrast to analytic induction, the object is more concerned with gathering as much data as possible rather than trying to account for all the data.

As can be seen from the synopsis of the stages of grounded theory, the emphasis is on developing categories out of the data, and there is some doubt as to whether this really qualifies as theory in any strict sense of the term. Moreover, the stress on the comparison of cases increases the quantity of data that is required. It is therefore perhaps not surprising that studies using the strategy tend to rely a great deal on informal interviewing as the main vehicle of data collection. To this end, and to facilitate the development of categories, there are now available a number of software packages based on the approach. In effect, what such packages do is categorise the interview responses according to criteria specified by the researcher.

Both of these approaches, analytic induction and grounded theory, arose in response to the pre-eminence of positivist methods in the shape of variable analysis. As we have already said, to a large degree the approaches argued on ground already established by variable analysis. Both shared the same objective – namely, the development of better theories which explained the patterns of social life – and the argument was essentially about which approach, the quantitative or the qualitative, did this better. However, many of the basic issues remained unresolved.

Conclusion

Qualitative approaches such as ethnography prided themselves on a 'bottom-up' approach which began by studying the lives of social actors who were, it was argued, the object of sociology. However, and despite its complaint against variable analysts' pursuit of quantification without regard to the nature of the phenomenon, the strategies just discussed 'buy into' much of what their proponents complained about in variable analysis. In the case of grounded theory, for example, the practical exigencies of trying to move beyond single cases to compare them placed a premium on resources and, as a solution, there was a tendency to focus on informal interviewing techniques and coding at the expense of extensive fieldwork. Though retaining a concentration on the single case and laying more stress on the importance of fieldwork, analytic induction similarly proposed procedures which involved the transformation of 'first order constructs' into theoretical categories to facilitate generalisations.

In crucial respects, the problem here is the objective of explaining by theorising and what this might mean methodologically. The issue is particularly pointed in the case of ethnography – though it surfaces in variable analysis – in the tension between the point of fieldwork, namely to observe and interact with parties to a setting, and the development of general concepts which might serve theoretical understanding. The tension arises, as we have already indicated, in the fact that the material the fieldworker will have collected will be closely derived from what he or she has heard, seen and talked about in the setting itself: that is, the 'first order constructs', the ways in which the members of the setting talk about and do the activities in which they are involved. It is these which, if we want to theorise, need to be transformed into the more technical concepts of theory.

> First order and second order constructs

We have already argued that the classic positivist approach uses a conception of the relationship between the sociological researcher and those being studied akin to that between the natural scientist and his or her subject-matter. In this conception, it is the scientist's task to identify regularities in the phenomena and develop categories and theories to express these. The only constraint on the researcher is the purposes and the requirements of the science, whatever it may be. This is not, however, the case with social phenomena for the identification of regularities in social life involves investigating phenomena which themselves partly consist in categories, categories which belong to the phenomena. Accordingly, any transformation of social phenomena for theoretical purposes will be a re-categorisation of phenomena that are already categorised, with these 'first order constructs' being vital to their being the phenomena that they are.

It is this which constitutes the tension between the 'actor's point of view' and that of the social theorist, and between their respective conceptions of social reality. As already indicated, the social theorist seeks to develop a generalised conception of social reality according to the requirements of logical coherence and empirical grounding. The members of society are also credited with a conception of social reality, but not one constructed according to the requirements of theory. Accordingly, it is to be expected that the two conceptions will differ. Moreover, there is a strong temptation to regard the theorist's conception as the more valid since it has been constructed according to criteria which are claimed to be objective. So, to the extent to which an actor's conceptions differ from those of the theorist, they are subjective.

> Tension between actor's point of view and social theorist

As might be imagined, this raises a host of problems which, in significant respects, are at the heart of the sociological enterprise. It is impossible to deal with all or even most of them at this point, except to note that many of them are epistemological and ontological in character and will be discussed elsewhere in the book. For now we want to raise some questions about the role of theory in sociology. As we say, at this point we want to raise questions rather than take a position.

That the objective of sociology is theoretical understanding is largely taken for granted within the discipline. It would be difficult to understand the fuss and bother over positivism, and method more generally, without the

> The theoretical purpose of method

realisation that these are directed at the development of sociological theory. By theory what we mean here are those formulations of general explanations which can account for the regularities of social life. As we have indicated previously, such offerings are highly variable, but all of them could be said to effect a contrast between describing and explaining: a contrast that is not as straightforward as it might seem at first sight.

One major consequence of positivism was to place problems of explanation first, and firmly so, on the methodological agenda. Of course, there is a sense in which one needs to describe something before one can explain, otherwise one cannot know what the explanation is an explanation of. Positivism realised this and also realised that science needs to be selective in its descriptions, hence Lazarsfeld's insistence on specifying the properties of social phenomena and operationalising these in terms of variables and their indicators. However, as we have discussed, the procedures which were devised owed more to the requirements of quantification than they did to some principled attempt to specify the phenomenon and its properties in order to determine how and in what ways in might be investigated. It was to avoid distortions of this kind that ethnography and other qualitative methods were devised.

It can be argued that one of the main objectives of the fieldwork orientation was to raise the problem of description to counterbalance positivism's emphasis

> Description versus explanation

on explanation. In effect, its argument was that one needs to know more about the daily life of social actors as carried out in real life settings prior to the attempt of theoretically explaining what it is they do.

However, we need to bring other considerations in at this point, in particular, the question of what is gained, in terms of sociological understanding, by theorising. If, for example, a fieldworker has adequately described a way of life, then what is gained by trying to explain facets of it in terms of some sociological theory? Let us try and put this a little more systematically.

One can say that we need explanations to resolve things that puzzle us. Why does rain fall but aeroplanes fly? Why do more men commit murder than women? Why did Mr X kill his wife? Why doesn't my computer work? Why don't contemporary teenagers like Bob Dylan? Why do women, generally, earn less than men? Why does alcohol make one drunk? Why are some people better at music than others? These questions, and they are of course but an infinitesimally small selection of the kinds of things that can puzzle us, require explanations, but what is not clear is whether they require theoretical explanations to resolve what puzzles us. Not, that is, unless one is inclined to regard any explanation as theoretical. To resolve the puzzle as to why the computer won't work, one needs a computer engineer to fix it. The question about aeroplanes and rain requires an understanding of aerodynamics and the law of gravity. Why did X kill his wife is asking for a motive that would have impelled X to do such a deed. The general point being that there is, to use a term from Alan Garfinkel, 'explanatory relativity'. That is, to put the point in a way germane to the discussion of sociological method, resisting the impulse to think that one form of explanation will suit all requirements, resolve all our puzzles and problems. This was an important aspect of the complaint levelled against positivism, namely, that it proposed a single form of explanation as paradigmatic of sociological explanation, one rooted in the HD format for theory. This the ethnographic approach challenged with its emphasis on the 'actor's point of view' but in ways which remained to be fully worked out.

> Explanatory relativity

There are two main tensions between qualitative research and variable analysis. The first is the tension between method as strict rule and procedure which defines sociological reality, and a method suited to the nature of the reality one seeks to study. In the first instance Blumer's arguments against variable analysis were corrective rather than radical. His argument that the concepts of sociology were 'sensitising concepts', including those specifying variables, suggested that progress in sociology toward a science of social life would be slow and the strategy one of continuous improvement rather than any kind of quick fix. However, given the focus on the 'actor's point of view' as at least close to the phenomenon of sociology, methods which were faithful to the nature of the phenomenon had to be the first priority. Hence the arguments for qualitative methods and ethnography in particular.

> Main tensions

The second tension, and one closely related to the first, is that between the actor's constructs and those of sociology, between a scientific version of social reality and social reality as experienced and understood by social actors. Positivism sought, in effect, a view of society that was similar to the way a natural scientist might view natural phenomena. The qualitative approaches we have discussed here take the view that finding out about the actor's point of view is the same as finding out about social reality.

Selected bibliography and suggested reading

- Good accounts of the Chicago School are Bulmer's, *The Chicago School of Sociology: Institutionalisation, Diversity and the Rise of Sociological*

Research (University of Chicago Press, 1984). Among the studies for which the School is well-known, though they are not always easily available, are Nels Anderson, *The Hobo,* University of Chicago Press, 1961; F. Thrasher, *The Gang: A Study of 1,313 Gangs in Chicago,* University of Chicago Press, 1927 and Paul Cressey's, *The Taxi-Dance Hall: A Sociological Study of Commercial Recreation and City Life,* AMS Press, 1932.

▪ General texts on symbolic interactionism include the two volumes of key papers edited by Ken Plummer, *Symbolic Interactionism, Vols. 1 and 2* (Edward Elgar, 1991). Hans Joas' 'Symbolic Interactionism' in A. Giddens and J. Turner (eds), *Social Theory Today* (Polity Press, 1987) is well-worth reading. The chapter on 'interactionism' in the authors' *Understanding Modern Sociology* (Sage, 2003) is a full account of the origins and development of the social thought of interactionism. Robert Prus, *Symbolic Interaction and Ethnographic Research: Intersubjectivity and the Study of Human Experience,* is a good textbook and brings the tradition up-to-date by discussing some recent field research.

Chapter 10

Explorations in the Actor's Point of View

Now we get to the tricky bit. The possibility of making the transition in ways of thinking about sociology that has been introduced in the previous three chapters is one that creates much disagreement that, in our judgement, is often due to confusion as to the changes being proposed. The issues involved here anticipate other, and equally confusing, developments that we will also deal with in turn, involving 'social constructionism' and 'post-structuralism'.

The chapter consists of two phases. The first discusses in general terms the major shift in sociological thinking proposed by interactionism along with our own approach to matters of theoretical dispute in sociology. The second phase develops in more detail some of the issues arising from the interactionist perspective, issues which have long preoccupied sociological thinking.

Methodological versus ontological thinking

What might help us make these complex developments less confusing is the general line of approach we have tried to use throughout this book. We are dealing with sociological theory as much in methodological terms as in – for want of a better word – ontological ones. Ontological considerations pertain to what is really the case. An example relevant to sociology might be the question: what is society made up of? As we have had occasion to notice, many different, often contradictory, answers have been given to questions such as these: 'individuals', 'social facts', 'social systems', 'social classes' and so on. Sociological disagreements often involve attempts to 'cut to the chase', so to speak, and directly fight over these ontologies. 'Is society really only an aggregate of individuals, or is it something more collective in nature?' is one of these disputes that has been running, in various forms, more or less throughout the history of sociology – and we have discussed aspects of it in Chapter 7 – and it is by no means dead.

Accordingly, if we wanted to start from ontological considerations – which is, after all, not an uncommon place to start in sociology – then we might posit for the interactionist approaches we are looking at here and in the previous chapter an ontology something like the following: 'social reality is an incessant flow of activities between people'. This is not entirely right but sufficiently simple enough for our present purposes. However, in our view much of the difficulty and *apparent* disagreement among sociologists would evaporate if we start, as we have been doing, with *methodological* considerations prior to 'ontological' ones. Doing it this way makes it plain that we cannot ask the question, 'what does social reality consist in?' outright as though it were a straightforward and quite unconditional question. For our part, we see it as a question that can only be asked on certain understandings.

Fully stated, the question must always be something like: 'For what purposes are we attempting to conceive reality, and in what ways is it most effective to do so relative to those purposes?' This is one of the reasons why we think that posing questions in this way would lead to the evaporation of many long and seemingly intractable sociological disputes. As should be blatantly clear from the discussion this far in the book, sociology is conceived in many different ways, and different conceptions involve different purposes. Think of the difference between Marx's purpose, which was to 'change the world', and the purpose of most other sociologists, which is to do what Marx condemned philosophers for, namely, 'interpret the world'. Very different purposes may require equally diverse ways of thinking about society. Thus, the conception we offered above – 'society as an incessant flow of activity between persons' – does not, on its own, make much sense. It remains to be seen what it would mean to think of society in that way. And, further, an important part of seeing what it would mean to think of society in this way might enable one to avoid, or bypass, a lot of the problems that others have encountered in trying to think of society in a systematic way. In other words, a large part of the answer to the question, 'why think of society as an incessant flow of activity between people?' is not given by asserting, 'Well, because society *is* an incessant flow of activity between people' but involves, instead, explaining why it would be sociologically useful to think of society in that way. And explaining that is really only describing the way of thinking that this conception facilitates.

A further aspect of this is that it is important to bear in mind that all arguments and recommendations in sociology should be prefaced by: 'For all sociological purposes …'. It would be unbearably tedious to put this phrase at the beginning of almost every sentence; nevertheless, we constantly need to remind ourselves that it is a rider which should govern all our deliberations. It is overlooked and forgotten at the risk of serious confusion.

Although this seemingly indirect way may seem an odd means of going about it, actually we are raising the issue of *the objectivity of sociology*. Let us consider what, for sociological purposes, a table – that is, a piece of furniture – might be. In other words, what sort of interest could a sociologist take in tables? There are a lot of

The objectivity of sociology

questions we could ask of tables: Is it made of wood or plastic? How many nails are there in it, or is it joined in other ways? Is it circular or oblong? However, questions like these do not seem the kind that would interest sociologists. Presumably there are answers that could be given to these and other questions of the same ilk. 'What make of table is it?', and if the answer is, say, Chippendale, IKEA or Habitat, there might be a stirring of sociological interest for, potentially, they say something about the people to whom the table belongs. These are recognisable makes of table and recognisable as implying a certain life style. Someone who furnishes in Chippendale must be very wealthy, whereas the makes of IKEA and Habitat function as what, long ago in sociology, were termed 'status symbols'. For sociological purposes we do not need to know what it is that makes Chippendale such an invaluable embodiment of fine carpentry skills. Even more basically, think what is involved in the very idea of 'a table'. For one thing it is the name of a physical object, and that is all many people think matters about it. Think further: what is involved in the name of an object. Certainly, 'table' implies a particular kind of construction – legs, a top, made of some solid substance and so on – but there is more than this. It also carries intimations of use and a response. Thus, tables come in kinds, often identified by their use: breakfast, dining, office, conference tables, bird tables, for example. All these kinds involve activities: eating, working on, gathering around, pecking. And the use implies a response – one sits at the dining table to eat, sits around a conference table to have a meeting … and so on.

The interactionists make the point that to name an object is to prepare for action, which is just an abstract way of stating what we have just said about calling something a 'dining table' as opposed to an 'office desk'. And this, they claim, is the kind of interest that sociologists can usefully take in material objects. Interactionists are interested in how people act, and take it that people characteristically act in response to – let is call them – situations. The tradition itself began by objecting to the stimulus–response model of actions as (though it came before variable analysis) two intercorrelated variables. Their objection was simple enough and, it seems to us, indisputable: while the behaviour of pigeons or rats might be understood by means of such a simple model, that of human beings cannot be so understood. It is not that persons do not respond to stimuli in the sense of there being occurrences – such as a traffic light changing from green to red – which occasion their action. It is, rather, that human beings do not respond to the stimulus merely as a physical occurrence. It is not the red colour of the traffic light as such that stimulates the braking of the car. The red light 'stimulates' the response but as a bearer of a cultural convention, as a signal of danger and as a sign to halt.

Further, not all people react in the same way to the changing traffic light. Drivers may draw their cars to a halt, but pedestrians now step out onto the road confident that they can cross safely, knowing that the traffic light applies to cars and not to them. Escaping bank robbers under hot pursuit do not screech to a halt at the red light. They have broken more serious rules than those which require halting when the signal is red.

Thus, there are two simple general points to emphasise:

- Human response to a stimulus is not a conditioned response to its physical properties as such, but to those properties in terms of the meaning or significance they have to the responding individual. Thus, for example, someone told that the table is a Chippendale may be much more careful about putting down a coffee cup on its top.
- The response to the same stimulus is not uniform. The meaning or the significance that the stimulus has does not depend upon its conventionally understood character alone, but also on the way in which it fits into the course of action in which the individual is engaged. The bank robbers understand perfectly well what a red traffic light is but in attempting to escape they care less about the consequences of jumping a red light than escaping.

Nowadays, many sociologists are concerned about the 'materiality' of social phenomena, often coupled with a complaint about earlier sociological approaches which ignored such materiality. The social action tradition, descending from Max Weber, and the interactionist approach coming out of Chicago, are often accused of a similar transgression, as though they were aiming to substitute the meaning or significance of a phenomenon for its material character: accused, in other words, of 'idealism'. Our methodological presentation of such matters ought to indicate that nothing of the sort need necessarily be involved in this approach.

> Materiality

Remember from our earlier remarks, our question is not, 'What does a red traffic light consist in?', but 'What are the sociologically relevant features of a red traffic light?'. Assuredly, red traffic lights consist of glass, metals, electronic wiring, timing devices and the rest, but these of themselves are of no interest to sociologists if their interest is in the capacity of such lights to provoke reactions in road users. From that point of view, the materiality of the traffic light is – excuse the pun – immaterial. From that point of view we might as well say that the traffic light consists in the meaning, the significance, it has for members of society and nothing else. In order to understand why people are stopping their cars at traffic lights, we do not need to know its engineering principles, just because the people who are obeying the traffic signals know little or nothing about these things.

The part which causes so much controversy is that some critics complain that the materiality of the thing disappears into its cultural and individual meanings. The logical consequence is that physical being evaporates out of all existence so that reality consists only and entirely in cultural meanings.

However, it should be clear that the argument is a methodological not an ontological one. It is made as a way of demarcating matters the sociologist needs to take into consideration which surely do not include – given the interest in why drivers brake – wiring diagrams of the traffic light junction box. This is not a remark at the expense of

> The methodological point of view

the physical reality of the traffic light which exists, is visible there at the road junction, but a claim that all that matters about it from the point of view of why people react to it in the way they do is the fact that it goes through its cycle of changing from red to green, which has cultural significance.

Despite such clarification there are many social theorists who feel that it is vitally important – because it affects the conception of what a sociological explanation is – that a foundational part of any sociological scheme should be an acknowledgement that there is a material world 'out there' which exists independently of the cultural meanings which shape much of our action. Material conditions, after all, may well affect actions and occasion reactions in ways that are not the products of cultural meanings. Germs made people ill even before we had any knowledge of them.

For us, the import of such ontological insistence 'cashes out' as a method-ological difference. Critics might insist that sociology must begin with the 'materiality' of the world outside of cultural conventions; our line is that we do not have to start there, though we can. Further, it is not as if the materiality of a table is somehow excluded from the understandings that person have of it: that it is an office desk leads to the expectation that it will be solid and stable enough to bear the weight of a computer, a stack of files, and so on. From this point of view, the adoption of scientific accounts of the table as a constellation of particulate matter, or as a function of engineering principles that maintain the solidity and stability of the table sufficient for the purposes it serves, does not bring us any closer contact with the object itself extricated from the cultural understandings of this as an office desk. In sum, it is not a matter of having either the material object or the cultural meanings. The concern with the object from the sociological focus on the actor's point of view is in terms of cultural understandings. A table divested of its role in people's lives and considered 'in itself' is merely a strangely arranged ensemble of wooden pieces.

From this point of view, the adoption of a natural science frame of reference does not remove us from the realm of meaning and interpretations. *Sociologically speaking*, the scientific frame of reference is exactly that – another point of view. We do not say, though some might, that it is *only* another point of view as though being a point of view must somehow, and necessarily diminish its status. The consequence of treating science, including natural science, as what in the phenomenological tradition would be called a 'scheme of specifications', can be confusing and troublesome and we can only set out very basic ideas.

Inset 10.1 Phenomenology

As a philosophical movement, rooted mainly in Europe, phenomenology takes as its objective the analysis and description of everyday experience as constituted in consciousness. It became influential in sociology – though not to any great extent – through the work of Alfred Schutz and his interest in the constitution of everyday experience: the life-world. For him this was the 'paramount reality' and the main focus of sociological inquiry. Social actors encounter the world as a 'pre-given' social world in which they interact on the basis of their common sense and practical knowledge. It is an experience in which the world is taken for granted and understood mainly in terms of 'typifications'. Schutz's work was greatly influential on Harold Garfinkel, whose ethnomethodology was built out of Schutz's more philosophical reflections.

The implications we want to pick out here are the primary ones. First, that the scientific point of view is among a plurality of points of view, and therefore, sociologically considered, the interest in science would be similar to the interest taken in any other point of view. Second, treating the meanings of science in this way is a way of identifying science as a domain of social action which will involve such considerations as differentiating, coordinating with and competing against other points of view.

Thus far we have sought to establish that:

- Variable analysis is akin to the stimulus–response model that interactionism initially set out to reject, in that it was concerned with establishing a uniform causal connection between a feature of the environment and persons' reactions to this.
- The stimulus and response are seen as independent of each other, as required by cause and effect relationships. Interactionism, by contrast, does not see the stimulus as identifiable independently of the way people respond to it.
- The root connection between the stimulus and response is provided by the assignment of meaning or, as it is often put, through an intervening process of interpretation.
- People's environment or 'reality' is 'perspectival'. It is identified and responded to through one or another of indefinitely many points of view.

Thus, one can see why Blumer's critique of variable analysis is not just a critique of it as a procedure for developing definitions and concepts suitable for formal theory, but for its conception of the actor. If, as interactionists such as Blumer argue, social actors are interpreting beings, then the variable analysis model makes no provision for the process of interpretation. In a way it is worse than this. The model not only makes no such provision but effectively obscures the fact that such a process is involved. This brings us to another key point:

- That a social phenomenon takes its identity – is the phenomenon that it is – only in a context of interpretation. This is a point often made another way as the claim that there is nothing intrinsic to some phenomenon which makes it into the stimulus that it is. There is nothing intrinsic in the red light that makes it a sign to stop; some other colour could have served just as well. Yellow, for example, is often used as a sign of danger in sites where radioactivity is present.

Unless, therefore, we are aware of the context in which some 'stimulus' occurs, we will not understand the relationship between that stimulus and the response to it, for we will not understand what the stimulus is and why it brings about the response that it does. It is this view which provides the rationale for Blumer's critique of variable analysis and explains why it is fieldwork, not social surveys, which enable social researchers to identify things in their context.

> Contextualism

It is the introduction of *contextualism* which, we think, is one of the major changes which extends more widely than the interactionist tradition and differentiates it from the tradition which culminated in variable analysis. The latter very much inherits an *atomistic* way of thinking, quite naturally since this had proven so successful in the natural sciences from which the tradition took its inspiration. By 'atomistic' we mean that the basic successful method is assumed to be that of understanding a phenomenon by breaking it up into its constituent parts, separating them out from each other, isolating each from the circumstances in which it is found so that it may be identified in its 'pure' form. Recall in this respect Parsons' 'analytic realism' and the analogy with chemistry.

Of course, it was not the interactionist tradition alone but a much broader movement within social thought which resisted atomistic thinking by insisting that the way to identify *social* phenomena was not to search for independently existing elements, but to recognise that social phenomena existed *relationally*. The identity of social phenomena hinged upon what they were related to. (We will meet the same idea in structuralism, though in a very different form and with very different application). This brings us to another element in the 'interactionist' tradition, and one reflected in the name. We have been talking about the way in which the individual's reaction to 'stimuli' is mediated by a process of interpretation as though this is all there is to social phenomena: that is, individual reactions to interpreted stimuli. However, interactionists would reject this, at least if it is understood as implying that social phenomena are interpreted by each individual independently of other people.

At this point we want to turn to Phase 2 of the chapter and begin by revisiting the idea of 'the actor's point of view'.

Revisiting 'the actor's point of view'

The 'actor's point of view' is the central phenomenon of inquiry for symbolic interactionism and, in different ways, for ethnomethodology. For both, one might say, social phenomena consist in nothing other than the actor's point of view – treating this, as we have been arguing, as a methodological not an ontological remark. It is a direct implication of the notion of the 'definition of the situation'. Members of society act upon the basis of their definitions of the situation or, as it is more commonly called, their interpretation. So, as we have said, fieldwork becomes a means of exploring the actor's point of view, and the guidelines set out in Chapter 9 indicate ways of filling this out.

However, the emphasis on 'definition of the situation' and interpretation has two potential and deep implications. The first is that social phenomena are interpretation 'all the way down'. That is, there can be no exemptions, no areas of social life which do not involve interpretation. Second is the question of whether the researcher's point of view is also just another interpretation.

> Definition of the situation

To remind ourselves, the positivist tradition took the view that objectivity was to be dealt with through method. The 'real world' is and *is only* defined through the application of an accredited scientific method. Only those propositions established through scientifically approved procedures can count as facts. Therefore, 'the real world' within which members of society act is nothing other than whatever is reported as a result of following the positivist rules of method. The sociologist knows, in ways that members of society do not, what the real world – the real society – is like.

Members of society act in this real world but they do so mainly through a 'veil of illusion', as Durkheim would put it. The success or failure of their actions is determined by the nature of the real world of which the members of society are largely unaware since they lack the mastery of scientific methods. Hence, how members' actions turn out does not depend upon their understanding and intentions, which further means that the kind of explanations members of society give to each other, their beliefs and intentions say, cannot be the proper explanation of why they do what they do. Scientifically identified causes need to be given for their actions. Hence, the sociologist is *privileged* to know the nature of social reality itself, and therefore able to give the true explanations of why persons act in the ways they do, and why their actions turn out as they do. This was one of the main motivations behind the desire to make sociology a science, from Comte, through Marx and Durkheim, to variable analysis: science will enable people to determine, for the first time, what people in society are really doing.

The counter to the above from those who make the 'definition of the situation' central to their picture of society is as follows. The picture that positivist science paints of the real world – of the real society – is not the one to which the members of society respond. The members of society do not respond to the 'real world' *per se* or, to put it another way, 'the real world' in the bare, in principle, physical, description that positivism gives of it. As explicated through the natural sciences and their methods, the real world is one of bare material facts, but members of society respond to the world that has meaning. Someone who runs away from a fire does not do so merely because it of its physical properties as a fire, but because of beliefs they have about what its being a fire means, what effects those physical properties can have on human flesh, because they fear that they will get burned. The reality of a fire as 'a threat of injury' is one of the things that is to be included as an instance of 'the meaning' of a phenomenon, and this is not something inherent in its nature as fire, but a feature of its relationship to people who would rather not get burned. The fire is *understood* as a threat, and it is this which results in the running away. A woman to whom the fire was the ritual funeral pyre of her husband might, in Hindu culture, voluntarily let it burn her. It is the interpretation of the situation that makes the difference, that decides the response.

As we argued in the first part of this chapter, none of the above disputes that natural phenomena exist independently of actors' definitions, or that they have been successfully studied using scientific methods. After all, fire does burn. The issue is entirely over the *relevance* of this to sociological study. To say something is irrelevant is not to deny that it exists. Moreover, social phenomena are, from the point of view of relevance to sociology, to a major extent made up of definitions of the situation.

The notion of 'definition of the situation' is not to be understood as a matter of there being 'a situation' which the parties to it then 'define'. The important step is to insist on *the identity of* the situation and its definition: the situation is, *for sociological* purposes, however it is defined by those in that situation. The situation consists in its definition, exists as a situation through its interpretation. In ethnomethodology this is characterised as the 'reflexivity of accounts'. Thus, a professional–client encounter consists in the reciprocal definition of one party as, say, 'a doctor', and the other as 'a patient'. This is a very different angle of approach from the one the positivists set out. There is no need for sociologists to define a 'real society' by properly scientific methods as a *starting point* for understanding how people act. The researcher's first, and in many ways only, task is to identify people's definition of the situation, for that identifies the situation in which they act. Hence, methods which are to capture social reality must take account of the way that situations are made up of definitions or interpretations. Social reality is, then, whatever the members of society define it as being. In which case there is nothing for a supposedly 'objective' scientific method to find out. As we have said previously, this is the point of fieldwork.

> Reflexivity of accounts

Objectivity and its temptations

'Objectivity', in the sense defined by the positivist tradition, is a matter of securing agreement among investigators. Different researchers using the same method should get the same results. The role of positivist method is to impose discipline, to eradicate the subjectivity of the observer. The capacity to observe events correctly is affected by the interference of various 'subjective'

> Dealing with subjectivity

features of individuals, such as their emotions, their own values, their partiality. It is well known, for example, that eyewitnesses can vary in their descriptions of the same event. They can be unprepared, surprised, frightened and so on, which inhibits their capacity to observe correctly. Method, in the positivist understanding, is there to inhibit the extent to which such factors interfere with the capacity for correct observation and recording. Part of the motivation for positivist methods was to repair the fact that sociological observers characteristically do not agree in their descriptions. If sociological observation is irresolvably contaminated by subjectivity, there will be none of the progress that method was meant to ensure.

One response to the above conclusion might be to embrace the subjectivity of sociology. Sociological research is a personal affair and the need in method is to make this much more apparent, to bring out the extent to which the sociologist's report is a personal response to a situation. After all, sociologists, too, are social beings and cannot rise above the realities of ordinary social life, cannot help but respond in some 'human' way to the situation and fate of the people they study. Further, the people they study are not inanimate objects but are thinking and feeling human beings who cannot be studied in a detached, objective and unfeeling manner. The research relationship is not an impersonal one, but an inter-personal one.

As we saw in Chapter 5, some feminist researchers, for example, explicitly adopt this kind of position arguing that the relationship between a researcher and her subjects has to be one of emotional equality (Stanley and Wise, 1982; Stanley, 1990; Skeggs, 1997). To separate reason and emotion as the condition for rigorous and objective research is a betrayal of the true nature of things, for research is a two-way process that affects both the researcher and the researched. Indeed, the researcher's biography is not something to exclude from research since it can be highly relevant to the research process rather than devalued as subjective.

A further implication of the recognition that social research is irreducibly subjective is that it is inherently perspectival. On the interactionist view, society is

> Problems of perspectivalism

an ensemble of perspectives, made up of different definitions of situations, and the sociologist's is just one more among the multitude. But if we allow this, then do we not seem to be condemned to relativism? Social reality is whatever it is defined as being by each individual. If individuals define it differently then there are multiple realities – as many as there are individuals – and each one just as real as any other.

Further difficulties seem to arise from the idea of subjective, multiple realities as leading to a kind of solipsism, the conviction that my own point of view is the only one I can possibly know. If society is only an ensemble of individual points of view – as many points of view as there are members of society – then all that one's point of view can be is precisely just one's own point of view. One cannot hope to capture any one else's point of view in its own right. One can only give one's version of someone's point of view, which cannot be the same as their point of view. There can be no appeal to a transcendent perspective that stands outside and above the hurly burly of multiple, multitudinous perspectives. Hence, all that one could really do is give voice to one's own perspective, dissociating oneself from any sociological practices that suggest otherwise. One must insist upon the personal, subjective character of one's research report in a way comparable to that in which novelists sometimes insist on the fictional nature of their text, design it in such a way as to undermine any appearance of attempting to give an objective, last-word version.

One seeming implication is that there is an essential 'politics' here. Since all points of view are distinct and autonomous, any appearance of universal generality or of a uniform social structure must be a denial of the true nature of reality, which is endlessly diverse, and must be the product of the imposition of some one point of view on others, of – at least – the suppression or obfuscation of points of view which dissent from the appearance of uniformity. The positivists, for example, were not trying to bring out the true nature of reality, but to disguise it.

> The implicit politics of research

This implication resonates with a more general tendency in the discipline to refurbish the critical thread in sociology, emphasising the hegemonic character of social phenomena: social reality is itself determined through a 'politics of experience'. The mode of analysis shifts toward seeing interaction as domination and control. As we shall also discuss in Part III, it also contributes to the 'crisis of representation', in that attention is drawn to the extent to which representation – in the way that Marx's critique of ideology condemns – seeks to generalise one point of view of reality as though it were the only possible point of view rather than one which is being imposed upon others. The representation obscures the conditions of its own production which, if investigated, will reveal the mechanisms by which alternative and dissenting voices or conceptions of reality are suppressed and excluded. This line of thought denies that there can be any determinacy in the characterisation of social reality; one cannot capture it with a single voice. The impression that it is uniform is a political outcome secured by the exclusion of the irreducible plurality of individual points of view.

> Crisis of representation

Toward social constructionism

Here one can see some of the lineaments of 'social constructionism' which has inspired an enormous amount of work, and controversy, especially as a result of its application to natural science and the claim that even natural reality is a social construction (Berger and Luckman, 1966; Barnes, 1977). It is a conception that will resurface in Part III, as will some of the issues about the 'single-voiced' as opposed to the 'dialogical' nature of social reality. For now all we want to point out is that it is a notion bound up, and confusingly so, with philosophical, critical and methodological matters, and we will try to develop the arguments against aspects of the idea insofar as they affect interactionist sociologies.

In simple terms, social constructionism takes the view that the nature of social reality, and sometimes the reality of the natural world, is 'constructed' (which means much the same as 'defined') in and through members' interpretative activity. This means with respect to natural and social reality that however they are defined, they are defined that way because of the way processes of interpretation or definition work, not because of their own intrinsic character – for, sociologically speaking, they have no such character.

Inset 10.2 Labelling theory

Labelling theory gained prominence within the sociology of deviance, being first put forward by Lemert (1951) and subsequently developed by Becker (1963). The theory claims that deviant behaviour is not simply the violation of a norm but any behaviour which is successfully defined as, or labelled as, deviant in some way. Deviance does not inhere in the act itself but in the responses of others to that act. Further, it is claimed that labelling amplifies the deviance. The deviant's response to the societal reaction, the labelling, leads to secondary deviation in that the deviant comes to accept the label of deviant and so becomes trapped in the deviant role. A major implication of the theory is that deviance is the outcome of the process of social control itself.

Labelling theory has also been used outside the domain of criminality to also illuminate the process of becoming mentally ill.

The basic objection to 'social construction of reality' by many critics of interactionism is that it not only implies relativism, but that at its very roots it is idealist. This is a criticism which often comes not only from positivists but also from anti-positivists, such as Marxists and post-Marxists, as well as those sociologists who share a Durkheim-style conception of social reality as equating with 'society' as a social whole or totality. In other words, social constructionism seems to imply for sociologists who cling to materialism, or to related positions, that social reality is ephemeral, to the neglect of the real causal factors which generate the inequalities, such as those of power and wealth, which so typify society.

What the dispute revives is a very old sociological argument that society is more than just a collection of individuals, which leads onto the issues of structure versus agency.

Structure versus agency from an interactionist perspective

To many of its critics, interactionism is understood to be saying that there is no such thing as society: there are only individuals, their definitions of the situation, and their actions. Interaction is between individuals. However, this picture of interactionism neglects its strenuous opposition to the idea that social reality can be composed into the properties and actions of individuals. After all, following Mead, it attacked the notion that there could be any psychology that was not a *social* psychology. The term 'interactionist' is meant to emphasise:

- the extent to which seemingly individual properties are not the primary data for sociology because they are extensively products of social interaction
- that social phenomena are collective in nature, subsist in the relations between individuals, and are emergent from interaction – which sounds much like Durkheim.

Even though the emphasis is on the study of people in face-to-face interaction, this is not intended to imply that society can only be recognised as the encounters of a small number of individuals. Erving Goffman is often accused of this fallacy. His fascinating books almost entirely involve the study of face-to-face – or as he called them, 'co-present' – activities and, as a result, he is often seen as a leading example of interactionism, with the conclusion that the approach only conceives of society as face-to-face encounters.

This, however, is a false impression, arising from a partial reading of Goffman himself and a very partial reading of the interactionist literature more generally. It is an obvious fact that very large and complex arrangements of *collective* action can be built out of face-to-face encounters, and that the interactions of very large numbers of different individuals can be connected up, coordinated and interrelated. Some of these patterns of action can be stabilised into the sort of official arrangements of the society that Marxists, Durkheimians and functionalists call 'structures'. However, it will only be understood how these structures are created, stabilised and operate if they are understood as complexes of social interaction created, sustained and renewed through the process of ongoing social activity.

Many critics persist in treating interactionism as if it were saying that society is the expression of a purely individualistic and subjective point of view. So, if social reality is what individuals define it as being, if it consists wholly and entirely in members' definitions, then any individual can define social reality in whatever way he or she chooses. Such a definition cannot be considered inadequate to any situation since it defines what the situation is. No individual can be wrong about any situation. However, this overlooks the fact that the notion of 'definition of the situation' is really shorthand for 'definition and redefinition of the situation'. Defining the situation unfolds over time, with one definition being tried out, found wanting, a new definition being ventured, and so on, and so on.

Still, for someone who misunderstands the idea in supposing that there can be no mistakes in definition – no mistakes, since it is what people define a situation as being which makes the situation what it is – then, equally, there can be nothing to constrain individuals' definitions. Which, of course, leads to the absurdity, and one often intended by critics, that someone could define a situation as one in which they could fly by just flapping their arms. If so, we should have to accept this since they have defined the situation in that way, and then they must be able to fly by flapping their arms.

Not only is this absurd, it is not what 'defining the situation' ever meant. Even more pertinently, the criticism claims that interactionism is premised on an absurd picture of human action as something which is exempt from constraint, upon which there is no external limitation. This is what leads to the charge of idealism: allegedly interactionism's picture of social reality is that it exists only in the mind of the individual. Interactionism cannot acknowledge any kind of external reality against which the individual's definition can be tested and through which external constraints can exercise a limiting influence. It is a picture of the social actor which flies in the face of sociological orthodoxy, namely, that social actors and their activities are constrained by supra-individual forces and structures which are external to and transcend the actor's standpoint. Moreover, this criticism is often conjoined with a presumption about the essential ingredients of this external social reality: namely, 'power', 'gender', 'ethnicity' and other structures of inequality.

Inset 10.3 Realism

Realism claims that explanation in both the natural and the social sciences consists in uncovering the real, underlying mechanisms that connect phenomena causally. Such mechanisms are often unobservable, hence realism rejects the positivist conception that causal relationships are to be identified as instances of observed regularity.

The above critique sees itself as 'realist' in two senses. It is realist about the existence of a mind-independent external world and also about the existence of a supra-individual level of social phenomena (Sayer, 2000). Society is something more than the aggregate of individuals. In such terms, interactionism stands indicted of two sociological crimes: first, that it treats society as if consisted only in the actions and interactions of individuals, and second that it exaggerates the capacity of individuals to determine the course of their conduct through their own volition, thereby denying the reality of social constraint.

The two alleged faults are connected, in that if there is to be any external constraint on the actions of individuals then it will need to be external to their consciousness as well as external to their actions and interactions.

Interactionism lacks, in other words, a recognition of the fact that individual actions are situated and constrained by the large-scale, supra-individual social structure.

It is difficult to make either of these charges stick on the basis of what is actually written within the interactionist tradition. In the example used earlier, of people fleeing from a fire, the point was made that from the point of view of understanding how and why people act in the way they do, how they came to be running from the fire, it is not the 'fire itself' which engenders the action. The relationship between the fire and the fleeing away is not like a causal connection between one pool ball striking another (Winch, 1990). The running away is occasioned by anticipation of the effects the fire will have if it gets too close. It is the fire *defined as a threat* that provokes the flight. Without this definition, people might just stand there waiting to see what might happen when the fire came close. There is nothing 'idealist' in saying that people often act upon the basis of their anticipations. For *sociological purposes* there is no point in seeking to identify natural or other phenomena 'in themselves' since this is not the identity which affects their actions. Such phenomena (a fire) affect actions (running away) only in their interpreted form (a threat). The insistence of the interactionists on stressing 'definitions of the situation' has been distorted as the idea that situations exist only in the heads of the members of society.

The struggle over structure and agency is conceived as an oppositional one between two extreme positions neither of which, we suggest, has ever really existed. On the one hand are those who emphasise the absolute self-determining power of individuals and, on the other, those who argue for the utterly constraining, even totally determining, effects of social structure. In terms of classic theory, it is supposed to be an opposition between the tradition of Marx and Durkheim, and that of Weber and the phenomenological tradition, but it seems to us to be much too simplified even for these familiar cases. It seems to be a fundamental dichotomy: a choice between society either as objective or subjective reality, or between society as the production of individual 'agency' or individual actions as products of structures.

> Structure versus agency

However, one way out of this seeming conflict is to understand the contrast as a matter of degree. Individuals are to some extent able to do what they want, but they are also to some extent limited by social structures in what they do. Society is both an objective and a subjective reality and individual actions are products of structure, but these actions, in turn, reproduce the social structure. Thus, one of the main theoretical ploys in recent years has been to replace the relationship between structure and agency as one of opposition with one of blending the two ideas. This ploy will be discussed more fully later in this chapter.

While this might seem a reasonable manoeuvre, the question remains: Does it capture a genuine schism drawn along the line that the contrast of 'structure' and 'agency' seeks to summarise?

There are two different kinds of issues involved here:

- Is the characterisation of, for example, the interactionist approach one which identifies its actual features?
- Does interactionism, when properly understood, actually suffer from these shortcomings?

We suggest that an accurate identification of interactionism's arguments undermines the idea that a supposed blending of structure and agency adds value to sociological thinking.

Let us return to the set of oppositions with which we began as summarised below:

Member's point of view	Analyst's point of view
Idealism	Materialism
Social reality as individual phenomenon	Social reality as more than product of individual actions
Individual actions as free	Individual actions as constrained
Face-to-face interaction	Large-scale organisation
Society as micro-phenomenon	Society as macro-phenomenon

There are some, as we mentioned earlier, who see the matter as making a choice between one side or the other. Those who argue for a synthesis of the two sides, for structure and agency, are perhaps more attached to these dualisms than the interactionist tradition has ever been. As we have tried to explain, the interactionist tradition does not place itself in terms of these oppositions, for it declines to construe matters in dualistic terms to begin with. Critics fail to recognise the extent to which the interactionist tradition, especially ethnomethodology, was dedicated to subverting standard philosophical and sociological dualisms. (George Herbert Mead, and the pragmatists who influenced his views, were dedicated to subverting the dualisms dominant in nineteenth-century philosophy, and it is a great irony that their late twentieth-century descendants are criticised for falling on the 'wrong' side of one or more of these pre-twentieth-century dualisms.)

We have already indicated how some can be misled by the notion of 'definition of the situation' into thinking that it must involve subjectivism, idealism and individualism, but also tried to give reasons why this implication does not follow. Let us now try to make the logic of this rejection of the dualisms a little more systematic.

The interactionist position

The aim of interactionism does not involve seeing the members and the sociological analyst as engaged in comparable determinations of social reality, such that there is a need to worry about aligning one with the other. While the central problematic is to capture the actor's point of view, the point is not to identify with that point of view – to accept or agree with it – but, rather, to understand how members of society, individually *and collectively*, come to form and act upon the definition of the situation, whatever that may be. On this conception sociology is neither more nor less than the portrayal of the ways in which definitions of the situation are formed and responded to.

The interactionists are arguing, with respect to the explanation of actions, that the insistence on a mind-independent external reality does not allow for the fact that it is only by virtue of its meaning, of the way it is defined, that the external natural and social world can figure in the organisation of *actions*. Of course, if some people define a fire as harmless and stand in its path, they will be burned, and burned *because of the way they have defined the fire*. To say this is not to say that they died because of their definition of the situation. They died because they were consumed by the flames. Their definition explains why they did not remove themselves from the threat; it is not a rival to understanding that it was the fire that killed them. (It is, of course, our assumption – that is, the definition that we, readers and writers, are taking for granted, that if someone remains in the path of an oncoming fire they will be burnt.) Thus, it is not a question of an alternative between a set of subjective definitions and a set of externally given conditions. Far from cutting off the definition of the situation from the given conditions, interactionists insist that for sociological purposes, the two just are inextricable. Sociologically, the given conditions, whatever they are, can only be 'known' via their definitions, and it is on the basis of these that action is formed.

Nor should it be supposed that there is a dichotomy between the definition of the situation and individual actions, as though 'defining the situation' were something that goes on mentally and prior to action. What makes the emphasis sociological is the fact that 'defining the situation' itself goes on in and through inter-action. It is produced through communication – as the titular emphasis on *symbolic* interaction tries to highlight. 'Defining the situation' is done in and through a flow of activity, and it is the depiction of a particular aspect of that flow of activity, the way in which that flow of activity organises itself to arrive at and further act upon a definition of the situation, which is the investigative business of the approach. Thus, understanding 'defining the situation' is nothing other than providing a depiction of social processes.

> Defining the situation as interactional

Interactionism also refuses to make a distinction between an individual with pre-given characteristics and social processes formed on the basis of such characteristics. The individual's properties are themselves derivative from the social process itself. Individuals are what they are – 'men', 'women', 'pensioners', 'drivers', 'medical students', 'lazy', 'beautiful', 'sick', and so on and on – because of their involvement in interaction. Ethnomethodology, for example, makes this point through its analyses of categorisation practices in which identities and categories are invoked in the course of naturally occurring activities (Sacks and Schegloff, 1979). *For the purposes of analysis,* there is nothing, including the characteristics of individuals, external to the social process.

Definitions of the situation are not worked up from scratch as if the individual defined the situation in a vacuum and, therefore, the situation could be defined in any way whatsoever. As a characterisation of what human life is like this is patently absurd, and it is absurd to interactionists, too. Defining situations is ongoing and begins in early childhood. It is located in the social process and, at any point in time, is only the latest stage in a continuous and unfolding flow of activity. Defining the situation is done in terms of what is given at the time, on the one hand, and available cultural resources on the other. The individual does not select the circumstances that require definition; these befall him or her. Nor is it imagined that the individual could *de novo* define situations at all. The individual is in possession of an accumulated set of socioculturally acquired interpretative resources, has available sets of received schemes of interpretation with which it is possible to assign a definition of the circumstances confronting him or her. Hence the massive emphasis interactionism gives to adult as well as child socialisation, to taking over new frameworks of definition through learning them from others.

In the preceding chapter we mentioned Schutz's notion of 'first order constructs', the concepts and categories, we might say, which comprise definitions of the situation. He sees this as an aspect of the 'natural attitude', that is, our ordinary experience of the world: an attitude in which the 'world out there' is presupposed and taken for granted at face value by the members of society. As Bittner summarises it:

> I, the perceiving subject who faces the world knowingly, know that as an object among objects I enjoy no special privilege. I come into being, endure, and perish as a thing among other things and even if I have it within me to look forward to redemption, it will not be in this world. However much I may have taken charge of my own life, the bare fact of my existence is just that, a fact over which I have no control. Moreover, a great many of the features of my existence are given in the just the same way as the fact of existence itself. And all of this is prior to either stoic calm or *angst* about it.
>
> (Bittner, 1973: 120)

In these words there is no suggestion that the social world is 'up for grabs'. The world of daily life is overwhelmingly characterised in terms of the mundane, the routine, the commonplace, over-and-again nature of the affairs that take place within it, and these affairs are commonly undertaken as the reproduction of standard situations carried through in matter-of-course ways. Indeed, Schutz's ideas and the standard Durkheimian conception of the given, objective and intractable nature of 'social facts' are very similar. The difference is that for Durkheim, and for traditional sociology more generally, the 'objectivity of social facts' is pronounced as the premise of sociological theory. However, from Schutz and Garfinkel's point of view this describes the standpoint of the member of society, one which, if correct, is oriented to the 'reality of social facts' as the starting point for understanding the character of our experience of the social world.

The individual is therefore plainly 'constrained' both by the circumstances that require definition and the resources that provide the means of definition. Moreover, it must be emphasised that the individual is constrained in defining the situation itself. 'Defining the situation' must not be understood as involving any kind of unilateral legislation, but more as the resolution of a problem, a problem embedded in and carried though in socially organised circumstances. It is a problem that must be solved with others to achieve a common definition of the situation and figure out what, practically, the social actor can do in these circumstances here and now.

However, the above argument should not be construed as implying that social actors are constrained only by their most immediate circumstances. The argument that interactionism cannot recognise that 'large-scale social structures' place limitations on what social actors can do – hence the need for micro and macro sociological theories to complement each other – is simply wrong.

> Interactionism and large-scale social structures

From an interactionist perspective, such critics are confused between what is external to the immediate situation and what is external to consciousness. The fact that the interactionist approach emphasises the *in situ* nature of action, its location in here-and-now, does not imply that persons in situations have no awareness of larger-scale social arrangements, or of their place in them. 'The situation in which the definition takes place' and the 'situation as defined' are not the same kind of things. Two persons, here and now, may comprise the site where the defining is going on, but it would not be adequately defined were it to exclude the fact, say, that they are employees of a major multinational corporation, managing its international financial transactions in order to figure out how the company would be placed in the event of an stock market downfall. The point is that 'large-scale social structures' patently do constrain people's actions, but they do so by virtue of their meaning, through the way they are defined and through the chains of interaction that make up the continuing affairs of collectivities.

The above arguments may have gone someway to correcting some mistakes about interactionist sociology and its supposed subjectivist and individualistic tendencies. However, as we have indicated, the issues were never simply about these. The charge of subjectivity is often wrapped up with a view which treated the social actor's subjective viewpoint as deficient in being unable to view society and social arrangements objectively. This issue touches closely upon that of the relationship between the social world according to the social actor and the potentially privileged picture of the social world according to the sociological theorist.

The relationship between actor's conceptions and theorist's conceptions

As we have stressed throughout, one of the main purposes for creating a sociological science was to bring objective knowledge to bear on the resolution of the various conflicts, tensions, sufferings and inequalities which had so marred the history of human society. This ambition was the spur for Marx, for Durkheim and, in its way, for the positivist project. What interactionist sociologies seem to do is foreclose on the possibility of objective knowledge produced by the application of appropriate methods of analysis and, hopefully, contribute to the remedy of such social ills.

Interactionist sociology's emphasis on 'definitions of the situation' and 'actor's point of view, even in light of the corrective arguments we have just reviewed, seem to support the view that whatever definitions of social reality the members of society come up with, there is no principled way in which this can be shown to be faulty. If there is no 'external reality' which shapes, even determines, actions to be uncovered by appropriate methods of analysis, then we have to accept that social reality is whatever the members of society define it as being.

The complaint is often coupled with the accusation that one of the major failings of interactionist sociologies is that they do not deal with 'power', 'gender', 'ethnicity', and the like, and are accordingly trivial and wilfully dismissive of the brute and sometimes brutal realities of social life. From what has been said earlier, it should be clear that interactionist sociologies do not deny any of these phenomena. Rather, they see their impact as products of interaction and definitions of the situation not as transcendent properties. They are not phenomena which, as it were, exist 'externally', independent of what the members of society actually do in their interactions.

In important ways, this particular criticism stems from the failure to understand the investigative stance of interactionism, in particular that of ethnomethodology. The point of fieldwork, of the 'bottom-up' approach, is to find out what social life is like, not to stipulate in advance of inquiry what will be found. Conceptions of power, gender, stratification, inequality, and the rest are ubiquitously part and parcel of the vocabulary in and through which we socially organise and make sense of the world. They are not by any means exclusive discoveries of sociological theory. The burden of Garfinkel's – along with Sacks, one of the founders of ethnomethodology – use of Schutz is to take his conception of the intersubjective experience of the social world, and *only that*, in order to see what kind of studies it allowed him to make of that world. Explicating the organisational properties of intersubjective experience rigorously means that concepts cannot be imported from 'outside' this frame, so to speak. Thus, rather than endowing concepts such as 'rationality', 'power', 'gender' or 'class' with a transcendental status as generally explanatory principles, ethnomethodology

> Interactionism's investigative stance

proposes to investigate them in the local and historical circumstances of their production (Lynch and Bogen, 1996).

Ethnomethodology goes further than this, however, and adopts a posture of 'indifference' to the versions of society propagated by its members. It sees itself as having no licence to criticise or evaluate these views from the standpoint of ethnomethodology. Of course, as citizens, ethnomethodologists are as variously politically aware and as sensitive to moral issues as any collection of people. But it is as citizens that they take political and moral stances, not as ethnomethodologists. In this respect, they concur with Weber's strictures against some of the academics of his day who paraded political views as if they were academic and objective (Weber, 1949).

> Ethnomethodology's 'indifference'

In this respect, ethnomethodology is perhaps stricter than symbolic interactionism which, to some extent, seemed more embarrassed about the charge of subjectivism made by the positivist project against fieldwork. Moreover, much of more prominent symbolic interactionist research had focused upon so-called deviant subcultures which, through the development of labelling theory for example (Lemert, 1967), had seemingly portrayed criminals as more sinned against than sinning. While this was not entirely fair, Becker did acknowledge that social research takes place within a living society in which people will take sides about many issues (Becker, 1967). The point is not so much for the researcher to avoid these as to be clear and open about his or her own commitments. In any event, many of the groups studied by symbolic interactionists were subordinate groups and less able to make their voice heard, and accordingly many took the view that is was no bad thing for ethnographic research to redress the balance somewhat.

Ethnomethodology's formal interest in the actor's point of view contrasts with symbolic interactionism's exploitation of the idea as one located in particular times and places. Symbolic interactionism's work was to render a version of society as seen from the point of view of people such as medical students, panhandlers, street walkers, photocopying technicians, police officers and store keepers. Ethnomethodology has no version of this kind. There is no other world but that of daily life and ethnomethodology's task is to identify and bring out, through analysis, the commonalities and differences, the competencies, the methods by which members endlessly produce daily life. It has no version of society of its own to compete with – to be better or worse than – that of the members of society.

The issue of the relationship between sociological theories and the pictures of society held by members is not one which has gone away. Quite the contrary. As we shall see in Part III, it resurfaces in a rather radical manner.

Conclusion

In this chapter we have reviewed some of the arguments which not only were critical of positivist sociology and social research methods, but also proposed an alternative conception of the sociological endeavour. The alternative approach stressed the centrality of the 'actor's point of view' as essential to the conception of the social. This was coupled with a critique of positivist methods which not only failed to adequately capture the interactional process of defining situations but, more than this, profoundly distorted the very phenomena they should have been investigating as sociological methods.

With the more systematic formulation of symbolic interactionism as an approach, an approach placing the actor's point of view centrally as the phenomenon of sociological inquiry, ethnography became almost mandatory as *the* method of research appropriate to the phenomena. It is in this respect that, occasionally, symbolic interactionism claimed that it was more scientific than positivism in that not only had it identified the phenomenon of sociology but also the means by which it could be studied.

We have also discussed some of the frequent and persistent misrepresentations of interactionist sociologies, in particular, their alleged idealism and relativism. This also gave us the occasion to discuss one of the more enduring of sociological debates, namely, that about structure versus agency.

In the next chapter, which concludes Part II, we want to build on what has gone before and address some issues which, we hope, will help prepare for the next part of the book.

Selected bibliography and suggested reading

- In addition to readings suggested in the previous chapters of this part of the book, more specific material relevant to this chapter includes, of course, Garfinkel's *Studies in Ethnomethodology* (Prentice-Hall, 1967). This is still the major source for ethnomethodology, though it is not an easy read for those coming to it new. Useful sources are W.W. Sharrock and R.J. Anderson, *The Ethnomethodologists* (Tavistock, 1981) and G. Button (ed.), *Ethnomethodology and the Human Sciences* (Cambridge University Press, 1991). The essay by Sharrock, 'The Social Actor: Social Action in Real Time' is especially relevant.
- Some of the realist literature, too, can be daunting. R. Bhaskar's *A Realist Theory of Science* (Alma Books, 1975) is one of the early statements but it is not easy going. Andrew Sayer's *Realism and Social Science* (Sage, 2000) is more straightforward.

Chapter 11

Data Collection versus Analysis

Trying to work through the ideas of 'definition of the situation' and 'actor's point of view' as the basis of a systematic empirical sociology is the distinctive characteristic of the approaches discussed in this part of the book. As we have seen, it was the rise of positivistic sociology in the form of variable analysis which did much to encourage the more systematic development of themes rooted in the early Chicago School and, somewhat later, in European phenomenology.

The idea that the way in which people understand their world is important to comprehending how courses of action became organised was not, of course, new to sociology. Marx's notion of 'ideology', for example, was more than just an acknowledgement that different ways of understanding the world in which social actors lived were critical for the patterns of behaviour in which they engaged; it also showed that these ways of understanding were themselves the product of structural forces lodged in the socio-economic base. Indeed, there was a strong theoretical suggestion that there was a causal connection between how people understood their world and their place within it, and the social structure: an idea which was to be a firm part of the agenda of sociological inquiry to the present day. Even positivism, through the measurement of notions such as 'attitudes', 'beliefs' and 'values', using variable analysis set itself the task of uncovering correlations between these and structural variables.

With the growth of so-called 'interpretative' sociologies came also a questioning of what sort of science sociology should be. As we have seen, symbolic interactionism directed sharp methodological criticism at variable analysis, a criticism which was to be reinforced by scholars such as Cicourel (1964) and, in many ways more tellingly, by fellow positivists such as Leiberson (1985) and Blalock (1982). It was clear that such criticisms could not be confined to techniques but amounted to a serious critique of the conception of sociology as an empirical science: a critique echoing many of the reservations expressed by Max Weber about positivistic social science.

In simple terms, the methodological debate centred around a distinction between the quantitative methods which call for objective, standardised, classificatory modes of inquiry and the more naturalistic qualitative modes of investigation which respected the everyday world of interaction. The difference was between those who approach the study of social life abstractly and objectively, and those who observe social life concretely and subjectively, between those who see the social actor on the one hand as a being determined by external forces, and on the other as a being acting with freedom and purpose. It also turned out that the label traditionally applied to the latter approaches as 'interpretative' was doubly appropriate in that it seemed to recognise that the sociologist could not be some independent, cold and calculating scientific observer but was also a human being who had to operate within society. In which case, the social scientist could not investigate the social world as if he or she were independent of it.

> Qualitative vs quantitative research

As should be no surprise, matters were not so clear-cut. The arguments advanced by Blumer, among others we have discussed, were not arguments about whether or not sociology could be a science, but against the positivist version – variable analysis – of social science. If anything, the argument was about the nature of social phenomena and how it might be investigated without the distortions introduced by positivistic methods. From this point of view, the problem was to find ways of bringing out the 'actor's point of view' and to do so methodically and systematically. In other words, it was not an opposition to the idea that sociology could be a science, but that, if it was to be then it would need to be a science that was faithful to its phenomena. Achieving that would, in Blumer's opinion, take a long time. What would such an alternative look like? Would it mean, for example, abandoning the familiar standards and objectives of science, such as objectivity, rigour and the search for generalisations?

As we have seen, symbolic interactionism, though passionate in its critique of variable analysis, turned out to be ambiguous in terms of how far it could dispense with positivistic assumptions about the methods of science. While it argued for a major shift in the focus of sociological inquiry toward examining the natural everyday habitats in which human beings lived their lives, in many respects it succumbed to positivistic criteria about hypothesis testing and theory building, and nowhere more so than in the approach of grounded theory. The methods were different but, in the end, they were seen as moving toward the same goals as variable analysis. Glaser and Strauss's methodological prescriptions, for example, stress theory as arising out of the research process itself in a continuous intermeshing of data collection and analysis. However, the symbolic interactionists' attitude to theory was far less full-blooded than that of positivism. If anything, they regarded variable analysis's strictures on theory development through hypothesis testing as

> Grounded theory

premature. The first priority for research was to obtain a better understanding of the phenomena of sociology and that, as we have said, could take some time. Their main objective could be said to that of discovery, finding out what is going on, rather than collecting data to test some hypothesis.

Nevertheless, it would be wrong to portray the differences between symbolic interactionism and variable analysis as one of outright confrontation – though it was in some quarters. If anything the dominant sentiment was to recognise that what each approach represented was legitimate and that much could be gained by combining them. In theory this led to the efforts at a synthesis of the 'micro' and the 'macro',

> Triangulation

and in methods to arguments for 'triangulation'. The notion of triangulation was intended to acknowledge that various methods had their own advantages and disadvantages, with the result that if research used only one method then this could, at best, offer only a selective picture. Accordingly research should ideally use a number of methods and then try to triangulate – the term is taken from navigation where a more accurate estimate of position is furnished by three or more fixes – the data collected from each method to give a better and less selective account. Such a strategy, of course, ignores the underlying rationale of each methodology by treating them simply as methods, rather than as methods which represent very different pictures of society and the social actor.

Among the positivist conceptions that symbolic interactionism retained was the emphasis on data collection as a crucial phase in the research process. True, the data was different, qualitative rather than quantitative, small rather than large scale, but it was seen as data nonetheless. Although symbolic interactionism did not see itself as concerned just with producing rich, qualitative descriptive accounts of social behaviour in a single setting, but also with generalising about social life, it remained cautious about its achievements, often describing its studies as 'exploratory' or, at best, providing a 'deeper understanding' of a particular setting.

One of the main problems that interactionism failed to resolve was to get out from under the yoke of positivism and variable analysis. As a result, methodologically speaking, it was always prone to trying to show how well it could meet the standards of scientific inquiry as effectively, if not better than, variable analysis: a stance which clothed qualitative research in the language and the rhetoric of positivist science to the neglect of pushing forward its own particular insight into the phenomenon of sociological inquiry.

Ethnomethodology's re-specification

A decisive break with the legacy of positivism came with ethnomethodology though it was not to prove greatly influential in the discipline. It did, however, have strategic effects in breaking the hegemony of positivist thought.

For positivists the major methodological problem was to devise methods of investigation which would reveal the objective reality of the social world. They assumed that by adopting detached approaches and objective procedures akin to those of the natural sciences, sociology could discover the law-like characteristics of the social world. The interactionists, however, viewed the social world, social reality, as the outcome of the interpretations and meaningful constructions of the members of society. To a degree ethnomethodologists take a similar stance but take it further by asking questions about the methods that members use in order to accomplish a sense of the world as having an external and object-like character. Social reality is, for ethnomethodology, a members' accomplishment.

As we mentioned in the previous chapter, Schutz's characterisation of the world of everyday life has close parallels with Durkheim's description of social reality as external, constraining and objective. Schutz's portrayal is intended as a description of how the world looks under the 'natural attitude', the standpoint of members of

> The natural attitude

society in their daily lives. The given and intractable character of the everyday social world derives not from specialist sociological knowledge but from the socially sanctioned facts which constitute lay sociological understanding and, from this point of view, are obvious to any member of society. In our ordinary lives we come across 'families', 'good neighbours', 'burglars', 'teenagers', 'authority', 'friends', 'statistics', 'pubs' and so on, and generally treat these in a taken-for-granted fashion as 'facts of life'. Indeed, if we did not take things like these for granted, and assume that others do the same, the social world would be chaotic and strange. Ethnomethodology argues that what Durkheim proposes as the nature of social reality is just what the members of society take for granted.

However, in order to understand the full radical import of this standpoint, we need to revisit some of the critiques which led to the turn against positivism with a focus more upon data and its analysis.

The turn against positivism

From a positivist point of view, the shift from the quantitative to the qualitative looks like a retreat. From a qualitative stance, however, it is rather a matter of facing up to some brutal facts about the actual state and immediate prospects of sociological inquiry. In simple terms, the argument is that if one wants to study social life with any degree of rigour then there is no choice but to use qualitative data.

Much of the criticism of positivism was levelled against variable analysis and the social survey. As we have also seen, there have been some defences of the social survey as well as complaints against the too sharp differentiation between quantitative and qualitative sociology. After all, much quantitative work relies upon qualitative materials, and much qualitative work can involve, if we may use the phrase, 'qualitative quantifications'. However, the objection to positivism is not to the social survey and quantification as such, but to these as the bearers of positivistic ambitions. Blumer's critique of the variable, remember, discriminated between effective uses of quantification and the excesses to which variable analysis was prone. It is more accurate to say that the objection was to a fixation on measurement than to quantification as such. Similarly, the social survey has its uses but, within sociology, these are limited and often mainly employed for administrative purposes rather than properly sociological ones. Which is not to say that administrative purposes do not have any point, only that their point is not sociological.

Moreover, in the absence of any agreed sociological theory, the results of social survey analysis often present further problems rather than solutions. The advantage of quantification and measurement was supposed to be that they would allow the testing of hypotheses and, through this, the resolution of theories. But, in actual fact, survey research raises pernicious questions of interpretation. 'What does the data show?' is a frequently asked question. In other words, and this is perhaps no surprise, the data produced by variable analysis was and is always in need of a great deal of interpretation to determine whether or not some hypothesis was satisfied. While questions also arise over data in natural science, these are not usually 'pernicious questions of interpretation'. This apart, the positivist programme was severely weakened, even though many of the methods which it supported are still alive and well. Social survey research goes on, as does statistical analysis, but these methods can no longer claim paragon status. They are no more notable than any other kind of sociological research even though they do carry considerable institutional weight in terms of the resources they can command.

One of the outcomes of the relegation of positivism to one among many ways of doing sociological research was a weakening of the close identification of rigour with the collection and statistical analysis of data. Although the demand for rigour had motivated the cultivation of the social survey and statistical analysis, the practicalities of research compromised its achievement. Realistically, the assumptions underlying the methods could not be sustained in practice, but had to be relaxed in order to get the research done in the first place. And for many this was a crossing of the fine line between relaxing constraints and abandoning them altogether.

However, as we have already argued, for some the turn against positivism was made in the name of rigour, as in the case of the critique of variable analysis by symbolic interactionists and, too, from ethnomethodology, an approach which had very radical ideas about both data and method.

The question of data

One of ethnomethodology's dissatisfactions with positivistic analysis was that, characteristically, it was not possible to examine the raw data. What was presented, for example in the form of statistical tables, was at best processed data. The data with which positivistic researchers actually work is, of course, qualitative. Consider the answers to survey questions. These are responses in ordinary language to questions asked in the same ordinary language. These are not, however, the materials presented to the sociological reading public. Excerpts from the odd interview may be cited, but almost all survey materials present too vast a body to be set out in the article that reports them (though these days they may be preserved in an archive for further analysis). The article will present these materials in a condensed form, transformed from the original qualitative mat-erials into a numerical format, commonly statistical tables. But how does this transformation actually take place?

Very often, for example, work of transformation is not done by the sociol-ogists who write the final report. It is commonly done by coders, people who are, in Julian Roth's nice phrase, 'hired hand' researchers assigned to do what is notionally a somewhat mechanical task (Roth, 1966). The main purpose of coding is to introduce a fairly mechanical way of giving numerical values to data and to have this done by disinterested parties in accord with protocols that are to be strictly applied. It should require no judgement on the part of the coders – if they are properly instructed in suitably strict coding procedures – to decide consistently that, given a particular piece of data, this or that number is to be entered in the corresponding place on the coding form. When the coding forms are completed, they can then be taken by the sociologist and run through the computer and manipulated statistically.

> Coding

Roth's expression 'hired hand research' was coined precisely to suggest that the commitment of those hired to do coding might be no more intense than that of anyone hired to do temporary drudge work. If sociologists took notice of qualitative sociological research about the work practices of such hired hand researchers in other occupations, one would expect the coders to be quite casual about fulfilling the requirements of their task. Nor is the work of trans-formation quite as mechanical as it is imagined to be. There is no assurance that the correspondence between the items of the qualitative material in the initial data and the numerical entry made in the coding sheet will be the same as that which it is supposed to be according to the manual of coding proce-dures. There is no assurance, that is, that the method of coding the data is capturing its actual structure in the ways that the manuals of coding intend that structure to be captured.

Garfinkel took an interest in what coders actually did when they were coding, in this case coding the files of a psychiatric clinic (Garfinkel, 1967). Among other things, the files contained reports of interviews between doctors and their patients. In Garfinkel's case, the coders seemed serious about their work and were attempting to do a good job. But there were two significant things which were noticeable about what they did.

- The coders were commonly unable to follow the coding instructions they were given, and were frequently unable to see how coding-according-to-the-rules could possibly capture the actual character of the structures of the interview talk they were given. They would have to make decisions as to how to code items of data in ways which would be a compromise between what the coding sheets allowed them to do and what was necessary to capture the actual character of the data they were coding.

■ More importantly still, in order to make the many decisions as to the best way to code the data from the point of view of the research project, they had to engage in sociological reasoning. To satisfy themselves that they understood what clinic staff meant by what they had written in the files, the coders had to draw upon what they themselves 'knew' about the way that psychiatric clinics work, about how they must work, about what psychiatrists could possibly do in the way of treating patients, and so on.

It is perhaps still commonplace to talk of survey data in its statistical form as 'hard data' suggesting that it has a definitive character, contrasting it with the 'soft data' of fieldwork. But if Roth and Garfinkel's arguments are justified, these mate-

> 'Hard' versus 'soft' data?

rials are not particularly 'hard'. One cannot tell, from the presentation of the data, how the figures have actually been arrived at, or whether the transformations are ones that should be allowed under the coding rules. Of course, as we pointed out in Chapter 6, if there is no isomorphism between the relationships presented in the data and the structures of the mathematics used to manipulate the data, then there is a serious problem about what the data shows apart from the mathematical relationships. In short, when reading quantitative studies in sociology, one does not know what the data was and, accordingly, cannot confirm for oneself that the way the data is presented gives an accurate picture.

From a positivist point of view, this is just another of the practical problems of quantitative research. The data is of such a quantity that no one could possibly examine it all, let alone carefully. Sociological researchers cannot afford to spend their time doing all the drudge work so, realistically, much of it has to be consigned to teams of hired hands. Again the paradox: this practicality is imposed by the unwieldiness of a practice which was recommended in the first instance as a principled solution to the very problems it is now treating as a practical restriction.

Further, dissenters can reasonably ask: what is the point of collecting such vast amounts of data if these can hardly be examined, let alone carefully? Why suppose that the only way in which to process sociological data is in bulk? The rationale of the positivist approach was to reveal and preserve the processes which transform initial data, to give them, so to speak, a transparent structure. The actual practice of bulk data analysis means, however, that these processes are obscured. Yet, the whole point of making them transparent was to enable their objectivity to be assured through assessment by the relevant scientific community. But if the data cannot be accessed, and the procedures by which they was transformed cannot be identified, then it is difficult to see how the goal of objectivity is met.

However, though by positivist standards it is an appalling step, there is a

> Ethnomethodology

rationale for presenting data in its raw form and also displaying the methods used in its analysis. This is precisely what ethnomethodology and conversation analysis set out to do: namely, to actualise the positivist aspiration to rigour. Of course, the idea of rigour is very different.

Ethnomethodology, unlike positivism and unlike other qualitative approaches, has no concern with what are thought of as methodological problems in the books on method. The concern with 'data collection', for example, which is so important to both quantitative and qualitative methods, is altogether absent from ethnomethodology. Certainly ethnomethodology presents and discusses data – hence must have collected it – but from its point of view there is nothing special about coming by such data. It is not as if it is acquired by professional training and skill. From ethnomethodology's point of view, there is no such thing as 'data collection'. Talk of data collection, as far as ethnomethodology is concerned, is talk of such things as, say, going to an evening class, videotaping the evening news, reading through records, hanging about a neurophysiology laboratory and so on. Going to evening class for instruction in Kung Fu or videotaping the evening news are things that 'anyone' can do, providing such things are practically available to do. Getting permission to do fieldwork in a laboratory is not something that is altogether different from what other people do. A successful laboratory is a bit like a tourist site, with all kinds of visitors being given tours, to have the work shown and explained to them; the fieldworker, from the point of view of the laboratory, is another tourist. Sociologists can research what goes on in a traffic court or in sanity hearings because, like other members of the public, they are entitled to sit and observe the proceedings. And, let us not forget, survey research is basically a matter of asking people questions, which goes on all the time – in social service bureaucracies, police emergency calls, tax offices and the like – where the questioning goes together with the filling in of forms.

While manuals of method go on about fieldwork, the importance of rapport, and so on, for ethnomethodology this is simply something that everybody is doing all the time: making relationships and getting along with other people – again, not a matter of advanced technical skills. 'Data', then, is not something that 'sociological methods' yield. The data is stuff that society itself makes available – what is found in an evening class in Kung Fu, what can be taped off TV, what can be witnessed or overheard in a courtroom, and so on and so on.

The question of method

If ethnomethodology has little truck with the idea of 'data collection' as this is typically understood, then so, too, it can have little enthusiasm for the notion of methods of research as typically understood. The ordinary phenomena which were pointed to earlier and which, to put it this way, are the data for ethnomethodology, are ones that are more commonly regarded as the starting point for sociological inquiry. The standard assumption, however, is that these phenomena are not encountered in their real settings for what they *actually* are. What they are can only be revealed through some kind of systematic analysis.

This issue we have met previously as the problem of the relationship between 'the member's' and the 'sociologist's' perspectives, although this time we will cast it in methodological terms. The orthodox sociological view is that the member of society is naïve with respect to the reality of social phenomena since the member has no methodological apparatus which will provide a systematic conception of the phenomena that members encounter in their everyday affairs. As Durkheim noted in his study of suicide, the members of society have a conception of what suicide is, but this is but a vague idea and certainly not a conception that can be used for scientific purposes. Such ordinary conceptions needed to be transformed for scientific purposes. However, as we have already noted, ethnomethodology raises serious questions about the ways in which supposedly systematic methodologies, of the kind that Durkheim sought to develop and that variable analysis proposed, actually process the 'raw data' that is fed through them.

The problem can be restated as follows. The idea that method defines the reality of the phenomenon can only be applied once a sound method is available. In sociology, however, there is a tension between compliance with a systematic method on the one hand, and on the other capturing the nature of the phenomenon purportedly represented in what the method produces. The complaint raised against positivism is that the gap between the method and the phenomenon is manifest in the method itself. The divergence, as we have seen, is manifest in the ways that the users of the method have to manage its application in numerous ad hoc ways in order to achieve what they regard as 'reasonable' rather than strict compliance with it. But how satisfactory can it be to insist on a method because it imposes strict discipline on data collection and analysis, and then to adopt a tolerant attitude toward constant infringement of that requirement?

The coding study again

In the coding study discussed earlier in this chapter, the point was made that classic sociological methods seek to transform 'raw data' into some codified form. Garfinkel was interested in the work done to achieve this: how the records of a psychiatric clinic could be codified according to as strict a coding scheme as could be devised. The rationale was to reconstruct the social structure of the organisation that generated the files, to determine how the clinic goes about its business, what kinds of things it members do, as revealed in what is written down in the files.

The contents of a clinic folder are an assortment of documents, and there is no general procedure for reading these so as to make a unique determination of what they actually record. One might suppose that the chronological order of entry might be a useful way of reading them. However, the coders found that they could not necessarily decide what the documents 'really meant' – what they actually said took place – just by reading them through in a chronological order. They would find that the meaning of a document that had been read would change in the light of what was read subsequently in other documents. What an expression might mean often only became apparent retrospectively: a case of the documentary method of interpretation. Furthermore, there were other relationships between the documents in addition to that provided by chronological sequence. Some documents, for example, could be 'played off' against each other.

Inset 11.1 Documentary method of interpretation

Garfinkel refers to the 'documentary method of interpretation' – a term he borrowed from Karl Mannheim – as the process by which a set of appearances, which may be objects, events, persons or symbols, are taken as evidence for some underlying pattern, while the postulated pattern serves as a guide for seeing how the appearances themselves should be seen. An example would be the ways in which scene of crime officers assemble the particulars of the scene – scratches on windows, fingerprints, clothes on the floor and so on – as evidence of a 'burglary' which, given this as a possible crime scene, is used to assemble the particularities as the evidence for a crime having been committed.

Garfinkel suggests that the documentary method of interpretation is a feature of common-sense practical reasoning. However, in no way does he suggest that it is a deficient form of reasoning. Rather, in his explorations of practical reasoning in a variety of domains, he claims that the classification or description of any behaviour on a given occasion as an instance of a particular type of action – for example defining the items mentioned earlier as evidence of a burglary – cannot be 'based on a set of specifiable features of the behaviour and the occasion but, rather, depends on the indefinite context seen as relevant to the observer, a context that gets its meaning partly through the very action it is being used to interpret' (Wilson, 1970). The evidence for the burglary could, for example, also serve as evidence of a different action – an insurance fraud might be one, or a very untidy housemate. The meaning, and hence the action that is being performed, depends upon the context. Similarly, the context itself is partly made intelligible by the meaning or the description given to the instances. It follows that any interpretation is always both retrospectively and prospectively revisable in light of 'further evidence'.

The point is that the collection of documents in even a single folder could be read in many different ways, yielding different possibilities about what they report as having occurred or actually been done.

However, the coding method does not allow those doing the coding to offer a variety of alternate possibilities as to what the record might show. It requires that the coder make a single, categorical entry with respect to what any single record shows. This cannot be decided from the record alone, and of course by the nature of the exercise the coders cannot undertake any further research to determine what the 'right' coding entry should actually be. However, the coders must decide! Accordingly, they decide on the basis of what they suppose that psychiatric personnel who made the entry must reasonably, plausibly, conceivably, credibly, responsibly have meant or done.

From the point of view of strict systematic method, then, one is in the following position:

- The method is designed to enable us to find out, from the clinic records, how the clinic works, what its social structure is. In actual use, however, it is from an imaginative reconstruction of how the clinic works that the coders are able figure out how to read the clinic files. The intended relationship is reversed.
- The intended and actual objects of inquiry have come apart. The intended object of inquiry is the day-to-day running of the psychiatric clinic, but what is provided in the coded data is the coders' imaginative reconstruction of what the order must be. By any standards these two are not the same.

Garfinkel's point is not just about coding but about sociological method more generally. It is not one, of itself, which disables the ventures which use these methods. On the contrary, his point is that the kind of ad hoc invention of imagined social structures is what enables such things as the completion of coding activities. This only becomes disabling insofar as the methods are intended to be used strictly. In that case, in Garfinkel's view, one comes up against a familiar dilemma. The problems he is pointing to cannot be fixed by more insistence on sticking strictly to the method. There is no unique way, for example, of reading an assortment of documents for their definitive meaning which can be given independently and in advance of reading the documents. Nor can one read an organisation's documents competently without already having some grasp of how the organisation operates. Therefore, either one sticks stringently to the method, as one is officially supposed to do, and then runs into what are effectively unresolvable problems. Or, one applies the method in a way which recognises the impracticality of its stringent application; that is, one persists with the method in a 'reasonable spirit', thereby detracting from the rationale for introducing the method in the first place.

Hence, the practice of coding the clinic files according to the method exhibits the coming apart of the intended and actual objects of study. It is manifested in precisely what it takes to do the coding in a way which enables the coders to feel that they have captured the reality of the clinic's work in their coding of the documents. The results of the coding, which provide the materials on which the sociological analyst will start to work, are therefore records of the clinic's actual working *only* as the 'good sense', imaginative reconstructions of these workings. But, of course, this is just what the method was originally contrived to avoid, what the coding rules and schedules are designed to prevent.

For Garfinkel, the point is not to set out to resolve these kind of problems – even supposing that they can be resolved – but rather to motivate the competent analysis of the 'raw materials' without benefit of some preconceived methodological scheme of how these materials are to be examined and understood. The overriding aim is to unite intended and actual objects of study. The key point of the coding study, and of several others of Garfinkel's papers, is to show that these are standardly divergent in sociological studies, in that what is actually studied and reported is often something other than what the study purports to talk about.

Abandoning methodology

From a number of sociological points of view, Garfinkel's arguments are unwelcome, and ethnomethodology has come in for perhaps more than its fair share of criticism. However, ethnomethodology does not see itself as methodologically disadvantaged by the lack of a specialised and distinctively sociological method. All that it feels that it has done is to dispense with a largely superfluous sociological preoccupation, namely, meditations on data collection. And in this respect it distinguishes itself not only from positivism but also from symbolic interactionism, with which it is occasionally grouped. As we have seen, symbolic interactionists are massively preoccupied with reflections on doing fieldwork and informal interviewing – their primary means of data collection – but one will search the ethnomethodological literature in vain for any sign of a concern with data collection as an independent topic. From ethnomethodology's point of view there is an extraordinary and disproportionate amount of attention given to data collection relative to the attention given to the analysis of the materials. Indeed, the distinction between data collection and analysis – that one first collects the data and then analyses it – is dispensable, not to say implausible. The question for ethnomethodology is not so much 'What do we make of the data we have collected?' as 'What is the data that we have collected data of?'

Perhaps we can appreciate these points better if we take regard of ethnomethodology's disaffiliation from the standard modes of sociological procedure and practice. In effect, it adopts a 'cut your coat to fit your cloth' method, one which most other sociological approaches resolutely refuse to adopt (and, according to ethnomethodology, this is the prime source of their problems). Insofar as the approach to sociological inquiry remains dependent upon preconceptions about the kinds of problems it can legitimately address, then it will continue to confront the methodological problem that ethnomethodology identifies. There is recurrently a gap between the topics that sociology proposes to talk about and the topics that its data can support. It is not usually possible to collect the kinds, quantities or qualities of data to capture the complex phenomena and problems that sociology purports to address.

A simple truth about sociology is that it is a resource-poor pursuit. Relative to the natural sciences it has very few resources to invest in research. Further, it is not a research-intensive activity. Few, if any, professional sociologists are engaged in full-time research – working around the clock on some occasions, as experimental scientists often do. It is much closer to a scholarly pursuit than it is to a research science in terms of the time and effort that its practitioners deploy. Accordingly, the amount of effort spent on any research topic will be relatively small and, most likely, superficial compared with what might be done with more time and effort. A good proportion of the research funding in sociology is spent on social surveys, but, as we have noted, the quality of survey data is limited. Consider the delight that Blau and Duncan exhibited at their ability to get some questions attached to the United States national census for their study of the American occupational structure (Blau and Duncan, 1968), and then consider how much of their book is devoted to trying to make up for the fact that they could only add a small number of questions. And, moreover, this is not to raise those aspects of the problem we have discussed to do with the relationship between what people say on questionnaires and what they actually do.

To put the point with a brutal simplicity, a main feature of sociological inquiry is that it claims to answer questions that it cannot, in research terms, really answer. It cannot collect data that is of the right kind of quality to solve the problem, and a major part of research effort goes into trying to make inadequate data serve the research purpose. It has been said that sociology is an interpretative discipline and so it is, in that one of its main problems is that of interpreting its data with respect to the problems it poses.

Ethnomethodology does not operate by assembling an agenda of questions in advance. Rather, it attempts to determine, from its materials, what questions those materials can answer. Rather than the question: how can these materials be used to say the kinds of things about society we want to say? It asks: what do these materials license us confidently to say about the social world? With respect to the kinds of questions ethnomethodology is attempting to answer, then, it is operating modestly but it is attempting to answer these questions rather than gesture at them.

Although it has given up the idea of 'methodology' as a distinct area of activity, this does not mean that ethnomethodology is recommending a disregard for method. As we have already pointed out, the idea of rigour is just as strongly influential for ethnomethodology as it is for the positivists. However, it is applied in a different way. The

> Rigour

whole point of eschewing methodology is to enable the idea of rigour to run right through its activities. Rigour is not something that can be achieved by following – or attempting to follow – a set of generalised methodological prescriptions. So, in place of a concern with data collection, ethnomethodology sets out to be an analytic pursuit focused upon the analysis of whatever primary materials might be considered to comprise 'data'.

For ethnomethodology's purpose it does not matter what the data are. If, as ethnomethodology is, one is concerned with the generic characteristics of everyday activities and the ways in which members make sense of the social world, then these are issues which can be considered using any instance of social life. There is no intrinsic merit in choosing one area of social life over any other. Dog racing will do as well as national government, filling out a form as well as socialising at a party. It really does not matter.

Further, there is no point in collecting large amounts of data that will not be used. The simple fact about field studies, for example, is that more materials will be collected than will ever be used in a final report. Field notes will contain far more things than one will ever talk about or write up. Audio or video recordings typically contain more material than can ever be seriously looked at. There is no merit in having large amounts of data that are not, cannot be, analysed.

So, for ethnomethodology, the data is the sort of stuff that can be cut out of newspapers, taken from document stores, videoed off the TV, tape recorded from phones or meetings, and so on. These kind of materials are preferable to fieldnotes – though often these will have to do – which are an impoverished recording of what video and audio can achieve. Nonetheless, the point is that data on social life can be easily collected. And one does not need very much of it. A few minutes of audio or video tape can be enough for analysis. Notice also that these are described as 'primary materials' in that there has been no change in the nature of the phenomena being studied. The phenomena do not appear after transformation into presentable and analysable data; they are not the kind that appear only through the sociologist's methodological and theoretical reworking of the materials. Rather, the phenomena are exhibited in the materials as they are exhibited in those materials. For ethnomethodologists, materials are, so to speak, to be found 'on the street' and the phenomena identified are also ones to be found 'on the street'.

Take the issue of bias in television news reporting. For most sociologists this would have to be something established by research. Some standard of what is to count as bias will have to be established and, then, numerous news broadcasts will have to be recorded and examined. Bias will then be determined by the extent to which the

> Example: bias in news reporting

results of the counting of such instances match against the standard of balanced coverage. 'Bias in television news' is, of course, an everyday phenomenon in that, routinely, various members of society complain about 'bias'. However, the professional inquirer's task is to ascertain whether or not such complaints are empirically justified. Ethnomethodology, by contrast, has no interest in deciding whether members' complaints about bias are justified, or even whether bias is or is not present in television news. Its interest would be in how the members of society can 'find' bias in news broadcasts. TV watchers do not make systematic catalogues of television programmes, protracted counts of recorded instances, yet they can find complainable cases of bias from their living room couch: how do they find such instances? Thus, ethnomethodology's question is: what kind of thing is 'bias' as encountered in everyday life, as something identified in the course of watching a TV news broadcast?

Ethnomethodology's interest in data, then, is very different to the standard one. It does not operate from a premise which supposes that we have to collect a thousand cases of, say, bias in order that we may begin to determine from them what bias really is. Rather, it begins from the very different premise that to put together a thousand cases we have to decide that each of the thousand cases can be relevantly included in the collection. Indeed, it was just this kind of problem which led to both Garfinkel and Sacks's early interest in suicide and dissatisfaction with Durkheim's treatment. Durkheim worked with collections of identified suicide cases in order to determine the factors which result in suicide. He had to begin with collections of persons already identified as suicides by compilers of the official statistics. However, the question for Garfinkel and Sacks was: how does an individual case come to be counted as a suicidal death in the first place? For them the issue was not a methodological one but a sociological one, a feature of members' practical reasonings. In short, the distinction between methodology and sociology collapses.

Methodical analysis

Ethnomethodology has been cumulatively dispensing with the standard assumptions about method made in sociology, and seeking to bypass the traditional problem of the relationship of theory to research. As we have already pointed out many times, the complaint is that theory and research are not integrated, and one reason for this is that they are treated as distinct activities as if theorising was done with the results of research. Ethnomethodology does not do theorising in the traditional sense. The output of ethnomethodology is not a theory of the kind sociology typically seeks but practices of methodical analysis.

Dispensing with a methodological apparatus is an upshot of the difference between ethnomethodology and 'constructivist' sociology and the kind of orderliness that their practitioners are interested in. Everyone agrees that social life is manifestly orderly. It is equally plain to positivists and other sociologists that everyday life is not a random affair. However, it is usually assumed that this readily available and obvious orderliness is only a rationale for the formation of a method capable of identifying a deeper and less apparent orderliness, one that can only be brought out by systematic analysis. Ethnomethodology's decision is to concern itself with the readily findable orderliness of social life.

Ethnomethodology has no truck with conceptions of science which are predicated on the idea that their objective is to uncover 'hidden' orderliness nor does it agree that the readily findable orderliness in social life should receive such perfunctory treatment when it in fact deserves sustained attention. That there is such anyone-can-find it orderliness is something that everyone takes for granted in their daily life. It is an obvious fact that, for example, when driving a car persons will obey a red traffic light and stop. They do not always do this, of course. Some jump or run the lights, but this is the kind of orderliness found in everyday life. It is not a strict 'whenever X, then Y' but a 'mostly X, sometimes Y' relationship. That persons typically stop for red lights is no news to anyone and most sociologists would say that the discipline should not occupy itself with this kind of trivial stuff that everybody knows. It should try and examine things that are less obvious. Ethnomethodology, however, takes the view that this response from sociologists – a lack of inquiring interest in such phenomena – is no different from that of the members of society. There is nothing distinctive in sociology's reaction, but rather than distancing itself from the ordinary members' everyday attitudes and outlooks, sociology is thoughtlessly incorporating just such attitudes and outlooks into itself.

Rather than incorporate the obviousness of a fact such as drivers stopping at red lights into its own approach, ethnomethodology prefers to reflect upon the availability of this and innumerable other facts about ordinary social life. Should not sociologists be struck by the fact that there is such a great degree of readily found orderliness in social affairs? Struck by the fact that any member of society can find orderliness in all aspects of social life? The interesting question is how they can do this? However rough and ready the kinds of orderliness people can find, it is the social order that they are finding. And finding social order is not something that is just done to sociology's subject matter; it is part of its subject matter. That is, 'finding social order' is done from within society, done by ordinary members of society, and done as part of the production of that same social order. Thus, it is entirely possible to propose, as a sociological topic, the finding of social order as an everyday affair. This is just the topic that ethnomethodology seeks to make its own. It is not one which has been identified or pursued by any other sociology to date and it is, furthermore, doubtful as to whether any other sociological approach could include this topic within their remit. Other sociologies take this ordinary, anyone-can-find-it orderliness for granted – indeed, they count on it – in order to pursue their own inquiries. Trying to attend to the activities of 'finding social order' would distract and disrupt the kind of practices in which they engage.

In the language of another tradition, the fact that members of society can find ordinary everyday orderliness in society is a social fact. That this kind of orderliness can be readily and everywhere found does not seem like an idle, ornamental fact, something which just happens to be the case independently of everything else about society. That persons can find ordinary everyday orderliness is integral to the organisation of society. Ordinary people are not hobbyist sociologists. It is not as if people took some time out from their other social affairs to do a bit of amateur finding of social regularities. If that were the case only some people would be aware of such orderliness rather than everyone knowing about them. It is not, then, as if people, in addition to the other things they do, do a bit of sociology on the side. Rather it is in the course of conducting their everyday

> Finding social order as everyday affair

affairs – shopping, driving to work, taking a vacation, losing money at the casino, taking a lecture course and so on – that they find this orderliness. Nor is this orderliness incidental to those activities. The activities could not be done without it. It is not as if, for example, we notice that members of society regularly stop at traffic lights. If you are a pedestrian, it is a fact on which you entrust your life. You may know that this regularity is not without exception, so you step out warily. If a driver fails to stop and nearly runs you over, you are entitled to feel indignant. In other words, the traffic light is a moral fact – again a parallel with Durkheim's proposal for the subject matter of sociology – and you feel entitled to be able to put your trust in red lights and drivers obeying their signals. You want to count on this regularity in order to 'cross the street'.

So 'finding social order' is part of organising one's everyday affairs, of getting on with those activities, in the course and part of which one is doing the finding of the social order. Ethnomethodology's chosen topic, then, is not some distinct, isolated aspect of social life, but about any, and therefore all, social activities. It will expect to find in each and every kind of social activity that members of society will be engaged in 'finding the ordinary orderliness' of that activity as an integral part of organising that activity. Studying how the participants in an activity participate in ordering it is, therefore, one way of conceiving what the study of social order might be. Developing that approach is a matter of studying any and all social activities from a particular angle rather than a matter of studying one aspect of those activities. The business of finding the ordinary orderliness of an activity is interwoven with the activities that are being found out about. One cannot really examine how someone 'finds out if it is safe to cross the street now' independently of examining how someone goes about crossing the street.

All of this means that ethnomethodology has no interest in constructing its own models of social structures and systems in the way other sociologies do. Accordingly, its depictions are not in any sense rivals to the models of social structures that, say, Marxists, functionalists, post-modernists and others seek to build. This is known as 'ethnomethodological indifference'. It does not matter to ethnomethodology whether these models are good or bad ones. Ethnomethodology has no

> Ethnomethodological indifference

way of deciding whether they are good or bad and has no criteria for assessing them. As far as it is concerned, such models and the work done to construct them is just another instantiation of ethnomethodology's interest in the way persons, including professional sociologists, find social order. The methods that professional sociologists use, such as reading documents, asking questions, hanging around places of work and so on, are from ethnomethodology's point of view, 'methods' that anyone may use.

The idea of 'good' or 'bad' data is alien to ethnomethodological studies. Anything can be subject to examination, including all the kinds of materials that sociologists collect and analyse. Of course, as we have said, its interest in such materials is not the same as that which sociologists would otherwise take. Ethnomethodology's interest in 'methods' is not in adding to their stock but in examining methods-in-use, in the ways in which people in practice find out about social order, in the ways in which finding out through the use of vernacular methods is done in and is part of the very social order that is found out about. It is because it is interested in analysing methods of this kind that we might term it 'metamethodological', and, because the use of these methods involves 'sociological reasoning', 'metasociological'. Sociological reasoning is, in ethnomethodology's terms, not something which is done *about* society but *from within* society and, therefore, constitutive of it. Ordinary members of society, no less than professional sociologists, engage in sociological reasoning. Integral to the methods that members of society use to find their way about society, find out 'what is going on' in actual social occasions, is their understanding of how the social order works, of what kinds of persons do what kind of things in what ways with what reactions and results. We have mentioned the way in which coders were forced to use their understanding of how psychiatric clinics actually work in order to decide what the clinic records 'really meant'. Such an understanding is, of course, a common-sense one about what psychiatrists do, what psychiatric nurses do, what record clerks and receptionists do, about what kind of things they can legitimately do to patients, what they could possibly write down, how they could express some things euphemistically, and so on and so on.

It is not a matter of endorsing these common-sense understandings but of noting that they pervade the practical decision making of all members of society. They are integral to and inextricable from the 'methods' that ordinary members of society use to figure out 'what is going on', 'what really happened', 'what might happen next', and so on. And ordinary members of society includes those who make their living doing sociology, including those who do ethnomethodology.

Harvey Sacks spoke of 'order at all points' in social life (Sacks, 1984). By this he meant that one can examine any elements of social life and expect to find orderliness in them. Which means that from the point of view of looking into the order that can be found, any point in the social order is as good as any other. It does not matter, in the way that it does to other sociologists, what kinds of phenomena, or what manifestations of them, one studies in ethnomethodology. From its point of view, it is meaningless to say that it cannot study this or that phenomenon, and pointless to complain that it has not studied this or that phenomenon. Failure to appreciate this is a failure to appreciate how drastically ethnomethodology breaks with 'constructive sociology'.

Conclusion

What we have tried to do in this chapter is describe the major re-specification of the sociological task made by ethnomethodology. Unlike other so-called qualitative approaches, it finally breaks with the conception of theory–method–data which has so dominated sociological research. Using phenomenological inspirations, it sought to develop the idea of the actor's point of view by treating the social actor as someone who has to employ common-sense methods from within the society in order to 'find out' how it works. Such practical methods are themselves constitutive of the ordinary orderliness that is social organisation. Ethnomethodology also eschews many of the traditional goals of sociology, especially theorising and striving to uncover the 'hidden order' of social life.

However, ethnomethodology has not been altogether successful in persuading fellow sociologists of the virtues of its case. Perhaps the main reason for this is its significant break with aspects of the sociological project which most sociologists were reluctant to abandon, particularly the idea that sociology should address important issues of history, society and social life. From its very beginnings sociology had set itself an ambitious agenda, nothing less than furnishing the means for the rational reconstruction of society. Though such an ambition was to prove very tough to realise, it burns as bright as it ever did, albeit in various guises, some of which we will discuss in the Part III. The formal sociology of ethnomethodology, with its focus on the ordinary visible orderliness of everyday life, its sociological indifference to moral and political issues, and its indifference to theorising, served to effectively marginalise it from the mainstream of sociology.

However ethnomethodology, along with the other approaches we have discussed in this part of the book, did help to elevate an issue which has become even more prominent in the last decades: namely, that of meaning. This notion had been centrally placed in symbolic interactionism, of course, and inevitably encouraged an interest in language. Of course sociology, and especially anthropology, had long had an interest in language, but symbolic interactionism had placed it centrally in its conception of social interaction as the medium through which the actor's point of view was articulated and conveyed, and the means through which courses of action were organised and understood. Ethnomethodology, though drawing on a somewhat different philosophical tradition – namely, phenomenology – also brought language in use to the fore as an ineradicable feature of social life. The use of vernacular language in practical reasoning and as embedded in interaction were central to its inquiries. Indeed, in conversation analysis, its interest in how categorising and description were done, how records were assembled and understood, how reports were made, how juries deliberated and so on displays a focus on ordinary language competence as an inextricable feature of sociality.

There were other interests in language which were very different but which became influential in the 1970s and 1980s which are the concern of the next part of the book.

Selected bibliography and suggested reading

▪ Again, reading cited in previous chapters of this part of the book is relevant, especially those mentioned in Chapter 10. Additional useful writings are

Sacks' 'Notes on Methodology', to be found in Atkinson and Heritage's edited collection, *Structures of Social Action: Studies in Conversational Analysis* (Cambridge University Press, 1984).

Part III

Critical Questions

Chapter 12

The Refurbishing of Critical Sociology

In this part of the book we aim to examine more recent developments in socio-logical thinking that seek to refurbish and reassert the critical posture of the disci-pline. In doing so they bring theory and philosophy to the forefront, though in European sociology these have never really been anywhere else. A major element in this refurbishment was a subtle critique of contemporary society and its domi-nant modes of thinking, especially its preoccupation with science, and particu-larly with positivistic science. Moreover, this attack on science was an attack not simply upon the institutions and organisation of science, as if somehow they were failing in their civic duty, but upon the very conceptions of knowledge which typified Western societies. The target was the very foundation of our ways of thinking and, as an inevitable consequence, the very character of sociology.

Let us begin by asking the question: Why measure sociology against the natural sciences at all?

The reason which motivated positivism was that the natural sciences were taken as the very paradigm of knowledge, the only real example of what it is to know something. They have a universal character in that what they say is true for everyone regardless of what individual persons happen to think is true. If one wants to say that one genuinely knows then there is no avoiding having to rise to the same standards as the natural sciences.

> Why a scientific sociology?

But are the natural sciences as final and as objective as they seem to be? Is it possible, in social life, to be universal and neutral in ways that the natural sciences claim to be? Or are we just uncritically accepting what the natural sciences claim about their status as the paradigm of knowledge? Might it be that the objectivity of science, its lofty aspirations and its undoubted great achieve-ments, are in fact a disguise for more down-to-earth sectional interests? But are we seeing science plain or are we seeing something wrapped in an ideology deeply embedded in our way of thinking?

What makes us think that the positivist conception of science – or any other for that matter – is the right one? The natural sciences grew out of social developments in Europe (though their origins were not confined to that continent) and, as such, were themselves products of history. In which case, why do we presume that we have fortuitously arrived at a conception of science which transcends historical and social change?

Marx had argued, like Hegel before him, that ways of thought and their associated conceptions of reality are shaped by their prior history, and that they are only fully understood when there is a self-conscious awareness of how they are part of this history and carry the marks of their time. By contrast, the positivist notion of the universalism of science proposed itself as transcending history. Its truths and 'facts' were universal and unchanging, the same for ever and in all places. Accordingly, if we apply its conception to understanding the social world, then that world, too, will be conceived – as the natural world has been – in terms of impersonal laws that cannot be changed by human will. They will be the fixed parameters of human life.

Of course, as we have tried to emphasise, positivists are not fools and even they accept that scientific change occurs. New theories come along, those found wanting fall by the wayside. What cannot change, according to positivism, is the very idea of science, the idea that the natural world works according to law-like principles, that facts about the natural world, once fully and finally established, are firm and enduring. They may be improved upon, honed and scoped, of course, but they will approximate the way that the world really is in itself, independently of how any human beings might imaginatively suppose it to be.

What we have here are two contrasting pictures, the positivist one and another which wants to recognise that human beings are more than the sum of their positivistic parts. If the truths of science are everywhere the same, then the positivist tradition tempts one into thinking that this must be so with respect to human beings, as it is for natural phenomena. There must be, for example, a general 'human nature' which is fixed and unchanging, and which therefore must have some common essence. But the idea that there is an invariant human essence is the idea which many critics of positivism find most unattractive about it. The importance of a historical conception is that what human beings are like cannot be shown through a description of what they are like now. We might find them now to be highly competitive, selfish, greedy, endlessly demanding more – as in a 'consumer society' – but we should not accept that this shows us what humans essentially are, that they have always been, or must necessarily remain, like this.

> An invariant human nature?

Moreover, overriding these empirical issues about the tension between human possibility and social regulation is the obligation of intellectuals – a particularly nineteenth-century European conceit – to expose the forces which inhibit human potential, if not to actually seek to abolish the social and political limitations. A conception of human nature based upon how we find human beings now would, at best, be partial and profoundly distorting.

It is not necessarily the claim of its critics that the positivist view is entirely false. Positivists might get many things right about how modern society actually works. Their mistake is to suppose that this is all there is to it – to treat historically local circumstances as though they represented the whole human condition. The positivist point of view, rather than standing as an obviously universal one, now begins to look parochial and limiting. Further, it is no accident that positivism tends to have this character since it is the product of a specific and distinctive historical development. It is built on the ideals of the European Enlightenment.

Critique of the Enlightenment

The Enlightenment ideal was, of course, mightily influenced by the successes of the natural sciences. The kind of control they have given us over nature is awesome if by no means perfect. This means that we are able to use the natural world greatly to our own benefit though we cannot transcend the laws of nature. As we saw in Chapter 3, achieving the same kind of scientific understanding of society, and control over the reconstitution of social affairs, was the dream of much of nineteenth-century social thought. Just as we can develop technologies to improve agriculture and industry, so we can improve society. The Enlightenment was basically formulated around the contrast between Authority and Reason. Its aim was to exempt all individuals from the dictates of authority and tradition, from obedience to the Church and Crown for example, so as to enable each individual to become an autonomous being, operating on the basis of his or her own capacity for reason. Thus, the growth of science as the most powerful embodiment of reason will enable each individual to achieve personal growth and freedom to their full realisation. This was the Enlightenment ideal.

Sociology was predominantly developed as a protagonist of Enlightenment ideas, but there were always counter-Enlightenment tendencies within it. Max Weber, for one example, was no Enlightenment optimist. In the 1960s these counter-Enlightenment tendencies were refreshed. In no small part stimulated by the Black Freedom Movement in the United States and the growing protests against the Vietnam War throughout the world, a number of philosophers and sociologists began to reiterate and develop a critique of modern thinking by reviving the arguments already mentioned about the historically grounded and limited character of positivist conceptions.

Herbert Marcuse, for example, a member of the Frankfurt School of critical theory, who became the intellectual mascot of the protest movements in the United States, in his book *One Dimensional Man* (1964) challenged the what he saw as the complacent tone of contemporary analyses of Western society. Such analyses proclaimed the 'end of ideology' in Western politics. This meant the end of politics centred on savage ideological disagreement of that typified the 1930s and led to the Second World War. The 'end of ideology' was brought about, in large part, by the post-war economic boom and the arrival of civil rather than confrontational politics following the defeat of Nazism and, at least in the West, the discrediting of the Soviet experiment. It was argued that the 'mixed economy' had effectively dissolved the tensions between the rival economic forms of the state-owned and private capital. Material prosperity had greatly softened if not eliminated the inequalities of wealth which gave rise to class divisions. Sociology, under the leadership of Parsons and Merton, had begun to think of itself as a successful and respectable discipline, holding the same position as other professions, especially those of law and medicine and, what is more, becoming responsible collaborators with the state and with business in helping to resolve the problems facing modern society.

Marcuse did not deny that society had become more affluent and less politically divided. What he did deny was that this state of affairs was conducive to human emancipation. For him, and for the tradition of critical theory to which he had long belonged and helped to form, the true aim of theory is never just knowledge for its own sake. Knowledge is required to help improve the condition of life, especially in respect of freedom (or, as it is commonly termed, emancipation). Helping the existing society administer itself better and more efficiently is not really a contribution toward this emancipation, but rather the reverse. Western societies might seem, to superficial and unquestioning analysis, as though they were free, certainly by contrast with the totalitarian dictatorships of the Nazi and Soviet kind. But this was the wrong perspective. It obscured the fact that totalitarianism, far from being defeated in the Second World War and the Cold War containment, was infusing the so-called advanced democratic societies themselves. These were becoming totalitarian albeit with a more benign face. These societies are not brutally oppressive but are oppressive in the sense that they impose a uniform existence and way of thought on all. They obliterate all alternatives to themselves both at home and abroad. The affluence of modern societies satisfies the material needs of individuals and thereby makes them contented. But the need for the excessive material benefits of the advanced economies are not genuine needs, spontaneously originating in the nature of individuals. They are 'false' needs created by the system and instilled into individuals by a mass-mediated culture as an essential requirement to maintain the markets for and the productivity of the industrial system. Though it may espouse in principle a commitment to freedom of thought and opinion, society is in practice restrictive in what it allows and accepts as thought and opinion. It is 'one dimensional' because it allows thought and imagination only within one dimension, namely, that which is needed by, and compatible with, the existing system.

> **Critique of modern society**

Inset 12.1 Critical theory

Critical theory grew out of the Frankfurt School, a group of Marxist scholars who, immediately prior to the Second World War, worked at the Institute of Social Research connected to Frankfurt University. Predominantly Jewish, most went into exile in the United States during Nazi rule. Their principle interests were the criticism of economism in Marxism and the elaboration of a critique of advanced capitalism. Later, Freudian psychoanalysis was incorporated into Marx's theory of society. Although the Frankfurt School did not originate the notion of critique – if anything this belonged to Hegel and Marx – they were to develop it by attacking the claims of 'instrumental rationality', especially the claim of natural science, to be the only form of genuine knowledge.

The contentment of post-war capitalism was really a passive conformism and its complacency reinforced by repressive tolerance. The system did not attempt to repress dissidence but, instead, while ostensibly allowing free expression, turned it into consumer products, into best selling books, television discussions, films, theatre and the like. Thus, dissent was tolerated but its teeth were pulled by its conversion into yet another commodity within the enveloping consumerist culture. As far as sociology was concerned, it was condemned for having, in the 1950s, bought into the dominant culture. Its 'professionalism' and 'respectability' were expressions of its own positivistic spirit. As a result sociology was unable to 'think outside the box' and fundamentally question the society of which it was part. Rather than opposing this 'velvet glove' totalitarianism, sociology more often worked directly with the state, the military and with business in their efforts to minimise the possibility of any alternative to the status quo through an ever more extensive rationalisation of work, administrative discipline over the population at large and the concentration of political control in the state apparatus.

The supposed connection between Enlightenment thought and the increase of human freedom was therefore being questioned. The association of knowledge – and we might as well say 'science' here – and freedom is superficial. In fact, the spirit of Western natural science is deeply infused with the spirit of domination. The rise of the natural sciences is marked by the exploitation of nature. Having achieved a domination (often ruinous) over nature through the natural sciences so that nature may only serve human material needs, the aim had become that of gaining the same kind of control over humanity. Individuals might be dominated, through the use of science, so that they too would serve only as the means for the increasingly effective fulfilment of narrow material needs.

Much of human and social science turns into administrative science, effectively ensuring that people 'fit into' society and its arrangements, are reconciled to their lot in life, obedient to authority, more productive, and thoroughly accepting of the way things are because they have been persuaded that this is the only way that things can be.

From this point of view, the social sciences were contributing to more sophisticated and indirect control over the industrial work force and the 'masses' more generally. Indeed, one of the major concepts to come out of the sociology of the 1960s (though it has older antecedents) was that of the 'mass society', a society in which the traditional constraints and supports of the publics of community, neighbourhood and free associations had been weakened by the mass media, consumerism and the nationalisation of social and political life – all of this prior to the new theme of globalisation. This state of affairs had created an undifferentiated mass population where individuals were isolated from each other and thus inhibited from acting collectively. However, this threatened the stability of pluralist democracies since those individuals, cut off from peer influence, were amenable to excessive influence by the mass media, so opening them to recruitment by extremist and totalitarian movements that could exploit these media (Kornhauser, 1959). In all this, science was not an innocent bystander but deeply implicated in and actively collaborative with the forces of human oppression by subordinating itself to the needs of the political and economic order.

There were a number of features of the human sciences which were singled out for critique:

- They were an important means of making people more docile and conformist. Therapies and related techniques would help to remove all traces of discontent and dissent, convincing people that their dissatisfactions were only psychological, and not a result of the real conditions of their lives. Individuals were to be 'adjusted' to the requirements of the productive system of modern capitalism.
- The sciences were also looking for ways of organising activities, especially in the work place, to enable more refined and complicated control of people's activities, so as to advance the development of more complex systems of work and eliminate conflicts and resistance. This was not merely the improvement of technical efficiency, but also the means of managing 'human relations' at work so as to 'adjust' people to the conditions of their workplace, preventing them from drawing the conclusion that it was those conditions that needed change.
- They also contributed to ideological pacification by generating the illusions that people lived in the best of all possible worlds, that their needs were being fulfilled within the narrow horizons of the debased pleasures of mass culture, that advanced capitalism is the fullest and most natural expression of human nature – of its supposedly universal and overwhelming urge for acquisition and material prosperity – and, accordingly, no need for fundamental change in the nature of such a society.
- All of this is a means of self-disciplining individuals rather than regulating them by external authority.

Marcuse's book, along with the more general critique from the Frankfurt School, testified to the success of capitalism – and the effectiveness of positivism – in its administrative arrangements, its subduing of the class struggle through manipulating the working class through its elaboration of a whole system of social control and incorporating that class into the advanced capitalist system. Positivism, and its associated methods, was part of turning Western society into a more and more thoroughly administered society.

Though springing from Marxist sources, such ideas nonetheless involve a significant retreat from the central idea of Marx's theory, namely that it is class conflict which is the essence of society, and that in modern society it is the working class which is the engine of change. Later members of the Frankfurt School of critical theory were resigned to the fact that the working class was not going to be any kind of revolutionary force. They were moving from traditional Marxian preoccupations with the economy to a concern with culture and the incorporation of Freudian psychoanalysis into the Marxist framework (Held, 1980). It was this concern with culture which helped to merge the Frankfurt School's critique with the critique of language emerging from structuralist thought, and it is to an exposition of this that we now turn.

Structuralism

Structuralists were initially no less aspiring to scientific status than the positivists in seeking to convert the social sciences into genuine sciences. However, for them the positivist strategy was misconceived, partly because it had followed the wrong model of science. Structuralism sought to work a major upgrading of social thought by following the example of the most successful human science – namely, structural linguistics – hence the label 'Structuralism'. In other words, language was seen as the basis for the study of social structures.

The background of structural linguistics

The great sociological theorists of the positivist programme, Parsons and Merton, did not take language particularly seriously except as an innocent – and entirely unexamined – medium of social communication. Neither gave much scientific regard to language, myth or literature. These were consigned to the cultural sphere. By contrast, European social thought came to regard language itself as a social structure reliant on the secure, but arbitrary, culture of the social group. Social structure became not so much a social thing but a representation of social experience, as it was for the Durkheim of *The Elementary Forms of Religious Life* (Durkheim, 1976). Collective social life is not merely represented by culture but is created by it. Our consciousness of the social world, even thinking itself, is the representation of social structures and the product of the accumulation of experience and knowledge in a social group. It was this, Durkheim maintained, that informed structural linguistics.

The aim of structural linguistics was to study the unconscious structure of language. Largely due to the influence of Durkheim, European linguistics had shifted their attention from individual language behaviour to that of the group or collective. Ferdinand de Saussure (1857–1913) applied Durkheim's notion of the collective consciousness to language. He divided language into *la parole*, or individual speech acts, and *la langue*, the rules of language. *La langue*, following Durkheim, he regarded as a social fact in being general throughout a language community and constraining individuals so that they are prevented from saying anything ungrammatical. However, the important step was to claim that linguistics ought only to deal with *la langue*, studying the common patterns shared by all speakers of a language. He held that *la langue* was a stable set of relations among linguistic entities, an abstract system independent of and distinct from speech itself. It was this idea of language as a self-contained system – a system whose elements were 'signs' and whose identity was determined relationally from within the system – which was Saussure's bequest to the structuralist tradition and to the further development of 'post-structuralism'.

| The Durkheimian influence |

Saussure had in mind a general science – semiology – which would encompass all the various sign systems used by humankind. Although language was the most important of these systems, semiology would include, for example, gestures, food, clothes and music among many others. 'Sign', in other words, can include not only words but any kind of meaningful unit in non-linguistic systems. Each sign consisted of two elements: the 'signifier' and the 'signified'. The former is the material element, such as the sound or the inscription on the paper that produces the word, and the latter is the mental element, the idea invoked by the sound or inscription. However, these two elements are thoroughly fused.

| Semiology |

The other important point to make is that signs do not stand for things in the world. They can be used to denote or name things in the world but the nature of the sign derives, and has to be understood as such, internally from the language system and not from anything outside itself.

Inset 12.2 Sigmund Freud (1856–1939)

Sigmund Freud's (1856–1939) psychoanalysis is important to social thought in his treatment of the conflict between the individual's instinctual gratification and the requirements of social order, or civilisation. The social order is the consequence of a compromise, and a delicate one at that, between sexual fulfilment, and the aggression which often accompanies this drive, and the necessary discipline conducive to a relatively stable social life. To put it simply: social life is made possible by the repression into the individual's unconscious, the often strong drive for sexual gratification which, in some cases, results in psychopathologies of various kinds.

Freud's theories have had an influence on social thought ranging from Talcott Parsons to Marxism. Parsons used Freud's account of personality development to provide the psychological basis of the socialisation process. However, he tended to stress the complementarity of the personality and the social system rather than focus on the tension between sexuality and the social order. The Frankfurt School used psychoanalytic theories to develop a materialist conception of the personality as a way of 'filling out' Marx's materialist analysis of society. Structuralists, such as Althusser and Lacan, regarded Freud's discovery of the unconscious as akin to Marx's discovery of the laws of modes of production.

This emphasis on the system connects Saussure to what was seen as the major contribution of Marx and Freud, namely, uncovering the forces which shape our history and ourselves of which we are unaware. As far as language is concerned, although our speech operates according to the structure of *la langue* it does so without our conscious compliance with it. We are unaware of the language system, even though it operates through our minds, for it does so in an unconscious way. It was applying this idea of a system of elements which received their identity from their relation to other elements in the system to understanding social life which was the central idea of structuralism.

It also represented a radical departure from positivistic conceptions of science. Structural linguistics was a successful science, it was argued, but it was not a quantitative one with all the problems of measurement. Rather, it was a formal discipline which had succeeded in understanding its chosen phenomena in terms of their form, and in identifying the underlying principles which generated that form as, for example, structural linguistics had identified a small number of basic and abstract elements that, in combination, could create all the sounds of human language.

It differed, too, from the positivist tradition in abandoning the 'atomistic' approach. The natural sciences had been very successful in understanding their phenomena by breaking them down so as to isolate their independent constituent elements. This was not the approach of structural linguistics. Its phenomena – the signs – could not identified in isolation for they consisted entirely in their relationships with other signs. The approach was intrinsically 'holistic'. They were to be identified by their place within some language system.

The importance of system

The basic point is simple: that any particular item plays a specific role in a language, or other sign system, is just an arbitrary fact. For example, it does not matter whether a chess piece is made from wood, plastic or cheese from the point of view of playing the game. A chess piece is not identified by the substance of which it is made but entirely by the part that it plays in the game. And so, too, with sounds and language. The sounds which are the constituent of spoken language are only arbitrarily bearers of meaning. In another language some other sound might have the same meaning as this sound in our language, or the same sound a different meaning. The nature of the sound itself does not matter from the point of view of meaning. What gives a sound its specific meaning is its relationship to the system of language and the part it plays in relationship to all the other sounds used in the language. So the language system is treated as a system of relationships: what matters is not any of the constituent elements of sounds or meaning, but the relationships between them. Indeed, the constituent elements, from the point of view of the system, consist of nothing but their relationships. The identity of each one is defined only in relation to others.

Thus, meanings are not to be understood by their materiality, such as the sound or the written form. The meaning 'monkey' may be constant across several different languages, expressed in each by a different word, and therefore cannot be identified with the sound/word combination that, in English, carries that meaning. Obviously, the capacity of different sound/word combinations to carry that same meaning must reside in the fact that *this* sound/word in this language plays much the same part as *that* sound/word combination in that language. What identifies their meaning must be abstracted from their substance, so to speak, and identified by their form; that is, the abstract pattern of connection they have to the other words in the system.

One main reason put forward for regarding structural linguistics as a successful science was that it had developed a systematic way of analysing the sound patterns for a language in terms of a small number of simple principles, and it was envisaged that this same systematic method could be applied to the rest of language such as its meaning. It seemed plausible, too, to argue that social phenomena are, in major part, meaning systems significantly derived from the cultural system. Extending the idea of structure to other symbolic systems was to be the life work of the French anthropologist, Claude Lévi-Strauss (1908–).

Claude Lévi-Strauss and the analysis of myth

Lévi-Strauss's major work was the structuralist analysis of the vast assortment of mythical tales told among the indigenous tribal peoples of the Americas. The aim of the analysis was to develop a thoroughly systematic method that would yield an overall order to the myths by showing how they derived from a small number of principles. However, his interests, as they eventually emerged after a long period of fieldwork in the 1930s, were not simply in myth but, rather, in formulating the basic structural laws of human consciousness (Lévi-Strauss, 1970a). Drawing on Saussure, he began to see anthropology as a semiotic discipline. His view was that the seeming arbitrariness and variety of culture to be found among the peoples of the world rested upon common mental structures which have a foundation in logical necessity. At first the interest was in the link between anthropology and linguistics, which changed into an interest in the links *beneath* anthropology and linguistics.

Lévi-Strauss was of the view that the human mind was everywhere the same. So-called 'simpler peoples' were no less intelligent than ourselves. Thought depends upon the brain and the brain must operate the same way in all human beings. Its operating principle is that of binary logic, which is the very basis of thought itself. Examples of binary relations include presence–absence, has–lacks, is–is not, up–down, does–does not, true–false, on–off and so on. Such binary oppositions provide one of the basic tools of logical thought. Saussure had earlier argued that the meaning of words depends upon the contrastive relations between them. For a simple example, if we take the colour words – 'red', 'blue', 'green' and the rest – rather than try to say what 'red' is by identifying the colour it refers to, we should, according to Saussure, under-stand its meaning in terms of its relation to other words. Meaning, to repeat the point, has nothing to do with a word 'standing for' something in the world, but is due to its place in a system of words. Accordingly, the meaning of 'red' is entirely internal to the language system.

What attracted Lévi-Strauss to Saussure's ideas was that they seemed to offer a way of moving from elements which themselves have no meaning – the sounds, or phonemes, of a language – to things which do, namely, the seman-tics of the language. Thus, the binary structure, embedded as it was in the mind, could characterise not only the

> The common nature of thought

structure of language but also that of culture. It could potentially do so in a thoroughly systematic way that could be applied to the whole range of cultures. The fact that cultures were very diverse was not to be discounted, but should not be taken as an indication that human thought is basically diverse. The human mind is grounded in the human brain and is everywhere the same. Thus, Lévi-Strauss concluded, diverse cultures must nonetheless reflect the basic, common nature of thought and, in each case, could be shown to be constructed according to the same finite code or structure. From the binary operations of thought the human mind is capable of creating meaning.

In the myths Lévi-Strauss studied, the 'elements' in the stories, the bearer's of the myth's meaning, are events, personages, animals, plants, animals and other natural phenomena, such as the sun and the moon. Consistent with the principles of structural linguistics, the bearers of the story's meaning are, of themselves, only arbitrarily related to that meaning. In another myth, another system, the same meaning could be fixed to a very different bearer. In one myth, for example, it might be carried by a bear, in another by an eagle. So understanding mythical stories involves working out the meaning of the different elements by virtue of their relationship to other elements in the system. The sky, for example, is a high place, whereas down on the ground is a comparatively low place, but not so low as beneath the ground. On top of a mountain is not as high as the sky, but not so low as 'on the ground'. Lévi-Strauss's analysis of mythical stories might notice that the characters in them go on various journeys, up into the sky, into the under-world, down river and so forth, and he argues that these events carry the meaning, within the myth, of 'vertical movement' (upward and downward) and, contrastingly, of 'horizontal movement' (across the earth and down the river). It might be in another myth that the sky features as a holy place, the dwelling of celestial beings and that, in relation to this, 'underground' is the location of the nether world. Thus, the one is now 'sacred' and the other 'unholy'. Through the interlocking of these meanings in the mythical stories, very elaborate structures of reasoning can be built.

Any element in a mythical narrative will have a place that depends upon which of its characteristics is the one operating as the arbitrary bearer of meaning. For example, an animal may play the role that it does by virtue, *inter alia*, of its habitat (land based/aquatic, lives in a hole/up a tree), its eating habits (carnivorous/vegetarian), its size, its status relative to humans (wild/domesticated), its temperament (gentle/savage), whether it is feathered or furred, and so on and on. Deciding which property is relevant requires consideration of its place in the overall narrative context, what other animals appear in the story, how their characteristics differ, and so on. If the animal in question is, say, a creature which flies and the other main creature that figures in the story is a fish, then it may be that the relevant contrast is between habitats, between sky and sea. But what exactly it is needs to be worked in each case in relation to the whole pattern of the myth's narrative.

Lévi-Strauss's method was not simply to enumerate the elements of the mythical tales. This was just a means to an end, that is, making sense of tales which otherwise might seem to make no sense to people like ourselves who do not live in societies where myth is a significant medium. He wanted to show that they were complex intellectual constructions, no less complex in many ways that our own scientific theories and mathematics. They were, when analysed, seen to be as much arguments as narratives, attempts to solve just the kind of intellectual problems and tensions which any human society faces about the problems of life and dilemmas of thought. For example, among many others: Why is there anything rather than nothing? How did humanity originate? Why is society divided into male and female? What is to be done with new newcomers to society, like children, and how are they to be controlled and made into responsible adults? What keeps the sun and moon in the sky and moving in their regular patterns? What determines the periodic rhythms of life?

The important difference between the 'savage' and the 'civilised' mentality is not the former's lack of desire for logical order, but that it is directed more to the concrete. The difference is akin to that

| Bricolage |

between the professional car mechanic and what the French call a *bricoleur*, a term usually translated as 'handyman'. The former possesses all kinds of tools specific to the work of fixing cars, while the latter is more of a generalised worker who has no specialist equipment but only a collection of materials and ready-to-hand tools for the variety of work he or she may be called upon to perform. The car mechanic has a standardised kit for fixing problems with cars. If called upon to fix a car the *bricoleur* will have to use whatever materials are to hand and adapt tools as necessary. The *bricoleur* is no less intelligent, no less logical in approach, than is the car mechanic. Like the *bricoleur*, the 'savage mind' – which has no ready-made logical systems such as formal logic and mathematics to hand – manipulates the events, flora and fauna which are to hand into stories. Myths are not just bizarre stories but, when properly understood, ways of working through, symbolically and indirectly, the same abstract and often intractable problems that our greatest thinkers wrestled with.

The main objective of the method was to bring out the logical structures underlying the myths to show that the apparently arbitrary sequences of events, superficially making up the story, are bearers of meaning which represent the things that stand in abstract logical relations. Decomposing the myths involved reducing the text to sentences, or 'mythemes', and looking for their relationships with others to bring out the patterns of logical connection and transformation.

In the first instance this uses the notion of 'binary opposition', identifying things in terms of their contrastive values, such as 'up–down', 'has–does not have', 'is–is not'. The titles of the four volumes of *Mythologiques* suggest the nature of the enterprise. To mention but one example, *The Raw and the Cooked* (Lévi-Strauss, 1970b). The two contrasting terms, 'raw' and 'cooked' comprise, respectively, natural and cultural states. Cooking is a cultural activity, an activity which changes something which is inedible into something which is edible – 'edible' and 'inedible' being another pair of contrasting terms. *The Origin of Table Manners* (Lévi-Strauss, 1978), to mention another example, concerns the difference between those who eat in a natural way, like animals, and those who eat in a 'civilised' fashion: that is, in a way that is culturally regulated. The contrast further serves to contrast animals and humans, but can also draw a line between different human beings, such as those who behave like animals, or in 'uncivilised' ways, and those who behave in a civilised manner.

Myths are layered and messages can be stated in different ways, and yet, underlying the diversity of myths are common logical rules. There is, for example, a difference between South American and North American myths in the ways things are represented. North American myths do not deal with the same subjects as the South American ones. Nonetheless, the same logical structure is at work. The idea of people as 'naked' or 'dressed' is, in North American myths, the equivalent of the ideas of 'raw' and 'cooked' in the Southern ones. So there is still an allusion to 'cooking' as, according to Lévi-Strauss, standing for the 'cultural' versus the 'natural'. The underlying logic is the same.

The important points about Lévi-Strauss's structuralism are as follows:

■ He is not attempting some kind of psychology of individual reasoning that describes the thought processes of the individual tribal member. Consistent with the tenets of structural linguistics with its focus on *la langue*, Lévi-Strauss is interested in the collective meaning system in which mythical thought moves.

■ Meaning is treated as an autonomous system. That is, it draws on a conception of language – and meaning – which constitutes a break with the more usual view that words stand for things: a break which, as we shall shortly see, has major consequences.

Further consequences of structuralist thought

An important feature of Lévi-Strauss's structuralism was that apparently it gave a systematic methodological cast to a notion which has had a long standing appeal in the social sciences, one cultivated by many of the titans of sociological thought, including Marx and Durkheim in sociology, and Freud in psychology. This is the idea that individuals are the creatures of systems and forces of which they are unaware. Take the linguistic analogy again. *La langue* is a system which exists independently of, and is greater than, any individual speaker of the language. Individuals move within the system to construct the individual sentences which make up their verbal expressions. But it is not individuals who decide what they mean by their words. What the words mean, and what the individual can possibly mean, is determined by the language system not by the mind of the speaker. Individuals are entirely unconscious of the system in which they are operating and which restricts what they can mean. Individuals do not control the language; the language controls them. It is this move which represents a radical break with Enlightenment individualism.

The structuralist conception of language is a radical break with the view that words stand for things and, accordingly, that their meaning is determined by their relationship to the external world. In some ways this sounds counterintuitive. After all, words are massively convenient. They can 're-present', stand proxy for, things which are not now present to us. We often call them symbols, meaning that they stand for something other than themselves. If we want to indicate to someone where there is food, we can point to an apple tree. If the tree is not in sight we can give verbal directions: that is, present the tree to another through words. The words, 'the apple tree in Frank's garden' 're-presents' the tree in its absence. Hence, words get their meanings for the things they 're-present'. But, according to structuralist thought, this is anything but a convincing view.

This is not to say that words cannot 'stand for things'. It is to say that the connection between the word and whatever it stands for is as arbitrary as the connection between the word and its sound. The connection is a conventional one. A different language may have a very different name for a certain thing, if it has a name for it at all. Therefore, the meaning of a word is not fixed by its

> Language as a self-contained system

connection to something outside the system of language, to some object in the natural world, but is entirely fixed within the language system itself. The notion of language as representation is superfluous to this conception since, by definition, in the structuralist approach the identity of the elements is determined entirely within the system, by nothing other than their relationship to each other. The system, therefore, is wholly self-contained.

As we have indicated, structuralist ideas within sociology provided a powerful counterweight to the social action tradition and its assault on positivism and its methods. Symbolic interactionism and phenomenology had argued that the displacement of positivism effectively transformed sociology into the study of social phenomena as constituted by meanings. For some this seemed to take sociology into much too individualistic, even subjectivist, a direction, treating individuals as being free to determine the meaning of social phenomena. What is more, this had sometimes come very close to abandoning altogether the aspirations to make sociology scientific. By contrast, the structuralist approach – as demonstrated by Lévi-Strauss – offered a strategy that could make sociology a study of meanings without sacrificing the major scientific insight of social science, even though rather old-fashioned, of structures as determinants of individual actions. The idea that individuals created their own meanings was pre-empted. Moreover, the approach could be highly generalised to analyse any cultural system, and was the seed of the idea that the study of cultural phenomena is akin to the reading of texts, understood of course as the attempt to determine how meaning is produced. The method could be applied to literature, film and history, and was a major stimulus to the formation of cultural studies as a distinct discipline. It could also be fused with the notion of ideology.

The notion of ideology, however, changed and in a way which was specifically identified with the structuralist Marxist, Louis Althusser (1918–1990).

Louis Althusser and the return to Marx

Classically, ideology had been conceived in terms of what people believed. Under Althusser's reconstrual, ideology is not to be identified with the ideas that people held or what they believed, but with the framework within which they thought.

Althusser was in harmony with Lévi-Strauss in being firmly convinced that the individual is not the unit out of which social phenomena are made. Systems, or structures, antedate the individual. He argued that the Marx's heirs had taken a wrong turning with the result that his achievement had been widely misunderstood. A proper structuralist science was to be found in Marx's writings. He had propounded the scientific doctrine – historical materialism – but this needed a complementary philosophy to go along with the science, which Althusser sought to provide. What was called for was a re-reading of Marx to identify the point at which Marx had made the 'epistemological break' from ideology to science proper. Such a re-reading, as Althusser saw it, was not unlike the manner in which a psychoanalyst attends to the speech of a patient giving it a 'symptomatic reading', attending not only to what is said but also to the 'silences'. Like a psychoanalytic patient, it must not be presumed that Marx himself knew the full significance of what he was writing. But a re-reading is not the only thing required. The re-reading must be based in a Marxist conception of science.

In brief, Marx's early thoughts were developments out of the raw materials of the thought of the time including the theories of his predecessors, such as Adam Smith and David Ricardo. Marx engaged in his own 'symptomatic reading' of these to produce his own theory. But this was a reconstruction of these ideas rather than an examination of the phenomenon, the nature of capitalism itself. It failed to transcend ideology into a fully-fledged science. According to Althusser, if a science is to emerge out of ideology then there must be an 'epistemological break', a point at which Marx begins to break out of the ideologies out of which the reconstruction has been built.

> Symptomatic reading of Marx

Science and ideology are rigorously opposed in Althusser. Not because they are rival occupants for the same space, so to speak, but because they view the world in very different ways. Science views the world impersonally. Ideology is typically seen – by Marxists and others – as a form of understanding which awaits displacement by a true scientific understanding. But for Althusser science cannot displace ideology since science has no space for individuals' personalised relationships to the world, and individual lives cannot be lived without such a relationship. Individuals have to represent their own relationship to the world, and since they cannot do this through science – which, by definition, is an impersonal point of view – they can only do this through the illusory forms provided by ideology. Ideology is indispensable to human existence and not something to be eradicated by the arrival of true science, even the Marxist one. In any case, 'the individual' is the creation of an ideology – that deriving from the Enlightenment – that makes people think of themselves as specific and distinctive beings.

At this point, Althusser presents an analysis of the ideology of capitalist society which strongly echoes that of Marcuse and others of the Frankfurt School. The ideology of capitalism may, in effect, create the individual as a distinctive and specific person, but its purpose in doing so is to maintain control over the society. It is not control by physical coercion, but by mental domination. The disposition of people to have revolutionary ideas is inhibited by instilling in them the kind of outlook that makes them compliant to the needs of capitalism. Although the state is in important respects a 'body of armed men', it is not only this but combines it with a repressive ideological apparatus which includes the educational system and even the family.

Althusser was later to deny that he had ever been a structuralist, and he had no particular use for the linguistic model which was of such importance to Lévi-Strauss and to other structuralists. Nonetheless, his ideas had an important impact, especially for what it seemed to promise in the way of Marxist-inspired analyses of the complexities of advanced capitalism.

Problems of structuralist method

One of the main objectives of structuralism was to banish traces of Enlightenment thinking, including the positivist programme. It proclaimed itself 'anti-humanist', rejecting the idea that the human individual is the 'atom' of social reality. Much of this argument was epistemological in nature. In effect it was an attempt to develop a persuasive invitation to look at social phenomena in structuralist terms. The fact that the movement drew upon reasonably well-established traditions in social thought – linguistics, Marxism, psychoanalysis, anthropology – lent it some weight, especially in Europe, well into the 1980s. Further, and parallel to the work of critical theory, it seemed to bring back the critical thread in sociological thought which the positivist project had – again seemingly – cast aside, along with an alternative way of achieving the positivist ambition of a properly scientific social science. Positivism itself, however, was argued to be itself a child of the ideology of the Enlightenment masquerading as a science.

However, structuralism, on the whole, was reluctant to abandon altogether the idea of a human science. One of the main problems with positivism was that it had the wrong notion of what a proper science should be. It had used the wrong exemplar. It had pursued measurement and quantification instead of trying to identify the logico-mathematical principles of the structures in which people were embedded and of which they were unaware.

But, and perhaps fatefully, a commitment to science brings with it a commitment to method, though not necessarily in the form in which the positivist project understood this as developing techniques of empirical investigation. From its earliest days, structuralist thought was committed to systematicity. The task was to identify the principles out of which structures were generated. Lévi-Strauss had spent decades of his life trying to tease out the multi-layered structures underlying mythical stories, though few of his structuralist colleagues were to have this kind of tenacity having, in truth, only superficial connections to the linguistic model he was developing. Nonetheless, the prospect of a science of semiology was enticing to some, notably Roland Barthes.

Barthes and the oppression of culture

Barthes had a much stronger kinship with Lévi-Strauss in his determination to make social science a semiological science. In the 1950s he began to explore semiology (Barthes, 1972). By the 1960s he was trying to put it onto a more scientific footing.

Barthes was both a sociologist and a literary critic and his overwhelming preoccupation was with language as writing, especially literary writing. His conviction was that culture was a convention and, moreover, a convention that was restrictive and oppressive, imposing conformity on the individual and inhibiting free expression. The recognition that culture was a matter of convention and, what is more, composed of signs, meant that one of the ways in which it oppressed was by concealing its own conventionality and presenting itself as immutable and unchanging.

Coming from a Marxist point of view, and thus critical of the dominance of the French bourgeoisie and their culture, Barthes tried to give this critique a new cast using the resources of semiology. Cultural expressions were not 'innocent'. He sought to reveal the manner and extent to which cultural signs passed themselves off as a reflection of natural realities rather than as conventional systems of signs. (Remember that the basic structuralist principle is that there is only an arbitrary connection between signs and any external reality. Thus, the connection of sign and anything it stands for is artificial.)

Critique of bourgeoise culture

Much of Barthes' writing was journalistic and some of his most influential works were critiques of 'mythologies' perpetuated by the French middle class and were analyses of various instances of popular culture such as all-in wrestling, eating steak and chips, and the Tour de France cycle race. The point was to show that our experience of things is never of the things themselves but is always mediated through culture. Thus, the wrestling bout or the cycle race are not things ingested raw but presented to us in stylised ways. The Tour de France is presented by the mass media in terms of devices drawn from a traditional literary form, the epic. The all-in wrestling match is an entirely stylised encounter in which all the signs of violence – blows, kicks, strangleholds, aggressive yells, cries of pain – are present but do not actually function as signs of the things they represent. The violence is wholly pretended, the signs of violence are pretended, and everyone knows that they are.

In some respects Barthes writings on culture are a refashioning in semiotic language of critiques made in the 1950s and 1960s about style and consumption as indicators of status (Packard, 1957, 1960; Riesman et al, 1951). However, he did try to take the analysis further.

Barthes was operating on two principles:

- The sign system is organised according to a 'code' which structures the signs and, therefore, our experience.
- All aspects of culture can be analysed as manifestations of a sign system, a means of sending messages or making statements. Eating and drinking, for example, though natural, are endowed with cultural meaning: steak and chips is a 'manly' meal, a taste for wine the mark of a 'civilised' person, and the ability to hold one's drink a 'proud French trait', and so on.

However, Barthes did attempt to give a more systematic exposition of the technical structure of the semiotic approach (Barthes, 1967), in addition to, though some years later, an equally systematic instance of its application to fashion (Barthes, 1985). Clothing serves the practical purpose of covering our body, keeping it warm and dry. But it does so in a culturally coded manner. The different kinds of clothing comprise the equivalent of the 'language system' by providing a collection of elements and their rules of combination. Bowler hat goes with pin stripe suit, grey tie, black shoes and similar attire. The particular clothing ensemble a person wears is like a statement in that language. The clothes one wears make statements about oneself. So far so good.

The systematic aspect of the study examines the way in which fashion magazines write about clothes. Barthes argued that each sign system had its own science, its semiology, with linguistics dealing just with language. Other sign systems are interwoven with language and, therefore, linguistics is the master scheme. It is this idea which premises his analysis of fashion writing rather than the clothes themselves. The cultural meaning of clothing is tied up with language not something distinct from it.

Thus, Barthes tried to analyse the underlying structure of written discourse, decomposing it into elements which were then recombined into the statements made by fashion writing. For example, using linguistic-like techniques, Barthes notes the ways in which items of

| Cultural coding |

clothing could be characterised in the categories of 'object' (O), 'support' (S), and 'variant' (V). A cardigan, the 'object', has a characteristic such as a collar, which is the 'support'. The collar may be a 'variant' in that it can be open or closed and, in fashion, the difference between the collar open or closed is a difference between the cardigan as 'sporty' or 'dressy'. Working this out rather elaborately, Barthes tried to show how fashion writing creates and recreates the 'world of fashion' as we know it: a world in which the important times are 'the evening', 'the weekend', 'the vacation'; the important events 'the party', 'the concert', 'the business lunch' and so on. Fashion writing also conveys ideological postures. For example, and bear in mind the time Barthes was writing, that young women did not have serious jobs, work was always shown as incidental to their lives, and so on.

Barthes at least tried to provide a systematic method for the structural analysis of culture but, as we shall see, he became increasingly dissatisfied what were to be seen as the limitations of structuralism. Among these were the manifold problems of meeting the requirements of systematicity and taking it beyond suggestiveness. In effect, and speaking methodologically, structuralism found it difficult to get beyond the aspiration to be a systematic semiological science.

This is not to say that it did not produce studies of interest. In many ways, it seemed to offer a systematic clothing for skills and sensitivities which had for long been the stock in trade of literary critics, historians and analysts of culture more generally, namely, identifying 'submerged' themes within various forms of narrative.

Wollen's *Signs and Meaning in the Cinema* (1970) provides a simple, illustrative example of the method as used in some films by John Ford. He argues that:

> The master antinomy in Ford's films is that between the wilderness and the garden. … It is crystallised in a number of striking images. *The Man Who Shot Liberty Valance,* for instance, contains the image of the cactus

rose, which encapsulates the antimony between the desert and garden which pervades the whole film.

(Wollen, 1970: 68)

Of the character Ethan Edwards in *The Searchers*, he says that he:

> is more complex. He must be defined not in terms of past versus future or wilderness versus garden compounded in himself, but in relation to two other protagonists: Scar, the Indian chief, and the family of home-steaders. Ethan Edwards ... remains a nomad throughout the film. At the start, he rides in from the desert to enter the log-house; at the end, with perfect symmetry, he leaves the house again to return to the desert, to vagrancy. In many respects, he is similar to Scar; he is a wanderer, a savage, outside the law: he scalps his enemy. But, like the homestead-ers, of course, he is a European, the mortal foe of the Indian. Thus Edwards is ambiguous; the antimonies invade the personality of the protagonist himself. The oppositions tear Edwards in two; he is a tragic hero. His companion, Martin Pawley, however, is able to resolve the dual-ity; for him, the period of nomadism is only an episode, which has mean-ing as the restitution of the family, a necessary link between his old home and his new home'.

(Ibid: 69)

The account of Ford's films is not in terms of their narrative and dramatic structures, but in terms of thematic elements. The natural phenomenon the cactus rose, for example, encapsulates the opposition between the cultivated garden and the wilderness and so, even though a natural phenomenon, repre-sents the social tensions between the wild and the domesticated ways of life. The recounting of *The Searchers* is in terms of series of opposed elements, all alluding to a persistent tensions in American thought between civilisation and the 'Wild West'. Thus, the film can be thought of as an exercise in thinking through the problem of understanding America's own nature, as a society which is becoming increasingly settled while having a conception of itself very much shaped around the idea of the 'Wild West'.

While such analyses may be suggestive they are a far cry from the aims of semiology to develop a systematic method of analysis. If anything it is akin to an invitation to look and examine language, culture, fashion, the social structure, film, literary productions, and more, semiologi-cally. However, what is missing is any strong claim that this way of looking at such phenomena actually does demonstrate that they are organised according to semiotic principles. But, in many ways, structuralism's ambitions were every bit as far-reaching as those of positivism in seeking to discover the general prin-ciples underlying the various instances of cultural products. Such a method

> Instances and generalities

would have to proceed on a case-by-case basis. One can only examine one instance of a film, a myth, a fashion magazine or other artefact at a time. One might hope to develop a collection of instances, as Lévi-Strauss did, and re-examine each of them in light of the others. The aim would be to develop a general method which could be systematically rather than suggestively applied to any case. Such a strategy – comparable to the one adopted by conversation analysis – gets away from the idea of sampling which infused, and confused, the issue of generalisation in the positivist project. Indeed, one can be completely general on the basis of a single case, providing that the general method can encompass *this* instance. If one's analysis of the case is correct, then any fully general account has to subsume this instance. One can project from the instance some completely general arrangements capable of producing it, for these are presupposed in the analysis of the instance. But one cannot assume from the beginning that this instance is representative of all such – that determination must await the examination of other instances. After all, gener-alities of method and analysis can be modified and revised in light of what is found from the analysis of other cases.

There is no quick way with cases. The analogy with conversation analysis is strong. One cannot count up cases and analyse them as a collection in the way that one can count up the answers to survey questionnaires. One needs to know what kind of cases they are and, in the case of structuralism, this involves nothing else than carrying out a structuralist analysis of each case. But work-ing out the systematic links proved to be extremely difficult. Moreover, from the outset it required buying into the structuralist conception of language and meaning – by no means an agreed-upon conception. Questioning this would, in effect, question the whole of the structuralist project.

However, this was not the main reason why structuralism collapsed or, better, moved toward post-structuralism.

The move toward post-structuralism

Even as the structuralist movement became the focus of international attention, in Paris it was already under criticism for not being radical enough. There was disappointment, too, with the failure of Althusser especially to give leadership to the student disturbances in Paris around May 1968. These were, as in the United States, interwoven with a condemnation of social scientists for their compliance with the 'military industrial complex', which also led to a deepen-ing distaste for the ambition to make the subject a science. Structuralism had placed great emphasis on the scientific nature of the exercise, which was displaced by the move toward 'post-structuralism', a label emphasising the combination of continuity and discontinuity. Barthes himself, by the late 1960s, abandoned the idea of making semiology a science and instead turned to the Text as an open political signifying practice directed against one of the central convictions of Western culture, namely, the idea of an organising Centre (Barthes, 1994).

Greatly oversimplifying, and an issue we will take up in the next chapter, eventually the move was provoked by the demand for 'reflexivity'; that is, the requirement that supposedly scientific analysis should be applied to itself in just the same way that it was applied to the activities of others. Post-structuralism was product of the consequences – and the problems – of applying structuralist methods to structuralism itself.

Outside Paris, in Anglo-American thinking, structuralism was a turning point that contributed to the breakdown of the prejudice against European social thought. Althusser's rehabilitation of Marx was especially crucial. Indeed, since the late 1960s, much of the initiative in social thought has shifted to the European development.

Structuralism initially was attractive because it offered an alternative conception of science to that on offer from those attempting to model the social sciences on the natural sciences, such as Parsons, Merton and Lazarsfeld. The adoption of a human science, linguistics, as the exemplary model was a refreshing move – even if contentious – offering the possibility of a formal, logical discipline rather than a quantitative one. This also offered resistance to what were seen by some as unsettling developments in social science. First of these was the emphasis on social phenomena as meaningful ones, and second, the development of individualist and phenomenological alternatives to systems thinking of the kind exemplified by functionalism.

The notion that social phenomena are meaningful and that understanding them required understanding the meaning they have for individual members of society was, in the 1960s, gaining some ground through symbolic interactionism and ethnomethodology. These approaches were seriously critical of any thinking which treated society as any kind of system, be it functionalist or Marxist. Such thinking was a form of illicit reification. In the eyes of some critics, these 'phenomenological' approaches – since they seemingly held that social reality existed in the consciousness of individuals – were convicted of rampant subjectivism. Structuralism, of course, accepted that social phenomena were cultural, and hence meaningful,

> The rejection of subjectivism

and that language was the bearer of meaning in social life. It drew a different conclusion, however, from that of symbolic interactionism and ethnomethodology. The need was to understand not the individual consciousness of meaning, but the objective systems of meaning from which the individual expressions of meaning were derived.

Structuralism was seen as a way of containing the threat of individualism and subjectivity in sociology, not least because it seemed to remove the critical impulse of sociology. Making the individual the focus of sociological attention came very close to saying – as indeed many subscribers to 'phenomenological' approaches, including Weber, did say – that sociologists had no more authority than anyone else to criticise social arrangements and the lives that people led. This was the business of the ordinary members of society. Structuralism, with its emphasis on systems of which the individual was unaware, not only defended system-type thinking against the encroachments of 'subjectivism', but gave a renewed credibility to Marxist conceptions such as ideology and, along with critical theory, refreshed the idea of political critique in sociology. But with post-structuralism this was to be taken much further.

Conclusion

In this chapter we have reviewed some of the arguments involved in the re-politicisation of sociology and, as part of this, the rejection not only of positivism but also the very mode of thinking which had created it and which had arisen out of the Enlightenment. This was especially pronounced in the thinking of critical theory, which seriously questioned the form of knowledge which had spawned science itself as repressive of human freedom and creating a society which was totalitarian in the constraints it placed on the freedom to dissent and create. This new totalitarianism was on the whole not brutal but, rather, benign in its repression as human lives became enmeshed in material comfort, intellectual complacency and narrow conformity to its modes of allowable thought.

As we shall see in the next chapter, this kind of critique was joined by a response to structuralism, an attempt to build a social science using the model of structural linguistics rather than, as positivism had tried to do, natural science. This movement, too, was an attempt to shed the legacy of the Enlightenment, in particular what it saw as its misplaced focus on the subject as the topic of a social science. For structuralists, as Marx and Freud had discovered, a proper science must discover the unconscious forces which drive people to behave and believe in the ways they do. However, and again as we will take up in the next chapter, structuralism transformed itself into post-structuralism as the effort to develop a systematic structuralist science proved not only difficult but, ultimately, self-defeating.

One final comment. As should be clear from what has been said, this reaction to positivism, unlike the symbolic interactionist and ethnomethodological responses, brought theory to the fore in sociological thinking. The triad of positivist methodological thinking – theory–method–data – is well and truly abandoned. However, theory is less about the formulation of general theories of the kind that the naturally sciences had developed (Lévi-Strauss is a possible exception here) and which explain the nature of phenomena, and more akin to a therapy or an illumination necessary for emancipating the members of society from the social order which constrains their thought and action. Readers are not to be persuaded by the force of the data correctly gathered and analysed, but by the force of the vision in the theory which enables them to see, possibly for the first time, the way things are. The aim is, though perhaps too much should not be made of this, revelation by the force of the vision rather than persuasion by the force of the evidence.

As we say, perhaps too much should not be made of this since none of the writers we have mentioned, or many that we have not, avoid detailed argument, the patient development of their case, the analysis of empirical examples and so forth. However, their writing has to be seen against the backdrop of the reaction against positivism and the proposal of an alternative to that philosophy. Accordingly, and to repeat a point we made at the beginning of the book, the main purpose of the studies is to demonstrate an approach, a point of view.

Selected bibliography and suggested reading

- For an introduction to the Frankfurt School and critical theory see L. Ray, *Rethinking Critical Theory* (Sage, 1993). David Held's *Introduction to Critical Theory: Horkheimer to Habermas* (Hutchinson, 1980), is extensive and thorough. Sharrock, Hughes and Martin, *Understanding Modern Sociology* (Sage, 2003) contains sections not only on the Frankfurt School but also on structuralism.
- Structuralism and its antecedents are not easy reading. R. Harris's *Saussure and His Interpreters* (Edinburgh University Press, 2001) is a useful account of the linguistic ideas which influenced structuralism. A short and accessible account is John Sturrock's *Structuralism*, 2nd ed. (Fontana, 1993). There are many more advanced guides available.
- Lévi-Strauss's corpus is extensive. His *The Savage Mind* (Weidenfeld, 1962) is a good place to start as is his *The Scope of Anthropology* (Jonathan Cape, 1968). *Structural Anthropology* (Basic Books, 1964) sets out the structuralist principles underlying his conception of what anthropology should be about. *Totemism* (Penguin, 1973) contains his attack on existing anthropological theories of totemism. See also *The Raw and the Cooked: Introduction to a Science of Mythology* (Harper and Row, 1970), *From Honey to Ashes* (Cape, 1973), *The Naked Man* (Cape, 1981). Edmund Leach's *Lévi-Strauss*, in the Fontana Modern Masters Series (Fontana, 1974, rev. ed.) is a good introduction.
- Barthes, too, has been a prolific writer. His *Elements of Semiology* (Noonday Press, 1967) sets out his ambitions for semiology. As might be expected, *The Fashion System* (Cape, 1985) contains his semiological analysis of fashion. *Mythologies* (Cape, 1972) contains journalistic pieces analysis aspects of bourgeois culture. *Empire of Signs* (Cape, 1983) analyses Japanese culture from a semiotic point of view. *S/Z* (Cape, 1975) is the reference for Barthes thoughts on writing and authorship.
- Althusser is not easy reading. His most famous work is *For Marx* (Penguin, 1969). But see also L. Althusser and E. Balibar, *Reading Capital* (New Left Books, 1970).

Chapter 13

Post-modernism, Post-structuralism

The developments we have been reviewing, and those we are about to turn to, are often seen as marking a major transition in the nature of thought: a breakdown in a way of thinking which, dominated by conceptions of natural science, had ruled the roost for three hundred years. It had been challenged before but never so widely and assiduously. This way of thinking is often identified as 'Enlightenment' thinking, a characterisation which is rather wider than simply identifying it with modern, that is post-1700, science. Nevertheless, it is a characterisation which highlights the connection between the scientific standpoint and political concerns which loom large in what follows. The Enlightenment took its name from the root idea that new scientific thought could contribute to the general betterment of human life by intellectually enlightened individuals, enabling them collectively to usher in an age of more enlightened relationships among human beings. We have now reached the point, it is claimed, of a deep and final disillusionment with these ideas. 'Modern' society was so extensively permeated by Enlightenment ideas that the disillusionment with them marks the end of that society and the emergence of a new one: hence, 'post-modernity'.

In getting to this point our emphasis on language has been growing stronger as we have reviewed the various dominant phases in social thought as, across a number of disciplines, the 'linguistic turn' took place. It is the elaboration of the linguistic turn in its different directions which has played a key part in the erosion of the Enlightenment idea.

The linguistic turn

The preceding discussion of structuralism and its adoption of linguistics as a model for social analysis, along with its treatment of social phenomena as linguistic in nature, points to the break with Enlightenment ideas. However, the emphasis on language as a constituent feature of social life and a topic for social thought does not provide the main significance of the 'linguistic turn'. Its prime importance is its attempt, in its various manifestations, to change the ways of thinking that had long been accepted in social thought, and to change them in fundamental ways.

It is important to understanding the radical nature of what is being proposed. It is an invitation to give up existing ways of thinking and to adopt quite new ones. This often makes the ideas seem bizarre and unconvincing. Many find them, simultaneously and rather contradictorily, both unintelligible and plainly wrong. However, such dismissive rejection often comes from critics who retain many of the established, even entrenched, ways of thinking and their criticisms, or so it seems to us, are both question-begging and unfair – even though they are criticisms of positions with which we ourselves have no great sympathy.

Post-modernism

A further element in much of the thinking we will be dealing with – and it is an idea found in different forms in Marx, Weber and Durkheim, and one discussed earlier – is that a specific way of thought is possible only under specific social conditions. There are preconditions to ways of thinking and in the absence of these conditions we cannot conceive of or take seriously some ways of thinking. Further, if the conditions which sustain a way of thought come to an end, then attachment to it will become weakened in that people will no longer be able to take its ideas seriously. Even if some sense can be made of them, they will seem incredible, even bizarre and stupid.

So, for post-modern social thought, the Enlightenment idea was possible only under a certain kind of society – modern society – which provided the conditions for the existence and success of Enlightenment ideas. But modern society had undergone fundamental change and, because of this, the props were removed from its entrenched way of thinking. Enlightenment ideas can no longer be taken seriously. As the name 'post-modernity' suggests, what follows 'modernity' is negatively characterised and consists in giving up conceptions definitive of 'modern society' rather than replacing them with some alternative and positive conception. We can see this in the example of architecture – which is where the expression 'post-modernism' first gained wide circulation – in reaction to a situation that had been dominated by a previous 'modernism'.

Originally 'post modernity' denoted an architectural style. It was not about developing an entirely new style – since the development of the 'new' was a preoccupation of modernity – but giving up on the 'tradition of the new', the relentless preoccupation with stylistic advance and progression. So the post-modern style does not have its own identity as one marked out by distinctive characteristics but, instead, differs from its predecessors by re-using their ideas but without taking them seriously, using

Post-modern preoccupations

them as pastiche or irony. By giving up on the idea that the succession of styles is an 'advance', post-modernism rejects the idea of progress. More generally, it rejects the idea of a division between 'high culture' and 'low culture' especially the implication that the former is superior to the latter. It rejects, that is, the notion that there is some developing historical logic that makes new architectural styles render earlier ones worthless. The idea of architectural progress was challenged by combining ideas from many different periods in its own style but without claiming that this was a new authoritative style of its own. Combining styles in this way effectively places them in quotation marks, accompanying them with a figurative wink of the eye and invoking them in a playful, pretend fashion. The words 'irony' and 'pastiche' are often taken as identifying prominent features of the post-modern attitude.

The same kind of attitude as found within architecture is taken toward the history of cultural ideas more generally. In the social sciences the idea of post-modernity was to prove immensely radical, encouraging a thorough cleansing of the remnants of the Enlightenment, especially of its deeply entrenched idea of rationality. The fact that the three century long Enlightenment hold on intellectual culture has begun to collapse – its ideas able only to live into the present as a caricature of themselves entirely lacking in the conviction they once had – signifies that the conditions that made them possible have also broken down. Certainly there had been major changes in the world, including:

> Post-modern society

- The collapse of Euro-American colonialism effectively destroyed the foundational economic basis of the modern world.
- It brought an end to the existence of an unchallenged centre to world politics which had been built on the dominance of the colony-based modern world economic order. The world's political structure has lost its classic form, but with no great hope of ameliorating the evident ills of the world.
- There is resistance to the very idea of a unified and universal world culture based on Euro-American values. New social movements, such as feminism, gay rights, the re-emergence of ethnicities as a primary basis of social identification, and the reappearance of traditional cultures in the form of religious fundamentalism, have challenged modernity's global legitimacy.

The ways of thinking of the modern world were rendered obsolete through the disappearance of the social conditions under which they could provide a credible way of thought. Lyotard, one of the prophets of post modernism, characterised the post-modern attitude as one of 'incredulity' (Lyotard, 1993). The idea of a 'centre' with an authoritative capacity to unify all thought through the adjudication of truth is one that reflects – is itself the product of – the existence of a political centre that unifies the world in subordination to it, and whose central position is uniquely privileged in the world that it rules over. With the crumbling of that world and its socio-political conditions, the idea of a centre ceases to be backed any longer by the reality of that world and loses its hold. In the absence of a centre, intellectual life loses its foundations, and certainty – so crucial to modern thought – ceases to be.

The other interrelated development is post-structuralism and it is to a discussion of its main themes of that we now turn.

Post-structuralism

Post-structuralism's name reflects the fact that it remains connected with structuralism but has moved on from the position the latter had reached in the 1960s. However, this is not a cumulative move forward that builds upon structuralism's achievements, so to speak. Rather, it subverts them by showing that the structuralist programme could not have worked out. It retains some key structuralist assumptions about language and basic Saussurean ideas as a launching pad for more radical thinking.

The structuralist project, post-structuralism argues, failed because of the nature of language itself. Language resists capture within the kind of analytic frameworks envisaged by structuralism.

> The problem of structuralism

Roland Barthes, for example, had been reluctant to publish his own thoroughgoing systematic attempt at structuralist analysis, *The Fashion System* (1985), because he began to doubt the point of attempting to reduce a pluralistic reality to one comprehensive, homogenising scheme of analysis. The post-structuralists called into question structuralism's basic assumption about language: that it consists in a systematic interconnection through definite and stable relationships between its units. If the interconnections within language were not stable and fixed but fluid, open ended and variable, then structuralist analysis could not work.

The point was not, however, to take structuralism's faults as lessons for establishing a better project to achieve the systematic completion that structuralism failed to attain. Instead, the lesson was that the whole idea of a definitive theoretical representation of reality itself was flawed. Attempting to provide a theoretical account of language – or, through language of reality itself – was like an animal trying to catch its own tail. The nature of language is such that it cannot portray itself, or anything else, in definitive theoretical terms. The temptation to think that theory can ever have the first or the last word needs to be undermined.

Post-structuralists are often accused of irrationality in being contemptuous of the conventional requirements of rational thought and, therefore, falling foul of those requirements, especially those

> The limits of logical thinking

of logic. However, although post-structuralists are quire capable of logical reasoning, they attach a very different significance to it than do their critics. They claim that if one commits oneself wholly to the demands of logical reasoning and attempts to push these through, then that attempt will inevitably run into trouble. The attempt to remain remorselessly logical will reach the limits of such reasoning and the aim of eradicating all inconsistency will begin to show that it cannot be fulfilled; it will end up in contradiction and paradox. Rather, and like the ethnomethodologists, the post-structuralists find that following through certain ideas insistently will eventually carry one to and beyond the limits of those ideas. When Jacques Derrida examines the work of Edmund Husserl (1859–1938), he does so by applying – so to speak – the logical screws to Husserl's argument, revealing that his ambitions are caught up in mutual contradictions and dilemmas. Husserl simply cannot have what he thinks he wants, namely, an account of the way language originates in thought. Husserl's attempt undercuts itself. In Derrida's view, Husserl's difficulties are of interest not because he was a great philosopher, but because his attempt to locate the pure origins of language in the mind is the same kind of urge that pervades the central preoccupations of Western traditions of thought.

Clearly, if Derrida is right in generalising his argument with Husserl, as he continued to do, then the idea of successfully eradicating paradox and contradiction to produce a consistent logically closed scheme – which was structuralism's own ambition – from any area of human thought is an illusion. The point is not to keep trying to effect such an eradication, but instead to bring out the inevitability with which such extreme projects of rationality will themselves turn into just the thing they seek to prohibit. These deficiencies cannot be repaired in such a way that an impeccably logical and thoroughly closed system can be constructed. Logic will turn against itself.

Both post-structuralism and post-modernism challenged one of the key ideas of the Enlightenment: that of progress toward full human freedom through the growth of rational understanding and a corresponding capacity to collectively control our own lives and destiny.

Recent history, it was claimed (and as we have discussed in the previous chapter), had demonstrated this to be an illusion. As Marcuse and others of the Frankfurt School had earlier argued – advancing ideas which experienced a resurgence in the 1980s and 1990s – the scientific spirit had not so much resisted authority as colluded with it. By attempting to bring many areas of human activity under its purview, science had not so much liberated individuals as created new forms of subservience by bringing more and more activities under the supervision of medical and related professions, industrial managers and state administrators. Its orientation was practical not emancipatory, and the practical interests which drove it were the interests of those who wanted to control and regulate life. The picture of science offered by positivism was an impoverished one, capable of capturing only superficial and partial truths. Foucault, for example, discussed the attempt to develop a scientific approach to sexual behaviour in nineteenth and early twentieth-century Europe, where the interest was in understanding sexual conduct not for purely scientific purposes, but for dominantly moral ones, ensuring that sexual needs could be disciplined to conform to the organisational requirements of society. He contrasted this with those societies where sex was cultivated as the 'art of love' and bound up with the self-development of the individual (Foucault, 1990).

However, this was not simply a reassertion of the orthodox Marxist argument about ideology. Although the reaction against positivism in the late 1960s might have been associated with a resurgence of Marxism, albeit transformed somewhat by the Frankfurt School and later by Foucault, the tenor of the new points of view was that Marxism as a revolutionary doctrine was no longer relevant. Latter-day capitalism, as a post-industrial society, had neutralised the possibility of an apocalyptic confrontation between the dominated and the dominators. As Foucault was later to argue, it was overly simple to think of society as divided between these two categories. To put it simply, it was power itself that was in charge rather than some group of powerful people. Modern society is essentially an administered society in which the tendrils of power finely penetrate all levels, even into the intricate details of who a person is and what he or she does. Much of that penetration is due to the aspiration to create human sciences. But, such sciences are usually largely comprised of moralistic preconceptions thinly disguised as scientific thinking. They seek knowledge that is useful in the administrative supervision of people. In treating conduct as a technical object for analysis and redesign, they seek to make activities more productive and effective from the point of view of employing, regulating and controlling agencies. The positivistic social sciences are only pretenders to scientific status, being little more than moralising cast in a scientific form.

> The administered society

But, if the tendrils of power permeate all levels of society, how can social thought itself escape and emancipate itself from their clutches? Harking back to our brief discussion of post-modernism, then if we are abandoning old 'modern' ways of thinking, abandoning the idea of progress in thought, what are we to do? If we cannot improve on previous theories and ideas, what is the point? This would seem to argue that we should give up altogether on the idea of social inquiry. However, this was not the stance taken, even though what was proposed constituted a major break with previous ideas of social inquiry – so much so that the very idea of the sociological project was jeopardised.

Lyotard's characterisation of the 'post-modern condition' as an 'incredulity toward grand narratives' referred to the loss of confidence in the all-embracing schemes of social thought, such as Marxism in particular, which were previously the repository of many hopes for freedom and emancipation. However, Marxism had not collapsed because it is was a false theory that might be replaced with a better one, but because the whole way of thinking which it instantiated was no longer able to retain its previous hold on us. Accordingly, it is not that Marxism's collapse leaves space for an alternative, improved theory or scheme;

> The incredulity toward grand narratives

it is the very idea of an overarching, all-embracing, comprehensively systematic scheme that Marxism aspired to be that no longer carries conviction. Its demise cannot, therefore, precipitate another scheme of the same kind.

It was their efforts to understand why such schemes had failed which led Lyotard and others to conclude that the ambition to develop a thoroughly coherent account of society and a narrative of its progress cannot possibly succeed. The need, then, certainly cannot be to carry on with the Enlightenment ambitions, but to expedite their full and final disintegration. All that can really be done is turn the ideas of the Enlightenment against themselves, bringing out their bankruptcy but without deluding ourselves that we are – in giving them up – losing anything of true value, or thinking that we need to replace them with anything more.

However, getting to this point entailed pushing through structuralist ideas to their logical conclusion and facing up to what became known as the 'crisis of representation'. Before we get to this issue we need to exposit some crucial steps on the way.

The impossibility of positivism

The post-structuralist critics did not have the positivist project specifically in mind in their critiques. It was but one example of the much more general tendencies of the Enlightenment scheme, and it was the broader tradition that provoked the post-structuralist/post-modernist reaction. This fundamental objection to Enlightenment ideas was, then, a much more generalised form of the objections we have already met with respect to the positivist project itself. Very grossly, the tradition created an impoverished conception of human existence, one which mistook the superficial, socially imposed and historically temporary characteristics of people as if these were definitive of what all human beings are and could possibly be. This failure was no mere oversight but a consequence of a concealed partisanship which becomes apparent when confronted with a critical theory.

The 'objectivity' to which 'rational thought' (for it is *this* which the Enlightenment prided itself on instantiating and advancing) aspired was challenged on two counts:

- It claimed that understanding human beings required the same kind of framework as that for understanding the natural world. However, human beings are not objects and, therefore, not to be understood in that way. An object can be understood without reference to its history, for its fundamental nature is not changed with the passage of time. Human beings are historical beings whose nature varies with time.
- It also involved the idea that a properly rational approach was neutral with respect to the divisions and conflicts between social groups, setting itself apart from judgements of value. Rational thought stands outside society. But, rational thought has been deeply implicated in society's conflicts,

perhaps without even realising how deeply it compromises its ideals by aligning itself with, rather than challenging, the values and the powers which prevail in society. The essential requirement of a separation between fact and value cannot be satisfied and never could.

Thus, the point of a 'critical' approach is precisely intended to reject the fact/value dichotomy and harness social thought toward critique of the status quo.

We remarked earlier that the intensification of this 'critical' reaction involved the politicisation of sociology. However, its exponents would argue that sociology was *already* politicised. The picture of rational thought as standing outside, even above, society's conflicts was deeply misleading, for rational thought was already aligned with authority.

This kind of attack on the ambitions of rational thought was not so much directed at its failure to attain its ambitions, but at their very possibility.

> The attack on the ambitions of rational thought

Enlightenment thinkers had supposed that acquiring knowledge meant replacing politics with knowledge, that is, science; but this was impossible. Social existence was essentially and entirely a matter of politics, of perpetual and pervasive contests for domination in which social thought could not but be implicated. However, the critical approach not only called for an overtly political approach to the social sciences in the sense of directly aligning themselves with elements in the social struggle – in the classic Marxist case with the working classes, or with dissident minorities in the case of post-structuralists – but also with respect to preconceiving the subject matter of the 'human sciences'. Society was conceived as political, and understanding it therefore entailed analysis of power relationships. In other words, there was a continuity between the mode of analysis and the subject matter. The ideal of 'objectivity' went out of the window as a pipe dream.

Rational thought had not so much reached the wrong ideas as sought a chimera. Its illusion was deeply rooted in Western traditions of thought and not easily resisted and dispelled. Accordingly, an effective critique required the uprooting of the whole way of thinking that philosophy, especially Enlightenment philosophy, had bequeathed to us. A central support of this whole illusion was the idea that language can represent reality as it is in itself. This, after all, was what science was about in the positivist scheme: namely, capturing reality. It was thought to be the language of science that would do this. It is only through the 'purification' of language, the elimination of the failings to which language is ordinarily subject – its vagueness, ambiguity, imprecision, affectivity and so on – that a language could be made which would be the vehicle for the true representation of reality.

However, rather than bringing language to a state of perfection by casting it into a scientific mode, such efforts involved an attempt to escape from the very condition of language, denying rather than fulfilling its essence. Rational thought, it was argued, had been basically non-sociological in its conceptions. It had conceived social phenomena as individual and intentional rather than as collective and unwitting. The kind of argument Marx and Durkheim, in their different ways, had advanced in classic theory on this point was now being reasserted. There was a similar reassertion of the doctrines of the founder of psychoanalysis, Freud, that individuals are extensively unconscious of the true nature of their motivations: rational thought deluded itself about the extent to which is was itself exempted from being shaped by both social and psychological forces that shaped all other thought. The re-assertion of these aspects of Freud's and Marx's doctrines led to the kind of argument Foucault made: power is a law unto itself rather than the result of any individual's intentions or actions and so cannot be understood in such terms. But, above all, rational thought presented a misconceived conception of language, in particular, that it could provide pure representations of reality, divorced from all unconscious social and psychological influences. This became known as the 'crisis of representation'.

The crisis of representation

This is a bundle of issues which will take some disentangling, so for now we will content ourselves with a brief introduction to some of the main ideas.

Richard Rorty (1980), in his *Philosophy and the Mirror of Nature,* argues that the standard 'modern' concept of the human mind, handed down since the seventeenth century, is like a 'glassy essence' which can serve as a 'mirror of nature'. This is, of course, metaphoric but it expresses the view that the mind is capable of giving a true reflection of nature, that what is seen in the mirror is an exact reproduction of what it reflects. Of course, the mirror can only provide a true reflection if it is not distorted in any way. So, pursuing the analogy, the mind can only reflect the true nature of reality if it is itself purely a reflecting medium, non-distorting and unsullied. However, the vehicle of thought is language, and the idea that the mind mirrors nature means that the true character of nature must be captured in language. What is sought, again metaphorically, is nature's own language, the *only* terms in which nature can be described if it is to be described correctly. It is, thus, as if knowledge of reality requires that the way nature actually is in itself dictates what the structure of any language must be if it is truly to depict how things really are in the natural world. If the language does not capture, does not represent, that structure then it cannot capture the structure of nature as it is in itself.

The bone of contention is that language can only represent reality-as-it-is-in-itself if language is formed entirely out of those features necessary for portraying reality-as-it-is-in-itself. But, what is being argued against this view is that language is formed through the influence of social and psychological needs and dynamics. Therefore, language cannot represent reality because it cannot be – to continue with the analogy – a true reflecting mirror of nature.

The crisis is in important respects a double one, though the two elements in it are deeply embedded in one another: a crisis of representation and legitimation.

The first concerns the ways in which the 'linguistic turn' makes problematic a major assumption of social inquiry, namely, that it can gain access to the lived world of social actors wherein its phenomena lie. If language cannot represent any reality as it is in itself, then this is no less true of social realities than it is of the natural world. Thus, the problems of social inquiry reach beyond those of technique and method and strike at the very basis of knowledge. For example, it jeopardises the idea that ethnographers can really report the lived experience of observed subjects since, in a non-trivial way, it is only through language, in a text written by the researcher, that any such 'lived experience' can be presented. Lyotard's proposed hallmark for post-modernity is our 'incredulity toward grand narratives', our inability any more to have faith in the all-inclusive stories such as those of Marxism. Such stories aspire to do what they cannot, to provide a general, unified account of society or even of the whole of history. But, it is being argued, this attempt goes against the very nature of society itself. Society is not a general unity and cannot be truly presented as such. Any story of society as a whole can only be put together at the expense of obscuring the extent to which society is divided, consists of many unresolvable differences and – incidentally, a strong resemblance to the Interactionist idea of society – is an ensemble of distinct, even conflicting, points of view. The only way in which society can be authentically viewed is as an irresolvable plurality that will only be distorted by attempts to compact it within an all-embracing theoretical unification: society is a cacophony, not even a polyphony, let alone a harmony, of voices. A 'grand narrative' simply cannot render all those 'voices' equally and equally authentically. To that extent, it will merely reproduce the 'marginalising', even the 'silencing', of voices that goes on in the society it attempts to represent.

> The crisis of legitimation

The crisis of legitimation makes utterly problematic the traditional criteria for evaluating research, by questioning the very notions of validity, generalisability, reliability and so on. If language cannot represent, then the very idea of checking what we say in our language against something – the data, the evidence – outside language is invalidated. The idea that we might advance criteria as to whether we have reported the facts accurately, done the research correctly, or faithfully captured phenomena becomes wholly meaningless.

However, as we have already indicated, there are a number of steps which precipitated the crisis of representation and we turn now to some of its sources within structuralism. It is important to note that these were not the only sources of the crisis.

Structuralist sources of the crisis

In structuralism, the relationship between language and external reality is arbitrary. The determinants of the identity and meaning of linguistic elements are internal to the language system itself. Thus, there is no connection between the structure of the language and any intrinsic structure of reality.

This view challenged the idea that we could match a language – theories and hypotheses – to the intrinsic structure of reality, the events, objects, processes in the world. This was supposed to be the business of science, which would therefore involve formulating the relationship between a language and the world as a non-linguistic phenomenon. Or, to put it another way, make statements about what reality is like so that they can be tested against reality itself. Science, on this view, is the attempt to approximate closer and closer to 'nature's own language', so that the things we say will more truly represent reality.

As we have seen, the structuralist argument invites us away from the view that the idea of meaning in language is to be understood as a relationship between language and reality, as if words get their meanings by standing for things, for example. Indeed, from this point of view the very idea that reality has an intrinsic nature is questionable. If there is such a thing, then it can only be known and described by using language, and that language is not fixed by anything external to it, least of all by the nature of reality itself. One might as well give up on the idea of their being an intrinsic structure to reality: it makes no difference whether one supposes that it does have such a structure or not, if one also supposes that language can never capture that structure.

At this point there are two strands which we need to examine. First is the structuralist twist given to social constructionism. The second is one which pushes the structuralist picture of language and meaning to destruction.

Social constructionism

The structuralist argument invites us away from the idea that the meaning is not fixed by reference to reality, but is, in the first instance, a matter of the internal relationships within the language system.

It is a view which seems counter-intuitive. Words do stand for things. The name 'Archie' stands for an actual, worldly and vicious cat: 'Archie'. The statement 'Archie is hungry' is a linguistic entity, but Archie is a cat, a non-linguistic entity. Therefore, whether 'Archie is hungry' makes sense depends upon the relation between a linguistic entity and a non-linguistic one.

At this point there is often a tendency to slip into talking about truth and insisting that for a statement to be true it must have a relationship to something in the world. However, the issue here is about *meaning* – the way words are able meaningfully to combine into statements – from which truth must be a derivative. Only meaningful statements can be judged in terms of their truth and 'compared to reality'. But, it is important to bear in mind, we can only have the sentence 'Archie is hungry' because we have the social practice of giving names to cats.

We are re-approaching the much misunderstood idea that reality is a 'social construction', or that 'reality is an effect of language' or, yet again, that 'discourse constitutes reality'. It is an idea that has a long lineage in sociology, with threads in Marx's notion of ideology, Weber conception of social action, the sociology of knowledge, the symbolic interactionist idea of the actor's point of view, and now the structuralist conception of language. What is being pointed to are the ways in which people's beliefs, conceptions, even their very perceptions, are shaped in and through the fact they are members of a particular society. At this level it has been a persistent idea in the sociological armoury of criticism of existing social arrangements. It has also provoked one of the enduring problems of sociology itself, namely, how it could transcend society as a form of form of knowledge. Indeed, in the hands of the sociology of knowledge, this problem was to have deep problems for the intellectual authority of sociology in that knowledge itself was seen as socially rooted (Mannheim, 1952; Bloor, 1976). Here what seems to be suggested is a strong form of such a thesis, to the effect that there is no such thing as a reality 'outside' our conceptions of it.

To take it generally, the thesis seems to put matters back to front. Material objects surely must pre-exist the language in which they are spoken about. Presumably language develops as we identify a need to speak about particular objects, identify them and endow them with a name. The idea that the name exists prior to its being endowed on some object sounds bizarre: cows surely did not come into being because the word 'cow' was invented.

However, this is to misunderstand what structuralism is saying when it claims that 'discourse constitutes its objects'. An 'object' is, from this angle, something which can be spoken about. Further, in structuralism the meaning of a word is not the object in the world it stands for. Its meaning is fixed by its relationship to other elements in the language system. What the 'object' can be depends upon how the words used to speak about it fits into the language system. This depends upon, so to speak, the space that the relationship with other words makes available to it. The language system is an impersonal one, and it is this that is the condition for its speakers to speak meaningfully, and not their personal, intentions of meaning. To understand how an 'object' comes into being is to understand how a language system develops, how new expressions, new things we can say and mean, come into language, such that individuals are enabled to speak of these things. Such changes are not the product of changes in the intrinsic nature of things or by individuals.

Let us look at this in connection with 'representation'. Is it being said that language cannot represent reality? Unfortunately, there can be no straightforward yes or no answer to this question. If we take 'to represent' to refer to language reflecting the intrinsic nature of reality, then language does not, because it cannot, represent reality in this sense. It is saying that the bequeathed notion of 'representation' has no role in understanding the nature of language and language change.

If by 'represent reality' we mean that we can say, 'The cow is in the field', and thereby truly say where the actual cow is, then it is not being denied that we can say such things. Our capacity 'to represent' the cow in the field is dependent upon the availability of a language system. No one is denying that we can do such things for we do them all the time. But this is not to 'represent' in the same sense that positivists demand.

Understanding how language changes is not, however, just a matter of understanding the language as a self-contained system of signs. Sign systems do not operate in a vacuum but within social arrangements. What use is the flag system of communication between ships at sea if no one has navies? Would there be such a system without navies? Thus, to understand how a language system changes is to understand how the social organisation within which the language system is embedded changes.

Consider the object 'mental patient'. The 'mental patient' is 'an object' that we talk about: 'he has been hospitalised', 'he is under the care of a psychiatrist', 'he has developed a dissociative identity disorder', 'he is being treated by Rogerian therapy'. These, and more, are all things that we can truly say of individuals who are, indeed, currently mental patients. They are persons 'in need of treatment', 'suffering from illness', 'curable through therapy', which are all elements of what it is to be a 'mental patient'. If we cannot talk of someone in these terms, then we do not have the object, the 'mental patient'.

Historically speaking, we did not have the object 'mental patient' in the Renaissance period. That is to say that we could not say then the kind of things we can say now about persons who are mental patients. In the Renaissance expressions like 'psychiatrist' would just make no sense at all, no one could possibly know what 'going to a psychiatrist' meant. There were, in the Renaissance, no 'mental patients' at all. This, we trust, is an utterly true but trivial point that no one would dispute. It would be bizarre to imagine that someone suddenly discovered mental patients by stumbling across one in a field and then decided that we need to find a name for them. Of course, in the Renaissance there were familiarly people doing the kinds of things that now lead to their being made into what we now call 'mental patients'. *Then* they were known as 'mad people'. The object 'the madman' is a very different object to that of the 'mental patient'. We can no longer speak about 'the madman' in the way that people could in the Renaissance. That is, the kinds of things that could be said about the former were very different then from those that can now be said about the latter. All this, we hope, is indisputable.

Between the 'madman' and the 'mental patient' we are dealing with a change because, in many ways, the two are the same kind of person that we now consider 'mentally ill'. There has been no change in the nature of individuals and their inclination to engage in behaviour that the rest of us consider troublesome or bizarre, to exhibit extremes of emotion and so on, but one 'object' has ceased to exist and another has come into being. The change is not produced because somehow the nature of the individuals who are these objects has changed, requiring us to find a new name for them. The need for the new object with its new name arises from the changes in the way in which we organise things and from the rearrangement of our ways of talking. We have moved these wayward individuals from the place they occupied in pre-Renaissance society, and have put them in a new position under the control of the medical profession which did not exist in the Renaissance. It is the need to find a *medical way of talking* that necessitates the

> Discourses

object 'mental patient' and, thus, it can be reasonably and plausibly be said that it is the change in the organisation of discourse that has produced the object 'the mental patient'.

Michel Foucault developed such ideas about the study of madness which, as we have noted, he made into a historical issue (Foucault, 1971, 1976). Although his thought owed much to structuralism, it has always been a standard critique of structuralism that it was ahistorical, that it sought to portray a timeless general structure within which meaning was possible. But it had little interest in how that structure came into being in the first place, why it possessed the form that it did, or how it may change. Foucault (1972) is making the capacity of a meaning system to 'constitute an object' very much a historical question: what is the transition from 'madman' to 'mental patient'?

The object the 'mental patient' does not pre-exist the formation of the discourse about it because the object consists in, or, as it is sometimes said, is constituted by, the discourses about it. Therefore, the object comes into being as the discourse about it develops. The formation of the object the 'mental patient' is not inevitable. There is nothing in nature itself that requires that we call these kinds of people either 'madmen' or 'mental patients'. There is nothing inevitable that, sooner or later, we come up with the idea of the 'mental patient'. We might never have formed such an idea and might, indeed, have developed a very different alternative idea to 'madman'. Indeed, a main part of Foucault's argument is that we can be very close to developing a different idea. That we have an object the 'mental patient' is an arbitrary matter from the point of the connection between the kinds of people we are talking about and the name that we call them by. That we call people by that name is entirely contingent. It might easily have been different. So, *in this sense*, there are no 'mental patients' in nature.

To cut a long and complex argument short, the essence of Foucault's case is as follows. The notion 'mental patient' is an idea connected with medicine.

> Foucault's argument

That 'madmen' came under the jurisdiction of the nascent medical profession was a touch-and-go matter. 'Madness' was not an illness, but perhaps a blessing from God. There is nothing that inevitably demanded a change from viewing it as a supernatural blessing to seeing it as a form of illness. However, the Renaissance idea of the mad person was disturbed by social and economic changes that, for all sorts of reasons, led to the treatment of all kinds of socially difficult persons – criminals, vagabonds and others – being enclosed together as a way of removing them from normal society. All kinds of difficult persons had been collected up and incarcerated. Questions arose as to whether this was the best way for dealing with them, indiscriminately and insensitively to the kind of troublesome people they were. Should 'madmen' be counted among the criminals or among the sick? There was no little struggle and, eventually, the argument for including them among the sick won out but, as in all social struggles, there was no necessity that one side win out over the other: everything depends on the circumstances and the balance of forces. The conflict actually could have gone the other way and turned 'madmen' into criminals, a very different kind of object. Neither the madman nor the mental patient can exist independently of a specific and contingently assembled set of social relations. Each of them is more than the characteristic behaviours of the individuals who comprise such objects. Each is implicated in a web of understandings of what their behaviours mean, what is to be done about them, what causes them to behave in such ways, who should be responsible for them, and so on and on.

Hopefully we have shown how the notion of 'social construction' does not involve turning good sense upside down, inverting the relationship between words and things in the absurd way its critics envisage. The transformation is, rather, in the direction of attention, away from inspecting 'the object' itself as psychiatrists do in their attempts to decide what characteristics identify the illness the patient has, what treatments are needed, and so on. The concern is shifted to identifying the conditions that make it possible for people to talk about sufferers from mental illness, for some to identify themselves as specialists in its treatment, to relate to organisational processes for dealing with the mentally ill, and handle patients as they do. The fact that people who do the things they do are attributed an illness may seem entirely natural, just as it may seem natural to place them under the supervision of medical specialists. But it is reflection on just those things that are taken for granted that conceiving things in terms of 'discourses' is meant to encourage. It should remind us that far from providing the obvious point of departure in thinking about those who seem to 'lack reason', the idea of them as 'mentally ill and requiring medical treatment' is, in fact, the end product of a complex, 300-year long process of social change. Likewise, there is no reason to suppose that the 'mental patient' is a permanent feature of our universe, that the discourses that now speak of the 'mental patient' will last forever and cannot themselves be transformed beyond all recognition. After all, even within the framework of 'mental illness' the discourse is changing all the time.

Replacing the idea of representation, then, is that of constitution. The representational relationship is thought to be between something that exists independently of and prior to the discourse and prior to it. But if it is reasonable to argue that these objects do not exist independently of or prior to the discourse, then it follows that the relationship cannot be one of representation. The formation of the discourse and the formation of 'the object' go together, and cannot be separated in the way that the idea of representation needs. What the discourse allows us to say comprises what the object can be.

> Constitution

At this point we need to consider the ideas of Jacques Derrida (1930–2004) who pushes structuralist conceptions to self-destruction.

Jacques Derrida and deconstruction

Philosophy is often taken as the West's leading attempt to think systematically and generally about reality. Indeed, the positivist programme in social research, as its label acknowledges, drew its inspiration from a particular philosophical approach. Derrida wants to question this assessment of philosophy by arguing from the nature of language itself.

His studies began with a logical re-analysis of Husserl's attempt to understand the meaning of signs as a purely mental phenomenon distinct from the materialities – the sounds or the marks – which are their bearers (Derrida, 1978). Husserl's approach is a good starting place for Derrida because of *both* its status as a major work of philosophy *and* its concern to understand the nature of 'the sign' and, thereby, language. Derrida concluded that Husserl's attempt to make meaning a mental phenomenon independent of the system of signs was a failure, but a failure indicative of a more general problem to do with the limits of thought itself. In essence, the problem is any attempt at thoroughgoing systematicity will inevitably breed inconsistencies.

The desire to identify 'pure' instances of phenomena is very much part of philosophical thinking. But the idea is an illusion. There can be no such thing as 'pure meaning' unmediated by material signs, for example. If we accept the structuralist account of meaning then it is inseparable from the system of signs. But, more crucially, specifying this system systematically is also doomed to failure.

The pointless search for systematicity

We began this book by emphasising the importance of systematicity as the basis for launching sociological projects. But now we are in the middle of an attack on the very idea itself. There would seem to be no point in looking for the pristine beginning point for a thoroughly systematic general approach, because not only is no such point to be found, but difficulties will arise which will infect the whole system. Inconsistency will be the constant companion of supposed consistencies. Take the case of 'making distinctions'.

Making distinctions

Derrida's early studies were of Husserl's attempt to understand the meaning of signs as a pure phenomenon of mind to which the distinction between thought, on the one hand, and speech and writing on the other was important.

Speech and writing, for Husserl, could not be 'pure meaning' because they were mediated through sound waves and a script respectively. However, speech is closer to pure thought than is writing in that the speaker whose thought the speech expresses is present to his or her own words. By contrast, writing carries a person's thoughts in the absence of the person. The thought which occasions the words is not present along with the written word.

Speech and writing

However, the distinction between speech and writing, Derrida notes, is not merely a distinction separating one from the other. It ranks them. On Husserl's rendering, speech is superior to writing because it is closer to presence. Such ranking is typical of philosophical distinctions more generally. They are not innocent. In any characteristic pairing one of the terms is valued over the other. In this case, as in many others, it is an aspect of the desire for 'pure presence'.

The desire to identify 'pure' instances of phenomena is very much part of philosophical thought. But if this is an illusion – just as the search for 'pure meaning' unmediated by signs is an illusion – then the philosophical project as we know it is in serious difficulties. Further, if we accept the structuralist conception of meaning, then it is not something separable from the system of signs. Hence, when we use a given sign with a particular meaning, this will depend upon what is 'not present' at the instant of using the sign, namely, the rest of the sign system. In which case, and in innumerable others, the idea of presence is brought down. Anything in philosophical thought which expresses a desire for presence is fatally flawed.

Making clear distinctions is indispensable to systematic thought. This is no less true of social thought than it is of philosophy. The least that distinctions should do is set things apart in different categories. But, claims Derrida, the idea of clear distinctions is no more sustainable than that of 'pure presence' or 'pure meaning'. The distinction between 'speech' and 'writing', for example, is required to separate two kinds of things which are different. But, insists Derrida, this is just what cannot be maintained. Speech and writing do not have clearly discriminable characteristics but have many in common. Indeed, rather than speech coming before writing – in a logical as well as a temporal sense – as is usually believed, with writing used to capture or copy down speech, it is writing that subsumes the idea of speech.

Derrida argued that both Saussure and the structuralists operated with a colloquial notion of writing as purely graphic, fundamentally phonetic and so representing the sounds of language. Speech, on the other hand, is assumed to be closer to thought and, accordingly, to the emotions, ideas and intentions of the speaker. Speech is thus primary and more original, and contrasting with the secondary and representative status of writing.

However, the claim that writing is purely phonetic or that speech is entirely auditory is difficult to sustain in view of the graphic nature of punctuation and the unpresentable silences of speech. Writing always includes pictographic, ideographic and phonetic elements and, accordingly, cannot be identical with itself. Writing is always impure and, in a sense, is more original than the phenomena it supposedly invokes. Writing is a trace, a mark, which is the precondition to all phenomenal forms. In a strict sense writing is virtual not phenomenal. It is not what is produced but it makes production possible.

In his thoughts on themes from literature, art, psychoanalysis and philosophy, Derrida is constantly trying to make apparent the 'impurity' of writing by using rhetorical, graphic and poetic forms of expression to alert the reader to the blurred boundaries between disciplines and subject matter. The impossibility of systematically separating the poetic and rhetorical aspects of a text at the level of the signifier, from its content, the signified, shows that supposedly eternal metaphysical principles have an ambiguous basis. A name, for example, does not refer to a simple, phenomenal object or person, because it has a rhetorical dimension that can be made visible by punning. Through punning, anagram, etymology and so on, names can be connected to one or more different systems of concepts, ideas or words.

The fact that words, phrases and sentences can be repeated in different contexts is the very quality, for Derrida, that breaks apart the signifier and the signified. If meaning is related to context, there is as far as the very structure of language no way to provide proof of a final meaning. Context is unbounded (Culler, 1983).

Moreover, as we have already indicated, the distinction is not between equivalent categories but between a primary and a subordinate one, with the latter treated as a degenerate form of the primary one. This means that since categorical distinctions cannot be made logically they will require enforcement. The distinction has to be imposed rather than brought out. Given that the secondary part is regarded as inferior, then it will in effect be marginalised, suppressed or even eliminated. Applied to persons, this will become a matter of oppressing them in order to make them conform to socially imposed divisions. One must, for example, be male or female, one cannot be both or neither of them. One cannot be somewhere in between, say, as a transvestite or a transsexual. To be one of these latter is to be an 'inferior' male or female.

The idea of systematicity is that of logically bringing things together without ambiguity and paradox. Derrida, however, is arguing that these cannot be avoided. Paradox and ambiguity are inevitable in language because there is no 'centre' from which meaning can be fixed. Husserl's notion was that meaning was fixed in the mind of the thinker, in the privacy of the mind. But structuralism rejected this idea as incoherent. Meaning is the product of a system and delimited within it; the meaning-identity of each element is fixed by its relation to each other entity. Now, however, Derrida is pushing the notion of language as a closed system to destruction. There can be no fixed and determinate meaning. The language system provides, in the structuralist scheme of things, a kind of 'centre' in terms of which meaning is organised. But there cannot be a 'centre' in this sense. Language does not comprise a closed system so, although meaning is generated in the relationship among signs, it is not generated in such a way that a set of determinate relationships between the elements can be fixed as defining any one of those elements.

Derrida takes his attack on the idea of a 'centre' toward the idea of 'the author'.

> Meaning

The demise of the author

An important legacy of Enlightenment individualism is the idea of the 'author' who produces texts, and for the purposes of the argument 'text' can include a play, film, painting, sculpture as well as the usual things meant by 'text'. Accordingly, understanding the text, characterising its unity, was seen in terms of an appeal to the author's intentions. The text, to put it another way, was a manifestation of the author's design. However, to structuralist and post-structuralist thinking, this idea of the author as 'a centre' is unacceptable in that it makes the meaning and unity of the text a product of conscious design. Understanding the generation of meaning by the structure of the language itself removes the author from this central position: the text becomes de-centred.

This was originally a view developed by Barthes in a libertarian move to diminish the 'oppressiveness of reading literature'. In Derrida's hands, however, the author is more than de-centred: it is dispersed. It is not merely a matter of removing 'the author' from the central role played in literary criticism and the analysis of texts, but of removing the deeper idea that there is a fully integrating meaning for the text. There is no reason to suppose that a novel, or a play, has any more unity than a philosophical text. To suppose that the parts of a text must all conform to a coherent plan obscures the extent to which the novel, for example, is divided against itself. There is no reason to assume that the novel, or any text, is a self-contained entity. Novels, for example, often contain allusions to other novels and works. In that case the meaning of some particular part of the narrative cannot be defined by its internal relations to other elements of the same text. Rather, it is defined intertextually in relation to elements in other texts.

> Decentring the author

Thus, the idea of the single, self-subsistent text under the author's control and unified by authorial design is abandoned. The figure of the author can be precluded from the examination of the text entirely. There is no need to refer to facts about the author's life or invoke the author's intention to identify the meaning of the text. The analysis, therefore, can focus exclusively on the text(s), upon the interrelations between the features of any focal text and all those others interwoven in it. The intertextuality of texts is an open-ended matter. The texts to which a given text relates are no more self-subsistent, unified entities than is the initial text. They are also intertextually constituted.

> Intertextuality

All of this means that there is no determinate meaning to be given to a single element since there are no fixed other elements to which it can be related. The analysis does not seek to bring together the features of the text within a single, unifying scheme but draws out, rather, the lack of unification and closure within the text, identifying both the inconsistencies and ambiguities and the intertextual linkages which can be found in any text. This is not a task which can meaningfully can be said to have an end.

Derrida initially referred to his way of proceeding as 'grammatology', but later came to term it 'deconstruction'. He was reluctant to describe it either as a theory or a method. Rather, its role was to undermine, revealing the chronic and irresolvable tensions in what might seem to be an integrated scheme or argument, showing that in each and every case there were unresolvable problems of fixing the meaning in a text, and unresolvable oppositions in systems of thought. Deconstruction is directed toward the subversion of texts in their own terms which is why Derrida does not wish to identify it as a method. It is a matter of approaching each text in its own terms, locating its focal concerns and bringing out the problems with them rather than applying some general method to each text. How to deconstruct the text needs to be worked out on each occasion. Hence, deconstruction does not lead anywhere.

The strategy of the approach is to seek to deal with problems by giving up on the assumptions upon which they are based, and refusing to replace them with any alternative, allegedly improving doctrines or assumptions. One might summarise the central thrust of deconstruction as being against finality. It is attempting to eradicate from our thinking the conviction that there is, that there must be, some definitive conclusion, some ultimate end, to our intellectual activity and, correspondingly, rejecting the conviction that there must be some unequivocally identifiable point of origin from which the phenomena spring – as 'the author' must be the point or origin of the text. The very notions of 'beginning' and 'end' as they are traditionally conceived are illusions or impositions, projections of our wish to find them in phenomena which do not have the unified or distinctive characteristics that we imagine they do.

Conclusion

The crisis of representation revived problems which had been raised quite early in sociology's development to do with the notion of ideology and its offspring the sociology of knowledge, and which were bound up with the ambition for a sociological science. Briefly, the issues concerned the foundations of knowledge. What marked science off from other claims to knowledge was that it was based on firm ontological and epistemological foundations. But if, as the notion of ideology proposed, conceptions of the world were shaped by history, then how could science be exempt from this process? If, as the sociology of knowledge proposed, knowledge itself was socially shaped, how could science itself be treated as socially detached from social causation? Since such problems were not empirical ones, the search for foundations had to look to philosophy. In the case of post-modernism and post-structuralism we have another attack on the idea of foundations, this time from the point of view of language and meaning.

If language can have no intrinsic correspondence with reality, if it can have no 'centre', then what sense does it make to speak of the foundations of knowledge? Without foundations social science has no legitimacy to speak authoritatively. Foucault's social constructionist arguments give us no basis upon which we might secure a privileged point of view. Derrida's 'deconstruction' of the Western philosophical tradition closes off that avenue for the search for foundations. It is a tradition unavoidably riddled with paradox and ambiguity. Indeed, in deconstructing pervasive philosophical shibboleths Derrida is showing that academic and everyday language bear within them presuppositions and cultural assumptions of a whole tradition of thinking. If there can be no principled escape from

> The loss of foundations

ways of thinking, no means of transcending our language, then social inquiry is in much the same position as any form of writing. Writing, in Derrida's conception, is always 'impure' and the boundaries between disciplines and subject matter inevitably and irreparably blurred (Derrida, 1978).

The crisis of representation as a fusion of post-modernism and post-structuralism is taken as striking at the very heart of the idea of a social science by questioning the very basis of western modes of thinking. In effect, the conclusion is that any mode of thought requires interpretation through and through. What is more the very act of writing, producing a research report, a monograph, a doctoral thesis, an ethnography, produces a 'text' and, hence, subject to the entire critical apparatus of post-modernism and post-structuralism. What the now-subverted Western tradition of 'rationality' does is to 'construct' others, excluding those who cannot be accommodated within the logically sharp distinctions its intellectual systems require. It downgrades them as inferior relative to the 'pure' kinds which do fit comfortably within the scheme. There is a redolence of Durkheim here, in the idea of defining ourselves, in our superiority, *against* inferior others. Since the idea of 'representation' follows from the illusory philosophical tradition, it also has to be abandoned. Therefore, the portrayal of others cannot be a *representation* of them, but will be a *projection* : the dominant tradition excludes the others (gays, ethnic minorities, women, whoever) partly by silencing them. It is the dominant tradition which creates the understanding of what others are like, for those are given no opportunity to be heard in their own right.

> The crisis of representation

Master narratives of social science reflect these facts, and thus must be seen as seeking to preserve the social order and obscure the privileged stances of the writers of social science. Others cease to be historical agents but are defined in totalising and universalistic theories that create a subject – the social scientist who is typically white, male, Eurocentric – that occupies the centres of power yet is treated as if existing outside time and space, as though it – and it alone – occupied a universal point of view (Giroux, 1991). There can be no such privileged standpoint since our own frames of reference come to be because we are social and historical creatures. Facts are not simply 'what is', and truth no longer that which corresponds to some unequivocal, uncontested facts. The world is constantly being constructed and since, in Foucault's terms, the tendrils of power are everywhere we can only approach this process critically. This does not mean opposition by creating other master narratives but by the subversion of the 'texts' that silence other voices. The word 'transgression' is valorised: the point is not to try to think of phenomena in ways which respect the requirements of logical regimentation, of capture within clearly delimited, mutually exclusive and universal distinctions. Rather it is to highlight the ways language resists the imposition

> Transgression

of this kind of discipline, and to draw out the embarrassment which the marginalised and oppressed represent to the grand narratives; the capacity to disrupt the categories of dominant modes of thought, and of the social relations that go with them, is highlighted. Academic research in the old, established understanding is, from this point of view, over. The point of academic work is to carry on a *guerrilla* war against the intellectual apparatus implicated with power, and thereby against the prevailing powers themselves (precisely the kind of resistance against and reaction to disciplinary power that Foucault talks of) – shifts within the workings of power, not a confrontation between the powerful and the powerless.

Selected bibliography and suggested reading

- None of the materials relevant to this chapter are straightforward reading. However, Kevin Hart's *Postmodernism: A Beginner's Guide* (Oxford, Oneworld, 2004), Catherin Belsey's *Poststructuralism: A Very Short Introduction* (Oxford, Oxford University Press, 2002) and James Williams' *Understanding Postructuralism* (Chesham, Acumen, 2005) are short, basic and clear introductions.
- Richard Harland's *Superstructuralism: The Philosophy of Structuralism and Post-structuralism* (London : Methuen, 1987) is an excellent, but more sophisticated guide to central ideas. Steven Best and Douglas Kellner's *The Postmodern Turn* (London, Guildford, 1997) and *The Postmodern Adventure* (London, Routledge, 2001) are also more advanced introductions. Mark Poster's *Critical Theory and Poststructuralism* (Ithaca, Cornell University Press, 1989) and Richard Wolin's *The Terms of Cultural Criticism: The Frankfurt School, Existentialism and Poststructuralism* (New York. Columbia University Press, 1992) are both good attempts to place the issues in relation to key ideas.
- For severe criticism of the whole idea of post-modernism and post-structuralism from two very different points of view, see Alex Callinicos, *Against Postmodernism: A Marxist Critique* (Cambridge, Polity Press, 1989) and Raymond Tallis, *Enemies of Hope: A Critique of Contemporary Pessimism: Irrationalism, Anti-humanism and Counter-enlightenment* (New York: St. Martin's Press, 1997).

Chapter 14

Discourses and Research

As we indicated in the previous chapter, the 'crisis of representation' had a profound impact on sociology. For post-modernists and post-structuralists it seemed that the ghosts of the Enlightenment had at last been laid to rest. The illusory quest for foundations and absolute truth had been exposed for the illusion it is. Derrida's dismantling of the 'metaphysics of presence', and the idea that knowledge and representation of the world requires a knowing subject, had not only laid to rest subjectivism in social thought, but had also shown that meaning was indeterminate, vague and devoid of fixed points of reference. For many the loss of foundations invited an extreme relativism, a refusal to countenance any talk of the truth or falsity of social theories, the denial of any relationship of correspondence between ideas and an external world; instead they claimed that the nature of the world is not so much discovered as socially or discursively constituted (Laclau and Mouffe, 1985). However, this did not mean an end to social thought or analysis. What it did mean was, at least on the face of it, a revision of the sociological project, and in some cases almost to the point where it dissolves as a distinctive discipline, as not only do disciplinary boundaries blur but core concerns become subsumed within something referred to as 'cultural studies'.

For present purposes there are two important consequences to note. First, that research methods as typically understood – never very high on the sociological agenda except, perhaps, during the heyday of positivism in 1950s and 1960s – fall even further down the list of major topics. The model of theory–method–data is rejected. But, as we shall see, not entirely. There are, for example, attempts to rethink qualitative research in light of the post-modern shift.

The second observation is that it would be wrong to see this shift as a unified movement (Mills, 1997). Indeed, such an idea sits uneasily with the post-modern spirit. Rather than a movement, post-modernism is perhaps more of a temperament or disposition – the word 'sensibility' is occasionally used – to dispense with the trappings of 'modern' science. Quite what trappings are to be dispensed with, and what the implications might be, depends a great deal upon the various allegiances to the diverse currents which constitute the 'sensibilities' of the movement. Many, for example, draw a distinction between post-modernism and post-structuralism even though there are similarities and overlaps. For others, the connections between the present movement and past traditions remain, with the former expanding and developing insights of the latter in the circumstances of a radically new kind of society. This is perhaps most evident in work arising from Marxism and critical theory. Matters are complicated further by the further interweaving of these traditions within, for example, feminism, literary theory and linguistics, to produce an extremely convoluted state of affairs.

Because the position is still in flux we cannot hope to do any more than illustrate some of the main ideas and approaches. However, let us begin by sketching out some of the key points of the post-modern 'sensibility'.

Common elements

First, post-modern social theory rejects Enlightenment assumptions about rationality, epistemology or any supposedly secure representation of reality existing outside a socially and historically conditioned language. Also, the idea that knowledge, to qualify as knowledge, must reflect an external language independent of reality is abandoned in favour of a conception which sees reality as socially or semiotically constructed.

> Reality as semiotically constructed

Second, as with ethnomethodology, the tripartite distinction of theory–method–data collapses as a framework for sociological inquiry. The positivist project was not only an intellectual failure but revealed as a major instrument of oppression. This does not mean an end to empirical research, though it could no longer see itself as the detached, impersonal and objective enterprise that positivism imagined. Much more important is 'theorising' as a form of analysis intended to bring out the hidden and oppressive presumptions of modes of thought, or discourses. The point is now to create disruption, stage confrontation and provoke self-reflection. The rejection of the idea that there can be absolute knowledge stresses, instead, the relativities of multiple perspectives arising from the fact that the researcher – like everyone else – is a person with a biography formed out of the historical conditions of society and thought. At its most extreme, a rampant constructionism is seen as running throughout thought. The aim of research is not so much knowledge as bringing to light what is excluded by the modes of thought in which 'knowledge' is framed – and this includes social thought. A great emphasis is placed upon 'reflexivity': the fact that social theory must apply to itself in just the same way that it applies to other social phenomena. There must be no privileging of one point of view over others.

> Theorising as form of analysis

Third, and related to the above, one of the principal themes is critique. Modes of thought, or discourses, are organised around practices of exclusion. However, exclusionary practices are subtle and complex. Ideologies, for example and to put it simply, inscribe themselves on our everyday experience and on our consciousness in ways we are unaware of. This not only makes objectivity harder, or impossible, to achieve but also means that a thoroughly self-conscious critical political stance is essential to see through ideology. Therefore there is much more self-consciousness about research and about the position of the researcher, which goes far beyond the strictures about bias and the importance of objective procedures insisted upon by positivism. In this case, it is an insistence upon a sensitivity to the manifold ways in which discourses and modes of thought, including those of science, constitute their objects and, accordingly, serve as ideologies of power. As mentioned, this results in arguments for the importance of reflexivity in research: that is, an effort to be more self-critical and aware of the implicit conceptions that can be brought to one's own research and writing. 'Writing' now becomes more than the simple act of putting pen to paper, but one of embedding interpretations within the webs of power. Writing is no longer simply a vehicle for the expression of interpretations but is itself an act of coercion.

> Importance of critique

Fourth, and again a point we made earlier, disciplinary boundaries are becoming increasingly blurred. Derrida's deconstructionism, for example, had argued that the distinction between philosophy and literature was unsustainable. In some respects this blurring of disciplinary boundaries was foreshadowed in a number of disciplines in reactions to the positivist project as scholars tried to break out of the straightjacket of scientistic thinking. Goffman, to mention but one example, had used literary devices, especially metaphors from the theatre and other domains, to convey his analysis. Geertz, a foremost anthropologist, argued that the boundaries between the social sciences and the humanities, had become indistinct (Geertz, 1973, 1983). Such disciplinary boundaries certainly could not be sustained in terms of a claimed distinction, as Durkheim tried to do, among phenomena in the external world that was each discipline's own particular focus. Rather, disciplinary boundaries were themselves aspects of the exclusory tendrils of power that permeated all modes of thought.

> Blurring of boundaries

It should not be thought that all the sociologists who would refer to themselves as post-modernists or post-structuralists would subscribe with equal gusto to all of these elements. Indeed, there are some who would subscribe to some of them even when resisting the idea of being described as post-anything. Much here depends upon the intensity and the grounds with which the ideas are argued. One does not need to agree with Derrida's arguments, for example, to concur that disciplinary boundaries are blurred or that the phenomena of sociology are socially constructed. Matters are indeed complicated and no more so in respect of the term which, on the face of it, seems common currency: 'discourse'.

Discourse

While this term is currently widely used in various disciplines and, in many of these uses, is a concept uniting what were previously diverse interests and traditions, it cannot be said that it has such a clear and definite meaning that it can perform this service. Its general and more colloquial sense refers to a conversation or speech. Some draw a distinction between discourse as spoken communication and text as written communication, while yet others would want to include both as discourse (Mills, 1997). One is likely to find such inclusive usages in sociolinguistics.

A use which brings us closer to the post-modern sensibility is closely connected with the first three of the elements discussed above. This is the idea of discourses as akin to what we might otherwise term 'modes of thought'. Whereas the latter term tends to be rather loosely employed – often to characterise the alleged typical ideas of a period for example – in the use of 'discourse' in this connection more attention is given to the notion that discourses embody an organisation of experience or way of looking at the world. To put it even more strongly: discourses constitute the world and our experiences of it. To put it another way: it is not so much that there are 'modes of thought' and the external world – and the task somehow to match the two – but that there are only discourses through which it becomes possible to experience and speak about the world. It is this kind of claim which constitutes a large part of the 'linguistic turn' in recent social theory. As we have said in previous chapters in this part of the book, this is far more than the claim that we use words to communicate and describe reality. It is, rather, to give primacy to language in the constitution of reality. There can be no knowledge of reality which is independent of language, or discourse. In that case *all* knowledge is discourse, including sociology and all other disciplines. It is taking this position seriously that, for many, constitutes the challenge of post-modernism and post-structuralism. A post-modern social theory is 'discursive' in not only reflecting and interpreting discourses but also reflecting upon the necessity and nature of interpretation itself (Lemert, 1997). It is this which requires giving up on traditional commitments such as belief in the subject–object dichotomy and sociology as a scientific source of knowledge. All that is left is a post-modern politics of fracture, confrontation and self-reflection.

However, discourse research is heterogeneous, roughly falling within one of two forms. The first is the analysis of discourse as largely a linguistically constructed entity; the second is discourse as a thought construction, as a dialogic process, and discourse as a mode of thinking.

Of course, neither of these is to be seen as entirely discrete and separate, not least because in both cases it is language, as talk or as text, which mediates between the discourses and the social life shaped by them. However, since both styles of research on discourses characteristically share a critical perspective on power and control and on ideology – or, alternatively, the ways in which our representations of the world in thought are shaped for us – there is a presumption that both these forms have an affinity. Certainly there is a widespread recognition within the discourse analysis research community that it does draw upon various traditions, including conversation analysis, sociolinguistics, the ethnography of communication, critical discourse analysis, Bahktinian research and Foucault (Wetherell et al, 2001). All of this makes it difficult to do justice to the variety of research styles which have emerged as part of the discourse analysis movement. What we try to do in what follows is to present a summary overview of three styles of research to give a flavour of the impact of post-modernist and post-structuralist thinking on social inquiry. We begin with a scholar who, in many respects, is the pre-eminent figure in modern social thought, Michel Foucault.

Foucault and the structure of discourses

Earlier, in Chapter 13, we discussed Foucault as evincing an interest in how discourses came to be, how the 'mad' became the 'mental patient'. However, Foucault's is not the conventional history of ideas. He rejects analysis that looks back upon our predecessors as any less enlightened than ourselves. His ambition was to rescue the people of the past from our condescension. Past ideas often seem bizarre, misguided even, maybe even unnatural to us, lacking the benefit of our own superior understanding. However, for Foucault, we think this way because we do not understand any better than our predecessors – as our condescension shows. Were we better attuned to the ways of thought of our predecessors, the things that seem strange to us would seem every bit as natural, as comfortable and as right as our ways of thinking are to us. At the same time we would realise that we are just as unaware as our predecessors of why we think as we do, of the ways in which our own thought is imposed upon us through the discourses within which we are ourselves entangled. In his last years Foucault described his work as creating 'a history of the different modes by which, in our culture, human beings are made subjects' (Foucault, 1982: 208) with a view, primarily, of getting us to drastically re-evaluate our own relationship to our language. It is this interest which leads him to extensive discussion of classification practices, dividing practices and self-subjectification practices.

Foucault used the term 'episteme' to refer to ways of thinking that characterised a particular epoch, though the notion was short-lived in his own thought (Foucault, 1970). By this Foucault meant the total set of relations that unite the discursive practices of a given period. He likens people who live within an episteme to those confined within a prison who are unaware of their confinement. They can only think within the episteme, not about it. They cannot consciously comprehend the episteme and nor can those who come later.

> Episteme

There is something of a paradox here. Foucault is attempting to get us to understand ourselves through understanding the epistemes of previous periods, yet suggests that it is impossible to understand previous epistemes. In fact 'archaeology', used in the title of one of his books, suggests that his purpose is to excavate the layers of preconceptions underlying previous periods of thought: that is, the widespread, unconscious structures not explicitly held by individuals but framing the possibilities of what those individuals can think and say (Foucault, 1972). Indeed, one of the ambiguities in his work, and a source of criticism by more conventional historians, is whether it is to be treated as genuine history or fable (Goldstein, 1994). He himself said that he was aware that what he was writing was 'fiction' but this did not mean 'that truth is therefore absent' (Foucault, 1980: 193), anymore than one would want to say that there could be no truth in parables or in novels. Foucault does, by his own admission, devise quasi-historical formations – 'the classical age', the 'disciplinary society' are two examples – and his case studies of prisons, clinics and the like are not so much offered as serious factual histories, but more as vivid illustrations of his motivating themes.

Nevertheless, his emphasis on discourse as thinking and saying, that thought is done in and through language, shows his continuity with structuralism. By contrast with Lévi-Strauss, however, Foucault's studies do not seek to identify any universal unconscious structures. Rather, they are concerned with specific configurations of discourses historically localised within an age and a region. It is because of this historical leaning that he did not affiliate himself with structuralism despite his affinities with it.

> Affinities with structuralism

Foucault used the notion of 'discursive formation' to emphasise that ideas cannot be divorced from language. Consistent with structuralism, he regards thought and language as two sides of the same coin. However, he does not want to treat thought as a mental phenomenon located in the privacy of the individual consciousness. To do this would have been to place the individual in the centre stage from which Foucault sought to displace it. Therefore he attends to what is explicit and public: what is said and what has been written. However, discourse is not just about language but is also about practice. Moreover, nothing exists outside of discourse. Although things can have a material and real existence in the world, they cannot have a meaning outside of discourse. It is discourses not things-in-themselves which give meaning and produce knowledge.

> Discursive formation

Foucault provides a battery of concepts for analysing the constitutive features of discourses. In the first instance a discursive formation consists of 'objects' – things that can be talked about. 'Mental patient' is an object of the discursive formation of modern psychiatry, something that can be talked about and acted upon in various ways, as we illustrated in Chapter 13. Prior to the development of this formation the object 'mental patient' could not be talked about. Additionally, the discourse has certain concepts for talking about the properties of the object, such as, to use the example of 'mental patient' again, various mental illnesses. Further, ennunciative modalities are ways of discursively marking the cognitive value of what is said. Within these modalities, 'themes' can develop. They are strands of thought relating to some given conception as, for example, the idea of evolution is a theme of biological discourse.

Foucault insists that a discursive formation is not to be thought of as an internally coherent entity. He uses the notion of 'field' to emphasise that a discourse is open to various possibilities and elements which are diversified and dispersed. His point is that the kinds of positions which seem to set individual thinkers in opposition to each other, are nonetheless contained within the same general discursive formation and operate under the formative influence of a common episteme. Thus, the discursive formation of psychiatry involves many different conceptions of mental illness and different notions of how it should be treated which are often at odds, if not in open warfare.

Foucault identifies four processes which determine the distribution of the 'field' of a discursive formation.

- *The formation of objects.* What things can be talked about within the formation, what can be introduced within it, and who controls the admission? Here 'grids of specification' provide the criteria for recognising, classifying and relating these objects as well as for distinguishing them from other objects. For example, within the discourse of psychiatry they involve symptoms which manifest particular types of illness such as schizophrenia, and the specific syndromes which are medically recognised, such as paranoid schizophrenia.
- *The formation of ennunciative modalities.* Just as not anything can be said within a discursive formation, so not anyone can say particular things. Some can be said only in certain kinds of settings, under certain conditions by certain people. Psychiatry, for example, involves giving diagnoses which are only properly given within the context of a professional relationship by qualified practitioners and must be based on their observation of the patient's behaviour. These rules also govern the formation of concepts regulating the relationships between statements, whether or not the statements are accepted, excluded or awaiting definitive assessment. For instance, the statements of the patient are often treated as symptoms and not as potentially true statements of actualities.
- *Procedures of intervention.* These regulate the way new statements can be produced or transformed, as when verbal expressions are translated into mathematical symbols, or spoken statements transcribed into written form. In psychiatry there are professional rules about who is qualified to describe and record a patient's symptoms in reports if they are to count as medically authoritative.
- *Strategies.* These are the development of themes, the selection and elaboration of certain lines of possibility, for example, treating mental illness through talk or through drug regimes.

The dispersion of statements across the field of a discursive formation can obviously be a complex matter, compounded by the interaction of one discursive formation with another, and with non-discursive constraints. In forming the concepts of one discursive formation, frequently another is drawn upon. For example, the idea of psychotherapy through talk drew upon the religious model of the confessional. Moreover, discourses are socially regulated. They are subject to the constraints of authority or normative regulation in respect of what they can say.

These general ideas notionally underlie Foucault's three early studies of madness, medicine and classification, though the details of the studies are not necessarily explicitly arranged around them. Nevertheless, the abstractions indicate the broad directions the studies took. Taken together, these three studies present an analysis of some of the main elements of the Enlightenment transformation of Western thought. Further, though Foucault may have delved into the archaeology of thought systems his studies are also underpinned by a conception of the pattern of social change from the sixteenth to the twentieth century – a pattern of change which broadly conforms to Weber's story about the progressive rationalisation and disenchantment of the modern world leading to what critical theory calls the 'administered society'.

It is not our aim here to write a summary of Foucault's opus but rather to try and draw out the main methodological aspects of his work.

What comes across very strongly is an impression that Foucault's is a work of theory, an extended attempt to carry through a reconceptualisation of the ways in which human beings are made into subjects by abandoning traditional historical narrative and other methods of analysis which are suspected of being party to the 'subjection'

> Theorising the ways in which humans are made into subjects

of individuals. Foucault spent long periods going through historical archives in France's national library, but his aim was not to produce a carefully summarised report of these researches, or to take them at face value – to the irritation of some historians, he ignored the usual convention of heavily footnoting his sources – but to provoke us into looking at such material anew for what it said about ourselves and about previous periods. For example, in his *History of Sexuality* (Foucault, 1990) he attacks the view that the advent of the modern era heralded in a period of prudishness and a repression of all talk of sex. On the contrary, according to Foucault, sex was much talked about, though not in the way we might today. The romance novels were but one example of such talk. Further, the new methods of the medical and the social sciences were becoming increasingly used to study those who deviated sexually from the norm as patients rather than their being lumped together with criminals. Power, in other words, was not so much tied to the actions of some elite, but permeated in the very methods of knowledge which achieved control through understanding.

One might say that Foucault is creating a framework, a fertile point of view, getting us to change our whole way of thinking about who we are, changing it to one which makes us intensely and generally suspicious of both the power and the knowledge interweaving with the oppressive character of state administration. It is certainly unlike conventional history. It is to take a deeply changed attitude in which, for example, it matters less what information an archival record contains than does the fact that the society is organised to keep records of what its members do. It is a point of view which other scholars can emulate, and many have done so, but there are no set-out procedures to follow by way of research design, methods of data collection or analysis. It is even a moot point as to whether it makes sense to speak of Foucault's approach producing findings or results. In important respects the work belongs to a long tradition of suspicion toward institutions and powers, and the aim of the analysis is not so much to achieve scientific objectives as provoke and disturb.

> Changing our outlooks

The politicisation of qualitative research

The second theme we want to discuss is the impact of post-modernism in qualitative research, mainly ethnography. The critique of qualitative research essentially boils down to three areas of contention (Bruner, 1993).

- Qualitative research is not objective, authoritative or political neutral.
- The researcher is historically positioned and locally situated.
- Meaning is radically plural and always open, with politics permeating every account.

However, when it comes to the practicalities of fieldwork it is difficult to see quite what differences these critiques make. The fieldworker's task still remains that of entering a situation, collecting what materials he or she can about the research topic in hand. The basic issue is a simple one: how to describe and interpret the experiences of others? It is at the point of reporting and in the 'writing' of the research that the main differences emerge largely as a consequence of the crisis of representation.

To remind ourselves, the crisis of representation raises the question of whether we can speak authentically of the other; whether we can say what others are truly like, or simply portray them in terms of our unwitting preconceptions about them. For some this requires a liberatory form of inquiry in which all responsibility is handed over to the others; that is, those members of the groups we are studying. They are to be encouraged to undertake their own social and historical investigations of themselves. Sometimes this means involving the others as co-authors, often constructing 'experimental or messy' texts where multiple voices speak (Marcus and Fischer,

> The crisis of representation

1986). The aim is to let these voices show themselves without interference and to let conflicts in the way different people see the world show themselves, without suggesting that any one of the views is *the* view. The reader is left to sort out those which speak to his or her personal life.

Recourse is often made to various literary devices – drama, poetry, fiction, autobiography, personal narratives – in an effort to make sure that other voices are heard and, in doing so, revising the role of the investigator as merely a connection between the field, the text and the wider community (Denzin and Lincoln, 1998).

Many find more troubling the issues to do with validity. Post-modernism casts doubt upon the possibility of establishing the final validity of any 'text' –

> be it theory, a research report, a method or other form – by imposing closer restrictions on the proliferation of meaning by adopting a set of rules concerning knowledge, its production and representation. To do so is, in effect, to attempt to assert the authority of

Validity

a 'text' and a regime of truth on the reader (Lather, 1993). Post-modernist thought is extremely sceptical of the authenticity of knowledge claims. In which case, thought must be endlessly alert to the ways in which power infiltrates language and must, therefore, be relentless in its attempt to strip any text of its claims to authority by 'undoing' it, highlighting the partialities, tensions and tendentious presuppositions of its own internal logic.

If validity is gone then values and politics hold sway. The task is to understand how power and ideology operate through systems of discourse, and how the meaning of texts play their part in shaping how race, class and gender pervade political conditions without having previously been explicitly acknowledged. A 'good' text is one that highlights how race, class and gender permeate the lives of individuals.

However, not surprisingly, there are differences in the implications drawn from post-structuralism and post-modernism. What has been called 'ludic

> post-modernism' sees social theory as limited in its ability to transform oppressive regimes of power since meaning is divided in itself and, accordingly, undecidable. Any attempt to interpret these ideas as pointing in a defi-

Types of post-modernism

nite political direction would be to go against the underlying assumptions (Ebert, 1991). Others, variously labelled 'oppositional post-modernism', 'radical critique-al theory' and 'resistance post-modernism', bring a more materialist slant by arguing that textualities are part of material practices and, as such, forms of conflicting social relations (Kincheloe and McLaren, 1994). In this latter view, the sign is always a site of competing, often conflicting, social relations which entails, in significant ways, that there is therefore always a conflict over meaning.

Given post-modernism's scepticism about the possibility of objective knowledge, it is hard to see any incentive for empirical research. Some, however, have attempted to bring a post-modern scepticism to ethnography. Much of this critique originated in anthropology inspired by its long-standing recognition of the problems of understanding and faithfully representing cultures unfamiliar to us, as well as an awareness of the often mixed agendas – a fascination with the different as exotic combined with a colonialist disdain, perhaps – affecting contact with other peoples. Such scholarship is accused of imperialism that is evidenced in terms of the identity of those who are studied and whose lives are written up in ethnographic texts. Why, for example, do we not know much about the lives of the rich? Why do we not study whiteness? There is, it is claimed, a form of cultural domination which infuses the anthropological enterprise (Fine, 1998). Anthropological texts – and we can add sociological texts – continually 'inscribe' largely imaginary representations of others, representations which stand in the way of being able to understand the others directly and properly. Under a veil of neutrality and objectivity, the reporter's own partiality and prejudices are concealed (Clifford and Marcus, 1986). Scholars seek to hide in their texts as if they were body-less, race-less, class-less, gender-less and had no interests to serve (Haraway, 1988). To put it another way: post-modern criticism aims at deconstructing what are regarded as Western meta-narratives of truth, along with the ethnocentrism implicit in the European view of history as the progress of reason.

> Ethnographic scepticism

In his *Schooling as a Ritual Performance* – a self-avowed critical ethnography – McLaren grounds his analysis in the post-structuralist claim that although the link between signifier and signified is arbitrary, it is shaped by historical, cultural and economic forces (McLaren, 1999). The school is a cultural site where there is a struggle over symbolic capital enacted in ritual dramas. The study argues that researchers are unable to introspectively grasp themselves or others without mediation through their positions with respect to race, gender, class and other locations. The main cultural narrative that defines school life is the resistance by students to the marginalization of street culture and knowledge. The visceral, bodily forms of knowledge, the rhythms and gestures of street culture are contrasted with the more formal and abstract knowledge of the school classroom. The informally constructed knowledge outside the classroom is regarded by teachers as threatening to the universalist, Eurocentric ideal of high culture that infuses the school curriculum.

There is, however, a tension within post-modernism and post-structuralism between deconstruction and the critique of ideologies. The latter owes much, as might be expected, to the Marxist tradition, and its aim to uncover the hidden forces and material structures that shape social life. In many ways it is an attempt to rescue determinism and the conflict view of society. Such a conception endorses the idea of foundations in the sense of grounding knowledge in something knowable outside the rhetorics of language. It clings to the Enlightenment framework. By contrast, the deconstructionist critique is not about offering a competing ontological framework but about looking at the historical, cultural and philosophical construction of frames, including those that invest critical ethnography (Lather, 1993). It is the latter which has stimulated the emphasis on 'writing' ethnography in almost a literal sense of this, that is, by 'disrupting' the conventional narrative construction of ethnographic reportage (Ashmore, 1989).

Critical discourse analysis (CDA)

This approach to discourse owes much more to the linguistic model rather than to the philosophies of deconstruction or the social theories of Foucault, though it does share some of the vocabulary and, of course, the objective of critique. Up to the 1970s most sociolinguistic research aimed at describing and explaining language variation and change, and the structures of communicative interaction (Gumperz and Hymes, 1972). Critical linguistics, first developed by a group based at the University of East Anglia, was an attempt to forge a connection between linguistic analysis and a social theory about the functioning of language in political and ideological processes, drawing upon the functionalist linguistic theory of Halliday (Halliday, 1985; Kress and Hodge, 1979). The approach rejected the treatment of language as an autonomous system independent of its use, as it did the separation of meaning from 'style' or 'expression'. Language was to be understood as gaining its character from its 'function' in the social structure. In many ways critical linguistics (later referred to as critical discourse analysis or CDA) extends the Sapir–Whorf hypothesis that the grammatical structure of a language embodies a particular world-view to variations within language which are reflected in the grammatical construction of texts. The aim is the critical interpretation of texts in order to recover the meanings expressed in discourse through the analysis of their linguistic structure and an understanding of their interactional and wider social contexts.

CDA is explicitly focused on the role of discourses in the production and reproduction of dominance and the challenges to it (Van Dijk, 1993). Dominance refers to the exercise of power by elites, institutions and groups that result in inequalities of such as class, gender, ethnicity and race. The aim of critical discourse analysis is to analyse the structures and strategies of text, talk and other communicative activities to examine what role they play in reproducing systems of dominance.

As a programme of research CDA has been set out as follows (Fairclough and Wodak, 1997):

- CDA addresses social problems.
- Power relations are discursive and grounded in material practices.
- Discourse constitutes society and culture.
- Discourse does ideological work.
- Discourse is historical.
- The link between text and society is mediated.
- Discourse analysis is interpretative and explanatory.
- Discourse is a form of social action.

Despite what looks to be a common focus, it is recognised within the CDA community that there are, and have to be, differences in emphasis as well as an acknowledgement that it is an interdisciplinary enterprise. Indeed, it is eclectic in drawing upon a variety of theories, methods and inspirations ranging over micro-linguistic analysis, conversation analysis, semiotics, social psychology and sociology, as well as Foucault's understanding of discourse (Wodak and Meyer, 2002; Wetherell et al, 2001).

The underlying assumption is that semiosis – all forms of meaning making – is irreducibly part of material social practices. A practice is a relatively permanent way of acting socially, as defined by its position within a structured network of practices. It is also a domain

> Semiosis

of social action which both reproduces structures and has the potential to transform them. They are arenas within which social life is reproduced, be they economic, cultural, political or everyday life (Chouliaraki and Fairclough, 1999). To put it briefly, CDA seeks to understand and explain the dialectical relationships between meaning and other elements of social practices.

Meaning, or semiosis, enters into social practices in the following ways. First, it is a component of the social activity itself. Part of doing a job, for example, involves using language in a particular way. Second, representations do not come from nowhere but are produced by social actors who participate in practices arising from their position in the social order and within the practice itself. Where persons stand in social relations affects how they represent things to themselves and others. Representations will therefore vary, depending upon the position of those who reproduce them. These representations will also be included in the practices within which they are produced. Accordingly, representations are to be understood as processes of social construction and reflexive self-construction, further shaping the social processes and practices of which they are part. Third, meaning enters into the performances of particular positions according to the differences in social class, gender, nationality, ethnicity, cultural membership and life experiences (ibid.).

Thus, the lives of the disadvantaged, for example, are represented through different discourses in the social practices of government, medicine, politics, and social science, are documented and talked about by politicians, civil servants, social workers and so on. The general idea is that these practices and their associated discourses are interconnected to make up a particular configuration that is the form of the social order, such as the level of the capitalist economic system or, at a more local level, the order of educational arrangements in a particular society at a particular time.

The important point for CDA is, of course, that not all discourses are equal but that they are articulated with each other in a structured way which involves the dominance of some discourses over others, as the discourses of politicians, administrators and other elites dominate those of the disadvantaged, even social workers. Some discourses are dominant, and some are marginal or even oppositional. Some discourses may become 'hegemonic' in legitimising the meanings which sustain relations of dominance, but they are always open to challenge and meet with resistance.

As we indicated earlier, CDA draws upon a variety of theories and approaches as well as methods of analysis. Fairclough (1995) sets out an analytic framework, along with examples, as follows:

1. *Select a social problem*
   CDA is problem based in the sense that it is aimed at illuminating problems with which people are confronted in their social life and, presumably, contributing to ways in which they may be overcome. CDA has emancipatory objectives and, hence, tends to focus on problems which confront those who are disadvantaged in some way – the poor, the excluded, the racially oppressed and so on. So, for example, one social problem is determining ways of organising the international economy in ways which do not increase the gap between rich and poor, options which are excluded from the political agenda by current discourses.

2. *Identify obstacles to problem being tackled*
   What is it about the organisation of social life which makes the problem resistant to solution? What is it about the network of social practices, the ways semiosis relates to social practices, the features of the discourse itself, which impede the finding of a solution to the problem?

   There are various levels of analysis which mark this stage. The obstacles to tackling the problem are seen, in part, as due to the social structuring of semiotic differences in orders of discourse. An example is the way in which, in the UK, many the public services such as education and health provision have been colonised by a managerial discourse. The obstacles are also partly due to the dominant forms of interacting and ways of using language in interaction, which also need to be analysed. It is this latter which makes use of various linguistic tools of analysis.

   For example, in an analysis of the foreword to a White Paper on competitiveness written by the British Prime Minister, Tony Blair, Fairclough draws attention to the ways in which processes in the 'new economy' are represented in timeless, ahistorical present. In terms of modality, statements about the 'new economy' are represented categorically, and authoritatively, as unmodalised truths – 'the modern world is swept by change', 'new technologies emerge constantly', 'new markets are opening up', and so on. In sum, change is authoritatively represented as lists of known truisms in the present, which are indifferent to place and social agency, and which must be responded to in certain ways. The 'new economy' is constructed as a social fact to which there is no alternative.

   The text also bears the familiar features of political rhetoric: it is more heavily oriented to 'ought' rather than 'is'; towards prescription and injunction for action; the agent is 'we' which oscillates in its reference between 'we, the government' and 'we, the British', though the reference usually remains vague. The text is full of short, dramatic sentences which could serve as soundbites – 'The modern world is swept by change', 'We must put the future on Britain's side'. It uses a vocabulary which highlights the will and energy of the agents, their commitment ('build', 'create', 'promote', 'forge', for example), and their collective vision.

The interactional analysis shows how the 'new economic order' is constructed textually as an inescapable fact of life. On the assumption that such texts are dominant and pervasive in various kinds of discourse, then there is a 'drip effect' which serves as an impediment to the consideration of alternatives which might solve the social problem identified at the start.

3. *Is the social problem 'needed' by the social order?*
Representations of economic change and the 'new global economy' as inevitable serve to help legitimise the new social order. They are also ideological in that they are misrepresentations – on the assumption that what has been socially created can be changed and is not unavoidable – and contribute to the reproduction of unequal relations of power.

4. *Identify possible ways past the obstacles*
By contrast, oppositional texts are likely to embody a very different discourse and display different properties of the kind selectively reviewed here. For example, it is likely that far from representing the 'new economic order' as inevitable, a fact of life, they will show it as something that can be changed because it is produced by agents who have their own interests – 'the big transnational companies'. Thus these texts open presumed truisms open to question, use a different vocabulary, and so on.

5. *Reflect critically on the analysis*
This stage involves thinking how the analysis can be used to tackle the problem which initiated it. In the case of CDA, this is likely to go beyond publishing academic papers and books to various forms of activism, writing more popular and accessible tracts and campaign literature. Above all, it involves thinking about how to relate such analyses to emancipatory goals.

In practice, CDA is much more complex than has been indicated here. It involves, for example, a much more subtle recognition that any text might well be a mix of discourse types, is open to transformations of various kinds, is produced in various ways for different kinds of consumption. There is also, again to mention some features briefly, the 'rhetorical mode' of the text, the use of metaphors, wording, the order of the discourse, and more. To repeat: CDA's aim is to fuse some of the techniques of linguistic analysis to bring out the ways in which discourses reproduce patterns of dominance in social life, which often involves – as illustrated above – how the use of grammatical forms is used to carry, or encode, ideologically loaded conceptions.

Perhaps more than any of the approaches we have briefly illustrated in this chapter, CDA in its manner of research at least bears many of the hallmarks of orthodox social research and thinking. It gives some emphasis to methods, to data, and presupposes that the analytic apparatus is capable of identifying real phenomena. Indeed, in this respect it departs significantly from Foucault. On the face of it, CDA accepts Foucault's claim that discourses have constitutive properties, in that both objects and social subjects are shaped by discursive practices. However, it insists that these practices are constrained by the fact that they take place within a material reality, a reality that consists of objects and social subjects that are constituted externally to the discourse (Fairclough, 1992). Studies of media discourse, it is claimed, which focus upon the interpretation of particular texts as well as upon how they are organised, paint a complex picture in which texts are being consumed, that is, interpreted, from different compliant and oppositional points of view. This makes problematic any simple and schematic conception of the way that media discourse affects those it is directed at. The way discourse is understood and the effects it can therefore have are affected by the way it plays into those social relations and interactions in which readers, viewers and others are already situated.

The constitution of social objects, it is argued, takes place within forms of social interaction between preconstituted subjects, forms of interaction which themselves influence the constitutive process. What is important for CDA is to understand the dialectic interaction that goes on between discursive practices and the preconstituted reality. It is in this respect that CDA, unlike Foucault for example, does not constitute a radical departure from modernistic thought.

Be this as it may, a major methodological issue with CDA is the work that the linguistic apparatus is purportedly adding to what are, in other respects, often fairly orthodox sociological analyses of the ideologies of power and domination. The linguistic analysis of the foreword to the White Paper briefly discussed earlier, for example, relies upon knowing that it is a White Paper putting forward the point of view of the political party in power and, accordingly, likely to be 'partisan' and to make use of 'rhetorical devices' to persuade, cajole and promote its point of view. It is not the linguistic analysis which, by itself, tells us this but the knowledge of the kind of social action it is: namely, the action of a government trying to give cogency to a point of view and using whatever legitimate devices it can to make the message attractive. Similarly, those who oppose 'the message' are likely to use devices which attempt to subvert its plausibility by, among other things, bringing out its partisan character. A great deal of extra-linguistic analysis is being brought to the linguistic properties of the texts in order to represent them as instances in the exercise of domination. The linguistic analysis on its own does not do this.

Concluding remarks

What we have tried to do in this chapter is present brief expositions of three forms of research done under the general rubric of discourse analysis. Despite their respective commitment to the notion of discourse, it is not clear that the approaches we have reviewed have, methodologically speaking, very much in common. Or, rather, it is not clear that they represent anything more than a casual synthesis which has what unity it has at the level of broad slogans and programmes. However, we do not offer this opening remark as necessarily a condemnation. After all, it would be difficult to think of any other attempt at such a synthesis in sociology which has succeeded in doing very much more than this.

Nowhere is this more apparent that in the use made by many sociologists of Foucault's ideas, especially his understanding of power. It would be difficult these days to underestimate the impact of Foucault on sociology, especially in the fields of health and illness, the sociology of gender and the body, and social welfare. In addition, it has been claimed that his approach not only breaks conclusively with modernity but also, in so doing, resolves many of the sociological problems arising from the spell of modernity, not least the agency/structure issue. However, it would be wise to exercise caution.

> Foucault's influence

The centrality of the concept of discourse in Foucault, along with its association with knowledge and power, makes it appear close to the kind of issues that the sociology of knowledge sought to address, in particular those to do with the social construction of knowledge (Fox, 1997). In Foucault's terms, 'discourse' refers both to the historically contingent practices which constrain human actions and what may be thought, as well as accounting for the fact that human beings actually *do* act and think within 'regimes of truth'. Hence the notion of 'power/knowledge'. For Foucault, power is not primarily repressive. Through the 'gaze' (i.e. through subjecting people to examination, inspection, surveillance), power is productive of 'effects of truth' in which certain knowledges become admissible or possible. Nevertheless, it can seem as if Foucault is offering a conception attractive to sociology which explains how the social impinges upon people's behaviour. It is the discourse of modern medicine which 'causes' persons to become 'patients', so to speak.

However, it is important to the principles of Foucault's analysis that he does not judge in any way the discourses of the past *or* the present. The problem with the present compared to past discourses is not so much its false assumption of having the truth– for every discourse shares the same delusion – but the condescension of the present vis à vis the past. As Hacking (1999) suggests, Foucault was a moralist whose concern was that of self-improvement, insisting that moralities are constructed by ourselves as moral agents, and it is only in loosing our condescension that we can emancipate ourselves to give us the freedom required as moral agents.

Describing Foucault as a moralist does not make him uninteresting sociologically. Indeed, and as we have pointed out, moralism in various guises has been a persistent theme in sociology for a long time, not least as a major element in the issue of values and their relationship to sociological thought and social research. It is a theme which certainly goes back to Marx and, before him, to the classical thinkers of the Enlightenment. And, of course, the approaches discussed here make a strong claim in favour of the idea that

> The moralism of sociology

values cannot be eliminated from social thought. On the contrary, since there are no foundations to knowledge, and since knowledge is socially constructed, knowledge cannot but be an act of power, of authority. Like all power and authority, it includes some and excludes others. The excluded are no longer just the oppressed proletariat of Marxism but now include women, ethnic minorities, the physically and mentally challenged, refugees and asylum seekers, gays and others.

One of the more salient aspects of this supposed shift from modernity to post-modernity in social thought is 'theorisation' as an explicit effort to analyse and expose the presupposition behind thought which oppresses persons by making them less than human. Queer theory, for example, drawing on post-structuralism, Derrida, Foucault and the psychoanalysis of Lacan, offers a critique of the epistemology which underpins most academic thinking about homosexuality. Though a somewhat amorphous body of thought, queer theory identifies the homo/hetero sexual binary, and its related opposition 'inside/outside', as a central organising principle of modern society. Applying these ideas to sociology, a queer perspective raises questions about the categories of identity and sexuality more widely while, at the same time, recognising the importance of culture as well as the practices of everyday life, especially its 'aestheticisation'. One claim is that one 'tendency' is a cultural challenge to 'heteronormativity' and destablising the homo-hetero sexual binary (Roseneil, 2000). It affects the population unevenly in being, in the main, an urban and younger generational phenomenon. Within new conceptions of intimacy, heterosexual relations have a less secure hold on the general population.

> Queer theory

On the face of it, such studies seem conventional enough. What we have is a proposed theory with connections to other literature and approaches, notably post-structuralism, and claims about how the proposed theory identifies one of the major axes around which our culture is organised. It then goes on to suggest how certain empirical facts about contemporary society can be explained in terms of the shifts in the culture of sexual relations, for example, the increased divorce rate which, it is alleged, represents the weakening of 'heteronormativity' and the culture of intimacy. However, and this is by no means uncommon in sociology, the connection between the theoretical account and the empirical illustrations (because they are no more than that) is simply one of possibility. Undoubtedly, changes in the divorce rate are due to cultural changes, but are these cultural changes of the kind suggested? Few, if any, others are suggested let alone examined. The whole thrust of the study is – and again this is typically of much of sociological research – the elaboration of a theoretical approach – on this occasion, motivated by explicitly stated political concerns.

The attack on Enlightenment thinking which characterised the post-modern and post-structuralist movements identified the 'crisis of representation' as the philosophical issue which implied the need for a wholesale reconstruction of social thought. No longer could it depend upon the illusion of secure foundations as knowledge, and nor could science itself. There can be no privileged standpoint for social science inquiries. Instead what we have is a thoroughgoing recognition that we are, along with our thought and the language which expresses it, social and historical creatures. There can be no escape from this fact of our existence. Academic research in the old, once established way is, from this point of view, over. The point now is to disrupt, dispel and attack the intellectual apparatus implicated in the subtle workings of power and knowledge toward emancipation.

Finally, one of the supposed effects of the rise of post-modernist social thought is the eradication of disciplinary boundaries, a move anticipated by Derrida in connection with the distinction between literature and philosophy. In the social sciences – especially in respect of a subject like sociology, which has never really had very firm boundaries with its related subjects – such as political science, economics, psychology, anthropology and history, there has been a long history of disciplinary imperialism or proposed interdisciplinary syntheses. Few have been notably successful. In the case of post-modern, post-structuralist social thought the unifying bond, the motivation for a synthesis of the human disciplines, has been the attention given to language by the respective disciplines. Although post-structuralism is, perhaps, the dominant view of language in this attempted synthesis, in fact there are an assemblage of influences from the more traditional sociolinguistics (itself an eclectic field) as well as the various understandings of the notion of discourse. In most cases it is difficult to see what the linguistic theories are doing other than offering a traditional critique of ideology in new clothes and in respect of new oppressed

Further, the idea that language is constitutive of the world is not quite the radical notion it may seem. There were, after all, more than just intimations of the idea in interactionism and later in ethnomethodology, but neither of these saw the need, sociologically speaking, to draw the devastating conclusions about the loss of foundations. In important respects, the 'loss of foundations' and the 'crisis of representation' are devastating in their consequences only if secure and certain foundations are seen as necessary in order for something to qualify as knowledge. If such foundations are not to be had, then it follows that there can be no such thing as knowledge true for all times and all places. We are condemned to a social and historical relativism. It is ideas such as these which are seen to be at the heart of the crises known as the science wars and the culture wars that have featured in intellectual life in recent years. They have provoked tremendous reactions from those who wish to defend science and its Enlightenment values and the superiority of Western rational culture against the tides of irrationality.

> interdisciplinarity

Selected bibliography and suggested reading

- Sara Mills' little book, *Discourse* (Routledge, 1997) is not a bad introduction to the diversity of approaches to discourse analysis.
- Foucault is a daunting task. His *Archeology of Knowledge* (Tavistock, 1972) is certainly worth reading as is *The History of Sexuality* (Penguin,

1990). Fox's article, 'Foucault, Foucauldians and sociology' (*British Journal of Sociology*, 49, 1998) is a good discussion of Foucault's influence on sociology.

■ Fairclough has written extensively on discourse analysis. See his *Language and Power* (Longman, 1989), *Discourse and Social Change* (Polity, 1992), 'Critical Discourse Analysis as a Method in Social Scientific Research' in Wodak and Meyer (eds), *Methods of Discourse Analysis* (Sage, 2001), which builds upon Fairclough and Wodak, 'Critical Discourse Analysis' in T. Van Dijk (ed.), *Discourse Studies: A Multidisciplinary Introduction*, Vol. 2 (Sage, 1997).

Chapter 15

Conclusion

In this text we have tried to bring out the main lineaments of the debates over methodology in sociology. Sociology has been very much our focus throughout. As we have said, many of the methods we have discussed are used in other contexts, and even though some of the critiques we have discussed – we have in mind here particularly those to do with the social survey and interviewing – are still of relevance in domains other than sociology, sociological preoccupations have been our prime concern.

It has also been a story whose 'ending' is really the present rather than a conclusion in which all the threads, subplots and diversions have been brought together into some resolution, happy or otherwise. Sociology, of course, goes on and, as should be clear from the story so far, it will no doubt change in the future. In what ways is impossible to say. Accordingly, in this short final chapter we want to provoke a number of questions – mostly about the how one might think of sociology and its practices – by standing back in a more reflective mode than hitherto. It would be impossible, at least for us, to present anything like a definitive statement of where the discipline, where sociological research, should go from here – although we will pass an opinion or two on this. Rather, and in keeping with what we hope we have achieved in this book, we want to encourage thinking about sociological reasoning.

For our part, and one of the main reasons for this book, we feel it important that sociologists remain conversant with the sociological tradition, and not simply as a catalogue of faintly amusing childhood peccadilloes but as a vital resource for understanding why sociology is so difficult to do well. All too often sociology can give the illusion of progress, as seen in the development of variable analysis, the attractions of structuralism, the disillusionment with the false gods of 'grand narratives', the 'linguistic turn'. These are just some of these 'progressive' steps we have discussed which have delivered, or will turn out to deliver, much less than the hopes invested in them.

One conclusion to be drawn from the above diagnosis of the state of sociology (assuming it is on the right lines) is that it is not worth doing. It does not go anywhere. Its hopes are constantly dashed. Sociologists can never agree on the right way forward. Its foundations are being constantly undermined. The list could go on. However, this is not a conclusion we want to draw even though, at present, the discipline as a tradition is in danger of losing its identity within an atmosphere which extols 'interdisciplinarity' or 'transdisciplinarity' as sociology becomes absorbed – perhaps colonised might even be an appropriate word – by cultural studies. Of course, there is no point to trying to maintain the identity of a discipline if it has been shown to be unrealisable, such as alchemy or astrology, but neither is there a point in trying to forge amalgamations simply for the sake of expediency. Of course, proponents of the post-modern, post-structuralist tendencies genuinely see this subsumption of literature, sociology, anthropology, art, architecture and human emancipation as the way forward by shedding the illusions of the past. Yet it must not be forgotten that this is just another point of view and, despite its current pre-eminence, it is not beyond challenge.

It depends, for example, upon a conception of language and meaning which is by no means uncontroversial. The philosophical conclusion that there is no way of fixing meaning leaves untouched the fact that, in our everyday lives and talk, this is a state of affairs that bothers us little or, to put it slightly more precisely, is practically managed in all kinds of prosaic ways. More fundamentally we do not have to begin from philosophical positions. In important ways, beginning from a philosophical position was one of the strategic mistakes of the positivist programme. Its 'top-down' approach was derived from philosophical conceptions of science which it then attempted to implement in procedures of social research, at the expense of the patient work needed to understand the phenomena it sought to investigate. It may well be that recent tendencies are in danger of committing the same error. And, after all, we do not have to subscribe to the particular philosophical account of meaning that present-day tendencies in sociology espouse. Wittgenstein, for example, would agree with the post-structuralists that there is (and can be) no fixity of meaning in the way that the structuralists had hoped for. For him what was paramount was language-in-use and there was no need to posit some underlying structure which determined meaning. Understanding language was more akin to understanding how to move pieces in a game. True enough, language was a system, but in no way a tightly integrated system of the kind structuralism posited. In which case, if there was no need to posit such a system in the first place, then the impossibility of describing and fixing that system is irrelevant. Wittgenstein would not have the problem the post-structuralists felt they had.

The purpose of the above point is not to offer an alternative account of meaning – Wittgenstein himself argued that there is no need for a philosophical theory of language – but to remind ourselves that, from a sociological point of view, using philosophy is an activity that needs to be done with more than just a little care. This is not to say that philosophical ruminations are incapable of providing valuable insights for sociology – after all, the founders themselves spent a great deal of time discussing philosophical issues – but what they cannot do is provide any foundations for sociology, or any discipline for that matter.

The issue of foundations is an important one not least for recent tendencies within the discipline. One of the major strategies against positivism was to attack its foundations, as in post-modernism and post-structuralism, philosophically and by showing that its thought was historically and socially conditioned. But, once again, we are in danger of letting a metaphor get out of hand. Surely enough, a building or a bridge needs foundations, otherwise it will collapse. What is less clear is why disciplines require foundations in this way. What does it mean, then, to suffer a loss of foundations?

We know the kinds of things it might mean in the case of buildings or bridges, but what about literature, history, physics, bread making, mathematics, acting, cigarette smoking and sociology? Take a strong example, that of mathematics. One of the activities that preoccupies mathematicians – one might even say that it constitutes their major interest – is proving their equations. If a formula is to be used in calculation, then mathematicians need to be assured that their reasoning is sound for the calculation to be correct. But what if, for example, it was shown that arithmetic could not be proved, what difference would this make to calculation? It might make some but it would hardly cause us to abandon arithmetic altogether. Arithmetic has proven itself practically in so many ways and in so many domains that the failure to *mathematically* prove the system of arithmetic would make little or no difference to us. It might make great deal of difference to mathematicians concerned with the problem, as well as provoking reflections on the nature of mathematics, but most of our practices which use arithmetic would be unchanged.

What might we say in the case of the other examples? Bread making surely has foundations. You cannot just mix anything together and make bread. Of course, to make bread there are recipes we have to follow in order to make a decent loaf but, again, this is not quite what we would understand the 'loss of foundations' to be referring to. In other words, we might begin to query quite what the question about the 'loss of foundations' is asking. Do we have to buy into the building analogy or the mathematical one or the bread-making one? There may well be others. Does the study of history have foundations? There were and certainly still are those who would seek to make that discipline into something akin to a science, even a sociological science, but this ambition remains a somewhat marginalised issue within history.

The point is that while there may be some activities or disciplines which require foundations – mathematics might be such a candidate – it is not clear that many things worth doing and thinking about require foundations of the kind that post-structuralism tries to prove cannot be had. But if there are many activities which do not require foundations, or have never had them, and which still remain viable and worthwhile, then do we face the problems that the 'loss of foundations' seems to imply?

Selected Bibliography

Abbott, A. (1998),'The Causal Devolution', *Sociological Methods and Research*, 27(2), 148–81.

Anderson, N. (1961)[1923], *The Hobo: The Sociology of the Homeless Man*, Chicago, University of Chicago Press.

Anderson, R.J., Hughes, J.A. and Sharrock, W. (1989), *Working for Profit: The Social Organisation of Calculability in an Entrepreneurial Firm*, Aldershot, Avebury.

Ashmore, M. (1989), *The Reflexive Thesis: Wrighting the Sociology of Scientific Knowledge*, Chicago, University of Chicago.

Atkinson, M. (1978), *Discovering Suicide*, London, Macmillan.

Ayer, A.J. (1959), *Logical Positivism*, New York, Free Press.

Barnes, B. (1977), *Interests and the Growth of Knowledge*, London, Routledge and Kegan Paul.

Barthes, R. (1967), *Elements of Semiology*, London, Cape.

Barthes, R. (1972), *Mythologies*, London, Cape.

Barthes, R. (1985), *The Fashion System*, London, Cape.

Barthes, R. (1994), *The Semiotic Challenge*, University of California Press.

Barton, A.H. (1955), 'The Concept of Property Space in Social Research', in P.F. Lazarsfeld and M. Rosenberg (eds), *The Language of Social Research*, New York, Free Press.

Becker, H., Hughes, E., Greer, B. and Strauss, A. (1961), *Boys in White*, Chicago, University of Chicago Press.

Becker, H.S. (1953), 'Becoming a Marijuana User', *American Journal of Sociology*, 59(3), 235–42.

Becker, H.S. (1963), *Outsiders*, Glencoe, Il., Free Press.

Becker, H.S. (1967), 'Whose Side Are We On?', *Social Problems*, 14(3), 239–47.

Becker, H.S. and Greer, B. (1957), 'Participant Observation and Interviewing: A Comparison', *Human Organization*, 16, 28–32.

Benney, M. and Hughes, E.C. (1956), 'Of Sociology and the Interview', *American Journal of Sociology*, 62.

Berger, J., Zelditch, M. and Anderson, B. (1966), *Sociological Theories in Progress*, New York, Houghton Mifflin.

Berger, P.L. and Luckmann, T. (1966), *The Social Construction of Reality*, Doubleday.

Bittner, E. (1973), 'Objectivity and Realism in Sociology', in G. Psathas (ed.), *Phenomenological Sociology*, New York, Wiley.

Black, M. (1961), *The Social Theories of Talcott Parsons*, Englewood Cliffs, N. J., Prentice-Hall.

Blalock, H.M. (1960), 'Correlation and Causality: The Multivariate Case', *Social Forces*, 38, 2146–51.

Blalock, H.M. (1961), *Causal Inferences in Nonexperimental Research*, Chapel Hill, University of North Carolina Press.

Blalock, H.M. (1968), 'The Measurement Problem: A Gap between the Languages of Theory and Research', in H.M. Blalock and A.B. Blalock (eds), *Methodology in Social Research*, New York, McGraw-Hill.

Blalock, H.M. (1969), *Theory Construction: From Verbal to Mathematical Formulations*, Englewood Cliffs, Prentice-Hall.

Blalock, H.M. (1970), *An Introduction to Social Research*, Englewood Cliffs, N. J., Prentice Hall.

Blalock, H.M. and Blalock, A. (eds) (1968), *Methodology in Social Research*, New York, McGraw-Hill.

Blalock, H.M., Jr. (1982), *Conceptualization and Measurement in the Social Sciences*, London, Sage.

Blau, P. (1960), 'Structural Effects', *American Sociological Review*, 25, 127–42.

Blau, P. (1964), *Exchange and Power in Social Life*, New York, Wiley.

Blau, P.M. and Duncan, D. (1968), *The American Occupational Structure*, New York, Wiley.

Bloor, D. (1976), *Knowledge and Social Imagery*, London, Routledge and Kegan Paul.

Blumer, H. (1954), 'What Is Wrong with Social Theory', *American Sociological Review*, 19, 3–10.

Blumer, H. (1956), 'Sociological Analysis and the Variable', *American Sociological Review*, 21.

Blumer, H. (1962), 'Society as Symbolic Interaction', in H. Blumer (ed.), *Symbolic Interaction*, Englewood Cliffs, Prentice-Hall.

Blumer, H. (1966), 'Sociological Implications of the Thought of George Herbert Mead', *American Journal of Sociology*, 71: 534–44.

Blumer, H. (1969), *Symbolic Interaction: Perspective and Method*, Englewood Cliffs, N. J., Prentice-Hall.

Blumer, H. (1971), Social Problems as Collective Behavior, *Social Problems*, 18, 298–306.

Bonjean C.M., Hill, R.J. and McLemore, S.D. (1967), *Sociological Measurement: An Inventory of Scales and Indices*, San Francisco, Chandler.

Boring, E.G. (1969), 'Perspective: Artifact and Control', in R. Rosenthal and R.L. Rosnow (eds), *Artifact in Behavioral Research*, New York, Academic Press.

Boudon, R. (1974), *The Logic of Scientific Explanation*, Harmondsworth, Penguin.

Boudon, R. (ed.) (1993), *Paul F. Lazarsfeld: On Social Research and Its Language*, Chicago, University of Chicago Press.

Bridgman, P. (1927), *The Logic of Modern Physics*, New York, Macmillan.

Brown, J.S. and Gilmartin, B.G. (1969), 'Sociology Today: Lacunae, Emphases, and Surfeits', *American Sociologist*, 4, 283–91.

Bruner, E. M. (1993). 'Introduction: The Ethnographic Self and the Personal Self', in P. Benson (ed.), *Anthropology and Literature*, Urbana: University of Illinois Press.

Bulmer, M. (1984), *Sociological Research Methods: An Introduction*, 2nd edn, Macmillan, Basingstoke.

Campbell, D.T. and Ross, H.L. (1970), 'The Connecticut Crackdown on Speeding: Time Series Data in Quasi-experimental Analysis', in E.R. Tufte (ed.), *The Quantitative Analysis of Social Problems*, Reading, Mass., Addison-Wesley.

Campbell, D.T. and Stanley, J.C. (1963), *Experimental and Quasi-Experimental Designs for Research*, Chicago, Rand McNally.

Child, D. (1970), *The Essentials of Factor Analysis*, London, Holt, Rinehart and Winston.

Chouliaraki, L. and Fairclough, N. (2001), *Discourse in Late Modernity: Rethinking Critical Discourse Analysis*, Edinburgh, Edinburgh University Press.

Cicourel, A.V. (1964), *Method and Measurement in Sociology*, New York, Free Press.

Cicourel, A.V. (1968), *The Social Organization of Juvenile Justice*, New York, Wiley.

Cicourel, A.V. (1973), *Theory and Method in a Study of Argentine Fertility*, New York, Wiley.

Clifford, James, and Marcus, G.E. (eds) (1986), *Writing Culture: The Poetics and Politics of Ethnography*, Berkeley, Calif., University of California Press.

Coleman, C. and Moynihan, J. (1996), *Haunted by the Dark Figure*, Buckingham, Open University Press.

Coleman, J. (1964), *An Introduction to Mathematical Sociology*, New York, Free Press.

Converse, J.M. and Schuman, H. (1974), *Conversations at Random: Survey Research as Interviewers See It*, New York, Wiley.

Culler, (1983), *On Deconstruction: Theory and Criticism after Structuralism*, London, Routledge and Kegan Paul.

Denzin, N.K. and Lincoln, Y.S. (eds) (1978), *The Landscape of Qualitative Research*, London, Sage.

Derrida, J. (1978), *Writing and Difference*, London, Routledge and Kegan Paul.

Deutscher, I. (1968), 'Asking Questions Cross-Culturally: Some Problems of Linguistic Comparability', in H.S. Becker, B. Geer, D. Riesman and R.S. Weiss (eds), *Institutions and the Person*, Chicago, Aldine.

Dijk, Teun A. Van (1993), *Elite Discourse and Racism*, London, Sage.

Dodd, S.C. (1942), *Dimensions of Society: A Quantitative Systematics for the Social Sciences*, New York, Macmillan.

Douglas, J.D. (1967), *The Social Meanings of Suicide*, Princeton, Princeton University Press.

Dowse, R.E. and Hughes, J. (1971), 'The Family, the School, and the Political Socialization Process', *Sociology*, 5(1), 21–45.

Dubin, R. (1969), *Theory Building*, New York, Free Press.

Duncan, O.D. (1984), *Notes on Social Measurement*, New York, Russell Sage Foundation.

Durkheim, E. (1952), *Suicide: A Study in Sociology*, London, Routledge and Kegan Paul. Trans. John A. Spaulding and George Simpson. First published 1897.

Durkheim, E. (1970), *Suicide*, London, Routledge and Kegan Paul.

Durkheim, E. (1976), *The Elementary Forms of the Religious Life*, London, Allen and Unwin.

Ebert, T. (1991), 'Political Semiosis in/of American Cultural Studies', *The American Journal of Semiotics*, 8(1/2), 113–35.

Edwards, A.L. (1957), *The Social Desirability Variable in Personality Assessment and Research*, New York, Holt, Rinehart and Winston.

Eglin, P. (1987), 'The Meaning and Use of Official Statistics in the Explanation of Suicide', in R.J. Anderson, J.A. Hughes and W.W. Sharrock (eds), *Classic Disputes in Sociology*, George Allen and Unwin.

Everitt, B. (1974), *Cluster Analysis*, London, Heinemann.

Fairclough, N. (1992), *Discourse and Social Change*, Cambridge, U.K., Polity.

Fairclough, N. (1995), *Critical Discourse Analysis: Papers in the Critical Study of Language*, London, Longman.

Fairclough, N. and Wodak, R. (1997), 'Critical Discourse Analysis', in T. Van Dijk (ed.), *Discourse as Social Interaction*, London, Sage.

Fielding, N.G. and Lee, R.M. (eds) (1991), *Using Computers in Qualitative Research*, London, Sage.

Fine, G.A. (1998), *Morel Tales: The Culture of Mushrooming*, Cambridge, Mass., Harvard University Press.

Fishman, P. (1990), 'Interaction: The Work Women Do', in J. McCarl Nielsen (ed.), *Feminist Research Methods: Exemplary Readings in the Social Sciences*, London, Westview.

Foucault, M. (1970), *The Order of Things: An Archaeology of the Human Sciences*, London, Tavistock.

Foucault, M. (1971), *Madness and Civilization*, London, Tavistock.

Foucault, M. (1972), *The Archaeology of Knowledge*, London, Tavistock.

Foucault, M. (1976), *The Birth of the Clinic: An Archaeology of Medical Perception*, translated from the French by A.M. Sheridan, London, Tavistock.

Foucault, M. (1980), *Power/Knowledge: Selected Interviews and Other Writings, 1972–1977*, New York, Pantheon.

Foucault, M. (1982), 'The Subject and Power', *Critical Inquiry*, 8, summer, 777–95.

Foucault, M. (1990), *The Care of the Self*. Vol. 3 of *The History of Sexuality*, New York, Vintage.

Fox, N. J. (1997), 'Is there life after Foucault? Texts, Frames, Differends', in A. Peterson and R. Bunton, (eds), *Foucault, Health and Medicine*, London, Routledge.

Friedman, N. (1967), *The Social Nature of Psychological Research: The Psychological Experiment as a Social Interaction*, New York, Basic Books.

Garfinkel, H. (1967), *Studies in Ethnomethodology*, Englewood Cliffs, N.J., Prentice-Hall.

Geertz, C. (1973), *The Interpretation of Cultures: Selected Essays*, New York, Basic Books.

Geertz, C. (1983), *Local Knowledge: Further Essays in Interpretive Anthropology*, New York, Basic books.

Giroux, H.A. (ed.) (1991), *Postmodernism, Feminism, and Cultural Politics: Redrawing Educational Boundaries*, Albany, State University of New York Press.

Glaser, P. and Strauss, A. (1967), *The Discovery of Grounded Theory: Strategies for Qualitative Research*, Chicago, Aldine.

Glymour, C. (1997), 'A Review of Recent Work on the Foundations of Causal Inference', in V.R. McKim and S.P. Turner (eds), *Causality in Crisis? Statistical Methods and the Search for Causal Knowledge in the Social Sciences*, Indiana, University of Notre Dame Press.

Goffman, E. (1983), 'The Interaction Order', *American Sociological Review*, 48, 1–17.

Gold, R. (1964) 'In the Basement – The Apartment Building Janitor', in P.L. Berger (ed.) *The Human Shape of Work: Studies in the Sociology of Occupations*, New York, Macmillan.

Goldstein, J. (ed.) (1994), *Foucault and the Writing of History*, Oxford, Blackwell.

Gumperz, J. and Hymes, D. (eds) (1972), *Directions in Sociolinguistics: The Ethnography of Communication*, New York, Holt, Rinehart and Winston.

Guttman, L. (1950), 'The Basis for Scalogram Analysis', in S.A. Stouffer, L. Guttman, E.A. Suchman, P.F. Lazarsfeld, S.A. Star and J.A. Clausen, *Measurement and Prediction*, Princeton, Princeton University Press.

Guttman, L. (1954), 'The Principal Components of Scalable Attitudes', in P.F.

Lazarsfeld (ed.), *Mathematical Thinking in the Social Sciences*, Glencoe, Free Press.

Hacking, I. (1975), *The Emergence of Probability: A Philosophical Study of Early Ideas about Probability, Induction and Statistical Inference*, Cambridge, U.K., Cambridge University Press.

Hacking, I. (1990), *The Taming of Chance*, Cambridge, U.K., Cambridge University Press.

Hacking, I. (1999), *The Social Construction of What?* London, Harvard University Press.

Hakim, C. (1987), *Research Design*, London, George Allen and Unwin.

Halfpenny, P. (1982), *Positivism and Sociology*, London, Allen and Unwin.

Halliday, M.A.K. (1985), *An Introduction to Functional Grammar*, London, Edward Arnold.

Hamblin, R.L. and Kunkel. J.H. (1977), *Behavioral Theory in Sociology*, New Brunswick, Transaction Books.

Hammond, P.E. (1964), *Sociologists at Work: Essays on the Craft of Social Research*, New York, Basic Books.

Haraway, D. (1988), 'Situated Knowledges: The Science Question in Feminism and the Privilege of Partial Perspective', *Feminist Studies*, 14(3), 575–99.

Heath, A. (1976), *Rational Choice and Social Exchange*, Cambridge, U.K., Cambridge University Press.

Held, D. (1980), *Introduction to Critical Theory: Horkheimer to Habermas*, London, Hutchinson.

Homan, R. and Bulmer, M. (1982), 'On the Merits of Covert Methods: A Dialogue', in M. Bulmer (ed.), *Social Research Ethics*, London, Macmillan.

Homans, G.C. (1961), *Social Behaviour: Its Elementary Forms*, New York, Harcourt Brace and Janovich.

Hughes, J.A. and Sharrock, W.W. (1998), *The Philosophy of Social Research*, 3rd ed. London, Longmans.

Hughes, J.A., Sharrock, W.W. and Martin, P. (1995), *Understanding Classical Sociology*, London, Sage.

Humphreys, P. (1997), 'A Critical Appraisal of Causal Discovery Alogorithms', in V.R. McKim and S.P. Turner (eds), *Causality in Crisis? Statistical Methods and the Search for Causal Knowledge in the Social Sciences*, Indiana, University of Notre Dame Press.

Humphreys, P. and Freedman, D. (1996), 'The Grand Leap', *British Journal for the Philosophy of Science*, 47, 113–23.

Kincheloe, J. and Maclaren, P. (1994), 'Rethinking Critical Theory and Qualitative Research', in N.K. Denzin and Y. Guba (eds), *The Handbook of Qualitative Research*, London, Sage.

Kolakowski, L. (1972), *Positivist Philosophy*, Harmondsworth, Penguin.

Kornhauser, W. (1959), *The Politics of Mass Society*, Glencoe, Il., Free Press.

Knorr-Cetina, K. and Cicourel, A.V. (eds) (1981), *Advances in Social Theory and Methodology: Toward an Integration of Micro- and Macro-Sociologies,* London, Routledge and Kegan Paul.

Kress, G. and Hodge, R. (1979), *Language as Ideology,* London, Routledge and Kegan Paul.

Kuhn, T. (1977), *The Essential Tension,* Chicago, Chicago University Press.

La Piere, R.T. (1934), 'Attitudes Versus Actions', *Social Forces,* 13, 230–7.

Laclau, E. and Mouffe, C. (1985), *Hegemony and Socialist Strategy: Towards a Radical Democratic Politics,* London, Verso.

Lather, P. (1993), 'Fertile Obsession: Validity after Poststructuralism', *Sociological Quarterly,* 34(4), 673–93.

Lazarsfeld, P.F. (1977), 'Evidence and Inference in Social Research', in M. Bulmer (ed.), *Social research Methods: An Introduction,* London, Macmillan. Reprinted from *Daedalus,* Journal of the American Academy of Arts and Sciences, Boston, Fall, 1958.

Lazarsfeld, P.F. and Menzel, H. (1961), 'On the Relation between Individual and Collective Properties', in A. Etzioni (ed.), *Complex Organizations: A Sociological Reader,* 2nd ed., New York, Holt, Rinehart and Winston.

Lazarsfeld, P.F., Pasanella, A.K. and Rosenberg, M. (eds) (1972), *Continuities in the Language of Social Research,* New York, Free Press.

Lazarsfeld, P.F. and Rosenberg, M. (eds) (1955), *The Language of Social Research: A Reader in the Methodology of Social Research,* New York, Free Press.

Lemert, C. (1997), *Postmodernism Is Not What You Think,* Malden, Mass., Blackwell.

Lemert, E. (1967), *Human Deviance, Social Problems and Social Control,* Englewood Cliffs, N.J., Prentice Hall.

Lemert, E. (1951), *Social Pathology. A Systematic Approach to the Theory of Sociopathic Behavior,* London, McGraw-Hill.

Lévi-Strauss, C. (1970a), *Introduction to a Science of Mythology,* New York, Harper & Row.

Lévi-Strauss, C. (1970b), *The Raw and the Cooked,* London, Jonathan Cape.

Lévi-Strauss, C. (1978), *The Origin of Table Manners: Introduction to a Science of Mythology,* Vol. 3, New York, Harper & Row.

Lieberson, S. (1985), *Making it Count,* Chicago, University of Chicago Press.

Lindeman, E.C. (1924), *Social Discovery: An Approach to the Study of Functional Groups,* New York, Republic Publishing.

Likert, R. (1932), 'A Technique for the Measurement of Attitudes', *Archives of Psychology,* 140, 1–55.

Lynch, M. (1985), *Art and Artifact in Laboratory Science,* London, Routledge and Kegan Paul.

Lynch, M. and Bogen, D. (1996), *The Spectacle of History: Speech, Text and Memory at the Iran-Contra Hearings,* Durham, N.C., Duke University Press.

Lyotard, J.-F. (1993), *The Postmodern Explained,* Minneapolis, University of Minnesota Press.

Madge, J. (1963), *The Origins of Scientific Sociology,* London, Tavistock.

Mannheim, K. (1952), *Ideology and Utopia: An Introduction to the Sociology of Knowledge*, London, Routledge and Kegan Paul.

Manning, P.K. (1982), 'Analytic Induction', in R.B. Smith and P.K. Manning, (eds), *Qualitative Methods: A Handbook of Social Science Methods*, Vol. 2, Cambridge, Mass., Ballinger.

Mapes, R. (1971). *Mathematics and Sociology.* Series: Foundations of Modern Society, London, Batsford.

Marcus, G.E. and Fischer, M.M.J. (1986), *Anthropology as Cultural Critique: An Experimental Moment in the Human Sciences*, Chicago, University of Chicago Press.

Marcuse, H. (1964), *One Dimensional Man*, Boston, Beacon Press.

May, T. (1997), *Social Research: Issues, Methods and Process,* Milton Keynes, Open University Press.

McKim, V.R. (1997), 'Introduction', in V.R. McKim and S.P. Turner (eds), *Causality in Crisis? Statistical Methods and the Search for Causal Knowledge in the Social Sciences,* Indiana, University of Notre Dame Press.

McLaren, P. (1999), *Schooling as a Ritual Performance: Toward a Political Economy of Educational Symbols and Gestures*, 3rd edn, Lanham, Md., Rowman & Littlefield.

Mehan, H. and Wood, H. (1975), *The Reality of Ethnomethodology,* New York, Wiley.

Merton, R.K. (1938), 'Social Structure and Anomie', *American Sociological Review*, 3, 672–82.

Merton, R.K. (1957), *Social Theory and Structure*, New York, Free Press.

Merton, R.K., Fiske, M. and Kendall, P.L. (eds) (1956), *The Focused Interview: A Manual of Problems and Procedures*, Illinois: Free Press.

Mills, C.W. (1948), *The New Men of Power: America's Labor Leaders*, Urbana, Il., University of Illinois Press.

Mills, C.W. (1951), *White Collar: The American Middle Classes,* New York, Oxford University Press.

Mills, C.W. (1956), *The Power Elite*, New York, Oxford University Press.

Mills, C.W. (1959), *The Sociological Imagination,* New York, Oxford University Press.

Mills, S. (1997), *Discourse*, London, Routledge.

Morgan, M.S. (1998), 'Searching for Causal Relation in Economic Statistics', in V.R. McKim and S.P. Turner (eds), *Causality in Crisis? Statistical Methods and the Search for Causal Knowledge in the Social Sciences,* Indiana, University of Notre Dame Press.

Nisbet, R.N. (1967), *The Sociological Tradition,* London, Heinemann.

Oakley, A. (1981), 'Interviewing Women: A Contradiction in Terms', in H. Roberts (ed.), *Doing Feminist Research*, London, Routledge.

Oppenheim, A.N. (1966), *Questionnaire Design and Attitude Measurement*, London, Heinemann.

Orr, J. E. (1996), *Talking about Machines: The Ethnography of a Modern Job*, Cornell, Cornell University Press.

Packard, V. (1957), *The Hidden Persuaders*, Harmondsworth, Penguin.

Packard, V. (1960), *The Waste Makers*, Harmondsworth, Penguin.

Parsons, T. (1937), *The Structure of Social Action*, New York, McGraw-Hill.

Parsons, T. (1952), *The Social System*, London, Tavistock.

Parsons, T. (1966), *Essays in Sociological Theory*, revised edition, London, Collier-Macmillan.

Parsons, T., Bales, R.F. and Olds, J. (1955), *Family, Socialization and Interaction Process*, Glencoe, Il., Free Press.

Pawson, R. (1989), *A Measure for Measures: A Manifesto for Empirical Sociology*, London, Routledge and Kegan Paul.

Pearson, E.S. and Kendall, M.G. (eds) (1970), *Studies in the History of Statistics and Probability*, London, Griffin.

Pearson, K. (1911), *The Grammar of Science*, 2nd edn, London, Adam and Charles.

Phillips, D.L. (1971), *Knowledge from What?* Chicago, Rand McNally.

Popper, K. (1945), *The Open Society and Its Enemies*, Vol. 1, London, Routledge.

Popper, K. (1947), *The Open Society and Its Enemies*, Vol. 2, London, Routledge.

Popper, K. (1959), *The Logic of Scientific Discovery*, 2nd English edn, London, Hutchinson.

Pruitt, D.G. (1981), *Negotiation Behavior, Organizational and Occupational Psychology*, London, Academic Press.

Prus, R.C. (1996), *Symbolic Interaction and Ethnographic Research: Intersubjectivity and the Study of Human Lived Experience*, Albany, State University of New York Press.

Pugh, D. and Hinings, C.R. (eds) (1976), *Organisational Structure: Extensions and Replications*, Farnborough, Saxon House.

Raiffa, H. (1982), *The Art and Science of Negotiation*, London, Belknap Press of Harvard University Press.

Rapoport, A. (1966), *Two-person Game Theory: The Essential Ideas*, Ann Arbor, University of Michigan Press.

Rapoport, A. (1974), *Fights, Games and Debates*, Ann Arbor, University of Michigan Press.

Ray, L. (1999), *Theorizing Classical Sociology*, Buckingham, Open University Press.

Reisman, D., Glazer, N. and Denny, R. (1951), *The Lonely Crowd*, New Haven, Yale University Press.

Rorty, R. (1980), *Philosophy and the Mirror of Nature*, Oxford, Blackwell.

Roseneil, S. (2000), *Common Women, Uncommon Practices: The Queer Feminisms of Greenham*, London, Cassell.

Roth, J. (1966), 'Hired Hand Research', *American Sociologist*, 1, 190–6.

Sacks, H. (1984), 'Notes on Methodology', in J. Maxwell Atkinson and John

Heritage (eds), *Structures of Social Action: Studies in Conversation Analysis*, Cambridge, Cambrige University Press.

Sacks H. and Schegloff, E.A. (1979), 'Two Preferences in the Organization of Reference to Persons in Conversation and Their Interaction', in G. Psathas (ed.), *Everyday Language: Studies in Ethnomethodology*, New York, Irvington.

Sayer, A. (2000), *Realism and Social Science*, London, Sage.

Schuman, H. and Converse, P. (1971), 'The Effects of Black and White Interviewers on Black Responses in 1968', *Public Opinion Quarterly*, 35, 44–68.

Schutz, A. (1962), *Collected Papers*, Vol. 1, The Hague, Martinus Hijhoff.

Shaw, C.R. (1930), *The Jack-Roller: A Delinquent Boy's Own Story*, Chicago, Il., University of Chicago press.

Skeggs, B. (1997), *Formations of Class and Gender: Becoming Respectable*, London, Sage.

Skinner, B.F. (1938), *The Behavior of Organisms*, New York, Appleton Century Crofts.

Skvoretz, J. (2000), 'Looking Backwards into the Future: Mathematical Sociology Then and Now', *Sociological Theory*, 18: 510–17.

Smelser, N. J. (1959), *Social Change in the Industrial Revolution: An Application of Theory to the British Cotton Industry*, Chicago, University of Chicago Press.

Stanley, E. and Wise, S. (1982), *Breaking Out Again: Feminist Ontology and Epistemology*, 2nd edn, London, Routledge.

Stanley, L. (1990), *Feminist Praxis: Research, Theory and Epistemology in Feminist Sociology*, London, Routledge.

Stewart, D. and Shamdasani, P. (1990), *Focus Groups: Theory and Practice*, London, Sage.

Stinchcombe, A. (1964), *Rebellion in a High School*, Chicago: Quadrangle.

Stinchcombe, A.L. (1968), *Constructing Social Theories*, New York, Harcourt Brace and World.

Stouffer, S.A., Guttman, L., Suchman, E.A., Lazarsfeld, P.F., Star, S.A. and Clausen, J.A. (1950), *Measurement and Prediction*, Princeton, Princeton University Press.

Stouffer, S.A., Suchman, E.A., De Vinney, L.C., Star, S.A. and Williams, R.M. (1949), *The American Soldier: Vol. 1, Adjustment during Army Life*, Princeton, Princeton University Press.

Strauss, A. (1978), *Negotiations: Varieties, Contexts, Processes, and Social Order*, San Francisco, Jossey-Bass.

Strauss, A. and Corbin, J. (1990), *Basics of Qualitative Research: Grounded Theory, Procedures and Techniques*, London, Sage.

Swarz, N. (1985), *The Concept of Physical Law*, Cambridge, Cambridge University Press.

Tannenbaum, A.S. and Bachman, J.G. (1964), 'Structural Versus Individual Effects', *American Journal of Sociology*, 69(6), 585–95.

Thomas, W.I. and Znaniecki, F. (1918), *The Polish Peasant in Europe and America*, Boston: Gorham Press.

Torgerson, W.S. (1958), *Theory and Methods of Scaling*, New York, Wiley.

Turner, B.T. and Williams, M.R. (1983), *Management Handbook for Engineers and Technologists*, London, Business Books.

Turner, S. (1997), 'Net Effects: A Short History', in V.R. McKim and S.P. Turner (eds), *Causality in crisis? Statistical Methods and the Search for Causal Knowledge in the Social Sciences*, Indiana, University of Notre Dame Press.

Turner, S.P. and Factor, R.A. (1994), *Max Weber: Lawyer as Social Thinker*, London, Routledge.

Turner, S.P. and Turner, J.H. (1990), *The Impossible Science: An Institutional Analysis of American Sociology*, Newbury Park, Sage.

Van Dijk, T.A. (1993), *Elite Discourse and Racism*, London, Sage.

Van Maanen, J. (1988), *Tales of the Field; On Writing Ethnography*, Chicago, University of Chicago Press.

Wagner, H.R. (1964), 'The Displacement of Scope: A Problem of the Relationship between Small-scale and Large-scale sociological Theories', *American Journal of Sociology*, 69, 571–84.

Weber, M. (1949), *The Methodology of the Social Sciences*, New York, Free Press of Glencoe.

Weber, M. (1964), *Theory of Social and Economic Organisation*, trans. A. Henderson and T. Parsons, New York, Free Press of Glencoe.

Wetherell, M., Taylor, S., and Yates, S. (eds) (2001), *Discourse as Data: A Guide for Analysis*, London, Sage.

Whyte, W.F. (1943), *Street Corner Society: The Social Structure of an Italian Slum*, Chicago, Il., University of Chicago Press.

Willer, D. (1967), *Scientific Sociology: Theory and Method*, Englewood Cliffs, N.J., Prentice-Hall.

Willer, D. and Willer, J. (1973), *Systematic Empiricism: Critique of a Pseudoscience*, New Jersey Prentice-Hall.

Wilson, T.P. (1970), 'Normative and Interpretive Paradigms in Sociology', in J.D. Douglas (ed.), *Understanding Everyday Life*, London, Routledge and Kegan Paul.

Winch, P. (1990), *The Idea of a Social Science*, 2nd edn, London, Routledge.

Wodak R. and Meyer, M. (2002), *Methods of Critical Discourse Analysis*, Thousand Oaks, C.A., Sage.

Wollen, P. (1970), *Signs and Meaning in the Cinema*, London, Thames and Hudson.

Wright, L. (1976), *Teleological Explanations*, Berkeley and Los Angeles, University of California Press.

Yule, G.U. (1911), *An Introduction to the Theory of Statistics*, London, C. Griffin and Company.

Index